PROMISE AND PROVIDENCE
the autobiography of
GOS EKHAGUERE

PROMISE AND PROVIDENCE
the autobiography of
GOS EKHAGUERE

Safari Books Ltd
Ibadan

Published by
Safari Books Ltd
Ile Ori Detu
1, Shell Close
Onireke, Ibadan.
Email: safarinigeria@gmail.com
Website: http://safaribooks.com.ng

ISBN: 978-978-59508-1-6 Cased
       978-978-59508-2-3 Paperback

DEDICATION

MY MOTHER: *you gave up everything so that I could have something.*

MEMBERS OF MY FAMILY: *you steadfastly had my back.*

MY TEACHERS AND SCHOOLMATES AT ALL LEVELS OF EDUCATION: *auld lang syne*

CONTENTS

FOREWORD 1

A great scholar and a good friend.

A number of years ago, I was able to organise a Summit Conference in Cape Town with the objective of having American and African scholars and researchers try to develop inter-continent joint degree programmes. One of the African participants was a representative from the Association of African Universities, based in Accra. At one point in the conference, two very well-known American scholars, who shall go nameless, made the suggestion that the problem with scholarship in Africa was that the African professors simply didn't put sufficient effort into their research. I could tell at this point that the meeting was in trouble. However, that representative from the Association of African Universities stood up to respond, and I can only say in the vernacular, he "tore a large one" out of the hides of those two American scholars; essentially by pointing out the differences in teaching loads, class sizes, lack of funds to collaborate internationally, and so on. That person, who took unquestionable risks in challenging these well-known Americans, was none other than Godwin Osakpemwoya Samuel "GOS" Ekhaguere.

For the rest of the conference, I had scholar after scholar, both Africans and Americans, telling me what an extraordinary contribution Professor GOS Ekhaguere had made to the entire proceedings. That was the beginning of my relationship with GOS, that has been cemented with many ventures that we've had together over the years, in the United States, in Italy, in Nigeria, in Kenya, and that first encounter in South Africa.

◊ ◊ ◊

Introducing GOS

My life, like many of my friends and colleagues, has been largely West of the Atlantic Ocean, in Canada and the United States. But I want to write a few words about GOS, because as I say above, he is not only "a great scholar but also a good friend". So, I want his achievements, activities and insights to be better known to like-minded friends, many of whom are mathematicians like GOS, others who have had considerable international experience, and those who would like to learn more about the life and activities of a distinguished scholar in the context of a career largely lived in Ibadan and Nigeria.

Most readers will know that what is today Nigeria, was colonised by England, but in 1960 did England (or the United Kingdom) see Nigeria become independent – when GOS was 13 years old.

It may come as a surprise to readers from North America that GOS was able to obtain his early schooling at a Catholic institution, the Immaculate Conception College in particular. There were numerous other Catholic secondary education institutions in Nigeria. His college had been founded by a number of members of the order of SMA (Societas Missionum ad Afros) from Ireland. Why this might seem unusual to many is that scholars from Ireland and not England were prominent in Nigeria at the time. Why this might seem strange is because in that era, Ireland or the Irish Republic was completely separate from England, and so one might have expected to read of the prominence of teachers and academics from England proper — thus more likely being of Protestant denominations rather than those from Ireland.

It may also come as a surprise and of interest that while in a period as a British colony, Nigeria was considerably influenced in higher education and religion by priests and educators from

Ireland. Perhaps there was an equivalent influence by British teachers, but it is fascinating and perhaps not well known on this side of the Atlantic, that Ireland and the Catholic Church had such an influence in Nigeria. It is interesting to note that at the ICC, manual labor after classes was required.

In order to gain entry into college, it was necessary to score well in the WASC (West African School Certificate) exams. Initially failing mathematics was not necessarily fatal but soon thereafter, that became a prerequisite for admission into certain programmes in Nigerian universities. Thus mathematics became of equal importance as English language. It was interesting in the narrative that the organisation of higher education in Nigeria at the time, that is, the 1970s, was interrupted by the internal so-called Biafra war. GOS later describes that he was taught physics by an American Peace Corps volunteer. At the time GOS was finishing his secondary school, his focus was what one needed to do in order to gain a teaching position in a primary or secondary school.

Continuing GOS' interweaving educational events with political events, he describes how 1966 impacted his learning of the results of his examinations from there the country had its first military coup deposing the nation's prime minister, Sir Abubakar Tafawa Balewa, resulting in the overthrow of the national government. Nigeria had only gained independence six years earlier, so this sent the country into a tailspin.

His performance in the WASC examination in 1965 was the best of any student from the ICC up to that point in time. He was subsequently awarded a scholarship and became an Immaculate Conception College Scholar.

His Path in Mathematics

After graduating from ICC, the principal suggested to him "Listen, GOS! No one else is taking mathematics. I think you should change your combination to physics, chemistry and zoology. This puts you on the path to becoming a medical doctor." This resonated with me, as at my first university, I was urged to switch to physics from mathematics, which I resisted.

GOS makes the very important point that "secondary schools are among the key drivers of national integration and cohesion because as boarders, we lived, learned and played together."

In Academia and The World Around

In reading GOS' autobiography, I was touched at how skilfully he managed to weave together a portrait of contemporary life in Nigeria and how it complemented his own development as a distinguished mathematician. I found the entire narrative very meaningful to me, since I have followed a somewhat similar mathematical journey, and have a very slight knowledge of Nigeria from several visits there.

It was through the Africa-wide Association of African Universities (AAU) that I first encountered GOS, as he served in several roles on the staff of that organisation – and I only learned in reading this that two of the scholars he interacted with were other notable mathematical friends of mine from the University of the Western Cape, South Africa: Loyiso Nongxa and the late Jan Persens.

The Math Community

Readers who, like me, come from the world of mathematics will find many common threads with GOS' mentors and several who have influenced me: one of my undergraduate math classmates, Barbara Keyfitz[1], had Peter Lax as her thesis advisor; another, Lon Rosen[2], had James Glimm as his thesis advisor and later collaborated

---

1   Barbara Keyfitz, University of Toronto Honours Math (known as MPC 6T6) classmate of the author. Former Director of Canada's national Fields Institute for Research in Mathematical Sciences; current Professor of Mathematics, Ohio State University.

2   Lon Rosen, also MPC 6T6 classmate of the author. Retired Professor of Mathematics, University of British Columbia.

extensively with Barry Simon – and I have been a guest speaker at the Abdus Salam International Centre for Theoretical Physics in Trieste, Italy – all of these were also colleagues and teachers of GOS.

GOS' PhD credentials are in the forefront of the international mathematics community. He cites, among others, persons who had influenced him in these studies: Glimm, Simon, and Salam.

Soon after his initial appointment at the University of Ibadan, perhaps ironically, he was assigned a telephone number 1729. This may not be striking or of interest to many readers, but it immediately jumps out at fellow mathematicians. The number 1729 is, according to legend, the number of a taxi in which the English mathematician Godfrey Harold Hardy arrived in a hospital in London where the Indian mathematician Srinivasa Aiyangar Ramanujan was on admission. When Hardy opined that the number was not very interesting, Ramanujan immediately pointed out that 1729 is the smallest positive number that can be written in two different ways as the sum of two numbers that are cubes:

$$1^3 + 12^3 = 1 + 1728 = 1729 = 729 + 1000 = 9^3 + 10^3 \qquad (!)$$

GOS points out that this number is sometimes referred to as a "taxi cab number" or Hardy-Ramanujan number.

But in addition to GOS' description of his career with such distinguished physicists and mathematicians, he draws a very insightful picture of the challenges in Nigerian higher education in the times as a British colony, the period when Nigeria became free of colonisation, and other initial struggles in a nation that experienced the Biafra war, and so on.

I am very grateful to GOS for having included me in describing a number of interesting events in his life, particularly for the expressions of gratitude that he offers, to which I can only say that my debt to him is infinitely greater. One very kind comment he has made about me is that on one of my visits to Nigeria, I learned from GOS and a colleague from the University of Ibadan that the first Head of Department at his university was in fact one of my professors, F.V. Atkinson at the University of Toronto, who was a very well-loved Professor of Mathematics and is highly regarded by my classmates, several of whom I have mentioned in this *Foreword*. It was my great honour to have filled in the blank by finding a photograph back in Toronto (with the assistance of another classmate, Jim Arthur[3]) of the late Professor Atkinson and forwarding to GOS and his colleagues so that it now hangs prominently in the Gallery of all Heads of Department of Mathematics at the University of Ibadan: Atkinson being the first, but now also including GOS among that number.

Professor Wayne Patterson, PhD (Michigan)

Retired Professor of Computer Science, Howard University,
former Director of the Cybersecurity Research Center,
Associate Vice-Provost for Research, and Senior Fellow for Research and International Affairs in the Graduate School, Howard University,
former Program Manager, Office of International Science & Engineering, National Science Foundation, Virginia, USA

---

3   James Arthur, also MPC 6T6 classmate of the author. Professor of Mathematics, University of Toronto, and Fellow of the Royal Society of Canada.

FOREWORD 2

An invitation to write a *Foreword* to the autobiography of an icon is a great privilege. And so when Professor Emeritus GOS Ekhaguere contacted me and requested that I should write a *Foreword* to this marvelous autobiography, I did not hesitate to agree. Shortly thereafter, however, I became puzzled: why me? A Political Scientist to write the *Foreword* of the memoir of a world-class Professor Emeritus of Mathematical Physics "with profound interest in axiomatic quantum field theory"? On deep reflection, I came to the realisation that GOS and I have some meeting points which make my choice for this assignment logical. These will become self-evident shortly.

Mathematicians are noted for their fascination with numbers, various abstract constructs or structures even in their various branches of *foundations, algebra, analysis, geometry,* and *applied mathematics.* But *Physics* was the author's first love and, incidentally, our first meeting point. To pure scientists, it is the study of matter, energy, and the relation between them and, in some senses, it is the most basic pure science whose discoveries find applications throughout the natural sciences.

As far as we are concerned in the Social Sciences, *Physics* is the natural philosophy and, whatever others readily attribute to Democritus and Pythagoras, two of the great originators of Political Science, Plato (427-347 BC) and his friend Aristotle (384-322 BC), not only had critical influence on the development of science in general but on *Physics* in particular. However, while Plato was more into mathematics at the Academy, and Aristotle concentrated considerably on logic and politics, they also collaborated in pioneering thoughts on politics as evident in Aristotle's treaties on *Politics* and Plato's being the architect of the great *Dialogues* and author of *The Republic* which derived from his conception of the ideal State. Is there any comprehensive philosophical scheme by GOS Ekhaguere? And where does he come in here as we touch on the torch-bearing ancient philosophers? It is simply that this ruminative and audacious author is one of the contemporary heirs to the legendary legacies of those inspiring ancestors.

Nobody in Benin, the capital city of Edo State of Nigeria, could ever have imagined that some unexpected turns of fate would play out to match talent with ambition to propel the ingenuity of a born star, an amazing genius, and throw him up before their very eyes as a colossus renowned for what drives the world. The memorable accounts contained in this autobiography provide previously unknown information about the author and close insight into his personal background, life experiences and monumental achievements as a scholar of international repute.

With the symbolism of the following simple equation:

My Life = Promise + Providence

GOS Ekhaguere, the Mathematical Physicist, presents the odyssey of his life in a fluid, scintillating prose. He captures the factors and forces that have been drivers of his life in this incisive and riveting chronology of an edifying life experience. From his early days through the pre-tertiary level education, the tertiary level education, marital life, service at various levels up to retirement and beyond, and the well-deserved rewards, we have here the liberal details of challenges along the way and the providential turning points. The graceful narration of the low and high points not only makes the book engaging but most revealing.

By enriching the kick-off of the autobiography with reference to the *Pre-Ogiso* and *Ogiso* eras, however, GOS would provoke some controversies. At least some historically sensitive descendants of

Edoland (or *Ubiniland*) would wonder why no reference was made to the theocratic ascendancy of the awe-inspiring *Idu* through whom an autocratic new order was designed and implemented by *Igodo*, one of his descendants who took the *Ogiso* title. That notwithstanding, we have in the following pages the circumstantiation and proof of *Promise* and *Providence* which sums up the life of an incomparable scion of a fearless and enterprising lineage.

GOS is among those who are passionately concerned about the imminent collapse of education in Nigeria, against the backdrop of government's policies and the attitudes of those in government, the quality of teaching and research and the dangerous products of the mushrooming tertiary institutions in Nigeria.

Having been born three days after the total solar eclipse of 1947 and performed meteorically in the Nigerian space, I pray that by Monday, 20 March, 2034 when a new moon, the earth and the sun are aligned in a straight line in space, with the moon completely obscuring the earth from the sun, GOS will still be on mother earth, mentoring and guiding the future's great scientists with his uncommon intellectual prowess. And may he also remain committed to salvaging Nigeria as a statesman for many more years in a nation in turmoil with its educational system in trauma.

Tunde Adeniran, PhD (Columbia), KJW, OFR, FCPA
Professor Emeritus of International Relations and Strategic Studies,
former Minister of Education and Ambassador Extraordinaire and
Plenipotentiary to the Federal Republic of Germany

FOREWORD 3

I was not too surprised when Professor Ekhaguere who is fondly referred to as GOS asked if I would write a foreword for this autobiography. I first met him through a mutual friend (now late), Professor Airen Amayo of the English Department, University of Ibadan, sometime in 1976. Thereafter it was as if Amayo sort of handed him over to me and then went on his way. Needless to say, our friendship has progressed like a train on rails since then. I must confess that at a personal level, I found GOS a gentle, quiet and easy-going personality. It was therefore not difficult to be friends with him.

Reading through the autobiography, I discovered many areas where we had similar experiences growing up. For instance, the arrival of free primary education in Western Nigeria in 1955, which miraculously saved his primary education, also saved mine. Like GOS, I too was taken ill, although not quite as seriously as his, during the finals of my secondary school certificate exams. In addition, during preparations for the 1979 elections, we found ourselves on the same team working for the UPN along with Professor Amayo and later as part of the Edo State Movement, Chaired by GOS himself, for the creation of the Edo State, which was launched at the Liberty Stadium in 1982.

I was particularly impressed about how detailed his narrative was. In certain instances, I felt it could easily have been a novelist telling the story. I found it interesting that even as a toddler, when he was told that he was not quite ready to begin his schooling, he protested in a way that compelled the school authorities to make room for this determined pupil. At the pre-tertiary level, we see him again choosing Mathematics over Zoology (and thereby passing up an opportunity for a career in medicine) rather than listening to the advice of his dear teacher at the Immaculate Conception College (ICC), Benin City, Fr. Donnelly. Seven years later, we see him insisting on undertaking a PhD thesis in Axiomatic Quantum Field Theory, at the Imperial College London, a relatively newer and apparently more challenging area of study in Mathematics, against what appeared to be (at that time) sound advice from his assigned supervisor, Professor Abdus Salam, one of the two 1979 Nobel laureates in Physics. In a way, it reminded me of the *Pangolin*, a scaly mammal that feeds on ants and termites (similar to and often regarded by some wildlife experts as South Africa's answer to the American Armadillo, another scaly ant eater). When this animal picks up a scent of an anthill several hundred metres away, and it begins to follow that trail, it is virtually unstoppable, until it gets to its targeted destination; should it encounter a cheetah or some other predator along its path, rather than being deterred, it folds itself up protecting itself with its scales. Eventually, not knowing what to make of this strange animal, the predator moves off its way. The pangolin continues this way until it arrives the anthill and begins to dig in, searching for insects to feast on.

The title *Promise and Providence* was demonstrated throughout his life trajectory even in cases where one would have thought that the requirement was small. For example, GOS came to my office one day and said that he had a mathematical conference in Switzerland and he did not know how to find the required funding. This was at a time when the university was visibly strapped for funds and nobody was being sponsored to conferences. I then told him that in a similar situation, Professor Ayo Bamgbose of the Department of Linguistics, University of Ibadan, had approached the then Vice-Chancellor of the institution, Professor Samson Olajuwon Kokumo Olayide, for help to attend a conference overseas for which he had no funding. The Vice-Chancellor approved, and he went for the conference. GOS quickly did the same thing and he was sponsored to attend the conference for which he required sponsorship in Switzerland. On his return, he brought me a nice little clock for which I was grateful.

On a lighter note it was impossible not to wonder if there was something in mathematics that guaranteed his success at the home front, in the field of study as well as in his various roles of leadership or authority in which GOS found himself.

Professor Emeritus Benjamin Ohiomamhe Elugbe, PhD, FNAL
former Executive Director National Institute of Nigerian Languages (NINLAN)
former President Nigerian Academy of Letters (NAL)
former Member, Nigerian Liquefied Natural Gas (NLNG) Advisory Board for the Award of the National Prize for Literature
former President of West African Linguistic Society (WALS)
former Member, Board of Directors, Bendel Newspapers Co. Ltd.
former Member, Constitution Review Committee (CRC) (Nigeria)

A Review of
Promise and Providence

Any review of the autobiography Promise and Providence by Emeritus Professor of Mathematics Godwin Osakpemwoya Samuel Ekhaguere (otherwise, GOS Ekhaguere), NNOM, must be set against the background of the author's renowned humility and established penchant for understatement. Enormous things happen in the 506 pages and 27 chapters of this phenomenal piece of work, which appear cast on a Homeric order. From its very beginning it attests to the interplay of mortals and immortals, in the affairs of men and of one man in particular – GOS Ekhaguere. Nothing could be more dramatic than that, or more evocative of the sweep of interpretive history. Yet, it is written with such linguistic sparseness, in an economy of words, which must be deciphered to unpack the grand dimensions of things written about. Paradoxically, it is this frugality of language that invests Ekhaguere's ideas and narration with such unspeakable atomic power and human appeal.

The aim of the book is stated at the outset. It is spelt out in a rather matter-of-factly tone of voice which shows that the author was not going to indulge the reader's hope for literary embellishments. In his first words, "This autobiography sketches some key aspects of my life journey." Period. There is no adornment. No elaboration. But the words "sketches", "some", "key", and "aspects" are unmitigated understatements, as this review would show. More than an autobiography, Promise and Providence is an engaged narrative of how history and critical reflection can shape the relationship between an individual and their society, and reconstruct their life aspirations. However, when that history is ineluctably guided by divine influence, then the vagaries of "a life journey" become the same things as the undulations of sea waves that bear a ship to a promised shore. I derive this seafaring metaphor from Ekhaguere himself, when he basically states the mathematical formulation that describes his life philosophy.

> Each earthling has some innate potential or promise. But the invariably nonlinear route to realizing or claiming a potential or promise will, in general, be different for each person. In the rest of this autobiography, I highlight the taut nexus between *promise* and *Providence* in my life. To this end, I narrate how Providence mercifully turned around for me certain negatively disruptive and game-changing situations, by furnishing me with awesome solutions to multiple unforeseen and apparently intractable life problems…As it is said, no boat without a sail can take advantage of any wind, no matter how strong. In navigating the numerous treacherous seas that I had to traverse in my journey through life so far, *promise* was my boat and *Providence* was my sail.

This statement could possibly pass as Ekhaguere's Principle. The ethnographic, oceanographic, philosophical, theological and mathematical significance and implications of this Principle are at the core of this review, and I shall return to them shortly.

In the meantime, as far as the stylistic choices of the book go, they exemplify what William B. Strunk (1869-1946) had promoted as the proper means of writing in his Elements of Style (1919). At page 19 of Elements, Strunk notes that "brevity promotes vigour" and, years ago, I added to my own copy my persuasion that it was also "a sign of mastery over the subject matter". Ekhaguere writes quite committedly with distinction and in the parsimonious tradition. But it is not likely that his parsimony was acquired through the parsimonious movement, which was a phase in social science writing during which the emphasis on brevity was paramount; Ekhaguere is not a social scientist per se. So, why does he write in this manner?

I must believe this style comes to him from Mathematics—a discipline whose lexical registers do not tolerate the superfluous. Unlike Literature, Mathematics has no room for drama, no space for suspense. However consequential its findings, they are rendered in cold cryptic calculi that brook no tension, intention or emotional flourish.

Nonetheless, the novelist's conversational mien is unmistakable in Promise and Providence. There is an Achebe there. Ekhaguere adopts this tone to make his dense material accessible to his audience; otherwise it would have remained a convoluted schema conveyed within a convergence of "taut nexuses". That would not have helped matters at all. The conversational tone is trustworthy. It delivers the core message with ease, under a historical leitmotif that arranges the material in a digestible logical flow and chronological sequence. In essence, Promise and Providence is what happened when a Mathematical rabbi borrowed tools from a literary writer to speak about his personal history and its underlying elements.

Following a neurologically sound strategy, Ekhaguere found it expedient to present his conclusion first, noting that his "ongoing earthly pilgrimage is amply symbolized by the following simple equation:

My Life = Promise + Providence".

Quite ostensibly, he retreated into the disciplinary territory in which he is a celebrated guru, namely Mathematics, to come up with a summary of his life philosophy by way of this "equation". For him, "The providential interventions transformed multiple fate-determining ordeals in my life into a series of modest achievements". At that point, he invites a philosophical scrutiny of his intentions. It is abundantly clear that this "equation" is couched in terms of Hegel's dialectical idealism, although the language used and the introduction of the question of ordeal makes his message distinctly Augustinian. But why does Ekhaguere run counter to the epistemology of John Locke (1634-1704) and his critique of any theory of innate ideas by submitting that "Each earthling has some innate potential or promise."

This idea of "innate potential" is inherently Platonic. In his Theory of Recollection, Plato had averred that human beings retained a remembrance of things they knew innately in their souls. Locke confronted this theory of innate ideas by noting that ideas that were often cited as innate were so complex that they could not be apprehended without learning. He (Locke) therefore wondered what the utility of innate ideas were, if we were not aware of these innate ideas. For him, whatever we thought of as innate had been deciphered through schooling and, in this way, was not innate at all.

Similarly, Locke would not have been satisfied with the prominence granted Providence in this work since, for him, God is not a universally accepted idea and can therefore not be held to constitute some part of innate knowledge. The Augustinian argument that every human being had a God-shaped void, which only God could fill, would have been an apt rejoinder but this autobiography establishes its philosophical foundations upon a contested pedal without moving swiftly to defend it.

At this point, the dramatic quality of the autobiography takes off. There is a continuous tension between explosive "fate-determining" histories and the moderation of a mathematician who must describe and, ultimately, own them. Ekhaguere comes across as a modest mathematical charioteer charged with the responsibility of guiding an experiential herd of horses from treacherous terrain belonging to arch-epistemologists like Locke to the greener pastures "innately promised" by God. He has done this charioting masterfully, albeit with such detachment as warrants a commentary on its own. The interesting fact, further to this, is that Ekhaguere is a master mathematician, an Emeritus Professor whose forte is in the field of epistemology for, as I noted years ago in a book of tributes written in his honour, according to Leibniz, Mathematics is the highest form of logic (Obono, 2017).

So, why does Ekhaguere not dwell at length on the thrills and frills of his emotional experience? Is it solely because he believes that his life is a product of the alignments of promise and Providence? Is that an adequate explanation? As I write this, I recall the times I served on policy formulation committees at the University of Ibadan, which Ekhaguere led. These were many years ago, but I distinctly recall thinking how this man had so much knowledge that his default attitude in his interactions with the world was by means of what I conceptualized as "engaged detachment". It was in reference to Ekhaguere that I first coined this phrase as I sought for ways of understanding how and why he could have so much commitment and passion about an enterprise and yet retain this ethereal air of equanimity about his person.

I suspect that it is a degree of that same engaged detachment that we find in the autobiography, which is also what makes the account so trustworthy and reliable. There is no push to persuade. But there does seem to be some ambivalence in the organisation of this crowning achievement. Reading through a second time, I still came away with the impression that, left to his own devices, Professor Ekhaguere would ordinarily not have gotten round to writing this autobiography. As he explains in the book, the COVID-19 lockdown of 2020 forced him to write this weighty tome. He says: "I wrote much of this book from March to December 2020, in the throes of an existential struggle to be unharmed by a novel, virulent and excruciating coronavirus pandemic, as one way of keeping myself busy and safe."

Yet, I am not too certain that I completely agree with this. I do not think that GOS Ekhaguere produced what could easily amount to his crowning achievement within nine months, or that the reason he had for doing so was to keep himself busy and safe. If it were that, then he could conveniently have taken up bee-keeping or snail production to stay busy, and Jiu-jitsu to stay safe. In my mind, the depth and breadth of his submissions in Promise and Providence show quite clearly that he had been ruminating over this autobiography subconsciously in his head for a long time. No specific timeframe can be placed on this, but it certainly extends beyond nine months. What I think Ekhaguere did within the nine months was to set down in visible written form the ideas he had been invisibly writing for many years before now, bringing order to the chaos. To use an analogy drawn from obstetrics, I would say that the gestation period of this work was far longer than the nine months it took for the birth delivery, and other elements of "autochthonous phytomedicine", to occur.

As I mentioned, I worked with Ekhaguere on several committees, which he led, and had the additional privilege of co-publishing with him on the impacts of underdevelopment on the quality of research. He has a highly developed sensitivity to matters of a moral kind. He might classify his achievements as being "modest" all he wants. That would not necessarily make them so. His achievements are extraordinary. Someone has actually said that "the Ekhaguere kind" does not pass through the same planetary system except at long intervals (Obono, 2017). He knows this, but his humility prevents him from openly acknowledging it. And, yet, he also knows that: "For everyone to whom much is given, from him much will be required; and to whom much has been committed, of him they will ask the more" (Luke 12: 48, NKJV). I believe that it is from this deep well of moral intelligence that Professor Ekhaguere stoked this intellectual fire and sustained it until it brought us this life-affirming ambrosia.

Speaking on his childhood, he shares difficult experiences of growing up in a working class family. His mother, uneducated and illiterate, gained some financial stability by performing child deliveries and other minor medical procedures using phytomedical approaches. His mother had a policy of treating her patients first and requesting payments only after the patient had recovered. Predictably, some patients did not return with payment, but this did not dissuade his mother from doing the same thing over and over again. Her humanitarian approach to interpersonal relationships exemplifies the difference between economic and virtuous wealth. Her economic situation did not deter her from being a virtuous human. This policy on payment has stuck with Ekhaguere as most important and foundational to his work ethic. It has left him with lasting lessons in personal ethical management.

Ekhaguere faced more than just economic instability during his childhood. In secondary school, he was forced to abandon his education due to a coup d'état in 1966. A national event instantly rendered him even more vulnerable. This demonstrates how economics and politics could intersect to create unstable grounds for childhood development. Earlier, he withdrew from school because his mother could no longer afford the fees. While these incidents showcase the suboptimal educational conditions for a child of low socioeconomic background, Ekhaguere was quick to recognize, and seize, the opportunity presented by the Universal Primary Education Programme instituted by Chief Obafemi Awolowo that allowed his return to school. His story is one of unending perseverance, courage, and good fortune. His rise to prominence in the Mathematics Department at the University of Ibadan demonstrates the heart that he showed and will to lift himself out of a working class background.

Having said that, the pertinence with which he recalls details from this background is not only incredible but also instructive. It is as though he sought to pay homage to every crop farmed by his single mother "such as cassava, maize, cocoyam, okro and our indigenous melon" as instruments of divine provenance in his life. These were the crops that sustained him – he who hawked kerosene for his mother "throughout the Nigerian Quarters at WAIFOR after school as from 4:00p.m.... [until] 7:00p.m. and 8:00p.m." For five straight years, commencing at age 7, Professor Ekhaguere was his mother's sales boy, until he turned 12. He hawked kerosene. This led to missed opportunities. He missed the co-curricular activities organised by teachers in the evenings after 4:00p.m. He could not join the Boy Scouts or the Boys' Brigade, which in his childhood eyes were the epitome of the sort of training needed by every progressive boy. It was too early for him to see the links between these organizations and a colonial mandate, and how those links cast doubt on their ethical neutrality on questions of race relations, even when he saw visual evidence of segregation and inequality in the divisions between the European Quarters and Nigerian Quarters at the West African Institute for Forestry Research (WAIFOR).

He regretted these things but remained committed to pulling his weight and making his contributions to domestic wellbeing. The experience of spending the first thirteen years of his life at the WAIFOR – which he calls "a veritable ecosystem of diverse nationalities, ethnicities, cultures, professions, and excellent resources" –situated him at the crossroads of opportunity and its denial. All around him, everything at WAIFOR seemed to reflect a European world at peace with itself, but his own internal "ecosystem" was in disarray. His apprenticeship in a vocational trade after he dropped out of school was the result of parental marital instability. His mother bore only him for his father, although she had three other children by a previous husband. His father was "indifferent to his education". He was a serial monogamist who would in due course send the young Godwin's mother away and take on another wife. His mother bore the costs of his education alone. For one gifted with such powers of perception, the trauma of this early period apparently never left him. But it did generate in him empathy towards others. The experience made him better, not bitter.

On this note of maternal intervention, who knows which new Benin hawker, aged 8 or so, would pick up this book in 2022, and find fresh reaffirmation in its pages? Should this account drift into the hands of a boy in a Soho slum, would it make a difference? The kind of mother that Ekhaguere had was a major factor in the ethical lifestyle he has chosen to lead. She appears numerous times in history, stabilizing a destabilized child, nurturing him to confidence. This maternal presence is a recurrent theme in the lives of many great people in the world today, such as an Obama, or a Carson. Alexander of Macedon. It should speak loudly to our society at a time of blurry role distinctions and the kind of familial disorganization that is behind my publication of "The End of Families" (Obono, 2019).

If there are any other young "Ekhagueres" out there, hawking not kerosene but oranges even at UI gates, or groundnuts from faculty to faculty, do they not deserve a stable family to enable them tide through this most destabilizing of experiences? If the parents abandoned ship, what would become of their biological passengers? We need to direct them to Providence and direct Providence to them.

As I wrote this section, my eldest son walked into my study, unannounced. He had just travelled in from his school, where he boards, to be with the family through the two-day holidays. His arrival reminded me of how about 18 years ago, when he was about 4 or 5, I had driven with him around the campus at about 10:00p.m. It was a familiar pastime of ours, only this time, I drove outside the school gates but really went nowhere. I swirled round at the intersection and headed back into campus, slowing down and stopping just before the gates.

As I expected, a young boy about my son's age emerged from the darkness beyond my son's window, hawking oranges. I left it to my son to decide how many oranges we should buy. He stated a figure. I surprised him by buying up every orange that the lad had. I tipped him, prayed for him, and asked him to go home, get some sleep, and be ready for school the next morning. He thanked me and ran off into the darkness. My son sat motionless as I quietly drove back to our home on campus. I gave him only a short talk about that anonymous boy who sold oranges in the darkness. I do not remember everything I told him but I do not think he ever forgot. Back home, I observed he could not bring himself to sucking the oranges. For all we know, that lad has a boat called promise and the wind behind his sails is Providence. He could be another Ekhaguere.

This, for me, is the purport of this autobiography. We mortals should be extensions of Providence on earth, much like Fr. Flanagan (Principal of Immaculate Conception College), or Professor Olumuyiwa Awe. We can make other people's dreams come true.

It is simply amazing that a child born and bred under the circumstances documented in Promise and Providence would find his way to Imperial College, London. This is nothing short of providential. How that event became a catalyst for his subsequent assent to the greatness he had evinced all along is a lesson in faith and fate but also on the value of a sterling work ethic and the need for endurance of all adversity with grace and equanimity.

Reading through sections of Promise and Providence as they concern the early life of Emeritus Professor GOS Ekhaguere, therefore, I am reminded of the reflections of British naval historian Cyril Northcote Parkinson (1909 –1993), who once said that:

> People of great ability do not emerge, as a rule, from the happiest background. So far as my own observation goes, I would conclude that ability, although hereditary, is improved by an early measure of adversity and improved again by a later measure of success.

Nothing could more eloquently describe the triumph over this "early measure of adversity" than the life and times of Professor GOS Ekhaguere. Depending on one's disposition, memories presented in this stark manner, without any attempt at, or interest in, whipping up sentiments, serve then to intensify pathos. Alternatively, and this is where it counts, they point to the significance of the message they convey—that throughout these events, the author was upheld by the hands of Providence. How else would you explain his not being qualified for primary school because he failed the arm-across-head test but was pushed forward to taking the aptitude test, which he passed; or the fact that the period he needed a father figure most was the time of his domestic disruption, which saw him living and working with a single mother?

This is indeed an extraordinary book. It possesses the biblical quality of the Book of Esther, in which Providence plays a decisive role in thwarting the machinations of Haman and other enemies of God's people, upon whom He had placed a promise, to deliver them from harm and bring them to an expected end. I believe the persuasion to write these two books came from similar sources. If Esther were to be renamed, a suitable title for it would have been Promise and Providence! Same difference!

Right from the title of this long-awaited autobiography to its Dedication — and the homage it pays to the named constellation of significant others in his life—the author, Professor Emeritus GOS Ekhaguere (NNOM) shows consistently that the cornucopia of realized promise that is the message of his life has been due less to human strategizing than the force of a Providential engagement. How a leading global mathematician would run all his calculations and arrive at God as his final answer to all the questions dialectically embedded in, and generated by, all possible answers is a mystery left unsolved by the author. I believe that, in a sequel to this autobiography, he must tell us how to make the engagement of Providence in our lives sure and secure.

In this sense, Ekhaguere's mathematical theology presents object lessons to an agnostic professoriate which has for long held the belief that the recognition of providential powers was incompatible with pure scientific analysis. My Christological reading of Ekhaguere's autobiography was preceded by a copy of *The Science of God: The Convergence of Scientific and Biblical Wisdom,* a book which, interestingly enough, I bought in a city called Providence while I had been a post-doctoral fellow at Brown University. That book dresses up Thomism in rich empirical accoutrements, and essentially disputes the idea that science was contrary to religion.

There are important similarities and differences in the approach adopted by physicist Gerald Schroeder in The Science of God to this unique aspect of cosmology, and Ekhaguere's approach to it in *Promise* and *Providence*. The former's empirical approach is immediately obvious. Schroeder deliberately uses a definitively discursive interdisciplinary methodology, drawing from the latest scientific evidence in biochemistry, astrophysics, and quantum physics, to show that science and religion were not just compatible but interdependent. He subscribes to a certain amoral binarism in which the products and the producer are at opposite ends of an equation, with the equality sign being the medium or bridge by which causality is established.

Ekhaguere, on the other hand, is instinctively transdisciplinary in his approach. He fuses all the evidence available in his illustrious life into a metaphorical bath of sulfuric acid (more or less supplied by Schroeder!) and points to the redundancy of dealing with contingent effects at the expense of a full focus on an Immutable Cause. His account dissolves the distinctions dependent on Providence by restricting the title of his book to the Primal Cause and the prophetic emanations of that Cause as they affected him. In the process, he (Ekhaguere) unified the universe. He tells the story of a single individual from an elevated ethnographic vantage point. Consequently, I would conclude that while Schroeder provided empirical demonstrations of the interdependence of science and religion, Ekhaguere took that discourse to an ontological plane by resituating it within what, for now, I will grant was an autobiography. Momentarily, however, I shall contend that Professor Ekhaguere has produced something much more than this. He has delivered to us an *autoethnography*.

His insistence on the primacy of God is not in any question. He clearly places God at the centre of his accomplishments when he wrote that:

> After my retirement, I was appointed, *through God's amazing grace* [emphases mine], to the life-long post of *Professor Emeritus of*

Mathematics by the Governing Council of the University of Ibadan, following a recommendation by the institution's Senate. I also had the *good fortune* [emphases mine] of winning the Nigerian National Order of Merit (NNOM) award, the nation's highest intellectual and academic laurel.

The interaction between the dependent human being and the contingent circumstances that then produced autobiographical outcomes are, in his view (and I am taking large liberties with an explanation of a theory or philosophy that even Ekhaguere might not be aware he had enunciated) become readily obvious to one. As I approach a conclusion of this review, it does indeed keep occurring to me that what Prof. Ekhaguere intended to produce was a thoroughgoing autobiography. But I cannot pull away from the fact that what he has achieved is not an ordinary autobiography. It is what anthropologists would call an autoethnography. Once Ekhaguere had committed himself to referring to his early childhood in the environment of a research institute as "a veritable ecosystem", the Freudian slip was out. The "biographical" content of the "autobiography" had become subsumed within a much larger ethnographic enterprise.

This explains why he seamlessly transits from WAIFOR to ICC, the premier university, and Imperial College, to his engagements in several professional bodies and formations of mathematical bodies, and the treatment of national politics as though these were the usual antecedents of an academic biographer. They are not. Ekhaguere's intuitive immersion in subliminal history is palpable as he narrates the subtle environmental influences that shaped his life as a person and scholar. It is at these points that the narrative begins to resonate with the multiple spiritualities of his diverse readership, who themselves are part products of the histories described. The continuous contention with that ecological perspective is what translates this work from being a mere autobiography into a constitutive autoethnography. Nowhere is he more autoethnographical than when he writes that:

I have also sketched my own perspective of some of the elements of the history of some of the educational institutions with which I was involved either as a student, teacher, researcher, visiting scholar or higher education administrator. In doing so, I have tried to furnish as many facts as possible, always with much sensitivity to avoiding an unwieldy presentation. It is my thinking that through progressive accretion of facts from similar sketches, by other alumni and alumnae as well as workplace colleagues, to complement the ones that I present in this book, the history of each of the institutions might be incrementally reconstructed.

Once the focus shifts, and is deflected away from the individual biographer to an account of external systems or institutions as the main subject, then the book has moved past the zones of autobiography and morphed into something much larger. The author's personal antecedents and a huge number of intellectual factors perhaps make it impossible for him to focus exclusively upon himself alone in this book, even when he is the worthiest candidate for that attention. He is a quintessential autoethnographer. His transdisciplinary mindset makes it easy for him to achieve this feat, within this eclectic realm of discourse. I extend my congratulations to him on this.

It is my submission that this book would probably go down as Ekhaguere's magnum opus. It is a far-ranging self-conscious and critically-aware chronicle of a swathe of history and how that shaped a distinguished human life. Thus, again, while the Science of God is interdisciplinary, Promise and Providence is the transdisciplinary compendium of a rich repertoire of experience that signals the dawn of a new ethos in the production of autobiographies. One would always expect that the summary of GOS Ekhaguere's life philosophy would be expressed in one form or the other of a mathematical dualism. In this sense, it is the equation of a pervasive moral force, which he charges with beneficence and, for convenience, calls "Providence".

As far as mathematical mantras go, this is a thick kind of equation. Two independent variables exist and both are located on the right hand side of the equation. The one *(promise)* is, however, a product of the other *(Providence)*. Both are treated as though they were coequal. Whether this dialectical contradiction is deliberate on Ekhaguere's part, or it is something serendipitous that inevitably emerged from his genius, even when it was not actively engaged to produce the kind of statement that this autobiography leads to, one cannot say. What one can say is that, in a nutshell, this is a stupendously engaging intellectual *tour de force*. The entire account suggests that the only knowable things are the permanent things, not transient ones. Thus, by identifying the "innate potential" that he always understood was placed upon his life by grace, Ekhaguere has produced a veritable autoethnography that invites us to acknowledge the Providence that had placed it there.

Professor Oka Martin Obono
Professor of Sociology and Ethnodemography,
Obol Kògbóónghà K'Ékpòn of Yakurr,
President, Yakurr Academic Society,
Chair, Case Studies Consulting Ltd.

References

Obono, Oka. 2019. The End of Families. In Eze Nwokocha and Funke Fayehun (eds.). *Concise Demography of Nigeria.* Ibadan: BumbleBee Publishing. Pp. 99-123.

Obono, Oka. 2017. A Quiet Introduction to Ekhaguere. *GOS Ekhaguere: A Multi-Perspective Glimpse into the Life of a Mathematician at 70.* Ibadan: NP: International Centre for Mathematics and Computer Sciences. Pp. 36-41.

Schroeder, Gerald. 1997. *The Science of God: The Convergence of Biblical and Scientific Wisdom.* Simon and Schuster.

PROLOGUE

The pen that writes your life story must be held in your own hand.
IRENE C. KASSORLA[4]

This autobiography sketches some key aspects of my life journey. It begins by documenting a number of my experiences when I was growing up in a research institute near Benin City. Those days were characterised by community cohesion, civic responsibility and collaborative collegiality, underpinned by ageless norms, values and precepts that were accepted by, and binding on all. The book also narrates some of the severe headwinds that I encountered during my struggle through the somewhat contorted Nigerian educational pipeline to acquire primary, secondary and tertiary education. This was in spite of the fact that, at each level of education, many of my teachers saw me as someone with much promise in the academic realm. Each predicament had the potential of quickly unravelling, in a somewhat Sisyphean way, every one of my previous achievements. Fortunately, at each crucial milestone in my life, Providence always intervened with awesome solutions that elegantly eliminated outstanding difficulties. The providential interventions transformed multiple fate-determining ordeals in my life into a series of modest achievements. As I do not think that my autobiography should be solely about me, I have also sketched the profiles of some of the many persons who contributed in multiple ways to make me who I eventually became.

---

4   Psychologist and author of the book: *Go for it! How to Win at Love, Work and Play,* published by Dell Publishing Company, Inc., New York (1985), ISBN-10: 0440127521, ISBN-13: 9780440127529.

Looking back now, I ask myself how it was that I had been so graciously favoured. As a result of timely providential solutions to several hard problems in my life, I attended one of the best primary schools in Nigeria, graduated from the nation's premier university and obtained my PhD degree in one of the best universities in the United Kingdom. Moreover, I had the good fortune of visiting, working and participating in a variety of academic and higher education activities in diverse universities around the world. After my retirement, I was appointed, through God's amazing grace, to the lifelong post of Emeritus Professor of Mathematics by the Governing Council of the University of Ibadan, following a recommendation by the institution's Senate. I also had the good fortune of winning the Nigerian National Order of Merit (NNOM) award, the nation's highest intellectual and academic laurel.

Through the events that are recorded in the following chapters, I have also sketched my own perspective of some elements of the history of some of the educational institutions with which I was involved either as a student, teacher, researcher, visiting scholar or higher education administrator. In doing so, I have tried to furnish as many facts as possible, always with much sensitivity to avoiding an unwieldy presentation. It is my thinking that through the progressive accretion of facts from similar sketches, by other alumni and alumnae as well as workplace colleagues, to complement the ones that I present in this book, the history of each of the institutions might be incrementally reconstructed.

I wrote much of this book from March to December 2020, in the throes of an existential struggle to be unharmed by a novel, virulent and excruciating coronavirus pandemic, as one way of keeping myself busy and safe. Globally, the pandemic swiftly precipitated lockdowns, border closures and flight cancellations, including widespread disruptions of educational and economic activities, with unprecedented adverse impact on both individual and national life.

PART I

EARLY DAYS

1

MY ROUTE INTO LIFE

several significant aspects of the history of the Edo people, who occupy a significant part of the Federal Republic of Nigeria, have been chronicled by multiple historians and other scholars. In chronological order, the history may be structured into the following three distinct eras: the pre-Ogiso era (before circa 900 AD), the Ogiso era (circa 900-1170 AD) and the Oba era, which began around the year 1200 and subsists till today. Knowledge of the governance structure, defense system and other strategic organs in the pre-Ogiso era is scanty, beyond the inference that some of the organs, however rudimentary or disparate, which were in operation during that era, might have been fundamental to the evolution of the Ogiso and Oba eras, about which there is ample documentation by multiple scholars. During the latter eras, the Edo people distinguished themselves by their chivalry, in the wars they fought, and by diplomacy, in their deft interaction with early missionaries and explorers, who were largely Europeans, as well as by their relatively advanced administrative and governance structures, including a high level of expertise in town planning that more than baffled many foreign visitors.

The famous Benin Empire flourished from 1440 to 1897. It was abruptly truncated in 1897 by the British Empire, after provoking an avoidable military confrontation with the Edo people. At the epicentre of the history of the Edo people is Benin City (6.3350°

N, 5.6037° E), which functioned dually as the capital of the Benin Empire and the seat of the Benin Kingdom. But the town was not always known by this name. During the reign, from 40 BC to AD 16, of Igodo, also known as Obagodo, the first Ogiso of Edo land, Benin City was called Igodomigodo, an eponymous derivation from Igodo. After the death of Igodo, his son, Ere succeeded him and reigned from AD 16 to AD 66. During Ogiso Ere's tenure, Benin City was called Ile. This name was changed to Edo by Oba Ewuare the Great, who reigned from 1440 to 1473. The name Benin City is a more recent appellation, adopted in 1914 during the tenure of Oba Eweka II, who reigned from 1914 to 1933.

In Japanese history, the name *Edo* also appears. It was the former name of present-day Tokyo, during the feudal military dictatorship established on March 24, 1603 by Tokugawa Ieyasu (January 31, 1543 – June 1, 1616). The period from 1603 to 1867 is called the *Edo period* in Japan. *Edo* was renamed *Tokyo* in 1868. It is seen here that the use of the word *Edo* by the Benin people predated its use by the Japanese by more than one and a half centuries.

Birth in Benin City

I was born in Benin City on Friday, May 23, 1947, a year marked by a total solar eclipse, the first after the Second World War. The eclipse occurred on Tuesday, May 20, 1947, and was observed in Benin City. The phenomenon began at 14:35 and ended at 17:15, a period of 2 hours and 40 minutes. But the duration of totality was only 3 minutes and 26 seconds. My mother described her experience of the spectacular solar phenomenon to me when I was very young. She recalled that at some time in the afternoon of that day, it appeared as though the sun was setting. That state of affairs progressed until total darkness, when the sun was completely obscured for some three and a half minutes. This kind of phenomenon, which had never occurred since her birth and of which she had no prior warning, was not only frightening and troubling to her but also caused considerable panic everywhere. "Total darkness in the afternoon? We all thought that the world had come to an end", narrated my mother. A solar eclipse is not an inexplicable event. According to physics, it occurs when a new moon, the earth and the sun are aligned in a straight line in space, with the moon completely obscuring the earth from the sun. The dates of future eclipses are, therefore, not difficult to calculate. The last total solar eclipse in Nigeria occurred on Wednesday, March 29, 2006, with only Oyo, Kwara, Niger, Zamfara and Katsina States lying along its belt of totality. The next total solar eclipse in Nigeria will occur on Monday, March 20, 2034, at precisely 18 minutes and 45 seconds past 10:00a.m. and its duration of totality will be 4 minutes and 9 seconds. Benin City will again lie along its path of totality.

Paternal Lineage

My father, Johnson Osayande Ekhaguere was born in 1904 at Orogho (5° 53′00″N, 5°58′ 00″E), located in the present-day Orhionmwon Local Government Area of Edo State, Nigeria. Recently, it has emerged that this town is endowed with oil and gas fields.

My grandfather's first name was Ekhaguere, an eponymous derivation from Ere, the name of the second Ogiso of Edo land. Ekhaguere means: a person [Ogiso Ere] whose predictions are always prophetic or someone [Ogiso Ere] endowed with uncommon perspicacity. Ekhaguere's father and mother were called Igunbor and Iwuamo, respectively. Reputed to be tough, highly articulate, fearless, and with zero tolerance for injustice, Ekhaguere was a native of Orogho, from the Idunmwunkhianmwan section of the town. In recognition of the indicated attributes, he was honoured with the much coveted title of the *Oka eghele of Orogho* (Youth Leader of Orogho) in his youth. He married three wives, each of whom bore him a child. The children, all since deceased, were Idelegbagbon (daughter), Osaghae (son) and my father, Johnson Osayande (son).

Ekhaguere died in 1933. My paternal grandmother Ihase, also called
Famiro, was born of Akure parents. Her father's name was Fatoke.
I have no knowledge of her mother's name. She had two children,
both male, for two husbands: one, my father, for Ekhaguere
and the other, Gabriel Eriamiatoe Aigbedion (1912-2007), for
Nugbasoro. She died in 1923. My father was quite close to his
mother. According to him, because of the excruciating hardship
that he was experiencing after his mother's death, he agreed to be
taken by one Osarenmwindamwen, a tailor, to Calabar in 1928 to
be trained in tailoring. He learnt the trade, became fluent in Efik
and remained in Calabar for some years before he was constrained
to return to Benin City in 1933, following the death of his father.
My father had six children from three different wives, namely:
Solomon, Martin, Godwin (myself), Enekpen (daughter), Oghogho
(son), and Ekogiawe (son). He was, however, not a polygamist in the
ordinary sense, since he did not have more than one wife at any time.
My paternal brothers Solomon, Martin, Oghogho and Ekogiawe have
all predeceased me. My father died in Benin City in 1990 at the age
of 86 years.

Maternal Lineage

My mother was Ogundemwingie Ekhaguere. She was born in 1900 at
Usen (6° 45′ 00″N, 5° 21′ 00″E), located in present-day Ovia South-
West Local Government area of Edo State, Nigeria. Usen is 40 miles (65
kilometres) from Benin City, driving along Benin-Sagamu expressway.
Her father's name was Edoh. The latter's father was Ogbebor, famously
called Ogbebor N'usen. My maternal grandmother was called Ebose.
She had four children, two sons and two daughters for Edoh, namely:
Edugie (daughter), my mother, Ovenseri (son) and Abbi (son). Born
in 1870 in Usen, Ebose died in 1971 in Benin City at the age of 101
years. My mother was basically a housewife, who was manifestly meek,
calm, compassionate and peace-loving, with an amazing capacity to
bond with almost anyone. She carried out her matrimonial and maternal
duties with passion. My mother had four surviving children, namely:

Rose (daughter), John (son), Mary (daughter) and myself. My maternal siblings have all predeceased me. She died in Benin City in 1986 at the age of 86 years.

Promise and Providence

Each earthling has some innate potential or promise. But the invariably nonlinear route to realising or claiming a potential or promise will, in general, be different for each person. In the rest of this autobiography, I highlight the taut nexus between *Promise* and *Providence* in my life. To this end, I narrate how Providence mercifully turned around for me certain negatively disruptive and game-changing situations, by furnishing me with awesome solutions to multiple unforeseen and apparently intractable life problems. The potentially progress-limiting circumstances would have severely undermined whatever promise the Almighty God had endowed me with or even rendered it entirely nugatory. As it is said, no boat without a sail can take advantage of any wind, no matter how strong. In navigating the numerous treacherous seas that I had to traverse in my journey through life so far, *Promise* was my boat and *Providence* was my sail. Accordingly, my ongoing earthly pilgrimage is amply symbolised by the following simple equation:

$$My\ Life = Promise + Providence,$$

which underlies the many awesome providential favours that I have been so fortunate to receive.

2

CHILDHOOD IN A
RESEARCH INSTITUTE

I spent the first thirteen years of my existence at the West African Institute for Oil Palm Research (WAIFOR), located 15 miles (24 kilometres) from Benin City. The Institute was a veritable ecosystem of diverse nationalities, ethnicities, cultures, professions and excellent resources. These attributes were exemplified by the presence of persons of European, Nigerian and West African origin as well as some other nationalities, a dedicated workforce, multiple institutional research programmes, high quality human and material capital for research, a conducive primary school education environment, efficient municipal services, including a rudimentary health service, and adequate recreational facilities. Growing up, fully immersed in that kind of social and research space, every child, including me, was meticulously mentored by the teachers and adults in the community, with no sensitivity to ethnicity. In those days, every adult regarded the mentoring of the next generation of youths as an integral aspect of his or her civic responsibility. Accordingly, it was not uncommon for an adult of some ethnic group in the community to bring to the notice of a guardian of a different ethnicity that (s)he observed the latter's ward behaving inappropriately and that (s)he had promptly disciplined the erring child. The guardian would express gratitude to the adult who had demonstrated such an altruistic concern for the proper upbringing of that child. Consequently, there was invariably no hiding place in the community for a delinquent child, as every adult could take prompt disciplinary action when the need arose. Through the collective mentoring system that was consensually entrenched in the community, children imbibed such ethereal values as honesty, truthfulness, diligence, respectfulness, forgiveness, integrity, kindness, compassion, competitiveness and self-control, which they in turn eventually infused in the community, as they themselves transformed into adults. Among other benefits, there was ethnic harmony: the community flourished and was the better for it.

Oil Palm Research

WAIFOR was established as a research institute whose research focus was primarily on oil palm (*Elaeis guineensis*). The Institute was later called the Nigerian Institute for Oil Palm Research (NIFOR). WAIFOR's predecessor was established in 1939 as the Oil Palm Research Station (OPRS), with Arthur F.W. Sheffield (fl. 1907-1958) as the pioneer officer-in-charge. His tenure was from 1939 to 1942. The OPRS was replaced with the West African Institute for Oil Palm Research (WAIFOR), which was created in 1951 by means of the Nigerian Ordinance No. 20. The pioneer Director of WAIFOR was Mr. Francis William Toovey, who had been the officer-in-charge of OPRS from 1947–1951. Born in 1911, Toovey's tenure was from 1952 to 1956. He subsequently became the Director of Glasshouse Crops Research Institute, Littlehampton, Sussex, England, established in 1954. He visited NIFOR in 1989 during the 50th anniversary of the establishment of OPRS. Following Nigeria's independence from Britain in 1960, the dissolution of the West African Research Organisation (WARO), a central outfit which conducted research in the British territories of Nigeria, Gold Coast (now Ghana) and Sierra Leone, and pursuant to the Nigerian Research Institutes Act No. 33 of

1964, the name WAIFOR was changed to the Nigerian Institute for Oil Palm Research (NIFOR) by the Federal Government of Nigeria. Under the Act, which also created the Cocoa Research Institute of Nigeria (CRIN), the Rubber Research Institute of Nigeria (RRIN) and the Nigerian Institute for Trypanosomiasis Research (NITR), NIFOR was charged with the:

> general duty of undertaking research into and providing information and advice relating to the production and products of oil palm and of such other palms as the Minister may determine.

As a consequence, NIFOR's research mandate was implicitly expanded to include kindred plants like coconut (*Cocos nucifera*), raffia (*Raphia farinifera*) and date (*Phoenix dactylifera*). The Institute quickly became a powerful magnet that attracted researchers in the biological, biochemical and allied sciences, and I recall that students from the School of Agriculture, Moor Plantation, Ibadan, established in 1921 but transformed into the IART in 1969 and affiliated to the University of Ife, Ile-Ife, visited WAIFOR annually for fieldwork. I became interested in the research enterprise from those early years.

In line with its core mandate and as a global centre of excellence in oil palm research, WAIFOR cultivated and maintained multiple oil palm plantations in other parts of Nigeria and some countries in the West African subregion. These were at the core of the Institute's research and development activities. The Institute also had a number of orchards, with oranges, grapes, guavas and other fruits. Fruits from the orchards were sold to workers at particular times of the year. WAIFOR was strict in matters of discipline. Nigerian workers were liable to be summarily dismissed if they, or their dependents, were convicted of taking fruits from the oil palm plantations or orchards. This kind of severe punishment was, however, never inflicted on European workers, who were always at liberty to pluck any kind of fruits as they wished without any consequences.

Life at WAIFOR

WAIFOR was a pleasing cross between a town and a village: it had the serenity of an elegant village while simultaneously exhibiting some of the modern facilities of a well-planned town. Streets and roads were always well maintained. Not all of them were tarred, except in the European Quarters and around the Institute's offices, which were remote from the Nigerian quarters. The road from Benin City through Evboneka to the European Quarters was also tarred. There was a water pumping station that supplied water to both the European and Nigerian quarters. In the early 1950s, electricity was also introduced throughout WAIFOR. This was quite revolutionary, as it eliminated the need to use oil lamps or lanterns in the night for household lighting.

There was also evident racial segregation, already alluded to above, reflecting the dominance of the Institute by Europeans who were in command of the governance and administration of WAIFOR: they directed research, held senior positions in the Institute and were at the forefront of decision-making. Moreover, they were housed in the so-called 'European quarters', a collection of well-built mansions of colonial type, secluded and remote from the quarters for Nigerians. The latter lived in houses, far away from the European quarters, which were organised by grade of appointment, according as the occupants were senior, middle level or junior members of staff. As one moved through the Nigerian quarters, it was not difficult to tell the cadre of staff which lived in the differently structured housing units: detached houses for senior staff and semi-detached houses for middle level and junior staff; there were also condominiums, derogatively called 'neighbour lines' in those days, for the lowest echelon of the junior staff cadre. Whenever a worker was promoted, he was assigned the kind of accommodation that matched his new grade. My parents lived in the Nigerian quarters, in one of the semi-detached accommodations for the junior staff cadre. With Nigeria's independence from the United

Kingdom in 1960 and the country's decision to become a republic in 1963, the population of expatriate workers in WAIFOR began to decline. What used to be the European quarters were unofficially, but more acceptably, renamed senior service quarters: they are today occupied by highly trained Nigerian experts and professionals.

Environmental Management

WAIFOR placed a huge premium on cleanliness and sanitation in the Nigerian quarters, in order to ensure a healthy and productive workforce. Tractors were deployed from time to time to mow the lawns, static pools of water were drained periodically and the environment was sprayed with DDT (Dichlorodiphenyltrichloroethane) to eliminate insects (especially mosquitoes), rodents and snakes. DDT was effective in reducing malarial morbidity and mortality in the community. But no environmental or human impact studies of the application of DDT was conducted in those days at WAIFOR. By contrast, in recent years, following a global outcry, triggered by the amply documented adverse environmental consequences of DDT use, its unbridled application was banned in May 2004, pursuant to the 'Stockholm Convention on Persistent Organic Pollutants', a global treaty, which restricted its application to malaria control. Other facilities which were enjoyed by workers in those days in the 1950s included uninterrupted electricity and pipe-borne water supply, scheduled waste collection, good health service, support for environmental sanitation and access to recreational amenities. These life-enhancing municipal services, hardly available in some big towns, let alone villages, in the Western Region of Nigeria in the early 1950s and delivered with steadfast attention to quality, relevance and reliability, were some of the fundamental prerequisites for a vibrant research establishment.

WAIFOR, therefore, was an ideal place in which to grow up: clean, scenic, multicultural, inclusive, collegial, sensitive to civic values, intellectually stimulating and world-class in its areas of specialisation. It was my good fortune to have spent my pre-teenage years in such an environment.

Travelling to and from Benin City

Before the mid-1950s, travelling to Benin City from WAIFOR was tedious and exhausting: to board a Benin-bound vehicle, one walked about five miles from the Institute to a village called Ugbogiobo, located along the Benin-Ibadan road, which was one of the routes of the famous Armels Transport Company of Benin. Similarly, returning from Benin City to WAIFOR involved travelling first to Ugbogiobo by means of a passenger lorry and then walking back to WAIFOR. As a solution to this problem and to enable the Nigerian workers to easily commute between WAIFOR and Benin City, the Institute introduced two daily free bus shuttles around 1956, with the Isiuwa Recreation Club, the community's hub of recreational activities, situated centrally in the Nigerian quarters, as the take-off point. The innovation was a great relief to all. The morning shuttle departed daily for Benin City at 8:00 am and returned to WAIFOR at 1:00p.m.; similarly, the evening shuttle departed daily for Benin City at 4:00p.m. and returned to WAIFOR at 9:00p.m. A prospective traveller would apply in writing for a seat. Many applications would be received daily but only about 40 persons would be selected to ride freely on each shuttle. Using the shuttles, staff and their dependents were able to carry out diverse activities in Benin City, such as purchasing merchandise for trading at WAIFOR, taking their wards to, or picking them up from secondary schools in Benin city, accessing services and medical clinics, delivering some services to Benin-based clients, watching athletic or footballing events or pursuing part-time studies in the city. I remember that members of my family, including me, rode on those shuttles from time to time in those days.

Community School, WAIFOR

As an indication of the Institute's commitment to the education of its workers' children and the raising of future generations of experts, some of whom potentially might be involved in administrative or scientific research activities in the Institute, there was a coeducational primary school at WAIFOR. Called Community School, WAIFOR (CSW), it was located in the Nigerian quarters, not far from the Isiuwa Recreation Club. Following Nigeria's transformation into a Republic on October 1, 1963, the name was changed to Community School, NIFOR (CSN), in 1964, and then renamed Isiuwa Primary School, NIFOR, several years later. The school was well-built architecturally, regularly maintained, properly staffed and adequately endowed with state-of-the-art teaching and learning resources. Probably as good as any of the primary schools in Britain and certainly much better than most primary schools in the Western Region of Nigeria in those years, CSW/CSN was the institution of choice for prospective pupils from such nearby villages as Ugbogiobo, Evboneka, Abumwere and the riparian Okokhuo, situated along the River Okhuo. Every year, the school performed excellently in the Western Region primary school leaving certificate examinations and its pupils were offered places in many highly competitive secondary schools in Nigeria.

Employment at the Institute

My father worked at the OPRS/WAIFOR/NIFOR from 1945 till his retirement in 1968. While still in service in the 1950s, he also engaged in tailoring on a part-time basis after his official work. But he could not carry out tailoring on a daily basis, because doing so depended very much on when he returned from work in the evening and how tired he was. That was because in those years, WAIFOR's modus operandi was to assign daily tasks to some categories of junior employees, which they were required to complete at the pain of losing the day's pay.

My father was highly regarded in the community as a competent tailor. As a child, I always looked forward to my Christmas and New Year dresses, which he sewed elegantly and were often significantly different in style and quality of tailoring from what other children in the community wore during such annual festivities. Although uneducated, one could see that he had a fairly high intelligence quotient, because he could make swift inferences, deductions and extrapolations when circumstances required such outcomes. He was also very witty, sociable, debonair and popular among his peers.

In the 1950s, married men managed their families in diverse ways, depending on their economic standing and professions. Many men in the villages were farmers. But as several crops such as yams, cassava, corn and rice were planted and harvested only once a year in those days, many farmers had incomes that were not only seasonal but often unpredictable. This posed huge financial problems in a large number of households. To cope with the challenges, some husbands adopted a division-of-labour approach. Accordingly, even if they had some civil service employments, men also cultivated farms and expected their wives to feed their households from the farms' harvests. Other household expenses were then deemed to be the responsibilities of the husbands.

As mentioned earlier, my father was husband to three women, in a nonpolygamous way, during three separate non-overlapping time periods. His first three children were male from two wives. The first wife had his first two children, both male. After separating from her, my father married my mother who had me for him. The first son, Solomon Amenaghawon, grew under the tutelage of my paternal uncle, Chief Gabriel Nugbasoro, who was an iconic primary school teacher in the service of the Roman Catholic Mission. If he had not lived with Chief Nugbasoro, it was unlikely that Solomon would have had any primary school education.

Solomon eventually became a skilful artist and graphic designer. In the 1960s, his business, called 'Super Signs', with its office on

Mission Road, was well known in Benin City and some other parts of the Mid-Western Region of Nigeria: it was the go-to company for services and artisanal capacity building in graphic art and design. Martin Osaretin, who was my father's second son, did not have an opportunity to acquire even a primary school education and hence was doomed to farming in the village, Orogho. But, through Providence, he would later be taken by a relation to Lagos where he became an electrician, flourished, set up a family, built a big mansion and had a large, lucrative pig farm. Solomon and Martin shared the same mother. I was my father's third child, from a different mother.

My Mother

My mother married my father in the year 1945 and moved from Benin City to join him at WAIFOR in that year. In addition to her other natural endowments, she was a versatile storyteller. From time to time after dinner, the family would persuade her to tell a story. As from the age of five, I began to understand and enjoy her stories. She would begin each story by first singing its accompanying song and then teaching us the chorus to the song. As she told a story, she would sing at appropriate intervals and we would respond with the chorus. She told us several stories over the years. The stories taught all of us a diversity of lessons about life and instilled some core values in anyone who listened to them. From my own perspective, the stories which made the most impact on me were, however, her moving and sometimes chilling accounts of her journey and travails through life. Often, she would be visibly distraught when narrating her odyssey and we, her children, would also be greatly upset. Let me sketch some of the things my mother told us about her life and also outline my own observations of some events concerning her as I grew up.

My mother was born and raised in Usen (6°45′0″N, 5°21′0″E), some 40 miles (65 kilometres) from Benin City. As was the practice in her days, she was quickly married off by her parents when she attained puberty. Her husband was also an indigene of Usen but was many years older than her. According to my mother, she resented the forced marriage and was often sad. That was her journey into womanhood. She longed for an exit from the marriage. But she soon became pregnant. Her mother, a practitioner of phytomedicine and traditional midwifery, was in charge of every aspect of her antenatal care. This was during an era of very high maternal mortality throughout Nigeria, principally caused by unmanaged high blood pressure during pregnancy, infection during childbirth and postpartum issues, all of which were largely beyond the competence of many autochthonous medical systems in those days. My mother safely gave birth to a set of twins in 1920. The arrival of babies normally triggered enormous joy and jubilation in a family and any community. Antithetically, the birth of the twins triggered pain and misery for my mother, her husband and her entire family. Why was that the case? Having twins in Usen in those days was an anathema, with grave consequences for the twins and their mother. My mother and her twins were taken to a forest, known to harbour extremely carnivorous animals, and asked to leave her twins there, turn around, move homeward and never to look backwards. That was the last time she saw her twins. To be forced by superstition to throw her twins to wild animals greatly traumatised my mother. This was the same kind of superstitious practice that the Scottish Presbyterian missionary, Mary Mitchell Slessor (December 2, 1848-January 13, 1915) laboured to successfully abolish in Calabar before her death. My mother never recovered psychologically from that heart-rending ordeal she endured so early in her life. Each time she narrated her tribulation to us, she would tearfully muse: "if those twins were the only children I was destined to ever have, I had been forced to pour away their lives as a libation to a weird, toxic and dehumanising superstition."

Abandonment of Marriage

My mother abandoned the marriage in which her twins were immolated, and left Usen for Benin City. That was not only because of her utter abhorrence of the forced marriage but also because, with the nonexistence of ultrasound scanning facilities in those days, she could not tell whether her next pregnancy would not again result in twins. In Benin City, she met and married Mr. Jonathan Okunoghae, for whom she had three surviving children in five births: Rose Atewe, John Osadolor Simeon (well known as JOS) and Mary Osatohanmwen. From her two marriages, my mother gave birth to seven children, with only three surviving: a set of twins and two female children had been lost to superstition and child mortality.

Separation from Second Husband

Some years after Mary's birth, my mother's marriage with Mr. Okunoghae came to an end because he had resolved to marry a younger wife. Thus, once again, destiny was forcing my mother to be on her own. She had custody of her three children and needed to fend for them. With no inkling as to where the requisite resources would come from, her new situation was enormously challenging. In 1945, she married Johnson Osayande Ekhaguere, a member of staff of WAIFOR, who would later beget me. She took her three children along with her to her new matrimonial home. My mother was a few years older than her new husband, my father. Along with her husband, she was incessantly the butt of deriders and traducers: some members of the WAIFOR community derided my father ceaselessly as a person who thoughtlessly married a woman much older than himself, while others traduced my mother as someone whose marriage would not produce any children as, according to them, she was well past her reproductive age. She was constantly under psychological onslaught by her traducers: a callousness that was liable to adversely affect many a woman's capacity to become pregnant.

Pregnancy by Amazing Grace

By Providence, my mother became pregnant in 1946 and gave birth to a son in 1947: me. As was often the tradition among the Edo people in those days, the names which many parents gave to their children sometimes depicted some fate-determining milestones in their own life trajectories before or during the children's conception and birth. My mother named me Ekhuemuenogiemwen, an Edo expression whose meaning is: my deriders and traducers have been shamed. The other names given to me were: Godwin, Osakpemwoya and Samuel.

NAME	MEANING
Godwin	friend of God or God's friend.
Osakpemwoya	God has washed away my suffering.
Samuel	heard of God or heard by God or asked of God or God has heard.
Ekhaguere	a person [Ogiso Ere] whose predictions are always prophetic or someone [Ogiso Ere] endowed with uncommon perspicacity.

Dumping of a Name

Out of my four forenames, Ekhuemuenogiemwen was the one by which I was popularly known at WAIFOR up till 1960, before I started secondary school education at the Immaculate Conception College, Benin City. From that year, I subtly abandoned Ekhuemuenogiemwen as one of my forenames. That was because, after much reflection over several years and in spite of the indescribable love I had for and received from my mother, I had arrived at the conclusion that the name had intrinsically nothing to do with me as a person but was simply a polemical response by my mother to all those who had gleefully humiliated, disparaged, derided and traduced her before my birth: I was unwilling to bear such a forename as a lifelong identifier and a perpetual reminder of the immense psychological pain that others inflicted on my mother.

My Extended Family Structure

By the age of four, I was fairly conscious of some features of the ecosystem in which I was immersed and growing. There were several children in our household at WAIFOR. It took me some years to know that I was the last born of my mother and the third child of my father, that I had three elder maternal siblings and that the other children were my nieces and cousins. But we routinely used the words 'brother' and 'sister' to describe ourselves, as if we were all from the same parents. It was my mother's fate to take on the onerous burden of raising all of us. With an entrenched culture of polygamy and no birth control scheme, poverty and suffering were palpable and widespread as women gave birth uncontrollably till menopause, with some mothering up to ten children, often without adequate and sustainable means of livelihood. Birth control was simply a fortuitous act of God, through which He either endowed a woman with only a small number of children, no matter how much she longed for more, or else He created her barren.

At WAIFOR, I was fortunate to grow up among other children of diverse religions and Nigerian ethnicities: Edo, Igbo, Yoruba, Efik, Urhobo and Ijaw, to cite only a few. In those days, no one saw the various ethnicities as constituting walls or contraptions for segregating the community into ethnically insular sub-communities but rather as salutary means of fostering community integration, cultural inclusiveness, continuous networking and national bonding. Every child in the community picked up some Nigerian languages other than his and was not only able to interact seamlessly with his peers but also made friends across ethnicities. In my case, some of the friendships that I was involved in during my pre-teenage years at WAIFOR have endured till this day.

PART II

PRE-TERTIARY LEVEL EDUCATION

3

ENTERING THE FORMAL
EDUCATION SPACE

Close to my sixth birthday anniversary in January 1953, it was time for me to begin my journey into education, which would become my lifelong enterprise. My father was largely indifferent to the education of his children. Although his first son, Solomon, acquired primary school education, that was by the grace of my uncle, Chief Gabriel Eriamiatoeaigbedion Nugbasoro (1912-2007), who was a primary school teacher in the Roman Catholic Mission (RCM) school system. It was therefore inconceivable that my father would take on the task of sponsoring my education. By contrast, my mother was determined that I must be educated to the highest possible level and was prepared to pick up the gauntlet. Her constant refrain was: "I am not educated. But I will ensure that my son is educated, no matter what it will take". This lapidary resolve by a woman with only modest means would later be tested, with an outcome that was potentially life-changing for me.

Enrollment for Primary School Education

In the 1950s and 1960s, an academic year for a primary and a secondary school ran from January to December, structured into three terms, each of 12 weeks. At the commencement of a new school year, January always marked the admission of prospective pupils to begin their primary school education programme. The first admission criterion was the arm-over-the-head test: a child would be asked to stretch an arm over his head until his fingers touched his ear on the opposite side. If a child passed the arm-over-the-head test, he would move on to the next stage, which involved testing the child's familiarity with the English alphabets and numerals. As there was only one primary school at WAIFOR, competition for admission was invariably keen. My niece, Patience Nosakhare Okuonrobo, the future. Patience Nosakhare Erhabor, and I, being the only children of primary school age in our household at that time, had been preparing to join the 1953 cohort of pupils. We were taught the English alphabets and the English numerals up to 100. We recited these over and over again, every evening for months, to reduce the likelihood of errors. My uncle, Chief Nugbasoro, usually spent some time with our family at WAIFOR whenever his school was on holidays. He was with us in December 1952 and joined in coaching my niece and me for the impending selection exercise. Other parents and guardians at WAIFOR also prepared their children and wards toward the competition for admission.

My first day at school was dramatic in some sense. My senior sister, Rose, the mother of Patience, took Patience and me to the Community School, WAIFOR, which was situated, at that time, in a temporary site, from which it subsequently moved to its permanent site in 1954. During the selection exercise, I failed the crucial arm-over-the-head test, as I was smallish, while my niece, Patience, who was one year younger but taller than I, easily scaled that hurdle.

I had looked with much enthusiasm to becoming a pupil. As a result, the tragic event of being rejected on account of my height alone was a devastating setback so early in my life. A child who passed the arm-over-the-head test was taken into a classroom, where his familiarity with English numerals and alphabets was evaluated. This was to ensure that a child's height alone did not determine admission; the child's mental preparedness for school life was deemed also important. Accordingly, there were children who were eventually rejected even though they passed the arm-over-the-head test. My niece easily passed the academic test: familiarity with the English numerals and alphabets. She was, therefore, enrolled along with other successful children for the 1953 school year. I wept inconsolably, when I was asked to try again the following year 1954. The school teachers around saw how distraught I was by their decision and began to be empathetic. They checked the enrollment numbers again and determined that there were a few places not yet taken up. I was tested on my knowledge of the English numerals and alphabets and passed. Ultimately, I was enrolled into Infant 1 as one of the pupils of the 1953 cohort. In those days, it took a child seven years to complete the primary school programme, because he would move from Infant 1 to Infant 2, and then through Standard 1 to Standard 5. In Infant 1 and Infant 2, a pupil acquired what amounted to an advanced type of nursery or kindergarten education. I completed my Standard 5 studies in 1959.

Providing Wards with Education

In the 1950s, providing their wards with education was a huge struggle for many parents and guardians. This was because of their low annual earnings which severely limited their capacity to sponsor their children and wards in primary or secondary schools. From 1907 to 1958, the Nigerian currency was the British West African Pound. Its subordinate denominations were: farthing (*anini*), half penny (*ekpini*), penny (*ikobo*), three pence (*itoro*), six pence (*esisi*), one shilling (*isele*) and one pound sterling (*ikponkpa*). One shilling was equivalent to 12 pennies and 20 shillings corresponded to one pound sterling. Money had value, as each of these denominations had economic relevance: there were items or services which could be procured with each of them. This contributed to ensuring that inflation was essentially nonexistent. After 1958, the Nigerian pound was introduced and used as the legal tender up to 1973, when it was replaced with the *Naira* and *kobo*.

In 1953, primary education was not free in the Western Region of Nigeria. The annual primary school fee at the Community School, WAIFOR, in 1953 and 1954 was about £3 (three pounds sterling). For many parents and guardians, this fee, corresponding to 60 shillings per year, was difficult to muster, because in the Western Region of Nigeria, the minimum wage, which took effect from October 1954, was five shillings per month or, equivalently, 60 shillings, i.e. £3 (three pounds sterling), per year. This meant that a parent or guardian who earned the minimum wage would be unable to enroll his child or ward in a primary school, if he did not have additional streams of income. The monthly income of a large percentage of the population was far less than the minimum wage. There was therefore a glaring need to do something about the primary school fee, if the minimum wage could not be higher. Otherwise, a vicious circle would be set up: poverty would put education out of the reach of many children of primary school age and lack of education would in turn fuel widespread poverty in the Western Region. This development-limiting conundrum was resolved by the Government of the Western Region to the relief of millions of parents and guardians.

Progress at School Work

With my admission in 1953 as a *bona fide* pupil of the Community School, WAIFOR, my mother defrayed my school fee of £3 (three pounds sterling) by paying £1 (one pound sterling) every term. She bought me a slate which served as my writing tablet and I joined my peers in Infant 1. Without my mother, I would never have had the good fortune of seeing the four walls of a primary school, let alone attending the several educational institutions which providence would subsequently see me through.

Academic and other activities kicked off in earnest on my first day at school and were sustained throughout the year. Learning was interesting: we were taken on a continuously fascinating journey into diverse branches of knowledge. Integral to our formation was every teacher's steadfast endeavour to etch multiple life-values, principles and morals into their pupils' genome. Our academic work involved identifying and writing the English numerals and alphabets, carrying out simple arithmetical operations such as addition, multiplication, subtraction and division of numbers, pronouncing simple English words, drawing, artwork, listening to Bible stories, reciting English nursery rhymes and participating in physical training. I was able to carry out multiple academic tasks. Because of what my teacher characterised as my nimbleness in understanding new concepts and correctly applying them, he gave me the nickname "KCMG", which is the abbreviation of the expression: Knight Commander of the Order of St. Michael and St. George, a British order established in 1818 by King George IV when he occupied the position of regent for his father, King George III. The nickname stuck for several years. The 1953 academic year soon came to an end, but not before the annual promotion examinations. I passed the examinations, achieving the first position in my class, and was promoted to Infant 2. At that time, the policy was that a pupil would not move from his class to the next class without passing the promotion examinations. Accordingly, there were some of my peers who unfortunately had to repeat Infant 1.

I was happy to be among the successful pupils who advanced to Infant 2 in January 1954, implying that I had, fortunately, not wasted my mother's hard-earned resources. We had a new teacher, different from the one who taught us in Infant 1. I continued to do well in my studies. I passed the end-of-year promotion examination, again coming top of the class and justifying my mother's investment on me. I was therefore qualified to advance to Standard 1, regarded by all at that time as a veritable marker of the beginning of the primary school certificate programme. While my academic performance was good and continuously improving, it represented a huge and excruciating financial burden on my mother: saving 20 shillings in three months was extremely challenging. My mother's resolve that she would ensure that I was educated at whatever cost was being severely tested.

4

A MARITAL QUANDARY

My mother reached her reproductive climacteric in 1949 and all prospects of further child-bearing were therefore biologically foreclosed. The development fuelled another swirl of mindless derision of my mother in the community, with many saying that they had always known that she was too old to have more than one child for my father. How was my father to address the situation? How was he to have more children, in a culture where fathering many children was ranked more important than wealth, as evident in such Edo names as: *Omosigho* (a child is more than money), *Omorodion* (a child takes priority over all other things), *Omosefe* (a child is more than riches), etc. He was miffed by the psychological brickbats that were daily hurled at his wife and the unsolicited counselling that he continually received from his peers to do something about the situation. With time, my father succumbed to the relentless pressure that was mounted on him from multiple quarters. The marriage was about to unravel.

An Additional Spouse

While in my second year in the primary school in 1954, my father notified my mother that, because of her age, he needed an additional wife. That decision was his way of dealing with the increasingly volatile situation. With polygamy as an entrenched component of the Benin culture, many married women were fully aware that, as their marriages progressed, there was a high probability that their husbands would decide to acquire additional spouses. My mother therefore spontaneously informed my father that he was at liberty to do as he pleased and that she was ready to act as a mother-figure to the new wife whenever she arrived. My father was very happy to hear my mother's generous and non-belligerent response, because he had expected some kind of opposition from my mother to his idea. A few weeks later, he informed my mother that he had identified a woman in a village not too far from WAIFOR, and that he would be making an introductory visit with some of his friends to the woman's family. Shortly after, he made the visit with a number of his friends. On his return home later in the evening on that day, everyone, especially my mother, was anxious to learn about the outcome of the visit, particularly information about when the new wife would be joining the family. But he looked utterly downcast. My mother set out his meal on a small table and urged him to eat. Somewhat reluctantly, he ate the meal. Then, once more, she asked him pointedly how the visit had gone. His reply amazed everyone. He said:

Everything would have gone well but you are now my problem.

Surprised by this reply, my mother asked: Me? What problem? How am I the problem?

Then he replied:

My friends and I met the woman's family. I was introduced as the suitor. After some discussion, the woman was summoned by her family to meet us. A beautiful lady soon appeared. She was told about our mission and then asked whether she was ready to marry me. She answered in the affirmative but with a caveat. She said that she was aware that I am married to an old woman and that she would not marry me as long as the old woman remained my wife. She emphasised that she was not ready to share her husband with an old woman. That is how you have become an obstacle to my progress. I would have brought my new wife home today but you have become my obstacle. My friends and I tried to convince her that you are like a mother to me and that you will diligently take good care of her and myself, but she bluntly refused to modify her position.

My mother was dumbfounded beyond description. After a while, my father revealed his position:

You have to go immediately! I want to move on with my life.

My mother tried to plead with him:

Let me go with you to the woman and assure her that I will be a good mate, even a mother, to her.

But he would have none of it. His mind was irrevocably made up. He had abruptly annulled their almost a decade-old marriage. Resigned to the dramatic change in her fortune, she begged to be given about a week to move out.

Joining the Category of Single Parents

After one week, my mother joined the category of single parents, the majority of whom were women. That was because of the inherent asymmetry in conjugal relations, fostered over the years by the patriarchal character of the Edo society: it was easy for a man to send his wife away, and acquire another spouse, but a woman could not act analogously. In those days, with scant attention to gender rights and sensitivity, female single parents, including widows, encountered a plethora of social and economic challenges. For many such parents, the main stressors were the loss of financial support, inadequate capacity to bring up their children, social relegation and heartless stigmatisation.

As already mentioned, these events occurred while I was in the second year of my primary school education programme at the CSW. My mother did not want to disrupt my schooling, which would have been the case if she had decided to move from WAIFOR to Benin City. On my part, I was much too young to understand the ramifications of the new developments in my mother's marital status. My mother searched for and soon found a one bedroom accommodation in a section of WAIFOR into which we all moved. By "we", I refer to my mother, three nieces, my sister Mary and myself. With the relocation, a new household, managed by a single parent, was set up. But with no guaranteed, steady or sustainable income streams, it was evident that the household had its work cut out for it, as it needed to labour very hard to ensure its survival in a highly challenging and rapidly changing economic milieu.

With very limited financial resources in our new home, as in several others in the community, the staple food was *eba*, made from cassava, as well as maize, plantain, yam and cocoyam, which were seasonal farm products. Rice was served only occasionally but always during Christmas and New Year festivities. Eggs and meat were sparingly given to us, as they were invariably reserved for adults, even though children were in much greater need of such nutrients for their development. The myth in those days was that giving eggs and meat to children was likely to trigger a potentially strong urge in them to steal such food items.

To meet our household feeding needs, my mother was into the small scale farming of crops such as cassava, maize, cocoyam, okro and our indigenous melon. She also tried her hands at petty trading. She would buy tins of kerosene, put their contents in bottles of different volumes (one litre, half a litre and one quarter of a litre) and arrange them in a rectangular open-top box. To support my mother's trade, I functioned as her sales boy: hawking the kerosene throughout the Nigerian quarters at WAIFOR after school as from 4:00p.m. I would normally return home between 7:00 and 8:00p.m.

My involvement in hawking began when I was about 7 years old and continued until I completed my primary school education in 1959, aged 12 years. There was no notion of child labour in those days: children dutifully carried out any chores that were assigned to them by their parents. As a consequence of the hawking, I acquired some elementary skills in salesmanship but, sadly, missed a number of priceless opportunities to participate in several co-curricular activities that our teachers organised from time to time for pupils of my age after school hours. In particular, as I was not available after 4:00p.m. each school day, it was not possible for me to be a member of the Boy Scouts (a movement that instilled some core values such as good citizenship, chivalry and outdoor survival skills in boys aged between 11 and 15 years) and the Boys' Brigade (an international Christian organisation that worked toward fostering Christian values in juveniles aged between 5 and 18 years). My mother made only a modest profit from the trade, much of whose proceeds she directed toward the family's upkeep. Additionally, she was adept in traditional midwifery, antenatal care, postnatal management, paediatrics and autochthonous phytomedicine. On account of her high proficiency in medical matters, she was the one that members of the community instinctively turned to whenever there were antenatal, birth delivery, postnatal and paediatric issues. As a result of her approach, competence and success, she was held in high esteem by all. But the income from her multiple endeavours was meagre, because of the poor economic endowment of many members of the community and her own approach to charging for her services. For example, she would say to a patient she was treating with her specially prepared herbal medicine: "I will not charge you now; when you are fully cured, you could give me whatever pleases your heart, because I treat but God cures". As her children, we were often unhappy about her approach. We saw her method as an invitation to poverty, because a number of her clients who were successfully treated never returned to show any gratitude. But she would say that she adopted the approach from her mother, who had taught her that a therapy would not be effective if a fee, especially one that was exorbitant, was collected upfront. Nevertheless, our single-parent household plodded on financially, one day at a time.

Concerning my father, his wife gave birth to a girl after about one year. She then abandoned the marriage and relocated to Lagos, where she subsequently married another man.

5

MY EDUCATION UNDER THREAT

It was in the third term of the 1954 school year that an event that had the potential of changing my entire life occurred. With sadness and a feeling of failure, my mother informed me that she could no longer pay my school fees because her sources of income were unstable, inadequate and even dwindling. For me and my mother, this was a colossal setback, whose consequences were difficult to fathom at that time. In spite of this development, I was still able to pass the promotion examination from Infant 2 to Standard 1.

Non-Formal Capacity Building

As a way of dealing with the potential consequences of her decision to end her sponsorship of my education, my mother informed me that I would have to learn a trade in Benin City, in lieu of formal education. The turn of events was overly dispiriting: it meant that as from January 1955, I would be left behind educationally by my peers. I braced up for my impending new status as a school dropout, occasioned

by poverty. But I was smallish and not at all ready for the
world of work, even as an apprentice. What trade would be
appropriate for me? Some of the common trades in those
days were buying and selling, tailoring, hair-cutting, carpentry,
driving, bricklaying and vehicle repairing. Sadly, unwholesome
financial circumstances, beyond my mother's control, were
constraining me to opt for apprenticeship or artisanal capacity
building in one or a combination of these trades.

Free Universal Primary Education Programme

January 1955 arrived and a new school year was beginning. As
my mother and I pondered what might be a fitting trade for me
to learn, an awesome providential solution to this hard-to-resolve
challenge suddenly emerged, through a novel and development-
fostering political initiative by Chief Obafemi Jeremiah Oyeniyi
Awolowo (March 6, 1909 – May 9, 1987). An iconic lawyer and
politician, Chief Awolowo was the Premier of the Western Region
of Nigeria from October 1, 1954 to September 30, 1960. In those
days, the Western Region comprised the present Oyo, Ogun,
Ondo, Ekiti, Osun, Lagos, Edo and Delta States. Chief Awolowo
had a huge passion for education, which he rightly saw as the
most powerful weapon in a nation's arsenal for transforming
the lives of its citizen's and moving them into prosperity. On
January 17, 1955, his government made primary education free
throughout the Western Region by launching its *Free Universal
Primary Education Programme* (FUPEP), underpinned by a set of
carefully planned initiatives developed by the Region's Minister
of Education, Chief Stephen Oluwole Awokoya (1913-March 15,
1985). With this miraculous and timely providential intervention, I
was able to continue my education in 1955. Following the welcome
introduction of the FUPEP, which was a game-changer for many
poor pupils like me, the total enrollment in primary schools in the
Western Region increased stratospherically from 456,600 in 1954

to 811,432 in 1955 and was 1,080,303 in 1959. Some of the knock-on effects of these developments were massive expansions in the number of primary and secondary schools, number of teachers and the number of education inspectors responsible for quality assurance in the schools in the Western Region. Additionally, there was also the introduction in the Region of secondary modern schools and technical colleges.

Progress through Primary Education

As I progressed from Standard 1 to Standard 5, I had the good fortune to be taught by highly professional teachers, some of whom had been well-trained in teacher training colleges. They were dedicated and industrious, had the requisite pedagogical skills, did not engage in ethical or professional misconduct, such as examination malpractice or sexual harassment of pupils which have become rampant in this day and age, and ensured that pupils imbibed the right kind of life values. For our academic work, the core subjects were English, Arithmetic, underpinned by mental Arithmetic, and General Knowledge, including elements of Civics, History and Geography, while the ancillary subjects were handwriting, drawing, crafts, gardening and physical training. Each class had one teacher who taught all the subjects throughout the academic year. A typical school day began around 8:00a.m. with a general assembly of all pupils and teachers. Any pupils who came late, especially those who were habitually late to school, received corporal punishment. Some pupils attended school from faraway villages and were liable to be late. The headmaster would lead the morning prayers, make some announcements and then dismiss the assembly. Thereafter, the pupils would march in single files to their different classrooms, where each teacher would conduct a roll call to determine which pupils were present on that day. The first academic activity was invariably mental arithmetic, whose fundamental aim was to test speed and accuracy: the class teacher would instruct his pupils to bring out their writing materials and then stand up with their backs to the blackboard. He would thereafter write ten questions on the blackboard, after which he would instruct the pupils to turn around facing the blackboard and attempt the problems for about fifteen minutes. The teacher would mark each pupil's answers, after which he would order all pupils to stand up again. He would then ask all pupils who scored 10/10 to sit down; then those with scores of 9/10, 8/10, 7/10, 6/10 and 5/10 would consecutively also be asked to sit down. The teacher would thereafter admonish any pupils who were still standing to work harder. I was very much at home with arithmetic and would already be sitting before pupils with a score of 8/10 were asked to sit down. Other subjects were also rigorously taught by our teachers, using both interactive and non-interactive approaches as well as several pupil-assessment techniques. We were introduced to a number of co-curricular activities like gardening, games, physical education and crafts. Through Civics, we acquired some knowledge about forms of government and the civic responsibilities of all citizens. I completed my primary school education in 1959, earning a First Leaving (Primary School) Certificate (Division A). Listed on my Certificate were: English, Arithmetic and General Knowledge.

All in all, the training that I was fortunate to receive at the Community School, WAIFOR, was robust, rounded and fit for purpose: it has proven to be the fundamental undergird of my modest contributions to higher education and several other fields of human endeavour in my continuing journey through life.

6

ACCESSING SECONDARY SCHOOL EDUCATION

At the beginning of the final year of the primary school education programme at the Community School, WAIFOR (CSW), teachers would unfailingly embark on continuously enlightening their pupils on some of the pathways to further education or vocational training in the country, notwithstanding the fact that only those pupils whose guardians had the resources, or might secure sponsorships from any of the country's governments (Federal, State of Local) or a variety of non-governmental organisations, could move forward with their educational objectives. In the 1950s, there were several types of educational institutions in the Western Region into which a person with a primary school certificate could seek admission: secondary modern schools, secondary grammar schools (also called colleges, high schools or academies), Grade III teacher training colleges, secondary commercial schools and technical colleges.

The Secondary Education Space

For their post-primary school education, the popular choices by pupils at CSW were secondary modern schools and secondary grammar schools. A secondary modern school offered a three-year programme of study to students who did not have the financial means to pursue further education at the secondary school level at the end of their primary school education programme. The government policy underlying the introduction of this tier of education was for it to be a pathway to the "teaching profession, trade centres, the police force and all trades and courses which required an age entry of not less than 15-16 years". On the other hand, a secondary grammar school offered a five-year programme of study and was modelled after a similar kind of institution in the United Kingdom. This tier of education served prospective students who had appropriate financial means or secured some kind of sponsorship from philanthropic individuals or organisations, missionary organisations, governments or the private sector. Secondary grammar schools prepared students for tertiary education in such higher education institutions as universities, polytechnics, colleges of education, nursing schools and ecclesial seminaries. The secondary modern school system and secondary grammar school system were linked: a student at a secondary modern school was at liberty to move during, or at the end of his course of study to any secondary grammar school, if he secured admission and had the requisite financial means.

Entrance Examinations

In my final year at CSW in 1959, the aspiration of many a pupil in my class was to have a secondary grammar school education because realising such a life-changing objective had the enormous potential of facilitating access to a multiplicity of employment and further education opportunities at home and abroad. I was not an exception.

In the 1950s, the ownership structure of secondary grammar schools in the Western Region of Nigeria was diversified: they were owned by the Federal Government, religious organisations, secular organisations, communities or individuals. Years later, Federal

Government-owned secondary grammar schools were renamed Unity Schools, as they were viewed as instruments for fostering national integration and peaceful coexistence. Admission into a secondary grammar school was normally through a two-stage selection process comprising a competitive examination and an interactive interview. In the case of Federal Government-owned schools, a nationwide common entrance examination was organised annually by the Government for prospective students. Similarly, schools established by religious organisations, secular organisations, communities or individuals also organised their own entrance examinations within their own institutions. Consequently, a pupil could attempt more than one entrance examination and might be successful in several of them. As the final stage of the selection process, schools invited candidates who passed their entrance examinations for interactive interviews after which they made shortlists of the candidates who would be offered admission.

I was in the 1959 graduating set of CSW, an apparently enormous achievement by every member of the set: we were at the threshold of a new phase of our lives. Unfolding in front of each of us were multiple life trajectories. Some of us were destined to end their formal educational journey at the primary school level and thereafter learn any of a gamut of artisanal trades. Others were sure to continue on the enviable path of further education, which could potentially increase the likelihood of their progressing to other levels of education.

Beginning from around the month of March 1959, several secondary grammar schools and secondary modern schools in Nigeria started sending announcements, accompanied with application forms, to our primary school concerning the dates for their entrance examinations for that year. As each announcement was received, the Headmaster asked interested pupils to purchase the relevant application forms from his office. The entrance examinations usually occurred between May and July. My intention was to purchase the application form for the

Immaculate Conception College (ICC), Benin City, a Catholic secondary school, established in 1944, with the motto: *Semper et Ubique Fidelis* (Always and Everywhere Faithful [to God and Country]). Before the deadline announced by our Headmaster for buying and submitting application forms, I approached my mother and requested for the relevant fee. After remaining silent for what appeared to me to be an unusually long time, she drew me to her side and said:

> I have the fee you have requested for. I know that if you sat for the entrance examination you will pass and be offered admission. But all that would be a waste of time and money because I do not have the wherewithal to sponsor you through college. It takes an awful lot of money to see a child through a college. We will need to carefully think about your next path through life. Not only persons who attended colleges have made it in life.

To convince me that I would eventually not lose too much in life if I did not receive a secondary school education, she launched emotionally into highlighting examples of several persons in Benin City who never had any formal education whatsoever but were nevertheless very wealthy, had gained recognition as notable philanthropists and were icons in the community.

My mother's delineation of her inadequate financial capacity vis-à-vis my educational ambition greatly depressed me. Although everything she said was true, the stark implication was that I might never advance educationally beyond the primary school level. Once more, there was the likelihood that I would be left behind by my peers. Was that the kind of life trajectory that Providence had mapped out for me to traverse in the coming years?

At school, my teachers expected me to be one of the first pupils to pick an entrance examination application form in respect of at least one of the multiplicity of secondary schools whose announcements had been publicised by our Headmaster. As deadline after deadline expired without me picking a form, my teachers were dismayed that a highflying and promising pupil like me might not be progressing to the next level of education. Whenever I was in the company of my classmates, I always avoided any discussion of the then imminent entrance examinations, especially whether or not I would be sitting for any of them. Several of my classmates took and passed the examinations and secured places in choice secondary grammar schools in Nigeria. At the end of our primary school leaving certificate examinations in December 1959, my classmates embarked on their secondary school education in January 1960. In my own case, throughout the year 1960, I stayed at home without attending any educational institution.

Another Round of Entrance Examinations

In March 1960, I received information that announcements by some secondary schools of their entrance examinations were already being received at the CSW. Moreover, some teachers in the school launched coaching classes for prospective candidates of the examinations. The classes were intensive and were usually for about a month. I requested for permission and was allowed to join the classes. The teachers, some of whom never had any secondary school education, were extremely dedicated and meticulously introduced us to all kinds of examination questions that we were likely to encounter. The coaching primed me not only for the year's entrance examinations but also for any other kind of examinations at the same level.

Meanwhile, the pressure that I exerted on my mother to allow me to participate in the entrance examinations was unrelenting. In the end, she yielded and I obtained and paid for the entrance examination form in respect of the Immaculate Conception College (ICC), Benin City. I passed both the examination and the subsequent interactive interview, and I received an offer of provisional admission around the middle of May 1960. To indicate acceptance of the offer, I was required to make a deposit of £8 (eight pounds sterling) within one month of receipt of the offer, i.e. by the middle of June. Pleased by my performance, my mother resolved to do everything within her means to sponsor my education at ICC. I was highly elated. What else did I want? Providence was re-mapping my life trajectory.

Converting a Provisional Offer of Admission to a Firm Offer

My mother began to work toward meeting the deadline for paying the deposit. I prayed fervently that the deposit would be paid. But two weeks to the deadline, no deposit had been paid. Similarly, ten days, one week and three days to the deadline, there was no evidence that the deposit would be paid. It turned out that my mother was trying to raise the £8. Then a day to the deadline, my mother informed my elder brother John that the deposit was available. My brother and I needed to travel the next day to ICC, Benin City, to pay the deposit. As my brother was obliged to be at work on that same day and close at 3:00p.m., the plan was that we would take the 4:00p.m. shuttle from WAIFOR to Benin City and then board a taxi to ICC to make the payment. The arrangement was fraught with several risks. For example, the shuttle to Benin might be cancelled, as sometimes happened, our names might not be on the list of travellers to Benin City on that day or the school might decline to accept deposits after, say, 3:00p.m.

My brother arrived home from work at about 3:30p.m. on the last day for paying the deposit. He took my letter of provisional admission and the deposit, and we both raced toward the shuttle terminal. But on the way, he suddenly realised that the deposit fee of £8 was not in his pocket. He searched frantically for the money, turned and started running in the direction of our house. The entire plan was about to unravel. Was this my destiny? Then, suddenly, he shouted: "I have found it!" This eureka moment was nothing short of the miraculous: Providence had again mercifully intervened on my behalf. My brother found the money by the roadside where it had fallen because, in the haste, he had apparently not put it properly in his pocket. We arrived at the shuttle terminal breathlessly. The officer who was boarding the day's selected travellers beckoned to my brother, saying: "I have called your name several times a while ago. Please board!" We were the last to board the shuttle.

Payment of the Deposit

We arrived at ICC at about 5:30p.m. on that day. Students were outside, manually clearing grass within the school compound. My brother beckoned to one of them and informed him that we had come to pay the deposit fee for my admission. The student said politely that he would fetch the Senior Prefect to attend to us. A young man soon arrived. He introduced himself as the Senior Prefect. Informed about our mission, he told us that the Principal was away from the campus at that time but that he would collect the fee from my brother and pay it to the Principal later on. The Principal was Fr. James Alexander Flanagan (January 1, 1920 – February 4, 2004), born in Belfast, Northern Ireland, UK. His tenure was from 1960 to 1961. The Senior Prefect's kind gesture saved my provisional admission, as it would have lapsed if he had not accepted to collect the deposit. We were extremely happy that we succeeded in paying the fee to the school and returned triumphantly to WAIFOR on the shuttle bus. In spite of our apparent achievement, no one really knew where the money to fund my education at ICC was likely to come from.

Fr. Flanagan was a priest of the Societas Missionum ad Afros (Société des Missions Africaines)[SMA], also called The Society of African Missions, in English. While writing this autobiography, I interacted with the Superior General of the SMA in Rome, Italy, as I acknowledge later. The SMA was established on December 8, 1856, in Lyon, France, as a Society of Apostolic Life, by the French Catholic prelate Melchior-Marie-Joseph de Marion-Brésillac

(December 2, 1813 – June 25 1859), an indigene of Castelnaudary, France. Some three years after founding the SMA, he died tragically from yellow fever in Freetown, Sierra Leone, a few months shy of his 46th birthday, barely 41 days after arriving in Freetown as the Vicar Apostolic of Sierra Leone. Bishop de Marion-Brésillac, whose remains are interred in France, was succeeded by Fr. Augustin Planque (July 5, 1826 – August 21, 1907). Before setting out on his voyage to Freetown, Bishop de Marion-Brésillac had enjoined Fr. Augustin Planque:

> if the sea and its rocks were to make this year my last, you would
> be there to see that the work did not get shipwrecked too.

Fr. Augustin Planque became the first Superior General of the SMA in 1859, a position he held till his death in 1907.

Dr. Andrew Nosa Igiehon

The ICC Senior Prefect who accepted to assist us was the future Dr. Andrew Nosa Igiehon (fl. 1939-2011). He sometimes rendered Nosa as Noser. Thirteen years after I first met him in 1960, our paths converged again in 1973 during my PhD research activities at the University of London. I valued the auspicious reunion greatly. I recounted how I encountered him in 1960 and his immense assistance at that time. The reunion fostered an eventually very taut friendship between both of us: Dr. Igiehon became my lifelong mentor, model and confidant. A devout and steadfast Catholic, he was the Chairman at the reception for my guests during my wedding ceremony in London in 1976. This kind, considerate, highly cerebral icon settled in London, qualified as a lawyer, obtained a PhD degree in Law, founded and operated the Pozihead Group of Companies and authored the trailblazing, bestselling 352-page book: *To Build a Nigerian Nation,* published in 1975 by Stockwell, Ilfracombe, UK, with ISBN-0722307144. His sudden transition in 2011 was an extremely painful blow to absorb by me, members of my family and every person who knew him.

Firm Letter of Admission to ICC

Following my success in paying the crucially important deposit fee, I was sent a formal letter of admission to ICC toward the end of June 1960, together with explicit details of the concomitant financial and other implications. The school provided the option of a resident or non-resident studentship: one could be a resident student in the school's boarding house or a day student. As my family was based in WAIFOR, some 15 miles from Benin City, the natural option for me was residency. This option implied an annual cost of £48 (forty-eight pounds sterling), with all key expenses covered: board and lodging, books, school uniform and access to basic medical treatment at the school's infirmary. In addition, there was a list of certain items that prospective resident students were obliged to bring with them. All told, the total financial implication was substantially north of £48 (forty- eight pounds sterling). It soon dawned on all of us in the family that the financial burden was far beyond my mother's modest means because of her low and few income streams. There was the option of borrowing the requisite funds. But even if my mother could secure adequate loans from some money lenders, who routinely charged usurious interest rates, to finance my first year at ICC, it was questionable whether such a strategy was sustainable. In the end, a way forward was not discernible. It was then painfully clear that a dead end had materialised: my vaulting ambition to attend a secondary grammar school needed to be permanently and irreversibly abandoned for precisely the same reason that had prevented me from access to secondary school education throughout the 1960 school year. A huge misfortune had once more become my lot! Although I was happy that my mother had done her level best to support the realisation of my aspiration, I was depressed that her strenuous efforts were effectively nugatory.

A Silver Bullet out of the Blue

While still struggling to come to terms with the sad and excruciating turn of events concerning my aspiration for secondary school education, my brother, through whose office letters were normally sent to me, received unexpectedly, toward the end of July 1960, a potentially life-changing communication from the Principal of ICC, Fr. Flanagan. He wrote that, based on what he characterised as my outstanding performance at the entrance examination, in which I had placed first, ICC had submitted my name as a candidate for the annual Western Region of Nigeria scholarships examination. Fr. Flanagan then stated that the examination would take place at Ibadan Grammar School, Ibadan, about two months from the date of his letter. The communication was pleasantly surprising since neither I nor anyone in my family had any inkling whatsoever that the entrance examination was also ICC's mechanism for nominating worthy candidates for the Western Region of Nigeria scholarships examination. Was this the silver bullet to end the financial difficulty that was undermining my educational ambition? Clearly, Providence was graciously handing me a timely lifeline toward the realisation of my ceaseless longing for a secondary school education. The divine gesture represented a huge challenge for me: it meant that the ball had again been thrown into my court, with the implication that everything depended thereafter, somewhat precariously, on how I would eventually perform in the scholarships examination in a distant town.

Scholarships Examination in Ibadan

The days passed by and it was soon September 1960. The die was cast: it was time to make the journey to Ibadan, a city which was reputed in those days as the most populous in Africa. My brother, John, and I travelled from WAIFOR to board a passenger lorry of the Armels Transport Service from Benin City to Ibadan. The journey was long: it took the better part of half a day to get to

Ibadan. We then took a taxi to Ibadan Grammar School, Molete, the first secondary school in Ibadan, established on March 31, 1913, by Rev. Alexander Babatunde Akinyele (September 5, 1875 – October 1, 1968). This clergyman and ardent educationist was the first Ibadan indigene to obtain a university degree, the first Bishop of the Anglican Diocese of Ibadan and the pioneer Principal of the school. The examination was scheduled to hold next day. At the school, the Government of the Western Region had already made provision for my board and lodging for one night. After he had handed me over to the school's officials, my brother left the school to secure overnight accommodation elsewhere. There were candidates from every part of the Region. On the next day, the examination was administered to us over some three hours. We answered multiple-choice questions in English, Arithmetic and General Knowledge. There was no interactive interview. Since the examination ended before two o'clock in the afternoon, my brother and I were able to leave Ibadan for Benin City on the same day. With the examination behind me, the next ordeal was waiting for its outcome.

The Long Wait

I was quite confident that I would pass the scholarships examination. But whether merely passing would be enough to secure a scholarship was unclear. Might a high threshold or cut-off mark have been set for a scholarship-earning performance? As the examination involved only multiple-choice questions, I expected the results to become available within at most one month, i.e. by the end of October 1960. But I received no information whatsoever about the examination at the end of that month. It was not at all clear what could have been responsible for the seeming delay in the release of the results. To me and my family, especially my mother, eternity piled on eternity appeared infinitely much shorter than each passing day that we craved for information about the outcome of the scholarships examination. What was happening? Was the situation God's way of saying that I was not destined to attend a secondary school? Was it that I failed the examination? Could it be that the Government of the Western Region had decided not to award any scholarships for the 1961 school year? These and kindred questions raced through the mind of every member of my family. But no one knew the answer to any of the questions. Moreover, there was the key question as to what our strategy should be if I did not secure a scholarship in the long run.

A Fallback Position

It was already November 1960. Information about the outcome of the scholarships examination was still very much unavailable. With the 1961 school year scheduled to begin in less than two months, it was imperative to develop and implement a fallback plan. I needed another pathway to continuing my education. Everyone in the family and the community reasoned that I needed to downgrade, by several notches, my lofty ambition to attend a secondary grammar school and settle for education in a secondary modern school. As conceived by the Government of the Western Nigeria, a secondary modern school education was apt for pupils who were "unable to gain admission to either the secondary grammar or technical schools, but who both desired and were in a position to pay for it". After assessing the overall annual tuition fee in a secondary modern school, my mother was confident that she could conveniently bear the financial burden of seeing me through the three years that I would spend in such a school. As already mentioned, with a secondary modern school certificate, I would potentially be on a trajectory to acquiring a qualification that could make me eligible for employment as a primary school teacher, policeman or an artisan, as envisaged by the Western Region's education policy.

The Secondary Modern School Option

With the firm assurance of unwavering sponsorship by my mother, I was persuaded to take a late entrance examination to a secondary modern school at Ugbogiobo, a village located about five miles from WAIFOR. I sat for and passed the examination which was held in November 1960 and was offered provisional admission. A firm offer of admission was predicated on my paying a deposit fee of £5 (five pounds sterling), before the middle of December 1960. This precondition for securing the admission was worrying to my mother, who was always averse to taking any financial risks. She did not know how wise it was to pay the new deposit fee, considering that a nonrefundable deposit fee of £8 (eight pounds sterling) had already been paid at ICC, Benin City. It was evident that if the new fee was paid, one or even the two deposits might eventually be forfeited. To hedge her risk and buy some time, my mother decided to request the secondary modern school for a deferment of the deadline for paying the deposit, promising to pay it along with the fee for the first term of the 1961 school year. The head of the school agreed to her proposal but warned that he could not guarantee that a place would still be available for me after the middle of December 1960, which was the deadline for paying the deposit. It then dawned on me that there was a nonzero probability that I could end up not taking up my admission at either ICC, Benin City, if there was an unfavourable outcome of the scholarships examination, or the secondary modern school, if all places had been filled by the middle of December 1960. In the situation, it seemed that I had essentially been entrapped between Scylla and Charybdis.

Lingering Uncertainty

As in the previous two months, at the end of November 1960, information about the outcome of the scholarships examination in Ibadan remained painfully elusive. Many reasoned that the happenings were an eloquent statement that I should settle for the secondary modern school whose entrance examination I had already passed. I was immensely confused. Had fate conspired to deal me a cruel hand at the time in my life when I needed all the support and luck possible? Questions of this type coursed incessantly through my mind. But I was utterly helpless. Then it was December 1960. But as in the preceding two months, there was still no news about the outcome of the scholarships examination. Things appeared to have finally come to a head. January 1960 was fully in our sights and the new school year would certainly begin.

A Providential Outcome

While it was true that we were already in the month of December 1960, we were only a few days into it: the month was not yet spent. As if this fact needed underlining, an overwhelmingly pleasing life-impacting event soon occurred: a list of the persons who were awarded the Western Region of Nigeria secondary school scholarships for the 1961 school year was published in a national newspaper in the first week of December 1960. My name was conspicuously on the list. The much awaited good news was brought to our notice by a family friend whose office at WAIFOR subscribed to the newspaper. The joy of my family and I was boundless. The coast was finally clear for me to realise my ambition to attend a secondary grammar school. Furthermore, my mother's decision not to pay the deposit demanded by the secondary modern school turned out, fortuitously and happily, to be the right one. With the nationwide announcement in a national newspaper, I achieved the unique feat of being the first pupil of the Community School, WAIFOR, since its establishment, to be awarded a Western Region of Nigeria scholarship based on a competitive examination. It was with great joy that we conveyed to the head of the secondary modern school at Ugbogiobo that Providence had graciously directed my academic path toward a secondary grammar school.

A Western Region of Nigeria Scholar

The scholarship, effective from the 1961 school year, was tenable throughout the five years of my education at ICC, Benin City, subject to satisfactory annual academic performance. Its value was £40 (forty pounds sterling) per annum for every Western Region scholar. In many secondary schools in the Western Region in the 1960s, the scholarship amount of £40 (forty pounds sterling) was adequate to pay fully for tuition, uniform, board, hostel and books. But that was not the case at ICC, Benin City, where the total amount for tuition, board, hostel, school uniform and books was £48 (forty-eight pounds sterling) per annum. As a consequence, in relation to the scholarship of £40 (forty pounds sterling) per annum, there was a shortfall of £8 (eight pounds sterling) per annum, which was to be defrayed by the scholar. My mother was happy to assume the implied financial burden, as paying the annual shortfall of £8 (eight pounds sterling) was, fortunately, well within her capacity. Moreover, payment of the shortfall in respect of my first year at ICC, Benin City, had already been made through the deposit of £8 (eight pounds sterling) that we all feared might potentially be forfeited. With Providence intervening decisively again to resolve a monumental challenge that would have adversely altered the course of my life, I was finally about to step on the next rung of the education ladder. I looked longingly forward to taking up my admission in January 1961 at ICC, Benin City, as a Western Region of Nigeria Scholar.

7

A DREAM COME TRUE

ollowing the newspaper publication after the *Daily Times* publication which indicated that I had been awarded a scholarship by the Government of the Western Region of Nigeria, I began to make preparations toward assuming my imminent status of a student at ICC, Benin City, in the 1961 school year. As I would be a resident student (a boarder), ICC had sent me a long list of items that I was to bring with me on my first day at school. On the list were shoes, cutlery, plates, drinking cup, bedding, cover cloth, personal attire, a towel, a bedspread, a cutlass, soap, a bucket and some other necessities. A number of these were optional while others were mandatory. My mother diligently procured the items and arranged them in a metal box that I would take to the school. The countdown to my first day at ICC had started. But what kind of institution was ICC?

The School Called ICC, Benin City

In 1960, the two foremost secondary schools in Benin City were Edo College, a Federal Government grammar school established in February 1937, and a Catholic institution called the Immaculate Conception College (ICC), into which I had gained admission. These two institutions engaged in a kind of positive rivalry that fostered competitiveness and cooperation.

Apart from ICC, some other prominent boys Catholic secondary education institutions in the Mid-Western Region in the 1960s were St. John Bosco's College, Ubiaja (established in 1920); St. Thomas Teacher Training College, Ibusa (established in 1926); St. Patrick's College, Asaba (established in 1937); St. Peter Claver College, Aghalokpe (established in 1950); Annunciation Catholic College, Irrua (established in 1955); St. Anthony's College, Ubulu-Uku (established in 1956); Ishan Grammar School, Uromi (established in 1956); Notre Dame College, Ozoro (established in 1957); St. Malachy's College, Sapele (established in 1959); and St. Pius X Grammar School, Onitsha-Ugbo (established in 1960). ICC was held in very high esteem by its peers and was the institution of choice for many prospective students.

The name ICC is linked to the Catholic dogma of the immaculate conception of the Virgin Mary, the mother of Jesus Christ. The school was founded in 1944 by Bishop Patrick Joseph Kelly (August 31, 1894 – August 18, 1991), born at Bearnacreagh, County Galway, Ireland. He appointed Fr. Andrew Patrick O'Rourke (October 16, 1913 – January 8, 1967), an academically outstanding SMA priest and educator, as the pioneer Principal of the College. Born at Gortbrack, County Clare, Ireland, Fr. O'Rourke studied at University College Cork (UCC), Ireland, and University College Galway (UCG), later renamed the National University of Ireland (NUI), Galway, Ireland, obtaining a BA (First Class Honours) degree in philosophy and education in 1937. Based on his excellent performance, he was awarded a scholarship which he eventually utilised at UCG to obtain a Master's degree in education in 1943. As an SMA priest assigned to Nigeria, a major country in what was consistently described derogatorily in those days as the 'Dark Continent', some were stunned and upset that Fr. O'Rourke would entitle his Master's thesis, somewhat inappropriately, as: *Psychological Factors Governing the Education and Culture of Primitive Peoples*. Once in Nigeria, he pursued his ecclesial and educational missions with thoroughness and excellence. His tenure as the Principal of ICC, which he helped to establish as a sound academic institution underpinned by the religious traditions of the Catholic Church, was from 1944 to 1947. In recognition of his impressive expertise in education, Fr. O'Rourke was appointed as an Adviser on Education to the Government of the Western Region of Nigeria in July 1955, with responsibility for policy formulation and implementation.

Modelled on the British colonial education system, secondary school education in Nigeria in the 1940s comprised three junior secondary years (Form 1, Form 2 and Form 3) and two senior secondary years (Form 4 and Form 5) as well as a two-year pre-university sixth form (Lower 6 and Upper 6). Many secondary schools in the country operated mainly at the junior secondary level or at both the junior and senior secondary levels. Before 1954, ICC had approval to operate at the junior secondary level and therefore could only admit students into the three classes of Form 1, Form 2 and Form 3. As a result, ICC was unable to present its students for the West African School Certificate Examinations, which every student yearned to attempt. To circumvent this impediment, ICC students, after completing their Form 3 studies, were transferred to St. Patrick's College (SPC), Asaba, another Catholic institution which had Government accreditation up to the senior secondary level, where they then completed their senior secondary school education. The SPC was also established by Bishop Kelly, with Fr. Anthony Mcdonagh (February 23, 1917 – January 23, 1994), born in Killeen, Claremorris, County Mayo, Ireland, as the pioneer Principal.

Fr. O'Rourke's successor as the Principal of ICC was Fr. Joseph Francis Stephens (September 4, 1915 – February 5, 1989), whose tenure was from 1947 to 1948. Born at Brockagh in County Galway, Ireland, he was awarded the BA degree in philosophy and education in 1937 after studying at the UCC and UCG. Fr. Stephens' tenure was marked by a consolidation and expansion of Fr. O'Rourke's achievements. From 1948 to 1949, ICC had

Fr. Michael Francis Drew (January 16, 1921- 15 June 1973) as its Principal. Born at Lackenstown, County Westmeath, Ireland, he also studied at both the UCC and UCG, and obtained a BA degree in education and philosophy from UCG in June 1942. Fr. Drew was succeeded by Fr. Michael Alphonsus Grace (April 30, 1918 - January 7, 1989), born at Traverston, County Tipperary, Ireland. His tenure was from 1949 to 1951. He died in Uromi in 1973. Like many other SMA priests, Fr. Grace studied at both UCC and UCG and obtained a BA in education and philosophy from the latter institution in 1941. He handed the reins of the office of Principal to Fr. Joseph Patrick Donnelly ((July 26, 1916 – June 11, 1992)), whose tenure was from 1952 to 1953. Following his death in 1992, the Irish Province of the SMA issued an obituary that sketched Fr. Donnelly's life journey. Born at Lisduff, County Roscommon, Ireland, the fifth child in a family of eight children, he also studied at UCC and UCG, like many SMA priests of the Irish Province. He obtained a BA degree in education and philosophy in 1937 from UCG. Some years later, he earned a BSc degree in physics and chemistry in 1944 and a higher diploma in education in 1955, both from UCC. Fr. Donnelly's was succeeded by Fr. John Henry Jones (September 11, 1923 – June 10, 1984) whose tenure was from 1953 to 1957. His university education was also at the UCC, where he earned the BA degree in English, History, Economics and Sociology. It was during Fr. Jones' tenure that ICC secured Government approval as a full secondary school in 1954. He died at the University of Benin Teaching Hospital, following a tragic freak accident at his residence in Ibusa, and is buried in Asaba. From 1957 to 1960, Fr. Donnelly was again the Principal of ICC. He was succeeded by Fr. James Alexander Flanagan (January 1, 1920 – February 4, 2004), who was in office from 1960 to 1961. Born in Belfast, Northern Ireland, UK, he obtained the BA degree in 1954 in Geography and Sociology, with English as a subsidiary subject. After Fr. Flanagan, the next Principal was once more Fr. Donnelly, who assumed office in 1961. He is largely the architect of the current ICC campus: between 1958 and 1960, before assuming office in 1961, he had skilfully negotiated and secured a large parcel of land for the new campus at the Third East Circular area of Benin City from the Omo N'oba N'edo Uku Akpolokpolo, Akenzua II (January 7, 1899 – June 11, 1978), a monarch who had a huge passion for empowering his people with Western education. Thereafter, the physical development of the site started in 1958; staff and students relocated to the new campus in January 1960. Fr. Donnelly, who had been Vice-Principal at St. Patrick College, Asaba (where Fr. Andrew Patrick O'Rourke was Principal) and at St. Peter Claver's College, Aghalokpe (where Fr. Michael Scully (April 3, 1900–May 13, 1959) was Principal), was the Principal throughout my student days from 1961 to 1967 at ICC. There was a stark difference between Fr. Donnelly, the teacher, and Fr. Donnelly, the school administrator. As teacher, he was calm and demonstrated an admirable mastery of his subject, namely: Chemistry, which he imparted to the students with excellent academic and pedagogical skills. As Principal, he performed his administrative role with charisma, consistency, fairness, unwavering decisiveness and laser-sharp focus on the implementation of the institution's mission and vision. With a majestic carriage and a no-nonsense visage that together exuded an aura of firm authority, control and professionalism in the discharge of his diverse functions, he issued orders that were unambiguous, mandatory and often time-bound. His decisions were final. No individual student ever mustered the audacity to defy Fr. Donnelly's commands; it was always: "Yes, Father". All in all, his leadership style fostered a safe, secure and conducive teaching and learning environment and helped to build a disciplined and hardworking student body, whose members were abundantly equipped, both spiritually and academically, to achieve significant successes in their life journeys after leaving ICC. Outside his teaching and administrative functions, Fr. Donnelly was kind, empathetic and supportive. For example, he had my back at an extremely turbulent phase of my life, as I will recount before long. His successor was Fr. John "JACK" Casey (February 11, 1931- March 2, 2015), who was the Principal from 1968 to 1969. He was born in Cork City, County Cork, Ireland. For his tertiary education, he attended the UCC, where he obtained a BSc degree in 1952. While at ICC, he was also the Chaplain to the erstwhile Military Governor of the Mid-West Region, Major General David Akpode Ejoor (January 10, 1932 – February 10, 2019). Fr. Casey was transferred to Ibadan in 1986. All the Principals at ICC from 1944 to 1972 were SMA priests.

My First Day at ICC

The much-awaited resumption day eventually arrived in the second week of January 1961, some four and a half months shy of my fourteenth birthday anniversary. I had a haircut at about 10:00a.m. on that day. In the evening, my brother, John, and I took the 4:00p.m. shuttle from WAIFOR to Benin City, arriving before 5:00p.m. Then we boarded a taxi toward ICC, whose location was along the Third East Circular Road, Benin City. Not long, we arrived at our destination: the Immaculate Conception College, Benin City. Setting my feet on the ICC campus as a *bona fide* student was, for me, an epic milestone: a lofty dream had materialised in my life. Remembering that retaining my scholarship was contingent on satisfactory academic performance annually, I prayed that God would endow me with whatever it would take for me to continue to enjoy the scholarship throughout the envisaged five years of my education at ICC. Numerous taxis and cars drove into the ICC campus and dropped off both fresh and returning students. The Senior Prefect, the genial, calm and helpful Thaddeus Ogboghodo, and some other prefects were on ground to ensure that all fresh students were accorded any assistance that they were likely to need. There were scenes of parents and guardians giving parting advice to their children and wards, stressing obedience to school regulations and steadfast devotion to their studies. I saw

1. My Father (1904–1990)
2. My Mother (1900–1986)

EULOGY

We lose, we realise not, our only Guide
But yet the bulk of us ignore the fact—
That all these years, alone he won
our pride, ?
With characteristic humour and tact
Safe in our bosoms his memory shall
rest,
Where ever we may go, the East
or west
Weep, Art Students, weep
Here goes a master,
When comes such another
If anyone deserves gratitude
Not reckoning on the magnitude
of the task undertaken by him,
None comes near, not even by a slim
chance, to claim univevent
acclaim.
Mr Murtagh, tho' time may run its course
To revere you we always shall
find cause.
          By Irusota
       (P. 7 O)

AN ANSWER TO THE EULOGY TO MR MURTAGH.
We really need not weep;
Though this we really can't help.
For the dictate of time he can't help,
Really then with him we must part
Life, you know, forces men apart
But the pain of parting,
To the joy of meeting again is nothing
Since nature allows no vacuum
Let's hope for just another him.
          By Aloysius Ekhayeme.

3. Eulogy to Mr. Gerard Murtagh by Bernard Irusota in 1966
4. My deceased friend, Dr. Gabriel Ehi Elubale Ojesebholo
5. Aloysius Ekhayeme's reply to Irusota's eulogy in 1966

6. GOS and Deborah signing the marriage register in London in March 1976
7. The officiating priest, Fr. Kersey, handing over the marriage certificate to GOS and Deborah in March 1976
8. The newly-wed couple in a group photograph with relations and friends in London in March 1976

9.   GOS and wife, Deborah
10.   GOS and his bestman, Andrew Babatunde Eke

some fresh students break into tears as their parents or guardians took leave of them. The campus was also festive, as returning students happily welcomed one another and seemed very much at home. Fighting back emotion, my brother handed me over to one of the prefects and then left to catch the shuttle back to WAIFOR. The prefect checked through a list to authenticate my admission letter. Satisfied with my document, he informed me that I had been assigned to the *Immaculate Conception College House,* which was more commonly rendered simply as College House. There were also the *St. Martin de Porres House,* simply called *Porres House* and *St. Matthias (Matiya) Mulumba House,* shortened to *Mulumba House.*

The ICC campus was an expansive swathe of land, split into two unequal parts by a section of one of the ancient Benin Moats. The larger of the two parts was structured into a football field, rimmed with some staff residential buildings, an administrative area that housed the Principal's office, staff common room, library and the school hall, a section for laboratories and another section for classrooms and dormitories. The latter were three huge one-storey buildings whose ground floors comprised classrooms while their upper floors functioned as the student residential areas. On the far side of this part of the campus and set majestically on top of a small hill dominating the Moat was the Principal's residence, which he shared with some other clerics (i.e. Catholic priests of the SMA) who were also teachers in the school. The second and smaller part of the ICC campus was an expanse of land, beyond the Moat, which the school used mainly for sporting activities.

With my box on my head, I was shown the way to College House. There were some fresh and returning students already in the House, unpacking, making their beds or simply chatting. I was allocated a bed space and a locker, and advised to take my feeding plates to the dining hall. The latter was large and contained many tables arranged in rows, with chairs positioned around them. I was assigned a table space and told that I was to maintain that sitting position throughout the year. I left my plates on the table and dashed back to the House to continue unpacking my belongings. I put some of them in the locker and left other items, which I was unlikely to need frequently, in my box before taking the latter to the boxroom. As I finished making up my bed, the school bell rang at about 6:30p.m.: it was, as we would learn from some of the returning students, an invitation to the dining hall.

All of us, returning and fresh students alike, headed toward the dining hall. Dinner had already been served in our individual plates. The meal comprised yam and stew containing some smoked fish. I assumed the sitting position allotted to me. A senior student was at the head of the table. A prayer was said by the Food Prefect, after which we were free to commence eating. It was my first time of using the threesome of spoon, fork and knife: at home, my fingers were my cutlery. I knew how to apply the spoon, especially when eating rice or taking pap made from maize, but I had never used the combination of fork and knife. This shortcoming was not peculiar to me, as I noticed that several other fresh students were also at sea regarding the proper use of their cutlery. The head of our table noticed our dilemma and asked the fresh students to watch him: he held the fork in his left hand and the knife in his right, and demonstrated how to use them. We struggled through the meal, as we tried to adopt the new mode of eating with implements rather than with our fingers. After about twenty minutes, another prayer was said by the Food Prefect to mark the end of the dinner. We then returned to our respective Houses to continue the process of adapting to our new environment. Our House Prefect assembled those of us who were fresh students and assigned to each of us a chore to be performed every morning.

Second Day at ICC

Our progressive immersion in ICC, as an academic, religious and social ecosystem, continued on the next day, beginning with students carrying out their morning chores or duties, followed by the Holy Mass and breakfast. All resident students were obliged to attend the Mass, irrespective of whatever (non-Catholic) religion they professed. After breakfast, there was an assembly of the entire school, whose total student population was about 200, where the Principal, Father Joseph Patrick Donnelly, addressed all students, with a special welcome message for the fresh students. The *de facto* Vice-Principal was Sir Augustine Ogbebo Emumwen (1914-2009).

After the assembly, the fresh students were distributed into two classes: Form 1A and Form 1B. I found myself in Form 1B, with a population of about 25. As students introduced themselves, I heard many names from a diversity of ethnic groups in the Western Region of Nigeria: Form 1B was a veritable microcosm of the Region. To me, two students did not need any introduction. They were Friday Ehiwe and Gabriel Aghedo with whom I sat for the scholarships examination at Ibadan Grammar School, Ibadan, in September 1960. There were only three Western Region of Nigeria Scholars among the approximately 50 fresh students in both Form 1A and Form 1B. Friday Ehiwe and Gabriel Aghedo were the remaining two and both of them shared Form 1B with me. I began to make friends with students, whether returning or fresh, with whom I was destined to spend a substantial part of the next five years of my life. Students addressed each other by their surnames. Moreover, every student was assigned an identification number (which would be called a matriculation number in a university). Mine was 676, a so-called *angel number*, which some have interpreted as symbolising compassion, empathy, selflessness, success, problem-solving capacity, honesty, gratitude and grace. Mathematically, 676 is a so-called powerful number, because it is one of the numbers N which may be expressed in the form $N=a^2b^3$, i.e. as the product of a square and a cube, where a and b are positive whole numbers that are equal to or greater than 1. Indeed, $676 = (26)^2 \times 1^3$, if one sets a=26 and b=1. Additionally, 676 is also the product of the squares of two prime numbers 2 and 13, i.e. $676 = 2^2 \times 13^2$. The terminology 'powerful number' is the creation of Professor Solomon Wolf Golomb (May

30, 1932-May 1, 2016), an American mathematician and engineer, renowned for his work on mathematical games. Powerful numbers have been studied by a number of mathematicians, including Professor Paul Erdős (March 26, 1913 – September 20, 1996), a renowned Hungarian mathematician, and Professor George Szekeres (May 29, 1911-August 28, 2005), a Hungarian–Australian mathematician. Over the years, I have maintained a deep attachment to the 'powerful number' 676.

To ensure that teaching and learning took off swiftly and smoothly, the school immediately began the distribution of books to students. Not long, it was the turn of Form 1B students to queue up for their books. Each one of us was given some textbooks in respect of several subjects, spanning the arts and sciences, and a number of bespoke exercise books, emblazoned with the ICC logo. In addition, we received such Catholic religious items as rosaries, missals and Bibles. Fresh students, like me, were also issued their school uniforms: white shirts and white shorts. Thereafter, we were all set to launch into academic activities. Some years later, these were changed to white shirts and navy blue shorts.

The teaching staff population was about 14 and diversified: there were Irish and other European nationals as well as Nigerians of multiple ethnic backgrounds. Like their Nigerian colleagues, the Irish teachers, both clerics and non-clerics, were specialists in a variety of subjects. All the clerics were SMA priests. The school was also gender-sensitive, as some of the teachers were female. I was extremely excited that I would be taught by Nigerians and Europeans. At CSW, all the teachers were Nigerians. Within a few days of our arrival at ICC, academic activities kicked into a pleasing rhythm that was steadfastly sustained throughout the year. Teaching occurred from 8:30a.m. to 1:30p.m. on weekdays. Our teachers were punctual, dedicated and professional. They helped to ensure that core norms, values and principles of ICC were incrementally etched into every student's DNA.

Environmental Sanitation Days

There were also some non-academic activities. At the end of academic work on weekdays, students had lunch from 1:30p.m. to 2:00p.m., followed by a one-hour siesta by resident students from 2:00p.m. to 3:00p.m. Then the period from 3:00p.m. to 4:00p.m. was study time. From 4:00p.m. to 6:00p.m., students engaged in games or environmental maintenance activities such as grass-cutting and litter-picking around the campus. Dinner was from 6:00p.m. to 6:30p.m., after which there was holy rosary session from 6:30p.m. to 7:00p.m. Evening studies started at 7:00p.m. Forms 1 to 3 students were obliged to retire to bed at 9:00p.m., while students in Forms 4 and 5 retired to bed at 10:00p.m. To use a phrase that has since become commonplace in Nigeria, every Saturday was ICC's 'cleaning and environmental sanitation day', which was steadfastly observed by the school, years before this kind of notion was introduced and implemented by the country's national and subnational governments. Immediately after breakfast on Saturdays, each House embarked on cleaning and sanitation activities. Between 10:00am and 11:00a.m., the Principal, Fr. Donnelly, would carry out a thorough inspection of the three Houses, their surroundings and what passed for student toilets, to assess their state in relation to cleanliness and degree of compliance with good sanitation practices. The so-called toilets were rudimentary pit latrines whose walls, doors and roofs were made of corrugated zinc sheets. Each toilet cubicle was a mini oven in the afternoon. There were no flush toilets for students. Keeping the latrines clean was overly challenging as they were unlit, thereby making their floors liable to being soiled at night by some students who might have been highly pressed or ill. At the end of the inspection, Fr. Donnelly would rank the Houses and issue strict instructions to each House about any areas that needed immediate or continuous improvement. The weekly exercise fostered a culture of cleanliness and good sanitation practices in the school and ensured a healthy, vibrant and intellectually alert student body.

Sundays at ICC

On Sundays, all resident students attended Mass at St. Joseph's Catholic Church, located along First East Circular Road, Benin City. Spruce and dapper in their uniforms, they would move in a double file from the school to the Church. Breakfast was after the church service. Thereafter, some students would participate in the ecclesial activities of the Legion of Mary (LoM) and the Patricians Society, with the Principal as the Spiritual Director. Typically, members of the LoM would carry out door-to-door evangelisation in pairs immediately after Church service on Sunday before the praesidium's weekly meeting some hours later. I would become a member of the LoM in my fourth year at ICC. My evangelisation partner was my close classmate, Joseph Ugbaja (RIP), who later specialised as a Veterinary Doctor. The LoM was founded on September 7, 1921 in Dublin, Ireland, by Francis Michael Duff (June 7, 1889- November 7, 1980), an Irish lay Catholic who worked in the civil service of Ireland. His Eminence Desmond Cardinal Connell (March 24, 1926 – February 21, 2017), Archbishop of Dublin and Primate of Ireland, launched the cause for Duff's beautification in July 1996, thereby entitling Duff to be addressed as the 'Servant of God'. To end the day on a Sunday, reciting the holy rosary and carrying out evening studies were mandatory for all resident students.

Some Variations

There were occasional variations in the foregoing schedule or course of school activities. One such variation occurred as follows: as adequate water supply on the ICC campus was generally a problem, provision had been made for a huge underground tank erected behind College House. It was filled with water from time to time by means of a rainwater harvesting system attached to the roof of the House. Whenever the water level in the tank was low, especially during the dry season, students fetched water for their personal use (bathing, washing their clothes, etc.) from a certain stream, whose name among students was 'River Okungbowa'. Student folklore had it that when ICC moved to its existing site along Third East Circular Road, the Principal sent out a search party to look for a river or stream, hopefully not too distant, that would be a constant source of water for the school. We were told that a student called Joseph Ogunseri Okungbowa (1939-2010) led the expedition that found a stream, within a reasonable distance from the school. ICC students then triumphantly and independently gave the name 'River Okungbowa' to the stream, not minding that the stream might not actually be without a name. On days when students went to River Okungbowa, the period for the activity was normally from 3:00p.m. to 6:00p.m.

Rules and Regulations

Fresh students were progressively introduced to the gamut of rules and regulations at ICC. I can state one or two of such rules and regulations. It was an anathema to communicate in a Nigerian language, which was derogatorily called 'vernacular': the punishment for violating this rule was a fine. There were also strict rules about leaving the campus. From time to time, the Principal would allow students to go to town by declaring a day-off, when students could, for example, visit their homes, replenish supplies, have their hair cut, repair their torn clothes or transact some other business. The time to leave the campus and the time to return were prescribed. At the end of a day-off, a roll-call of students was done to determine if there were any students who did not return on time or at all. A student who breached the prescribed time to return was punished. Apart from days-off, a student who had a pressing and cogent need to go to town would be issued an exeat by the Principal, with the times of egress and ingress meticulously inscribed. There were rules against stealing, bullying, fighting and other misdemeanours. Examination malpractice was a very serious offence, which was also regarded as utterly disgraceful. Many of the rules and regulations were implemented by the prefects, as they were continuously in close proximity with the students, without bothering the school authority.

First Year at ICC

My first year at ICC was the most exciting in my life. I was away from home, lived with my peers, no longer engaged in street-hawking, was well-fed daily and received good education. During the period, my peers and I were diligently taken through a process of life-impacting inculturation within ICC's iconic cultural space of discipline, collegiality, sportsmanship, hard work and focus on academic excellence, underpinned by a solid moral and religious foundation. I was healthy, happy and able to cope with my studies. I engaged in a wide range of co-curricular activities that all students were expected to participate in. I made new friends among my peers and seniors. Some of those friendships have endured till today. The school was orderly and conducive to learning. Advancing from one Form to the next was conditional on satisfactory academic performance. At the end of the year, I placed first among all the students in Forms 1A and 1B and was thus ready to move to Form 2. I looked forward to becoming a Form 2 student, a sophomore.

Form One 1961: GOS seated second from left. The three
Government of the Western Region Scholars in the class were:
GOS, Gabriel Aghedo (seated fifth from the left)
and Friday Ehiwe (fourth from the right
in the back row)

8

ONE SMALL STEP UPWARD

The new school year started in January 1962. The Senior Prefect was Emmanuel Osadebamwen Woghiren, a well-built student with charm and charisma, who easily commanded the respect and cooperation of all students. Like several of my peers, it was gladdening that I had left Form 1 behind and was a Form 2 student: we were no longer freshmen, a humbling but highly motivating characterisation. As my new status as a sophomore gradually sank in, it was somewhat traumatic to learn that student X or student Y, who was my peer in Form 1, would not be returning or would be repeating the class, apparently on account of unsatisfactory academic performance. The school quickly settled down to the clockwork rhythm of the diverse activities that characterised, enriched and were positively shaping student life at ICC.

There were twelve teachers in the school in 1962, as depicted in a staff photograph taken in December of that year. They were Fr. Joseph Patrick Donnelly (Principal), Mr. Augustine Ogbebo Emumwen (Vice-Principal), Judith Elizabeth Danielson (née Frese), Fr. Jeremiah (Gerry) Joseph Crowe, Mr. John Encmoh, Mr. Peter Ebedi, Mr. Owen Gerry Murtagh, Mr. Gilbert Cain, Mrs. Florence Osaze Ukponmwan Guobadia, Ms. Esther Erwin, Mr. Liam Gleeson and Mr. Joseph O'Connor.

Teachers at ICC in 1962. Rear: left to right: Joseph O'Connor,
Liam Gleeson, Owen Gerard (Gerry) Murtagh, Gilbert Cain.
Front: left to right: Fr. Jeremiah (Gerry) Crowe, Judith Elizabeth Danielson (née Frese),
Augustine Ogbebo Emumwen, Fr. Joseph Patrick Donnelly (Principal), John Enemoh,
Florence Osaze Ukponmwan Guobadia,
Peter Ebedi, Esther Erwin.

Mrs. Danielson was an American Peace Corps member. She served
at ICC, Benin City, from 1962 to 1964 as Biology teacher. From
1958 to 1973, she was the wife of David (Davio) Arthur Danielson
(December 3, 1938-August 27, 2018). David, who arrived Benin
City with his wife, Judith, was also a Peace Corps member. He
taught Biology and English Language at Edo College, Benin City,
from 1962 to 1964. Judith and David had their first child, Robin
Sarah Adesode, in 1962 in Benin City, and included the Benin
name Adesode as one of the child's forenames. The child's birth
made global headlines, as she was the first American Peace Corps
baby to be born overseas. Before their divorce in 1973, the couple
had two other children: Benjamin Darius Stiles, born in 1964, and
Maria Amy Ellsworth, born in 1966.

Mrs. Florence Guobadia was the wife of the solid state physicist,
Dr. Abel Ibude Guobadia who, in 1987, was appointed Nigeria's
pioneer Ambassador to the Republic of Korea and, in 2000,
the Chairman of the nation's Independent National Electoral

Commission. She taught me mathematics as a Form 2 student in 1962.

In those days, many of us knew most of our teachers only by their surnames, often with no knowledge of their forenames or initials. In 1962, close to 70% of the academic staff population was Irish, with Nigerians and other European nationals forming some 30%. Accordingly, the Irish clerics and teachers shouldered a considerable proportion of the burden of teaching and administration at ICC. My thinking in those days was that Ireland must certainly be a hugely populated country for it to be able to send large numbers of clerics and other professionals to Nigeria to assist in key areas of national development like religious formation, education and medicine. Actually, in terms of population, Ireland was, and still is, a relatively small country: its population in 1962 was merely 2.8 million while that of Nigeria was about 47 million. I eventually found out that the SMA, which sent out the clerics and had been working in several countries in Africa for decades, was motivated by service to humanity. In 1962, Nigeria was just emerging from colonisation and was highly underdeveloped by all development indices. As I write, Ireland's population is just over 4.8 million while that of Nigeria is about 200 million: thus, while the population of Ireland is yet to be twice its 1962 figure, that of Nigeria has more than quadrupled. In spite of the evident huge disparity in the populations of these two countries, the Irish Province of the SMA remains very active in supporting Nigeria's development efforts, within the ambit of its (SMA's) vision and mission statements.

Form 2 in 1962: GOS is seated third from left

Form 2 in 1962: GOS, participating in a school opera,
is standing fourth from left in front row

Many of our teachers carried out their work with a strong commitment to excellence. They implemented the prescribed curricula with diligence, ensured that they were themselves truly masters of their subject areas, graded student assignments on time, developed and administered relevant tests and examinations, prepared reports on student academic performance, general conduct, social interaction and physical health, enforced ICC's rules, norms and values, supervised diverse student extra-curricular activities and ensured as much as possible that no student was left behind. To ensure that these and kindred outcomes were substantially achieved, the school held every teacher individually liable for any dereliction of duty or a poor realisation of the prescribed academic and non-academic objectives.

We were equipped with socialisation, relational and teamwork skills. At the end of the 1962 school year, I moved to Form 3 with many of my peers.

College Anthem

1962 was a defining year in the history of ICC because it was the year when its anthem was composed and adopted. The composer of the 'College Anthem' was Fr. Jeremiah (Gerry) Joseph Crowe (July 19, 1926-June 9, 2003), who thereby bequeathed an invaluable piece of his intellectual property to ICC and posterity. Shown below are some photographs in which he appears. On arrival at ICC, Fr. Crowe was surprised that, eighteen years after its foundation, the school did not have an anthem. The reason for the glaring omission was not known. Nonetheless, mindful of the unique character of ICC and conversant with the rich history of Benin City, the institution's host community, Fr. Crowe took on and successfully accomplished the daunting task of eliminating the anomaly. As a glimpse into the life of this cleric and teacher, let me provide a rapid sketch of his educational apostolate in West Africa, especially Nigeria.

Commonly called Gerry within the SMA sphere, Fr. Crowe's parents were Bridget (née Whyte) and Patrick Crowe, who was a tram-conductor in Dublin. He was ordained on June 14, 1950, at St. Colman's Cathedral, Newry, County Down, Ireland, by Eugene O'Doherty, Bishop of the Diocese of Dromore. In 1954, Fr. Crowe was appointed to the Diocese of Ondo, in the present-day Ondo State. The Bishop of the Diocese, Thomas Hughes, assigned Fr. Crowe to the staff of St. Augustine's Teacher Training College,

Akure. In 1958, Fr. Crowe was transferred to Oka in Akoko, Ondo State, where he founded a secondary school for boys called St. Patrick's College in January 1959, with an enrolment of over 100 pupils. While carrying out his duties and responsibilities, there were disagreements between him and his Bishop. Moreover, St. Patrick's College was racked by incessant student disturbances. Discomposed by these circumstances, Fr. Crowe requested to be transferred out of the Diocese of Ondo. His request was granted. Accordingly, in October 1962, he was assigned to the Diocese of Benin City, where he joined the staff of ICC. Fr. Crowe, who obtained his BA degree in 1953 from UCC, Ireland, after studying History, Sociology and English, was poetic and liked composing music. His stay at ICC was inordinately brief: he was a member of staff for only one term, during which time he taught English Literature to my class. But before departing ICC, he left a large and indelible footprint: he composed the College Anthem and I recall that he taught my class how to sing it in 1962. After leaving ICC at the end of 1962, he became the founding Principal of St. Benedict's College, a secondary school for boys, at Igueben, Edo State. Following a request by him, he was granted permission in 1967 to join the SMA's British District, which was at that time working toward attaining provincial status. Fr. Crowe became a founding member of the British Province of the SMA, established in February 1968, with its location in Manchester, England. Able to communicate in English and French, both orally and in writing, he returned to West Africa in November 1972, worked in Francophone Ivory Coast (present day Cote d'Ivoire) till July 1975 and then returned to England. During his apostolate in West Africa, Fr. Crowe pioneered several initiatives. Consequently, associated with his name are such achievement-depicting phrases as "founded", "founding Principal", "founding member" and "composed" which amply characterise this cleric's creativity and impactful leadership. Due to ill health, he retired in 1991 and lived in the SMA House at Anson Road, Manchester, England. Born on Monday, July 19, 1926, in Tram Terrace, Clontarf, in the Archdiocese of Dublin, Ireland, Fr. Crowe died suddenly on Monday, June 9, 2003, and is buried in Manchester, United Kingdom.

Fr. Crowe at his ordination in 1950   Fr. Crowe in retirement in the 1990s

College Anthem
Composed in 1962 by
Rev. Fr. Jeremiah (Gerry) Joseph Crowe, SMA (1926-2003)

1. Our school's conception college
    And it's placed in Benin town
    A place that's rich in history,
    For many miles around
    We built our school around a moat
    And having placed it there,
    We named it after Mary mild,
    And sought her loving care.

2. The students come from miles around,
    To learn and work and pray,
    And yet there's time for everyone,
    To laugh and sing and play
    There's joy and fun and happiness,
    And peace ashining through,
    Because we're placed beneath the shade
    Of Mary's mantle blue.

3. The days pass by and students too,
   Exams are passed and then,
   The boys no longer stay as boys
   They take their roles as men.
   But still they live and still they pray
   And keep in mind always,
   That they're beneath God's mother's love
   As in their student days.

9

TWO CRUCIAL YEARS

The 1963 and 1964 school years were crucial for my classmates and me. At ICC, every Form 2 student looked forward to attaining Form 3, the mid-point of his academic trajectory in the institution. In 1963, I achieved that dream. As the halfway point of my journey through secondary school education, Form 3 was a unique milestone in my upward academic mobility. A student's performance in Form 3 was a crucial criterion that was employed by the school when deciding whether he would specialise in either the Arts or Science subjects during his remaining two years of training. Moreover, 1963 was remarkable in several other ways, one of which was the epochal constitutional reconfiguration of Nigeria into four federating regions, through the creation of the Mid-Western Region. Celebrated by all the inhabitants of the new region, the development had, nevertheless, the ominous potential of adversely affecting my educational journey.

The school year began in January 1963. As usual, the institution welcomed new teachers and fresh students, as well as returning students and teachers, to its fold. A number of the teachers who taught us in Form 2 had left. As continuing students, we longed for a rapid disclosure of the subject specialties of the new teachers. Very quickly, the full range of academic and co-curricular activities kicked-in. We continued to receive tuition in the same subjects that we studied in Form 2 but with much enlarged scope and greater depth.

An Audacious Student Protest

Our Senior Prefect in 1963 was the future Catholic priest, Fr. Theophilus Ewaenosetin Uwaifo. Ordained on Sunday, December 27, 1970, he was born on December 12, 1941 and died on Sunday, All Saints Day, November 1, 2015, after an illustrious career as a priest and educationist. He was a brilliant student, academically always among the top of his class. Endowed with preternatural oratorical prowess, his leadership skills and approach were inspiring, even if somewhat radical. He demonstrated exemplary courage whenever there was need for such. For example, he was remarkable for being the first student to ever lead an open protest at ICC, where strict adherence to school rules and regulations was at the core of student development. At ICC, it was unthinkable that a Senior Prefect, whose duty included helping to defend and enforce the school's rules and regulations in all circumstances, would be at the forefront of any kind of uprising. The audacious protest occurred in second term of 1963, an evening before dinner. The students' grievances were about the variety, quantity and quality of the food that was served in the dining hall. Although almost all students secretly supported the protest, only a small number actually participated, afraid that they might be identified and severely punished by the school, possibly by expulsion. Faced with a Hobson's choice between my inalienable right to participate in a demonstration that had the potential of improving my welfare and the imperative of adhering to the unwritten school convention on how students should present their grievances, I openly joined the protest, although realistically apprehensive that if I were expelled from ICC, it would inevitably be the end of my education forever. The protest was peaceful, non-violent and non-destructive but merely boisterous and attention-seeking. As the unprecedented action continued, with songs, dancing in front of the dining hall and clanging of empty bottles and cans, the Principal soon became aware of the unusual situation so we all expected his response to be nothing short of drastic: we feared that the heavens were about to fall. Then, he summoned Uwaifo to his office. After discussion, or negotiation, with the Principal, Uwaifo emerged with an air of victory: the Principal, who was apparently unaware of the state of student feeding and was probably never apprised of it, readily agreed to implement the students' demands. It was a profound victory and Uwaifo had pulled it off. As a consequence, those of us who participated in the action had amazingly escaped, by a whisker, the huge punishment that might have been our lot for what would have been characterised as gross insubordination. I did not witness such a protest any more throughout the remaining years of my student life at ICC.

During his life time, the priest and educationist in Fr. Theophilus Ewaen Uwaifo shone brilliantly: apart from his sacerdotal duties, as a Chaplain at St. Albert the Great Church, University of Benin, Benin City, and as the founder of an active prayer ministry in Benin City, he was at various times the pioneer Provost of the College of Education Iyaro, Benin City, which was subsequently called the College of Education, Ekiadolor, but later renamed Tayo Akpata University of Education, Ekiadolor, and the Pro-Chancellor and Chairman of the Governing Council of Ambrose Alli University, Ekpoma. With the aura of a sage, his charisma was captivating. In his homilies, often tinged with a hue of radicalism, he exuded enormous courage in his somewhat fiery criticisms of the many irreligious and permissive tendencies that had become immanent in the Nigerian society.

Co-Curricular Activities

Apart from the unprecedented student protest that I recounted above, academic and co-curricular activities went on smoothly throughout 1963 at ICC. In regard to co-curricular activities, the school was adequately equipped with facilities for student participation in many games and campus-based secular and religious societies, such as the chess club, debating club, Legion of Mary and the Patricians Society. I participated in several debating and chess contests. In later years, I was also a member of the Legion of Mary and the Patricians Society. Moreover, I took interest in table tennis and football. In table tennis, I plied the game with such students as Isaac Uhunmwagho, Victor Oshodi, Abel Agbontaen, Harris Enabulele, Federick Ilabor (RIP), John Igbinedion, Ephraim Osubor, John Ogbeide, Paul Ordia, Peter Kagbala and Daniel Ogbomo, with the English Language teacher, Mr. Owen Gerry Murtagh, as the table tennis coach. As a member of staff at ICC, I would later assume the role of table tennis coach in 1968. In that year, the team included such players as Abel Agbontaen, Joseph Uujamhan, Ben Okobaro (RIP) and Daniel Ogbomo. In football, where I featured as a goalkeeper, I played in one of the junior teams, but not in the school's first eleven. At that time, some of my team mates were Andrew Osahon Adeghe, Harris Enabulele, Dennis Okungbowa, Felix Ogbeide, Cletus Obahor and Latifu Adeoti. In later years (1968, 1969), Felix Ogbeide, the future medical doctor and deft player, would become the captain of ICC's first eleven team, winning multiple laurels for the school.

Form 3 in 1963: GOS is seated sixth from right

Baptism and Confirmation

At the time we were admitted into ICC in 1961, many students were not yet baptised Catholics. In particular, I was not a baptised Catholic, although I had been attending the Catholic Church at WAIFOR since 1953. From 1961 to 1963, all students in my set studied the Catholic Catechism as part of our religious formation. The 'Penny Catechism' contained 370 questions, with accompanying answers. The questions ranged from introductory ones like question 1 and question 28 which were 'Who made you?' and 'What do you mean by a mystery?', respectively, to deeper questions like question 277 and question 327 which were 'What is the Holy Mass?' and 'Which are the four sins crying to heaven for vengeance?', respectively. We were expected to memorise the questions and answers. Around June 1963, the Principal, Fr. Donnelly, announced that those of us who were yet to be baptised were required to go to the Holy Cross Cathedral, Mission Road, Benin City, for a catechetical examination toward baptism. With much trepidation, my classmates and I presented ourselves for the examination. We were all anxious to exit the category of catechumens. The examiner was Fr. Vincent Boyle (February

21, 1920-January 29, 1999), who was well known at that time at the Holy Cross Cathedral. Using a copy of the catechism, Fr. Boyle asked question after question. We were neither expected to supply a wrong answer nor fail to provide an answer. In the end, I passed the examination and Lawrence Ojeogwu, a fifth form student, acted as my Godfather. In November of the same year 1963, my classmates and I took the catechetical examination for the sacrament of confirmation and passed. The confirmation ceremony was performed by Bishop Patrick Joseph Kelly (August 31, 1894 – August 18, 1991). Another fifth form student, Matthias Ogunsuyi, acted as my Godfather. Having received the fundamental sacraments of baptism and confirmation, I had been fully inducted into the Roman Catholic Church.

Creation of the Mid-Western Region

It was also in 1963 that a major constitutional restructuring of Nigeria occurred. That was the outcome of a prolonged and steadfast agitation by the people of the Benin and Delta Provinces to be constitutionally excised from the Western Region and be named the Mid-Western Region. To achieve this, a constitutional referendum was mandatory. Relying on the Mid-Western Region of Nigeria Act 1962 that eventually mandated the referendum, the latter was held on Saturday, July 13, 1963, supervised by Gabriel Edward Longe a Barrister-at-Law. The referendum question, which required a Yes or No answer, was the following:

> Do you agree that the Mid-Western Region Act, 1962, shall have effect so as to secure that Benin Province including Akoko Edo District in the Afenmai Division and Delta Province including Warri Division and Warri Urban Township area shall be included in the proposed Mid-Western Region? [Ben Obi Nwabueze: *A Constitutional History of Nigeria*, C. Hurst & Co. Publishers, London, 1982 - Constitutional history - 272 pages, page 136, ISBN: 0905838793, 9780905838793]

By the Act, for a positive outcome, it was mandatory that not less than 60% of the registered voters in the Benin and Delta Provinces must have voted affirmatively. At the end of the referendum, out of the 654,130 voters in the Federal Electoral register of 1959, over 89% voted affirmatively for the creation of the Mid-Western Region. The Region came into existence on August 9, 1963, with Benin City as its capital. The Mid-Western Region has the unique distinction of historically being the only federating unit of Nigeria that was ever created constitutionally: all the States in Nigeria that were created after 1963 were through military decrees, devoid of any constitutional process. Governance of the Mid-Western Region commenced swiftly, following the establishment of an Administrative Council with Chief Dennis Chukude Osadebay (June 29, 1911-December 26, 1994) as its interim Administrator from August 1963 to February 1964, and, subsequently, as its elected pioneer Premier from February 1964 to January 15, 1966: Chief Osadebay's premiership was terminated on January 15, 1966 by a military coup. The eventual realisation of the goal of creating the Mid-Western Region and installing its Government were epic events, which had the potential of opening up new vistas in development activities, with unprecedented impact on the expansion of employment and education opportunities within the entire Region.

From Western Region to Mid-Western Region Scholar

The new configuration of the national political space caused me some anxiety. What was my fate as a Western Region Scholar? Would the Mid-Western Region assume responsibility for my scholarship? Would I be required to seat for another scholarships examination? These and related questions coursed persistently through my mind. When I asked the Principal, Fr. Donnelly, some of these questions, he counselled that we needed to wait a while to see how events would unfold. By the beginning of the next school year in January 1964, it became evident that responsibility for funding my scholarship had been seamlessly transferred to the newly established Government of the Mid-Western Region: I had thereby become one of the pioneer Mid-Western Region Scholars. I maintained the status till the completion of my education at ICC in 1965. Concerning the school's administration in 1964, the Senior Prefect was Wilfred Osuala and his Assistant was the future Professor of Biochemistry, Anthony Uyiekpen Osagie (June 7, 1947- May 22, 2013), two extremely brilliant and admirable Fifth Form students.

In 1964, Form 4 was structured as Form 4A and Form 4B, representing the Science class and Arts class, respectively. Students were allowed to make their own choices concerning which of the two classes to join, provided that the options were compatible with their individual performances in the examinations at the end of their Form 3 studies. I advanced to Form 4 in 1964, the last year before my West African School Certificate Examinations (WASCE).

Career Choice without Much Guidance

Deciding whether to opt for Form 4A or Form 4B was a tough responsibility because, firstly, there was no formal institutional career guidance for students; yet we were essentially being asked to chart our career paths. For example, at ICC in 1964, students could only enroll for some or all of the following twelve subjects: English Language, Latin, Oral English, English Literature, Bible Studies, History, Mathematics, Physics, Chemistry, Biology, Art and Health Science. Thus, a subject like Economics, that is key to a diversity of careers in such sectors as banking, insurance, accountancy, economic consultancy, civil service, international organisations, universities and research institutes, was unavailable to students. With an institutional career counselling programme, the set of available subjects in the school might have been different or expanded. Secondly, for some students, all was grist that came to their mills: they could join either of the two classes and do very well. I was assigned to Form 4A: the Science class. Toward my WASCE, I opted to take lessons in the following seven subjects: English Language, English Literature, Bible Studies, Mathematics, Physics, Chemistry and Biology. ICC had the human and material resources to provide effective teaching in these subjects: the laboratories were adequately equipped and there was no mismatch between teacher and subject. All was set for the hard work that both teachers and students must implement throughout 1964, as students endeavoured to realise their perceived career goals.

The 1964 academic year went smoothly for me, both academically and healthwise, and ended in December of that year, marked by a vacation for students. Simultaneously, the 1965 academic year beckoned, as we had only a few weeks for the vacation.

Members of College House in 1964: GOS is seated second from the right

1962 ICC junior football team: goalkeeper GOS (third from left, kneeling), captain Andrew Osahon Adeghe, standing third from right, and student coach Matthias Ogunsuyi standing, first from right

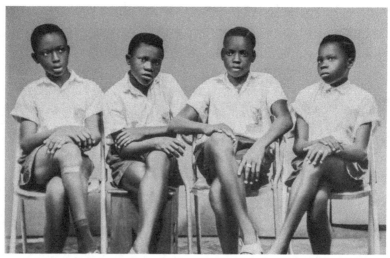

(L-R) Andrew Adeghe, Cletus Obahor, GOS and Andrew Akatugba in 1962

1964 ICC table tennis team: GOS seated, first from right.

10

PREFECT OF MATIN DE PORRES HOUSE

At the completion of each academic year, the tenure of every student officer of the school also came automatically to an end. A new set of student officers, mainly from the fifth form, would then be appointed by the Principal at the beginning of the following academic year. Every student looked forward to the identities of the in-coming student leaders. As was its tradition, ICC groomed some of the potential student leaders, who it was discreetly considering for key positions such as those of Senior Prefect and Assistant Senior Prefect. The grooming normally involved sending the putative in-coming Senior Prefect and Assistant Senior Prefect to a leadership training course in early January at the beginning of a new academic year.

Man O' War Bay

The leadership training was usually conducted at the Man O' War Bay, established by the British in 1951 and originally located in British Southern Cameroon. As junior students, it was always intriguing to listen to the narration by senior students who had undergone the Man O' War Bay training about their experiences, which included tough paramilitary exercises and drills as well as seminars on citizenship, leadership, integrity, self-discipline, self-reliance, selfless service, patriotism and national consciousness. The core activities of the Man O' War Bay have since been subsumed under those of a larger entity called the Citizenship and Leadership Training Centre (C&LTC), created in 1960 by the Citizenship and Leadership Training Centre Ordinance, to which Sir James Wilson Robertson, Governor-General and Commander-in-Chief of the Federation of Nigeria, gave his assent on September 16, 1960, a few days shy of October 1, 1960, Nigeria's Independence Day. The ordinance was subsequently transformed into Decree No 38 (viewed legislatively as equivalent to an Act) which took effect from December 11, 1989.

The C&LTC, an affiliate of the global organisation called Outward Bound International, whose motto is: *To Serve, To Strive and Not to Yield*, was originally a parastatal of the Federal Ministry of Youth and Sports. Following the United-Nations-mandated plebiscite of Saturday, February 11, 1961, British Southern Cameroon opted, by an affirmative vote of 70.5%, to be integrated into the French Cameroon, rather than Nigeria. The unification was effected on October 1, 1961, subsequently christened the *Unification Day* and observed as a public holiday, to form the Federal Republic of Cameroon. Consequently, in 1963, the Man O' War activities were moved to Shere Hills, Jos, in Plateau State, Nigeria. Since then, the C&LTC has created the following additional seven Man O' War training schools: Sea School, Apapa, Lagos State, South West (1964), Forest School, Port Harcourt, Rivers State, South South (1977), Hill Top School, Awgu, Enugu State, South East (2002), Desert School, Fika, Yobe State, North East (2002), Rock Land School, Kotorkorshi, Zamfara State, North West (2002), Women Unit, Otu-Jeremi, Delta State, South South (1975) and the Mobile Unit located at the C&LTC Headquarters, Gudu District, Abuja, Federal Capital Territory.

1965 leadership training at St Patrick College, Asaba: GOS seated in
the front row, fourth from right, with the late Stephen Imasuen Nosakhare Ekunwe standing,
second from left, in the third row.

Participation in Leadership Training

At the beginning of an academic session in January of each year,
students were always curious to know who had been sent by the
school to participate in the Man O' War Bay training. In December
1964, shortly after I returned home for the end-of-year vacation, I
received a letter from the Principal, Fr. Donnelly, stating that two
of us had been nominated to participate in a one-week leadership
training course at St. Patrick College, Asaba. This was not one
of the two Man O' War Bay training schools, which were Shere
Hills, Jos and Sea School, Apapa, in those days. My companion
was Stephen Imasuen Nosakhare (SIN) Ekunwe (June 1, 1948 –
December 21, 2016). Ekunwe and I participated in the five-day
training activities, which comprised seminars on leadership and
citizenship during plenary sessions followed by scenario analyses
in groups. There were no paramilitary exercises or drills. For
me, the training greatly enhanced my capacity for leadership and
substantially boosted my understanding of the manifold roles that
I was expected to continually play as a citizen of Nigeria.

Prefect of Martin de Porres House

Toward the third week of January 1965, the school resumed for the first term of the 1965 academic year. On the resumption day, the ICC campus bustled with life and activities, with students connecting again with their friends and narrating interesting tales of how they spent their vacation. After carrying out some environment-improving chores in the morning of the next day, there was Holy Mass, as was customary. At the end of the Mass, conducted by the Principal, Fr. Donnelly, he asked students to wait for some announcements. He then reeled out the names of the student officers for the 1965 academic year. In particular, my classmate Stephen Imasuen Nosakhare Ekunwe, the future Professor of Cellular and Molecular Biology at the historically black Jackson State University, Jackson, Mississippi, USA, whose research focused on colon and prostate cancer, was assigned the office of Senior Prefect. I was given the portfolio of Prefect of Martin de Porres House, named after the Peruvian, mixed-race, Dominican brother, Juan Martin de Porres Velázquez (December 9, 1579 – November 3, 1639). De Porres is the patron saint of mixed-race people, African-Americans, hairdressers, barbers, innkeepers and public health workers as well as all persons who struggle for racial equality and social justice. He was beatified by Pope Gregory XVI (September 18, 1765 – June 1, 1846) in 1837 and canonized by Pope John XXIII (November 25, 1881 – June 3, 1963) in 1962. The other student officers in 1965 are indicated in the following table.

STUDENT OFFICERS IN 1965

Office	*Officer*
Senior Prefect	Stephen Ekunwe†
Assistant Senior Prefect	Frederick Ilabor†
College House Prefect	Anthony Amadasun
Mulumba House Prefect	Lawrence Ohiowele
Porres House Prefect	GOS Ekhaguere (till May 8, 1965) & Michael Uchidiuno (from May 8, 1965 till December 31, 1965)
Food Prefect	Andrew Iloh
Time Keeper	Thaddeus Daniel Hart
Games Prefect	Paul Guobadia
Library Prefect	Bernard Irusota
The Sacristan	Sylvanus Airhauhi†
Football Captain	Joseph Igbinosun†

† = deceased

Some Characteristics of my Appointment

My appointment was unconventional in several ways: it therefore surprised me and many students. Firstly, it was customary that the leader of a House was appointed from among the Fifth Form members of the House: I was not a member of Martin de Porres House. I had been a member of College House from my first day at ICC, i.e. from January 1961 till January 1965, when the appointment was announced. I did not expect that I would be assigned a post that would ever require my relocation from College House. Many a student saw my appointment, which involved the deployment of a student from one House to head a different House, to which he did not belong, as probably the first in the history of ICC. Secondly, there were several eminently qualified Fifth Form members of Martin de Porres House who were looking forward to be appointed as Prefect of Martin de Porres

House and were therefore, understandably, quite upset and miffed by my appointment. Thirdly, whereas I knew all the students in College House and they also knew me quite well, my knowledge of the members of Martin de Porres House was comparatively superficial. Finally, I was somewhat smallish whereas many of the members of Martin de Porres House were relatively much bigger than I: consequently, I worried about how I would get everyone in Martin de Porres House to carry out House duties at my behest, without constantly reporting uncooperative students to the House Master or the Principal. In spite of these concerns, I moved my belongings from College House to Martin de Porres House, as required by my appointment, and I assumed leadership.

My Duties as House Prefect

As I had indicated previously, ICC had three Houses: Martin de Porres House, College House and Mulumba House, named after Matiya Mulumba (1836 – May 30, 1886), one of the martyrs of Uganda, who was beatified in 1920 by Pope Benedict XV (November 21, 1854 – January 22, 1922) and canonized in 1964 by Pope Paul VI (September 26, 1897– August 6, 1978). St. Mulumba is the patron saint of chiefs and families (he was himself a chief of several Ugandan villages). Each House was contained in a huge two-storey building, whose ground floor comprised classrooms while the first floor was a large dormitory. The school's governance structure was quasi-federal: the Principal, his staff, including the House Masters, and the principal student officers, especially the Senior Prefect, formed the central or apex administration while the Houses were the quasi-federating units. Each House had its own quasi-independent administrative structure, with the House Prefect as leader. As House Prefect, my duties and responsibilities included, but were by no means limited to, the following: being a role model to House members by exhibiting exemplary conduct; ensuring the effective and problem-free administration of the

House; galvanising House members into a cohesive and united team with a cooperative spirit; organising House members to be able to participate competitively in extra-curricular events such as inter-House debates and sport competitions; ensuring that the House performed highly in any competition among Houses; ensuring that the dormitory and its surroundings were clean at all times, ensuring that members presented themselves neatly at assemblies; furnishing House members with timely information when necessary; attending problem-solving and planning meetings of House Prefects; and carrying out any other assignments, duties or directives by the school administration. Associated with these tasks were distinct metrics which the Principal employed for assessing performance.

Going about my Duties as House Prefect

My first initiative was to set up a framework for implementing my duties and responsibilities, by identifying and appointing some students as leaders of certain House activities. Within a few weeks, a routine was in place and House members knew what their daily duties were. Every Saturday was an *environmental sanitation day*, when the following set of activities would take place. Each House was obliged to ensure that its surroundings and dormitory were in the cleanest possible state. Moreover, on a rotational basis, Houses would take turns, one Saturday at a time, to clean the communal pit toilets. By 9 am, students would have moved to their dormitories and stood by their beds. The Principal would then undertake an inspection of the dormitories and award marks to each House. He would subsequently move on to also inspect the toilets. The Prefect of the House whose turn it was to clean the toilets would be put on the spot, if the Principal adjudged the toilets not to be clean enough. From time to time, a House Prefect ran afoul of the lofty standard of cleanliness of the toilets envisaged by the Principal. As Prefect, I applied myself to the effective discharge of my duties and responsibilities, in spite of the circumstances, including my initial concerns listed above. A sore issue was always the state of the pit toilets. There were about 30: for over 200 students, including day students, in the three Houses. Given the sometimes dire state of water supply on the campus, several of the pit conveniences were occasionally badly soiled, especially at night. On week days, it was sometimes difficult to use some of them because of their bad state: occasionally, one needed to open door after door before finding a good toilet. But every Saturday, all the toilets were to be transformed and made spick and span for the Principal's inspection.

Removal from Office as House Prefect

On Saturday, May 8, 1965, the usual activities on an *environmental sanitation day* were carried out on the campus. On that day, it was the turn of the Martin de Porres House to clean the toilets. I sent a team of students to clean the toilets and I carried out a pre-inspection to verify that the job had been properly done. We were then ready for the Principal's rigorous inspection. Following a familiar routine, after inspecting the dormitories and its surroundings, the Principal, together with the Senior Prefect and all the House Prefects, moved on to check the toilets. As the inspection proceeded, we all soon found about three freshly soiled toilets: some students, maybe badly pressed, had rendered nugatory the meticulous work that had been done. The Principal did not take kindly to what he saw: he scored my House poorly and instructed that the affected toilets be cleaned up. Although highly disappointed, I easily associated myself with the Principal's uncompromising and strict stance: it was his fundamental duty to ensure a clean campus and a healthy and safe student population. But it would have been utterly unthinkable to lock up the pit toilets before inspection and disallow students, irrespective of their circumstances, from using them simply because they had been freshly cleaned. In the evening of the same day, the Principal showed up at the student refectory during dinner and proceeded to address all of us. He alluded to the state of the campus and what students and their leaders should always do. He then made the following statement:

> I have decided to replace GOS as Prefect of Porres House. But because he is a brilliant student, I will give him another post. He should return to College House.

These words still ring in my ears. They will continually ring in my ears. In today's political parlance in Nigeria, it would probably be said that GOS was impeached, even though my appointment was not through an election. The Principal ended by immediately naming my successor as Michael Uchidiuno, who was also a member of College House at that time. As I will soon narrate, not long after my removal from office, my circumstances changed so dramatically that it was no longer expedient or feasible for the Principal to appoint me to another position: fate was about to deal me a very heavy hand.

11

A NEAR SISYPHEAN ORDEAL

I was a substantially healthy child during my primary school days. Only occasionally did I fall ill. One of such illnesses sometimes manifested as very high fever, probably caused by the malaria parasite. In those days, my parents would apply the bloodletting treatment: my chest would be lacerated with a sharp razor blade, blood would ooze out of the cuts, a peppery powdery substance would be rubbed into the lacerations and then I would be laid some distance away from a fireside. Subsequently, I would be given some soup made from pepper, *oziza* (Piper guineense) and dried fish. That kind of therapy, which was also used in Europe up to the 18th century, was invariably traumatic. But by the next day, as was usual with kids, I would be up and running again with my peers.

My Health Status at ICC before 1965

I was also very healthy, until almost midway through my Fifth Form, the last year of my secondary school education. I was fond of playing table tennis. This was one game that made me happy, since there were many other sporting activities in which I could not participate effectively because I did not possess the relevant skills. From around 1963, when I was in Form 3, I was well known in the school as a table tennis player. There were many other good table tennis players in the school in those days, as I had indicated in a previous chapter of this book. I also played football, functioning in the position of goalkeeper. I expected everything to be blissful throughout 1965. I had no inkling that the expectation might not be realised. But it was not until close to the middle of the year that it became manifest that 1965 would, for me, be very different from every other year before it: a cataclysmic health upheaval, enormously disruptive and potentially life-changing, soon occurred in my life.

Preparation for Final Examinations

The final year of my secondary school education at ICC was 1965. Academically, I was a confident and audacious student, who never missed an opportunity to engage his teachers intellectually, with a view to acquiring more knowledge from them beyond the normal classroom experience. My teachers were always very much aware that I was perpetually ready to engage them intellectually, whenever I could not agree with the rationale for some of their academic arguments. To some of the teachers, whose feathers I occasionally ruffled academically, I represented some pain in their teeth: a toothache. Nevertheless, my teachers and peers accepted me for who I was: they all knew that I always did things my way.

The final examinations were to be administered by the West African Examinations Council (WAEC), a board established in 1952 and headquartered in Accra Ghana. The examining body would thereafter issue the West African School Certificate (WASC) to each successful candidate. Time appeared quite fleeting: it was already May 1965, only a few months away from the final examinations which would begin in November. Most of the fundamental aspects of the prescribed curricula in the arts and sciences, as relevant to my set, had been meticulously covered by our teachers before the end of the second term of our final academic year. All students were engrossed in continuous revision, under the supervision of the respective subject teachers. The strategy was to get students to attempt as many past questions as possible in the different subjects. Tests were periodically administered by our exceptionally diligent teachers, after which they normally highlighted key points and potential pitfalls. No student could afford to waste any time during that crucial game-changing phase of their secondary school training. Above all, it was utterly inconceivable that any student would be absent from school so close to the final examinations. Every student was in a heightened examination mode. But for me, the game was about to change abruptly and fundamentally. Indeed, as I wrote elsewhere:

> Every now and then, as we travel along the never lonely one-way high street from mortality to immortality, we realize that the game changes, sometimes abruptly, with God as the game-changer. No earthling will ever know when the game will change or how the game will change.

Illness deals a heavy hand

In the boarding house at ICC, evening studies normally started at 7:00p.m. for all students. Then students in Forms 1 to 3 were obliged to retire to bed at 9:00p.m. while bedtime for the senior students in Forms 4 and 5 was 10:00pm. During the timespan from 7:00pm to 9:00pm or 7:00pm to 10:00pm, as the case may be, students attended to academic assignments or engaged in independent studies. Our dormitories were upstairs, above the classrooms. As I was often tired after playing table tennis, I ensured that I always quickly completed my assignments and then instead of waiting till 10:00pm like other senior students before retiring upstairs for the night, I would occasionaly sneak upstairs to bed. Before other students retired at 10:00pm, I would have been deeply asleep. So it was on Wednesday, May 12, 1965: I was in bed around 9:15pm, in contravention of school rules which prescribed 10:00pm as bedtime for senior students. I experienced nothing unusual. I soon slept off. Not longer after, the first few students to enter the dormitory were confronted with a frightening sight: they found me in an unusual and awkward posture on my bed. Afraid that something calamitous might be happening to me, my successor as the Prefect of Martin de Porres House promptly contacted the Principal, Fr. Donnelly. The Principal assumed that I had already relocated to College House. As he drove toward College House, he was informed that I was still in the Martin de Porres House. Wasting no time, he was promptly by my bedside. Fr. Donnelly observed me and told the bewildered students that there was no cause for alarm, explaining that I might merely be experiencing a nightmare. As if to buttress his explanation, I woke up normally in the morning, hale and hearty, completely unaware of the dramatic occurrence during the night. Morever, no student, including my close friends, spoke to me about the incident. The day was Wednesday, May 12, 1965, a bright and potentially nice day: it was like every other. The usual academic workflow quickly kicked-in after the customary morning activities, prayers and breakfast. I participated in the class activities like other students. At break time, I moved toward the school's notice board to read the latest publications. Then, I had a seizure. The school had apparently not experienced an event like that before. With the new incident, which was utterly humiliating and enervating, it was highly probable that what had transpired overnight could also have been a seizure: an existential and unprecedented health cataclysm was erupting in my life. But the school and I thought that the two incidents were together merely a one-off occurrence. So, I went about my normal student activities with no serious concern or reflection on the emerging new state of my health.

Apart from academic work which was its cardinal focus, ICC also encouraged a diversity of co-curricular activities such as sports. From time to time, the institution was involved in inter-school sporting competitions. Toward the end of May 1965, ICC had football and table tennis matches in Sapele, Delta State, where it was to take on a rival school, St. Malachy's College, Sapele, a boys institution established in 1950. As the best table tennis player in my school and, arguably, also in the Mid-West at that time, I was the arrowhead of the table tennis team. I was not in the football team. The two teams travelled to Sapele in a single bus, eager to settle a longstanding supremacy contest with the rival school. We were accompanied by two of our teachers, both Irish, one of whom was the table tennis coach, Mr. Owen Gerard (Gerry) Murtagh: they travelled in the same car.

The table tennis match was the first to be staged and our school easily defeated St. Malachy's College. Next was the football contest. As I moved out to the balcony of the hall where we had the table tennis match, still in jubilant mood over our decisive victory, I suffered a seizure. This highly distressing and embarrassing event, far away in another school, was awfully disconcerting to me. Was this going to be the trajectory of the rest of my life? The two accompanying teachers quickly got me into their car, in my unconscious state, and headed toward our school in Benin City. It was on the way that I regained consciousness. I recall asking the teachers why I was in their car and not the bus in which the teams travelled to Sapele. They replied that I was ill and they decided to take me back to school. But what exactly was happening?

Withdrawal from School

The news of my sad experience in Sapele spread quickly throughout ICC on our return to the campus. Nonetheless, undeterred, I continued with my studies next day. But about midday, a student came to my classroom during break time, requesting me to teach him how to solve a certain mathematics problem. In the course of explaining the solution steps to him, I experienced another seizure: in broad day light and in the full glare of some of my classmates. When I recovered consciousness, the student who I was helping with the mathematics problem had fled. He was one of the students who I had attracted to ICC in previous years. I did not know what actually happened. Again no one discussed the incident with me: neither the student, who would later in life become an expert in the financial services sector of the Nigerian economy, nor the school authority. The incident was clearly one too many. On the same day, my family was informed about the happening by a concerned day student from our school. That was the first time that my family became privy to my illness. Till date, I do not know the identity of the empathetic student. My family was greatly alarmed and took the immediate step of dispatching my elder sister, Rose, to ICC to bring me home. I hurriedly left the school with my sister, taking nothing and not even informing the Principal, Fr. Donnelly: all I had were the clothes I wore when my sister arrived. It was surprising to many that the Principal did not view the way I was whisked off the campus without his approval by a woman, who was unknown to him, as a grave violation of school rules, regulations and security. As it appeared, the Principal had judged my situation to be truly grave: it was therefore neither the time to wield the punitive hammer nor be rigidly officious. By an awesome act of providence, that particular seizure was the last that I ever had in my life.

With my illness occurring barely six months to my final year examinations and as continuing with my studies was no longer an immediate priority, the challenge was how to deal with the condition and somehow save my secondary school education. My family raced to find a way round my predicament. Days passed by, and then weeks: there was no sign that I would be returning to school. A life-disrupting health tsunami was sweeping away all my dreams. Was I about to fall off the education cliff? Was I finally about to be left behind by my peers? Every day and night, I writhed in unending psychological pain. I remembered the hymn which contains the following inspiring lines:

Have we trials and temptations?
Is there trouble anywhere?
We should never be discouraged,
Take it to the Lord in prayer.

My constant prayer was therefore:

Come Lord Jesus,
My light is dying;
My night keeps crying.
Christ, come quickly: there's danger at the door.

But how would this pernicious existential assault be eventually neutralized?

To me, a Sisyphean ordeal appeared to be playing out. Was all that I had achieved rolling down a slippery slope or being sucked into a black hole? Quite suddenly and sadly, my life had become so forlorn and directionless. I reflected constantly and somewhat deeply on the multiple characteristics of a typical journey through life, including some of the rare events that may disruptively supervene by happenstance. Things appeared palpably cloudy in my life. But surveying some earthly occurrences and their impact on several life journeys that were eventually quite remarkable, I consoled myself by philosophising: if the skies were always cloudless, there would never be any rain, with its manifold benefits and blessings. I realised that although every rainfall is preceded by a cloud; one should actually only be wary about the clouds that give rise to no rainfalls but, antithetically, turn out to be quite disruptive. Were the clouds that I was experiencing likely to foster any beneficial outcomes in my life?

A Concerted Problem-solving Effort

My family launched a frenetic flurry of problem-solving enquiries and consultations aimed at achieving a possible relief to my ailment. Countless ideas were proffered by many family friends and well-wishers. The proposals ran the gamut from banal speculations to serious treatment plans.

In the first week of June 1965, my cousin, Mr. Dauda Lawani, an iconic primary school teacher and son of my mother's elder sister, informed the family that he had identified someone who hard a herbal treatment for the condition. This was a kind of breakthrough. On Wednesday, June 9, 1965, my cousin and I travelled to meet the herbal specialist, a man, who lived at the outskirts of Benin City. He received us and laid out what the therapy would entail: he would administer a phytomedicinal preparation, composed of some herbs and other substances, to me. The immediate effect would be that I would go through a cycle of vomiting, which would eliminate the cause of my illness and I would be free for all time.

Very early in the morning on the next day, I was handed the preparation in the form of a drink. I vomited multiple times throughout the day. Going by the specialist's explanation the previous day, the illness should then be well behind me after the therapy. Would time prove him right? My cousin and I returned to Benin City on Friday, June 11, 1965, after two nights in the specialist's home.

Throughout the whole of June 1965, I experienced no seizures whatsoever and it seemed that the specialist's claim was holding. But over time, a fundamental impact of the illness was that I had become a recluse, always holed up in my mother's room.

On June 30, 1965, another perspective to the search for an end to my illness materialised. On that day, at about 11 am, I was summoned by my mother from her room to meet our school Principal, Fr. Donnelly, fondly called JD, who had come to see me. He had driven all the way from ICC, located along Third Circular Road, to my residence located along Siluko Road. I was highly apprehensive. Had JD come to hand me a letter terminating my studentship? If not, why would he come to my residence? I emerged from the house with much trepidation and greeted him. He said:

GOS, come with me. I am taking you somewhere. I'll bring you back.

I hopped into his Volkswagen car and he drove off toward the city centre. He turned into Mission Road and then Dawson Road. Finally, he drove into the premises of St. Philomena Catholic Hospital, established by Bishop Patrick Joseph Kelly in February 1941. The Hospital was chiefly a maternity home whose medical staff comprised a number of Irish Reverend Sisters and Reverend Mothers, with professional training as medical doctors and nurses. JD took me to an office occupied by one of the Rev Sisters and said to her: "This is the student I spoke to you about: my best student. His name is GOS." The Rev Sister greeted me and asked me to take a seat. As she began to ask me some questions, JD left the hospital to attend to other matters, probably as a way of giving me adequate time for my interaction with the Rev. Sister. After a meticulous questioning, the Rev. Sister informed me that I would have to come back the next day, without eating, for some tests. By the time JD returned, I was done with the consultation. He then drove me back home and delivered me to my family.

On the next day, I was at the hospital for the tests. Some blood and urine samples were taken from me for the required tests. Close to the end of the day, the Rev Sister received the results of the tests associated with the samples. She then explained to me that she did not think that my seizures were epileptic seizures, adding that they appeared to be provoked seizures. I did not understand what she meant but the phrase stuck permanently in my mind. She said that she was putting me on some drugs. Without asking for money, she then handed me about four different medicines, one of which had to do with boosting my very low blood sugar level. I am sure that JD must have paid the fees for the consultation, tests and medicines. The Rev Sister asked me to take the medicines in a certain order at about the same time on each day throughout July and visit her again after four weeks for a check-up. I adhered to the prescription. Thus, unbeknown to me and my family, my school

Principal, JD, was so concerned about my predicament, especially about the real likelihood that I might not be completing my secondary school education, that he had independently also been searching for a remedy. When I narrated all that had transpired at the St. Philomena Hospital, my family was full of gratitude for the overly empathetic and proactive JD. I took the medicines throughout July as prescribed and visited the St. Philomena Hospital once a month during each of the months of August and September. Throughout the four months of June, July, August and September 1965, I experienced no seizures whatsoever. The hospital gave me the "all clear" and everything was fine again! More spectacularly, from June 1965 till date, I have never had any seizures. At all times, God wins! He often uses mortals to achieve His lofty plans for us. This is plainly in fulfillment of His solemn promise:

> He calls to me and I answer him: in distress I am at his side, I rescue him and bring him honour. I shall satisfy him with long life, and grant him to see my salvation. *Psalm 91: 15-16, New Jerusalem Bible*

My debt to Fr. Donnelly, for so paternally having my back during a period of crisis and uncertainty in my life, is unquantifiable. By contrast, my other teachers literally stabbed me in the back, through their attitude which did not move the needle in the direction of any kind of empathy or solicitude for me during my unprecedented medical ordeal, in spite of the fact that I was a highly visible student at ICC, right from my first day in the school. The experience taught me a lot about human relations, even at that age. Thirty (30) years after its establishment in 1941, the St. Philomena Catholic Hospital, Benin City, became a full-fledged hospital in 1971, with specialties in the areas of Obstetrics and Gynecology, Dermatology, Hematology, Paediatrics, General Surgery and Internal Medicine.

Medical Explanation of the Nature of Illness

In 1965, I knew neither the medical meaning of a seizure, especially of a provoked seizure, nor of its aetiology. But with the advent of the internet as a knowledge resource and the availability of search engines, it was eventually possible for me to unravel the meanings and aetiology of the medical conditions. I found the following explanations:[5]

> A *seizure* is abnormal electrical activity in the brain that happens quickly. It may go nearly unnoticed. Or, in serious cases, it may cause unconsciousness and convulsions, when your body shakes uncontrollably.
>
> Seizures usually come on suddenly. How long and serious they are can vary. A seizure can happen to you just once, or over and over. If they keep coming back, that's epilepsy, or a seizure disorder. Less than 1 in 10 people who have a seizure get epilepsy.
>
> Seizures can happen with no explanation, but there are also conditions and events that can bring them on, including: stroke, cancer, brain tumors, head injuries, electrolyte imbalance, very low blood sugar, repetitive sounds or flashing lights, as in video games, some medications, like antipsychotics and some asthma drugs, withdrawal from some medications, like Xanax, narcotics, or alcohol, use of narcotics, such as cocaine and heroin, brain infections, like meningitis, a high fever, COVID-19.

With regard to the meaning of the expression provoked seizures, another websitecontains the following definition:[6]

> A *provoked seizure* is also called an *acute symptomatic seizure*. The term "acute" implies a relatively sudden onset and/or relatively short duration. Acute symptomatic (provoked) seizures are generally defined as:
>
> 1. Seizures that stem from an identifiable cause. This is in contrast to cases of epilepsy, or recurrent seizures, many of which have no readily identifiable cause.

---

5   https://www.webmd.com/epilepsy/understanding-seizures-basics
6   https://study.com/academy/lesson/what-is-a-provoked-seizure-definition-treatment-guidelines.html

2. The cause is sudden in onset and/or transient in nature.
3. They are seizures that occur at the time of the event or relatively shortly thereafter. How shortly thereafter depends on the event itself, but generally speaking it can be up to a week after the event.

The web page also explains that:

> The causes for a *provoked seizure* can be sudden or transient events like head/brain damage from something like a ski accident (think: hitting a tree), a stroke, an electrolyte disturbance such as one that causes hypocalcemia, or low levels of calcium in the blood, a metabolic disorder, such as one that causes hypoglycemia, or low blood sugar, an infection of the brain, an adverse reaction to a medication, alcohol or drug withdrawal, the consumption of a toxin.

As if to corroborate the Rev Sister's diagnosis made decades ago, I also found the following[7]:

> But not all people who appear to have seizures have epilepsy, a group of related disorders characterized by a tendency for recurrent seizures. ... However, non-epileptic seizures look like true seizures, which makes diagnosis more difficult.

Up till this day, I could never thank my cousin Dauda and JD enough for having been used by God to pull me out of a potentially life-destroying abyss. In total, I had three seizures in my entire life, all in 1965 between May 11, 1965 and May 30, 1965; i.e., as I write now in 2021, my last seizure occurred some 56 years ago. In 1965, I needed considerable fortitude to move on in life, as some even openly gloated over my predicament. Indeed, there were several ignorant perspectives of my situation in the school in those trying days which were aimed at putting me down, without knowing that only about 1 in 10 people who experience seizures might be epileptic. I was not. Over the years, I have largely achieved my life

---

7   https://www.webmd.com/epilepsy/guide/understanding-seizures-and-epilepsy#1

objectives, as many things eventually turned very auspicious for me in my life trajectory. Moreover, I have had the good fortune of being able to play fundamental roles in facilitating the achievement of the life goals by many persons who regard me as their mentor, teacher or confidant.

Back to School Again

My prolonged stay at home, from May to September 1965, during the search for some kind of remedy for my illness, engendered a number of adverse collateral consequences. The foremost of these was the utter disruption of my preparation for the West African School Certificate examinations. Having lost all of May to September 1965, during which time my fellow students were focused on their studies, and with the crucial examinations billed to start in November 1965, the fundamental issues were whether I should resume my studies and appear for the examinations; whether I would be emotionally fit for the examinations and whether the Principal would agree that I should participate in the examinations. These matters were carefully considered by all members of my family. After some discussion, it was agreed that I should be the one to provide answers to the first two questions. Of course, I promptly declared that I was ready to appear for the examinations and that I was emotionally strong. Concerning the school's position, it turned out that JD, our school Principal, was even more eager than my family to see that I wrote the examinations.

With the coast clear for me to return to school, my family was, nevertheless, much concerned about the form that this should take: should I return to the boarding house or attend school from home? After some consideration, my family decided that I should stay away from the boarding house. But it was quickly realised that attending school from home as a day student, i.e. travelling daily from Siluko Road to Third East Circular Road, would be extremely challenging for me, in addition to being fraught with potential dangers. My family then decided to search for and rent some accommodation for me, as close as possible, to the school. Luckily, such an accommodation, comprising one bedroom, was found and promptly rented. But then one more issue remained to be addressed. Would I be able to combine the task of daily cooking with preparing for my final examinations which were barely two months away? All the arrangements that had been painstakingly made to enable me to resume schooling would rapidly unravel if this question could not be satisfactorily addressed. While ways of dealing with this conundrum were being considered, my niece, Patience, provided an amazing solution. She said:

> I will go with him to the school. I will help with the cooking to enable him to study for his final examinations which would be concluded by mid-December 1965.

These infinitely altruistic declarations and commitment threw the whole family into prolonged jubilation, with endless praises for Patience. My gratitude to Patience is eternal: till this day, I continue to hold her in high esteem for her uncommon and exemplary selflessness during a momentous period of my life.

1965 November/December WASC Examinations

In the last week of September 1965, Patience and I moved into the bedsitter rented for us just outside the school fence. Every month, my mother provided the funds for our rent, board and upkeep.

Adequately equipped by my mother with the fundamental prerequisites for meeting the challenges ahead of me, the ball was then in my court and my fate was in my hands. I was living through a defining phase of my life. I quickly devised and then steadfastly implemented a compact work plan that enabled me to carry out my preparation for the 1965 November/December WASC Examinations in as an effective and result-oriented manner as was feasible under the circumstances. As I pressed on with the task, I rapidly found my rhythm academically and became increasingly hopeful of a potentially good performance. But how well I would perform was not evident to me.

As soon as I was through with the examinations in mid-December 1965, I moved to NIFOR to stay with my mother and elder brother, John. The results of the examinations were released by WAEC in March 1966. I obtained the best result not only in my set but also in the history of ICC up till that point in time.

I would be remiss if I failed to refer to the conduct of some of my friends during my predicament. I had essentially two sets of friends in the school. The first set comprised students for whom I was the inspirational magnet that pulled them into ICC. If I were attending a school other than ICC, it was certain that they would also have striven to attend the same school because of the role model status they ascribed to me. They gained admission into ICC from Benin City, NIFOR and some other cities. They were at various levels of their studies, lower than mine and hence they rarely interacted with me. But I still saw them as my friends. In this category was the student who I was helping to solve a mathematics problem when I had a seizure. Unfortunately, during my travails, I received no form of empathy from this set of my friends. I was quite surprised and confused by their unexpected apathy. As soon as everything was fine with me again, they reconnected with me. I overlooked their excruciating insensitivity to my plight when I needed them most and accepted their friendship till this day.

The other set of my friends comprised a number of my contemporaries in ICC in those days. Most of them were my classmates. Painfully, I did not receive any empathetic "how are you doing?" or "get well soon" visits from them: I was quickly forgotten by them. This was infinitely shocking to me. By contrast, ICCOBA65, my set at ICC, is today well organised, proactive, collegial and empathetic, holds monthly virtual and physical meetings where matters concerning its members and alma mater are discussed, felicitates with members during their joyful moments, sends delegates to visit members with health challenges, provides welfare assistance to members in need of such and gives financial support to the relations of deceased members. Time certainly changes many things.

Writing this chapter in 2021, I repeatedly asked myself what made it possible for a "wretch like me" to be alive till today, considering that I could have been dead in 1965, some 56 years ago, or condemned by fate to such a lowly life that the thought of writing an autobiography like this would have been a mere pipe dream. I recognised over the years that it is undeniably my unmerited God's grace that "hath brought me safe thus far" and that "grace will lead me home."

12

OUR TEACHERS IN 1965

At ICC, as I had indicated or implied in some of the previous chapters, teachers were noted for their exemplary dedication and commitment to the thorough discharge of their assigned curricular and co-curricular responsibilities. There is no doubt that without such educationists, I would probably not have attained a significant height in my journey through life. This chapter is a rapid tribute to my industrious teachers of 1965. Forty (40) of us formed the 1965 cohort at ICC. A list of the members of the set is presented in the following table. I am saddened that, with the inexorable march of time, some of my 1965 classmates are since deceased.

THE 1965 WASC SET AT ICC					
S/N	FIRST NAME	SURNAME	S/N	FIRST NAME	SURNAME
1	Sylvanus	AIRHAUHI†	8	Andrew	EKE
2	Imuetinyan	AJAYI	9	Godwin	EKHAGUERE
3	Frederick	AKPATA	10	Stephen	EKUNWE†
4	Anthony	AMADASUN	11	Sam	ENOMAH
5	Benson	ASEMOTA	12	Richard	FADAKA
6	Augustine	EBUEKU†	13	Peter	GIEGBEFUMWEN†
7	Anthony	EGBE	14	Paul	GUOBADIA

15	Thaddeus	HART	16	Louis	IDAHOSA
17	Pullen	IDELEGBAGBON†	18	John	IGBINEDION
19	Joseph	IGBINOSUN†	20	Francis	IGBINOVIA
21	Frederick	ILABOR†	22	Andrew	ILOH
23	Bernard	IRUSOTA	24	Paul	ISEGHOHI
25	Thaddeus	JONAH	26	Peter	MOLOKWU
27	James	OBAKPOLOR	28	Joseph	ODIVRI†
29	Peter	OGBEIDE†	30	Lawrence	OHIOWELE
31	Victor	OKENYI	32	Clifford	OLOTU†
33	Edward	OMOROGBE	34	Jude	ORONSAYE
35	Patrick	OSUBOR†	36	Roderick	SMART
37	Michael	UCHIDIUNO	38	Joseph	UGBAJA†
39	Isaac	UHUNMWAGHO	40	Alexander	VLACHOS

† = deceased

To write this chapter, I needed to have a fairly good description of each of my teachers at ICC. This is because, as students, we knew our teachers mainly by their surnames: we had no information about their ages, degrees, universities attended or their co-curricular interests. These descriptors became crucial in this task. Our teachers were Irish, Nigerian, British, American and Indian. How could I now acquire the information in respect of each of my teachers, multiple decades after leaving ICC?

A number of our teachers were priests who belonged to the *Societàdelle Missioni Africane* (SMA), translated as *Society of African Missions*, with its headquarters in Rome, Italy. I have previously sketched the founding of this society of apostolic life, dedicated to evangelising and serving in Africa as well as in other territories with people of African descent. My first thoughts were to launch a systematic search for as much information as I could gather about the early lives of the priests. Accordingly, I contacted Fr. Fachtna O'Driscoll who became the *Supérieur Général* in 2013 of the SMA, which is based in Rome. Prior to 2013, he had served in Nigeria and was later the Provincial

Superior of the Irish SMA Province from 2001–2013. In early 2019, I requested Fr. O'Driscoll to supply me with a list of the SMA Irish priests who taught at ICC during the period from 1961 to 1967. His response was prompt and helpful, writing:

> I have passed on your request to the Provincial leader in Ireland. They should have such information in the archives there. I do not have it here in Rome. [E-mail of Friday, January 18, 2019]

As a result, in no time, I received a message from Fr. Michael Mccabe, the incumbent Provincial of the SMA Irish Province since 2013, conveying a list of some priests who taught at ICC, with the caveat that it was not possible to:

> provide the dates at which these SMA priests taught there because the Archives here don't have records of the College.

Fr. Mccabe's list contained just five names: James Alexander Flanagan (January 1, 1920-February 4, 2004), Joseph Francis Stephens (September 4, 1915-February 5, 1989), John Henry Joseph Jones (September 11, 1923-June 10, 1984), Christopher Columbanus (Colum) Mckeogh (November 16, 1934-June 2, 2011) and Joseph Patrick Donnelly (July 26, 1916-June 11, 1992). But only the last two were known to me, because the other three did not teach at ICC during the period from 1961-1967 that was of primary interest to me. The archivist at the SMA Irish Province who supplied the list was Fr. Edmund Hogan SMA. Thereafter, I worked with Fr. Hogan to obtain information about some other SMA priests who also taught at ICC. For all these, my debt to the SMA headquarters in Rome and the SMA Irish Province is truly unquantifiable.

My Teachers in 1965

I see my secondary school education as the defining cornerstone of my academic development: the path toward my lifelong career in higher education was largely shaped by the wholesome training that I had the good fortune to receive at ICC. To all my teachers, many of whom ignited in me an unquenchable yearning for knowledge, I owe an indescribable debt. In this chapter, I provide rough sketches of the identities of some of the teachers who taught me in 1965, with profound professional devotion to their duties and responsibilities.

History

I studied History at ICC only from 1961 to 1963, i.e. from Form 1 to Form 3. The subject was taught by Mr. Augustine Ogbebo Emumwen. He obtained the Grade II Teachers Certificate in 1938 at St. Thomas Teachers Training College, a Catholic institution, established in 1926 and located in Ibusa in the former Western Region. The site of his alma mater is today occupied by the Federal Government Girls College, Ibusa, which opened its gates to its pioneer set of 264 girls on Saturday, May 13, 1995. Mr. Emumwen earned the Grade I (Senior) Teachers Certificate in Geography in 1948. He was the *de facto* Vice Principal during most of his period of employment at ICC, Benin City. Subsequently, he taught at St. Paul's Minor Seminary, Benin City, from 1975 to 1981. When students were asked in 1964 to indicate their preferred subjects for the WASC examinations scheduled for November/December 1965, I dropped History. Although, in terms of scores, I was doing well in History, I observed that I would have to spend increasingly more time on History than on Mathematics or Physics, if I was to remember the numerous dates and their associated events, aware that there was no formula or algorithm for mapping events to dates. Several students in my set, especially those in the Arts class, included History among their subject combinations. Mr. Emumwen was a meticulous tutor with a huge wealth of teaching experience: he compiled his history notes with care and often dictated them to students during class. From 1960 to 1974 when he was employed at ICC, he lived on the school compound with his family in a bungalow that was not far from one of the two official entrances to the school. Born in 1914, Mr. Emumwen died on Friday, June 19, 2009.

Bible Knowledge

I received teaching in Bible Knowledge throughout my secondary school education at ICC. As I progressed from Form 1 to Form 5, the teachers who taught this subject included Fr. Peter Thompson, about whom I will make some statements soon. Bible Knowledge was not declared as compulsory, either by the WAEC or ICC, but every student instinctively knew that it was incumbent on him to include it as one of his final year subjects. Accordingly, all forty of us in the class sat for Bible Knowledge in the WASC examinations in 1965. In teaching the subject, there was much emphasis on the Catholic perspective and interpretation of biblical events. Our teacher in 1965 was Mr. Michael Ojo, experienced, diligent and approachable. At the 1965 WASC examinations, seventeen students earned distinctions in Bible Knowlege. I was one of them, with a score of A2, a distinction. But the star of the class was James Obakpolor, who scored A1, the ultimate distinction, in the subject. He was the lone person who earned A1 and also the first student to achieve that feat in the history of ICC up till the year 1965.

English Language

In the 1960s, a candidate was not entitled to the West African School Certificate if he failed English Language, no matter how well the student performed in other subjects. As a consequence, secondary schools paid a lot of attention to the teaching of this fate-determining subject. In 1965, English Language was taught at ICC by Owen Gerard Murtagh. Concerning his name, Murtagh wrote me in September 2019, some 53 years after he left ICC in 1966, as follows:

> My full name is Owen Gerard Murtagh. The Owen [and] Gerard are my Christian names. I had an uncle Owen. I prefer the Gerard rather than the Owen name. Everyone calls me Gerry, the informal one. Please call me Gerry.
> *[Source: E-mail of September 18, 2019 to me from Mr. Murtagh.]*

Writing to me about his immediate family, he disclosed:

> I was born on March 14, 1937, in County Cavan (in Ireland), one
> of three boys and six girls — "one father, one mother", to use a
> well remembered Nigerian phrase.
> *[Source: E-mail of September 18, 2019 to me from Mr. Murtagh.]*

Distinguished by his lush signature beard throughout his
appointment at ICC, he was an Irish graduate of English who
studied at the University College, Dublin and Trinity College,
Dublin. After graduation,

> I got a job ("Permanent and Pensionable"!) in the Vocational
> School in Cavan Town.
> *[Source: E-mail of October 9, 2019 to me from Mr. Murtagh.]*

He held the position for two years. How did he become a
teacher at ICC? His answer to me is:

> I heard that the SMA priests in Cork were looking for volunteers
> to work in Benin City, Nigeria.
> *[Source: E-mail of October 9, 2019 to me from Mr. Murtagh.]*

The rest is history. Gerry had an approach to the teaching of
the subject that some would characterize as bordering somewhat
on the unusual. As an example, he would stop reading an essay of
several pages if he found a certain type of error anywhere in the
writing, even if the mistake occurred in its very first paragraph.
He would write "I stop here" somewhere at the margin of the
offending paragraph. In the category of what students quickly
christened "I-stop-here errors", were statements like:

> Although he speaks good English, but he makes many spelling
> mistakes,

> *instead of*

> Although he speaks good English, he makes many spelling
> mistakes,

> *or*

> The three front-runners were neck to neck throughout the race,

instead of

The three front-runners were neck and neck throughout the race.

It was always frustrating when one's essay was not graded simply because there was an error in its, say, second or fifth paragraph of a three-page essay. Was Gerry's strict enforcement of his I-stop-here rule probably a smart stratagem to reduce the relatively heavy burden of grading some forty long essays each week? Fortunately, his steadfast firmness had the beneficial outcome of spurring almost every student to be meticulous about his grammatical expressions. And as if to authenticate Gerry's seemingly unorthodox pedagogical technique, results of the 1965 WASC English Language examination revealed that several students, including myself, earned distinctions in the subject. Moreover, a student, Bernard Osasere Irusota, the future administrator and barrister, who exhibited a somewhat preternatural command of the English language throughout our training at ICC, shattered the glass ceiling by effortlessly earning the best possible result: an A1. That was a feat that had never been achieved in the school up till that point in its history.

As I have said above, Gerry left ICC in 1966. In his September 2019 correspondence with me, he spoke nostalgically about his stay at ICC:

> GOS, I have been sad for over half a century over leaving Nigeria so soon. It was partly because I felt I should go back to Ireland, something to do with getting a pensionable job. I remember well the day I left ICC. The school gathered on the football field. Father Donnelly presided, Bernard Irusota made that lovely, very kind speech — and I made my great mistake. I left. I left and lost so many friends. I loved working in ICC and I loved being in Nigeria. I met recently a Nigerian man who was working in a local hospital. We sang the Nigerian National Anthem together — the old, old (Nigeria, we hail thee).
>
> *[Source: E-mail of October 6, 2020 to me from Mr. Murtagh.]*

He also recalled the following incident:

> Once I was driving back to Benin from Sapele and my car was
> stopped by the army. An officer examined my cheque book (the
> stubs showed that I had written a cheque for 2.50 sterling. I was
> hardly up to something for Biafra). Standing opposite me some
> yards away was a young soldier, holding a rifle pointed in my
> direction. I was not amused. The officer handed back my cheque
> book and walked away. The young soldier stood there, his gun
> still pointed in my direction. "Hello, Mr. Murtagh", he called out
> to me. It was amazing. He did not shoot me, and I drove off to
> Benin much relieved. Sixty years later I am still wondering who
> the soldier was.
> [Source: E-mail of October 23, 2019 to me from Mr. Murtagh.]

In spite of the apparent air of uncertainty about his future
in 1966, he did not head straight to Ireland but toward another
African country. He held a teaching appointment for some years at
St. John's Teacher Training College, Lilongwe, Malawi. Thereafter,
he joined the staff of a Marianist institution, called St. Laurence
College, located in Loughlinstown, County Dublin. Named after
St. Laurence O'Toole (1128 – 1180), a former Irish bishop, the
College was established in 1967, by the Cincinnati Province of the
Society of Mary. It morphed into a co-educational institution in
1973. About his role at St. Laurence College, where his students
called him "Uncle Gerry", he informed me that:

> I taught English, was Head of English for a number of years,
> but I also taught Latin and Classics, which I thoroughly enjoyed.
> [Source: E-mail of September 18, 2019 to me from Mr. Murtagh.]

He has been active in the Classical Association of Ireland (CAI)
and the Classical Association of Northern Ireland (CANI). At St.
Laurence College, Gerry was revered as an inspirational English
and classics teacher who made students read the *Odyssey*, one of
Homer's epic poems, fostering in them a love for the legendary
Greek and Roman poets, Homer and Ovid, through "his unswerving
passion" for classical literature.

Outside teaching, Gerry was also a passionate anti-apartheid campaigner. As one example of his activities, he wrote the following to me:

> Probably the best thing I did was at the time of apartheid in South Africa, I joined an anti-apartheid group here. "Buy no South African goods". At the school I set up a "Black and White" group, and once we held a black and white day when instead of the normal school uniform (green), students were free to wear black and white. I am sending you a battered photograph of the group. I called it the *Mary Manning Group* because, Mary, who worked in Dunne's Stores, refused to sell South African goods. This caused a sensation. There was a great march through the streets of Dublin, and my *Mary Manning Group* took part in the march. In due course, apartheid ended. Nelson Mandela came to Dublin and was made welcome. He became a Freeman of Dublin City.   I was very honoured myself to be invited to be one of those to meet him.
> *[Source: E-mail of January 3, 2020 to me from Mr. Murtagh.]*

During our student days at ICC, Gerry was our table tennis coach. But unknown to many of us at that time, he was also a deft chess player. After returning to Ireland, he participated in several chess congresses in that country and won in a number of competitions. Some past students of St. Laurence College recall that Gerry operated a chess club after school, as a co-curricular activity for staff and students. Gerry, who was a bachelor during his employment at ICC, is married to Eileen Mary (nee O'Connell). He retired from St. Laurence College in 2002. As I write, Gerry lives with his wife Eileen in Foxrock, a suburb of the city of Dublin.

Seated in the middle of the front row is Gerry Murtagh,
as table tennis games master in 1963. GOS is standing,
first from left, in the second row.

Eulogy by Benard Irusota

We lose, we realise not, our only Guide.
But yet the bulk of us ignore the fact,
That all these years, alone he won our pride.
With characteristic humour and tact,
Safe in our bossoms his memory shall rest.
Wherever we may go, East or west,
Weep, Art students, weep.
Here goes a master,
When comes such another?
If anyone deserves gratitude,
Not reckoning on its magnitude
of the task undertaken by him,
None comes near, not even by a slim chance,
to earn universal acclaim.
Mr. Murtagh, tho' time may run its course,
To revere you we always will find cause.

Response by Aloysius Ekhayeme

We really need not weep,
Though this we really can't help.
For the dictate of time he can't help.
Really then with him we must part.
Life, you know, forces men apart.
But the pain of parting,
To the joy of meeting again is nothing.
Since nature allows no vacuum,
Let's hope for just another him.

Source: Email sent to me by Gerry Murtagh on February 8, 2020.

English Literature

English Literature for the WASC examinations and the General Paper for the HSC examinations were taught in 1965 and 1966, respectively, by Fr. Peter Thompson, an SMA priest. A native of Scramogue, County Roscommon, in the Irish province of Connaught, he was born in Dublin on Saturday, July 4, 1936. Fr. Thompson was a member of staff of ICC from 1964 to 1973. He was a quiet and hard-working teacher. At the 1965 WASC examinations, many students, including myself, had distinction in English Literature. I also made a distinction in the 1967 HSC examinations in the General Paper. Apart from his academic duties, Fr. Thompson also served as the Master of the Mulumba House at ICC and as a Chaplain at the St. Maria Goretti Girls Grammar School, Benin City, a Catholic institution for girls established on March 4, 1959, by Bishop Patrick Joseph Kelly (1894-1991). Before 1973, his mission in Nigeria straddled the educational and the apostolate, as he diligently combined the duties and responsibilities of a school teacher and of a priest. When I asked him about his experience at ICC, Fr. Thompson wrote me in February 2019, saying:

I greatly enjoyed my time there and I hope that I helped some
students in those years.
Source: Fr. Thompson's email to me dated February 1, 2019

Fr. Thompson was the Principal of ICC from 1971 to 1972. He
had succeeded Fr. Patrick Aidan Anglin (July 26, 1934 - May 19,
2012) who was the Principal from 1969 to 1971. Fr. Anglin was
born and baptized in Belfast. Laicized in the Catholic Church in
December 1973, he married in 1974. When he died in 2012 at
Tournagee, Kingsland, County Roscommon, Ireland, former Fr.
Anglin was survived by his nuclear family comprising his wife Mary,
daughter Marianne and sons Oliver and Colum. On July 5, 1973,
the Catholic Diocese of Issele-Uku was established as a suffragan
diocese of the Archdiocese of Benin. Fr. Anthony Okonkwo Gbuji,
born on October 29, 1931, was ordained on September 30, 1973,
as the pioneer Bishop of the new diocese. This development had a
direct impact on ICC, because Fr. Thompson was appointed as the
pioneer diocesan Secretary of the Diocese of Issele-Uku. I recall
that before he assumed office as Diocesan Secretary, we met him in
1973, as I shall relate later. Upon returning to Ireland, Fr. Thompson
was elected as one of the delegates to the Irish Provincial Assembly
in 1978. During the Assembly, he was elected as a member of the
Irish SMA Provincial Council and served as Bursar up till 1983. He
was also the House Bursar of the SMA Formation House of the
British Province located in New Barnet, London, UK, succeeding
Fr. Robert (BOB) O'Regan (January 18, 1915-August 21, 2012)
who had carried out some of his missionary activities in Benin City.
As I write, Fr. Thompson lives in the SMA House in Dromantine,
Newry, County Down, Ireland.

Biology

This subject was taught by Felix Agun, a university graduate with
a BSc degree. He was industrious, cool and approachable. He did
his best to professionally impart the subject to his students. Several
students, including myself, had distinctions in the subject in the

1965 WASC examinations. Unfortunately, I could not find much information about him, compared with other ICC teachers who are described in this book.

Chemistry

In spite of his enormous administrative duties, the Principal, Fr. Joseph Patrick Donnelly (1916-1992), taught this subject. He attended the University College Cork (UCC), Ireland. From the institution, he obtained a combined BA degree in Philosophy and Education in 1937, and a combined BSc degree in Physics and Chemistry in 1944. He returned to UCC eleven years later in 1955 to earn a higher diploma in education. Many students, including myself, had distinctions in Chemistry in the 1965 WASC examinations. I had the best result: an A1, which was an outcome that had never previously been achieved in the school before 1965. Fr. Donnelly was a seasoned educator, who played no small role in the establishment and operation of several secondary schools in the defunct Mid-Western Region of Nigeria. He was the Principal of ICC during three separate periods: 1952–1953, 1957–1960 and 1961–1968. In 1945, while teaching Mathematics, Elementary Science, Religious Knowledge and English, he was also appointed Vice-Principal of ICC, where Fr. Andrew Patrick O'Rourke (October 16, 1913-January 8, 1967), born at Gortbrack, Miltown Malbay, County Clare, Ireland, was the pioneer Principal. In 1952, Bishop Kelly gave Fr. Donnelly the crucial assignment of reorganizing St. Peter Claver's College, Aghalokpe (established in 1950) to meet governmental requirements for approval. He successfully implemented the assignment in his capacity as Vice-Principal to Fr. Micheal Scully (April 3 1900–May 13, 1959), the pioneer Principal of the College, who was born at Derrybrien, County Galway, Ireland. Fr. Donnelly established the High School Certificate programme in ICC in 1966, and left the school in 1968. In July of that year, he was elected as the Vice-Provincial, with Fr. Lawrence Patrick Carr (May 12, 1920–

September 12, 1976), born at Blackrock, County Dublin, Ireland, as the Provincial, of the SMA Province of Ireland. Following the unexpected death of Fr. Carr in 1976, Fr. Donnelly assumed the post of Provincial and served in that capacity for two years. In 1979, he returned to Nigeria, preferring the Archdiocese of Kaduna to the Archdiocese of Benin, because he felt that the Church was less firmly established in the Kaduna Archdiocese than the Benin Archdiocese to which Archbishop Patrick Ebosele Ekpu (born on October 26, 1931 at Unuwazi, Uromi), had urged him to return. He was in Kaduna until March 1990 when his health faced some challenges and he was evacuated to Ireland. During his last years in retirement, Fr. Donnelly was scourged by a painful and debilitating illness which he endured with fortitude and faith. Shortly before his death, he said the following to one of his colleagues:

> I joined the SMA in answer to a call from God. I went to Nigeria as a messenger of the Gospel. All my work there was to fulfill that call as well as I could. I was sad when illness compelled me to leave Nigeria[6] — but I thank God for using me to bring His message of hope to many Nigerian people. The work is God's.
>
> *Source: Obituary by the SMA Irish Province*

I have christened some sets of students educated at ICC as the *Joseph Patrick Donnelly Generations*, or simply the *JD Generations*, of students. These are the cohorts of students who were in ICC during the three tenures of JD as Principal from 1952–1953, 1957–1960 and 1961–1968. Among the *JD Generations* of students is the 1965 set to which I belong. This cohort, which was vastly positively impacted by JD's tenure as Principal, helped in the physical development, through manual labour after classes, of what was then the new ICC campus into which the school, originally collocated with the St Paul Minor Seminary at the Airport Road, Benin City, had relocated in January 1960. Moreover, in implementing his epic project of introducing ICC's Higher School Certificate programme in 1966, it was to the 1965 cohort that Fr. Donnelly strategically and confidently turned when recruiting many of the pioneer students. All told, the cohort was positively disruptive of several myths and academic folklores that had been pervasive at ICC for many years: it left large and indelible academic footprints on ICC's inexorable development into an iconic pre-tertiary Catholic educational institution. The demise in 1992 of Fr. Donnelly, a highly dedicated SMA missionary and educator, was painful to many Nigerians, especially the *JD Generations* of students.

Mathematics

In the 1960s, unlike the case with English, failing mathematics was not equivalent to failing the entire final year public examinations, namely the WASC examinations. But some years later, securing credit passes in both English and mathematics became a prerequisite for admission into certain programmes of study in many Nigerian tertiary education institutions. This placed mathematics on the same level of national importance as English. In 1965, our mathematics teacher was Fr. John "Jack" Casey who was born in Cork, County Cork, Ireland. He obtained the BSc (Hons) from UCC in 1952. He began his teaching career at Ishan Grammar School, Uromi (established in 1956). Apart from teaching at ICC, in Benin City, from 1964 to 1969, he also taught at St. Peter Claver College, Aghalokpe (established in 1950), Notre Dame College, Ozoro (established in 1957), and Annunciation College, Irrua (established in 1955). While at ICC, Fr. Casey was the chaplain to General David Akpode Ejoor (January 10, 1932–February 10, 2019), who was the Military Governor of the Mid-Western Region of Nigeria at that time.

    In 1969, Fr. Casey was recalled to Ireland to teach at the SMA College, Ballinafad, County Mayo, for one year. While in Ireland, he studied for the Higher Diploma in Education at the UCG. He attempted to return to Nigeria in June 1971 without success because he was not granted a visa. This was partly because of the

Nigerian Government's reluctance to issue visas to missionaries as a consequence of the alleged involvement of some of them in the Biafran war. While waiting for the situation to change, Fr. Casey studied French in Dublin and in Lyons, France, before returning to Benin City in January 1973. He then went on to join the teaching Staff of St. Patrick's College, Asaba, where he distinguished himself as a brilliant teacher of mathematics. In 1986, Fr. Casey transferred from the Mid-West of Nigeria to the diocese of Ibadan in Western Nigeria. He returned finally to Ireland in August 2000. The performance of my set in the 1965 WASC mathematics examinations was trailblasing: several students, including myself, earned distinctions in the subject. Additionally, a student, Isaac Izogie Uhunmwagho, the future First Class Honours (Teesside University, Middlesbrough, UK) graduate of Mechanical Engineering and an icon in the transportation business in Nigeria and West Africa, who always displayed the phenomenal ability to make mincemeat of almost every mathematical problem throughout our training, naturally bagged the best result in the subject, namely A1. That was an accomplishment that had not been achieved in the school before 1965. Fr. Casey succeeded Fr. Donnelly as Principal. His tenure was from 1968 to 1969. Born on Wednesday, February 11, 1931, in Cork, Fr. Casey died on Monday, March 2, 2015, in Ireland.

Physics

In 1965, our physics teacher was Robert "Bear" Hornady, an American, who served in ICC from 1964 to 1966 under the Peace Corps scheme. The latter, which still exists, is a volunteer organization established by President John Fitzgerald Kennedy (May 29, 1917– November 22, 1963) in 1961. Peace corps members carried out diverse developmental activities throughout Nigeria from 1961 to 1976 and from 1992 to 1995. Among his peers, Hornady's nickname was "Bear". Before joining ICC, he obtained the BS degree in Physics in 1962 from the Department of Physics and Astronomy, University

11. The University of Ibadan main gate in the 1960s
12. The University of Ibadan main gate since the 1990s
13. GOS, standing second from right in the second row, at the Functional Analysis Conference held at UI in 1977

14. (L-R) Mrs. Eugenia Abu, Prof. Ayo Banjo and GOS during the selection of the winners of the Ford Foundation Teaching Innovation awards in 2007

15. GOS, standing first from right in front row, at a conference in Ascona, Switzerland in 1985

16. GOS, standing third from right, as a member of the University of Ibadan Governing Council in 1995

17. Our daughter at her graduation at the University of Hull, UK, with MSc in Business Management in 2009
18. Me, my wife and our daughter at her graduation at the University of Hull, UK, with MSc in Business Management in 2009
19. GOS, wife and Prof. K.R. Parthasarathy at a conference in Chennai, India, in 2010

20. GOS, sitting third from right in front row, at a conference at the Institute of Mathematical Sciences, Chennai, in 2010

21. (L-R) GOS, Prof. K.R. Parthasarathy, his wife and Deborah at the International Congress of Mathematicians in Hyderabad, India, in 2010

22. GOS, and Prof. Huzihiro Araki at the International Congress of Mathematicians in Hyderabad, India, in 2010
23. My wife and I at my Inaugural Lecture in 2010
24. University officials at my Inaugural Lecture in 2010

25. (L-R) GOS, standing third in front row, at a conference at The Bellagio Center, the Rockefeller Foundation, Bellagio, Italy, in 2011
26. GOS, standing 4th from left in front row, at an International Seminar on the Management of Higher Education Institutions, Israel, 2013
27. GOS at Registry marriage of his daughter in Northampton, 2013

28. GOS and wife at daughter's marriage at the Our Lady Seat of Wisdom Catholic Church, University of Ibadan, 2013

29. GOS and wife with in-laws Prof. and Prof. (Mrs.) Ekanem during their children's marriage at UI, 2013

30. Marriage of my daughter and her husband at the Our Lady Seat of Wisdom Catholic Church, University of Ibadan, 2013

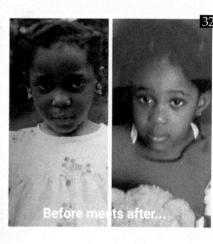

Before meets after...

31. Daughter and her husband take the marriage oath, 2013
32. My daughter Etin (left) and her daughter Idara (right)
33. Daughter and husband receive their marriage certificate, 2013
34. My investiture as a Fellow of the African Academy of Sciences in 2014

35. President of NMS, Prof. N.I. Akinwande, performs the investiture of GOS as Fellow of the NMS, 2016

36. GOS receiving the insignia of Fellowship of the NMS from the President Prof. N.I. Akinwande of the NMS in 2016

37. At my investiture as a Fellow of the Nigerian Mathematical Society in 2016

38. Group photo with the President of the NMS, Dean of Science, my wife and colleagues at my investiture as a Fellow of the NMS, 2016

39. My daughter, her husband and children, with me and wife, 2021
40. GOS and wife, Deborah
41. My wife, her mother and my daughter, Etin
42. Etin and her husband, Dr. Ekanem, cutting the cake at their traditional wedding in 2013

43. Deborah and daughter, Etin
44. Etin and her husband, Etiowo, together with the bridesmaids, the twin sisters Chioma Kanu and Chisom Kanu, at their traditional wedding in 2013
45. (L-R) Deborah, Heidi Adodo, Godfrey Adodo and Etin in Germany in 1998
46. GOS, seated first from left, attending a conference in Chile in 1999

47. (L-R) Prof. Julius Okojie, GOS and Prof. Anthony Osagie attending the 10th AAU General Conference in Kenya in February 2001

48. Joan Dassin (third from right in front row, founding Executive Director of the Ford Foundation International Fellowships Program (IFP)) and GOS (first from right in second row) attending an IFP meeting in South Africa in 2002
49. GOS (fifth from right in front row) attending a conference at the Maastricht School of Management, the Netherlands, in 2000

of Nebraska, Lincoln, USA. After returning to the USA in 1966, he went on to earn an MS degree in Physics in 1968, also from the Department of Physics and Astronomy, University of Nebraska. In 1973, he bagged the PhD degree in Plasma Physics from the University of Maryland, College Park, Maryland. MD. Hornady was an effective, competent, approachable, problem-solving and result-oriented teacher. Only one student, Isaac Izogie Uhunmwagho, had a distinction in Physics in the 1965 WAEC Examinations. I scored a credit (C4) in the subject, the only course in which, to my surprise, I did not obtain a distinction. Born on Friday, January 27, 1939, in Lincoln, Nebraska, Hornady died on Thursday, August 21, 2008. In absolute deference to his wish, he was cremated and his ashes were spread over Monterey Bay in California.

13

HSC STUDY AT ICC

By August 1965, I was close to the end of my secondary school education at ICC. From around April of that year, the school continuously displayed on its notice boards a constant stream of announcements, by many secondary schools from various parts of Nigeria, indicating the dates of the entrance examinations to their HSC programmes. I showed no interest in any of the announcements, as I was painfully aware that I would not have the financial resources to move on to the next level of education. Instead, my thoughts were riveted on how I would quickly secure a teaching appointment in a primary or secondary school or a clerical job in a company or a government establishment after leaving ICC in December 1965.

Then, unofficially, we began to receive information about ICC's intention to also introduce a HSC programme beginning from January 1966. The unofficial eventually morphed into the official when the Principal, Fr. Donnelly, announced formally that ICC was expanding its academic activities to include the provision of HSC education. Fr. Donnelly fixed a date for the entrance examination and decreed that all final year students were to be candidates. Unlike external candidates, we were not required to pay any entrance examination fees. I participated in the examination, as I had no other option, but quickly erased the event from my mind because of my circumstance and the reasons that I had mentioned above. My cardinal goal was to pass my WASC examinations in flying colours, as a way of enhancing my chances of employment in the labour market. The remaining part of 1965 soon came to an end: the final year examinations were completed in December 1965 and I became an alumnus of ICC. I moved to NIFOR, to join my family, while waiting for the results of the WASC examinations to be announced nationwide.

The First Nigerian Coup d'Etat

The year 1966 was a significant watershed in the annals of politics in Nigeria. As I awaited the results of my 1965 WASC examinations, the political landscape of the country changed dramatically: on Saturday, January 15, 1966, Nigeria's first military coup d'etat was staged by a set of military officers, resulting in the overthrow of the Federal Government of Nigeria. The Government had been formed after the national parliamentary elections of December 30, 1964 and March 18, 1965. The bloody putsch, which was led by one Major Patrick Chukwuma Kaduna Nzeogwu, who was born in Kaduna on Friday, February 26, 1937, and died at Nsukka on Saturday, July 29, 1967, sent the nation into an unprecedented political tailspin. A gloomy pall of uncertainty blanketed Nigeria, which had gained its independence from Britain less than six years earlier on October 1, 1960. It was not at all clear where the country was headed. General Johnson Thomas Umunakwe Aguyi-Ironsi (March 3, 1924-July 29, 1966) emerged as the Head of the Federal Military Government of Nigeria. One of his principal acts was to issue the Unification Decree No. 34 of 1966, dated May 24, 1966, which abolished the federal structure of the nation's political union and replaced it with a unitary system.

Inauguration of the ICC HSC Programme

The worrying state of the nation did not, fortunately, disrupt educational activities. The proposed HSC programme at ICC took off in January 1966 as planned. The pioneer students were recruited from ICC and some other secondary schools in the Mid-Western, Western and Eastern Regions of Nigeria. ICC's 1965 cohort formed the core of the pioneer HSC class. At the WASC examinations, the institution's 1965 set, trailblazing and comparatively star-studded, had established an exceptional institutional academic record, obtaining the best results since the creation of ICC, with 38 of the 40 students (i.e. 95% of the students) scaling the examinations in record-setting grades. I was not privileged to witness the unique day that marked the historical inauguration of the HSC programme at ICC: I was far away at NIFOR, writing and transmitting applications to organisations and establishments, in search for employment. One of the institutions that received an application from me was the St. Paul Minor Seminary, Benin City, where I was seeking the post of a mathematics teacher. But none of my applications was accorded any response whatsoever. With no means of continuing my education and no prospect of employment, it was as though my life had come to a screeching halt.

Results of the WASC Examinations

Toward the middle of March 1966, the results of the WASC examinations were released nationwide. As a school, ICC performed very well: with 95% of its students passing the examinations. Moreover, it emerged that I obtained the best overall result in my set. My performance was also the best at that point in time by any student since the establishment of ICC. It was therefore overly sad that, as a consequence of financial indigence, there appeared to be no avenues for me to take advantage of an evidently good academic performance to join the newly established HSC programme at ICC or pursue any other kind of tertiary education. While I had already fully resigned myself to fate, a window of opportunity miraculously materialised: two delegations travelled all the way from Benin City to NIFOR, where I was staying with my family, with two separate messages for me.

Two delegations with two offers

The first delegation comprised a Catholic priest who was the Rector of the St. Paul Minor Seminary, Benin City, one of the institutions to which I had sent applications without any reply. The Rector was Fr. Maurice Gabriel Maguire; he held the position from June 1961 until June 1966. He was instrumental in the establishment of the Saints Peter and Paul Major Seminary, Ibadan, following its transfer to Ibadan on January 31, 1957, from Benin City. Training at the St. Paul Minor Seminary was originally up to the Sixth Form. As a result of student dissatisfaction with Fr. Maguire's management style, the first-ever revolt in the Seminary, tagged *Maurice Maguire Must Go* by the students, occurred from Friday, October 22 to Saturday, 23, 1965. The revolt was led by the Sixth Form seminarians and supported by almost all the other seminarians. As a result of the unprecedented upheaval, fifty-eight (58) students, including all the Sixth Form seminarians, were expelled and the Sixth Form was abolished in that year, thereby limiting the scope of the non-ecclesial academic courses of the Seminary to that of a normal five-year secondary school. The academic status of the Seminary has remained unchanged since then.

Born in Belfast, Northern Ireland, UK, on December 16, 1917, Fr. Maguire was one of six boys and two girls. He died at the Oluyoro Catholic Hospital, Oke-Offa, Ibadan, on March 2, 1993, and was buried in the grounds of the Brother Roman Centre, Ekpoma, Edo State.

During his visit to my residence at NIFOR, the Rector (Fr. Maguire) indicated that the Seminary had received my application but waited to have adequate information about my performance in the WASC examinations before taking any action. He said that following the release of the results of the WASC examinations,

> I paid a visit today to the Principal of ICC, Fr. Donnelly, to enquire about your performance and he told me that you had the best result in your set.

He asked whether I was ready to take up an appointment as a mathematics teacher at the Seminary. He also added that he was well aware of another message for me from Fr. Donnelly. He then gave me the responsibility to recommend a suitable substitute if I was not in a position to accept his offer of employment.

The second delegation was an emissary from Fr. Donnelly. He was asked to do two things: to take the Rector to my house and also to deliver a message from Fr. Donnelly to me. The two delegations had first visited my residence at Siluko Road, Benin City, and upon learning that I was at NIFOR, some 15 miles (24 kilometres) away, the Rector, in whose car the delegations rode, then insisted that they must proceed to NIFOR to meet me. The message from Fr. Donnelly was that the school was ready to award me a scholarship, if I was interested in the newly introduced HSC programme at ICC. Thus, simultaneously, I had two interesting offers on the same day: an employment and a scholarship.

It was clear that the more attractive offer to me was the scholarship. I speedily wrote to Fr. Donnelly to thank him for the offer of a scholarship and to convey my grateful acceptance of his kind life-changing academic lifeline. With the providential offer, I became an Immaculate Conception College Scholar or simply College Scholar. To the Rector of St. Paul Minor Seminary, I tendered my gratitude for his kind offer of employment but declined the offer for reasons which he fully understood. As the Rector had requested me to recommend a suitable person who could be appointed, in the event that I did not take up his offer, I recommended, without any reservation, a classmate called

Roderick for possible employment. The Rector verified the name and academic profile of my nominee, especially his WASC results, with our Principal, Fr. Donnelly. I was glad that Roderick, whose paternal grandmother was the elder sister of Bishop Samuel Ajayi Crowther (circa 1807 -December, 31, 1891), was subsequently employed by the Seminary. But Roderick spent only three months in the employment of the Seminary before joining the Ministry of Agriculture and Natural Resources of the Mid-West Region. For some fifty years, Roderick had not been in any kind of interactive contact with me but we knew of each other's life progress. Hence, I could not intimate him with the foregoing, until May 3, 2020, when I was lucky to receive his telephone number from a mutual classmate of ours. His response, when I informed him that I was instrumental to his employment at the Seminary, was not entirely surprising and was the following:

> Thank you brother, all these years, I had thought it was
> Mr. A. Emumwen who recommended me to the Rector.

It was logical for Roderick to think that it was Mr. A. Emumwen who recommended him for the teaching position at the St. Paul's Minor Seminary, as Mr. A. Emumwen was the husband to Roderick's maternal aunt. Roderick subsequently became one of the pioneering students of the Institute of Agricultural Research and Training, Moor Plantation, Ibadan, which was affiliated to the University of Ife, later known as the Obafemi Awolowo University, Ile-Ife. Graduating from the latter in 1971, Roderick returned to the Ministry and subsequently transferred his services to the Rubber Research Institute of Nigeria (RRIN), Iyanomo, Benin City. In 1977, he was chosen to pursue a one-year postgraduate course in Rubber Technology at the Rubber Research Institute of Malaysia Processing Instructors' Training School – Course 13. He graduated with distinction: the first African student to earn such a laurel. Back home, Roderick was transferred from the Benin City head office to head the Rubber Research Institute Station in Abia

State. Beyond his official obligations, Roderick's contributions to the welfare of his staff and workers and the consequential impact on the economic activities of the neighbouring communities remain legendary. Roderick retired statutorily from the Rubber Research Institute in 2001 after 35 years of meritorious service. He currently owns a consultancy outfit on Rubber Technology and related issues, spanning the rendering of agronomic services to rubber plantation owners and establishment of rubber processing factories in the rubber growing States of southern Nigeria.

Back to School

Concerning my returning to school, the easy part was my acceptance of the scholarship offer in March 1966, one full term after the commencement of the HSC programme at ICC. That meant that I had missed one term of schooling and its associated academic work. How would I catch up? I put this question to my friend, Gabriel Ojesebholo (1949-2015), the future orthopaedic surgeon, who had his secondary school education at the Annunciation Catholic College, Irrua, Mid-Western Nigeria, and was one of the pioneer students in the HSC class. He assured me that I would eventually make up for the lost time, saying that most of the HSC students did not concentrate very much on their studies as they eagerly awaited the WASC results. The rule was that students who did not obtain a credit in each of English and mathematics would automatically be asked to withdraw. With my friend's encouragement, I joined the HSC class in April 1966 as a College Scholar. My choice of subjects was: general paper, mathematics, physics and chemistry.

Political Volatility

As the months rolled by, 1966 was increasingly politically volatile. The elites in Northern Nigeria had characterized the January coup as a purely Igbo coup, allegedly intended to eliminate non-Igbo people from the military, the political class, the civil service and other strata of the Nigerian society. It was clear that a backlash was inevitable. Predictably, a counter-coup, also called the re-match coup, masterminded by a set of Northern military officers occurred on Friday, July 29, 1966. General Johnson Aguiyi-Ironsi was killed and Lt. Colonel Yakubu Gowon was installed as the military Head of State. The inexorable accretion of bitterness, resentment, turmoil, xenophobia and revenge killings in Northern Nigeria after the first coup d'état combined with the new development of another forceful change of government to effectively fuel an ethnic cleansing of Southern Nigerians, especially the Igbo people, who lived in Northern Nigeria during those turbulent days. The diverse events progressively propelled the nation down a slippery slope to a potentially brutal civil war that eventually erupted about a year later.

Academic Work in Turbulent Times

The country's political waters became murkier by the day. Although the highly dynamic situation did not bring academic activities in schools to a halt, ICC was nevertheless adversely impacted. The implementation of the newly introduced HSC programme by the school became very challenging, as ICC had a substantial number of non-Nigerian teachers from the USA, Ireland and India. Some of the foreign teachers, especially the USA Peace Corps members and non-clergy Irish staff, left the school after the second coup d'état of July 29, 1966. The dilemma was then how and from where to recruit persons who could teach the various HSC courses. Unfortunately, not many of the teachers at ICC at that time had the competence to teach HSC courses. With the latter comprising both science and arts subjects, and with no good prospect of recruiting qualified teachers, a dire situation emerged. Students were largely idle. That they were becoming frustrated was evident. Fr. Donnelly realised that he needed to act fast before the cookie crumbled: apparently he had not foreseen how difficult it would be to recruit qualified teachers for the new HSC programme. In a rather deft move, he arranged for all the HSC Arts students in our set to be transferred in the third term of 1966 to St. Patrick College (SPC), Asaba. This is a Catholic institution established in 1944. Originally called St. Augustine College, Asaba, the name was changed to St. Patrick College, Asaba, in honour of Bishop Patrick Joseph Kelly (1894 – 1991). Among the Arts students who had to move to SPC were: Anthony Osagie Egbe, Aloysius Ekhayeme and Bernard Osasere Irusota. I was lucky that it was not the Science class, to which I belonged, that was relocated to SPC, Asaba. Otherwise, my HSC education might have ended abruptly, if my College scholarship was not transferrable to SPC. With the Arts students apparently moved to safety, what was to become of the HSC Science students? Would these also be moved to another institution? Luckily, the Science students were allowed to continue their programmes of study at ICC. If that was not the case, the laudable project of making HSC education accessible at the institution would certainly have unravelled. Numerically, the students were 25, including me. In the following table, I display the full list of the 25 Science students. They completed their programmes of study in December 1967 at ICC, as the school's pioneer HSC graduates.

THE 1967 PIONEER HSC GRADUATES AT ICC

S/N	FORENAMES	SURNAME	S/N	FORENAMES	SURNAME
1	Vincent Uwafiokun	AIHIE	14	Nathaniel	SADO
2	Sylvanius	AIRHAUHI†	15	Thaddeus Osaretin Edosomwan	JONAH
3	Anthony Eluemunor	ARINZE	16	Cyril Akporuere Chukwuemeka	ODU†

4	Patrick Godwill	ASEMOTA	17	Fidelis Fade	OGUNTIRIN
5	Dennis Inobemeh	ASUMU†	18	Gabriel Elubale Ehi	OJESEBHOLO†
6	Patrick Osemenkhian	EBEA	19	Victor Osagie	OJO
7	Augustine Omoruyi	EBUEKU†	20	Eugene Edenomehi	OKPERE
8	Godwin Osakpemwoya Samuel	EKHAGUERE	21	Joseph Omolathebu	OMAMEGBE
9	Stephen Imasuen Nosakhare	EKUNWE†	22	Pius Olatunde	OMOREGIE†
10	Anderson Godwin	EMOKPAE	23	Augustine	ONIGHO
11	Thaddeus Daniel	HART	24	Michael Nwalie	UCHIDIUNO
12	Frederick Chukwuemeka	ILABOR†	25	Godwin Gregory	UWADIALE
13	Andrew	ILOH		† = deceased	

I was the only one in the Science class whose combination of subjects was mathematics, physics, chemistry and general paper. Other students' combinations were either chemistry, physics, zoology and general paper or botany, chemistry, zoology and general paper.

One day in September 1966, Fr. Donnelly summoned me to his office, and we had the following conversation:

Listen, GOS! No one else is taking mathematics. I think you should change your combination to physics, chemistry and zoology. This puts you on the path to becoming a medical doctor.

Father, I don't want to be a medical doctor!

It's not possible for me to appoint a mathematics teacher for only one student. It's too expensive. You may go, GOS! I'll think about this problem.

A few days later, I was again summoned to the Principal's office.

I've found a solution to the problem. I have reached an arrangement with Edo College: you'll take your mathematics classes at Edo College, and the physics and chemistry classes here. Okay?

Yes, Father!

That's all.

Thanks, Father.

Before I could start the classes at Edo College, Fr. Donnelly summoned me again to his office.

I've reconsidered your taking mathematics classes at Edo College. I know you can pass mathematics without any help from Edo College. I'll give you some past HSC mathematics questions and you should study mathematics on your own. If you go to Edo College for mathematics classes, they'll take the credit. ICC should get the full credit, GOS!

Yes, Father!

I pursued my academic activities with commitment and diligence, studying mathematics on my own while receiving tuition only in physics, chemistry and general paper.

In January 1967, I was in the Upper Six class of the HSC. But at the beginning of August 1967, a new threat to my educational pursuit suddenly materialized. On May 30, 1967, following several months of continuous political tension in the country, the Eastern Region, which was under the leadership of Lt. Colonel Chukwuemeka Odumegwu Ojukwu as the military administrator, declared that it had seceded from Nigeria and named itself the Republic of Biafra. In response, the Federal Government, under the leadership of Lt. Colonel Yakubu Gowon, launched what it called a "police action" on July 6, 1967, to deal with the apparent violation of the country's territorial sovereignty.

At the outset of the conflict, not wanting to alienate its Igbo population which was substantial, the Mid-Western Region adopted a nonaligned stance and did not allow the Federal army to use its territory as a staging post against the Biafran army. Schooling and other activities in the public and private sectors continued normally in the Region without any disruption. But some four months to the envisaged completion of my HSC programme, the Region was invaded on August 9, 1967 by the Biafran army, ousting the government of the Military Administrator of the Mid-Western Region, Lt. Colonel David Akpode Ejoor (January 10, 1932-February 10, 2019), who then fled to Lagos. With the benefit of hindsight, the surprising military invasion was an existential strategic blunder by the controversial Republic of Biafra. The invading army was commanded by Lt. Colonel Victor Adebukunola Banjo (April 1, 1930-September 22, 1967), a Yoruba man from Ijebu-Ode in the Western Region, who had been appointed the General Officer Commanding the 101st Division of the Biafran army. To govern the Mid-Western Region which his troops had brazenly occupied, Lt. Colonel Ojukwu appointed one Major (Dr.) Albert Nwazu Okonkwo, a medical doctor, as the territory's Military Administrator on August 17, 1967. With the patently imprudent invasion of the Mid-Western Region in spite of its neutrality, a full-scale civil war erupted. Several schools in the Mid-Western Region were transformed into barracks by the Biafran soldiers, schooling activities stopped and most of the foreign teachers at ICC left to their countries. It was no longer certain that I would complete my Higher School Certificate programme. If I was unable to move forward with my education, the prospects were that I would probably end up in life as a low level clerical officer or a school teacher but not the Emeritus Professor of Mathematics that I would later providentially become. Fortunately, the invasion which started on August 9, 1967, ended after only six weeks, because the Federal troops, under the command of Lt. Colonel Murtala Mohammed (November 8, 1938 – February 13,

1976), vanquished the Biafran troops on September 20, 1967. But, comically, the Mid-Western Region had been declared the Republic of Benin in the early hours of the same day September 20, 1967, by Major Okonkwo, who assumed the new title of President. In a section of his broadcast to the people of the Mid-Western Region, he declared:

> I, Maj. Albert Nwazu Okonkwo, Military Administrator of the territory known as Mid-Western Nigeria including the air space, territorial waters and continental shelf, mindful of the powers vested in me under Decree No. 2/1967 of Mid-Western Nigeria and other subsequent decrees, do hereby declare the said territory of Mid-Western Nigeria as the Republic of Benin, autonomous and completely sovereign. The Republic of Benin will perform all functions of a sovereign state, make any laws, enter into any treaty with any other sovereign state, prosecute war against the enemy, make peace and agree to enter into association for common services with any Region of the former Federation of Nigeria. The Republic of Benin shall collaborate with the Republic of Biafra in all military matters. We shall honour all international treaties and obligations, support the OAU, and as soon as possible apply for membership of the UN. We would like to retain our association with the British Commonwealth of Nations and support any other organisations dedicated to peace, the concept of self-determination, freedom of the press, speech, movement and worship. God bless you and long live the Republic of Benin.

The Republic of Benin existed for only a few hours. The Biafran Army was roundly defeated in the battle of Ore, in the Western Region. That was a huge calamity that greatly unsettled the Republic of Biafra. Lt. Colonel Ojukwu saw the defeat as a betrayal, aimed at toppling his administration, by some of his trusted officers: Colonel Banjo, Major Emmanuel Arinze Ifeajuna (1935- 22 September 1967), Major Philip Alale and Major Samuel Agbamuche (Agbam). These persons were tried by a military tribunal, convicted of treason and sentenced to death by a firing squad. The sentence was swiftly implemented on September 22,

1967 in Enugu, the Biafran capital. Banjo and Ifeajuna had the ranks of Brigadier-General and Lt. Colonel, respectively, in the Biafran Army.

Close to three decades after Colonel Banjo's execution, a member of the University of Ibadan non-teaching from the Registry, called Taiwo Joyce Banjo (nee George), of the Creole ethnicity, born on January 27, 1932, in Kissy, Freetown, Sierra Leone, served briefly in the Department of Mathematics as the Departmental Secretary. She was punctual, deligent, peace-loving, fair-minded, genial, godly and religious. At that time, she worshipped at the Scripture Pasture Christian Centre (SPCC), Ibadan, established by Pastor Dr. Olubi Johnson. In pursuit of her evangelisation outreach on behalf of the SPCC, she invited me on several occasions to worship at the SPCC but as a Catholic, I could not honour her kind invitation. Just before I assumed office as the Head of Department on August 1, 1993, she was redeployed to another section of the Registry. Prior to her leaving the Department of Mathematics, I had found out that the amiable lady, who died some four years later on March 2, 1997, was the wife of Colonel Banjo, about whom I have written above. There was another occasion when I interacted with one of Colonel Banjo's children.

About a decade after the passage of Mrs. Banjo, I worked closely with her daughter, Professor Olayinka Omigbodun, the first female professor of psychiatry in Nigeria, and the latter's husband, Professor Akinyinka Omigbodun, an obstetrician and gynaecologist, who were principal investigators of some projects, funded by the MacArthur Foundation. The interaction was between 2008 and 2013 when I was the MacArthur Grant Liaison Officer of the University of Ibadan. The Omigbodun's are the first couple to occupy the office of Provost of the College of Medicine of the Nigeria's premier university since its foundation in 1948: Akinyinka was in office from 2006 to 2010 and his wife, Olayinka, assumed office as Provost in 2020 for a four-year tenure. With the defeat of the Biafran Army in the Mid-Western

Region, school activities resumed at ICC at a frenetic pace, aimed at completing the syllabus before the onset of the final examinations. Born a Nigerian on Saturday, November 4, 1933, the arrowhead of the dismantled Republic of Biafra, Lt. Colonel Chukwuemeka Odumegwu Ojukwu died a Nigerian, and not a Biafran, on Saturday, November 26, 2011, almost 41 years after the end of the Nigeria-Biafra war. On the other hand, well over three million Igbo people died as Biafrans, and not as Nigerians, during the thirty-month long secession.

Academically, things moved smoothly for me after the liberation (to use the popular term in those days) of the Mid-Western Region by the Federal Government from the Biafran Army. I successfully completed the HSC programme in December 1967.

Some of the 1967 HSC students at ICC: GOS is seated on the fence on the left.

Adding All Things Up

My secondary school days, from 1961 to 1965 (Form 1 to Form 5 classes) and HSC days from 1966 to 1967 (HSC Lower Six and Upper Six classes), represented a defining period in my existence. They opened up new vistas for me in such areas as social relations, cultural integration, group learning and the seamless acquisition of a multiplicity of real life skills. Those were the days of my continuous immersion in a whole new reality involving search and discovery, disbelief and faith, challenge and success, competition and cooperation, hard work and leisure, action and consequence as well as youthful deviance and formative discipline. When I attended the primary school at WAIFOR, I knew all my classmates, since they were either from WAIFOR or some nearby villages. By contrast, my fellow students at ICC were predominantly from various parts of the Western, Mid-Western and Eastern Regions of Nigeria: I met a number of them for the first time in my life at various times during my programme of studies. It was therefore easy for me to form the opinion that secondary schools are among the key drivers of national integration and cohesion because as boarders, we lived, dined, learned and played together, slept collectively in the school's dormitories, carried out school chores collaboratively, discharged assigned administrative roles with team spirit and participated in multiple skills-building and character-enhancing co-curricular activities with much sportsmanship. In that engaging social, religious and academic bubble, ICC inculcated in every one of its students an assortment of attributes such as communal living, team spirit, leadership traits, sportsmanship, cultural and ethnic tolerance and coexistence, empathy, a lifelong bonding with peers and contemporaries, patriotism and institutional loyalty. These fundamental values, which are evidently at the core of nation-building and national unity, figuratively coalesced into a unique gene, marked by a deep nostalgic attachment and sensitivity to ICC, that was somehow automatically inserted into the genome of every old boy of the school. Upon completion of his programme of studies at ICC, every former student assumed the status of a *de facto* member of the Immaculate Conception College, Benin City, Old Boys Association (ICCOBA), which has branches around the globe. Members of ICCOBA are found in eminent positions in the private and public sectors of their chosen countries of residence, as iconic and innovative game-changers in their different spheres of specialisation.

A Surprise Offer of Appointment

Before leaving ICC in December 1967 at the end of my HSC studies, Fr. Donnelly summoned me to his office and said the following:

> I am appointing you a member of my teaching staff. I know that you will pass all your papers with good grades. So, I will pay you the salary of an HSC holder with effect from the January 1968 without waiting for your HSC results.

I thanked him for his kind consideration and gladly accepted the offer of appointment, together with his decision to pay me the salary of an HSC holder, even though I did not officially, as at that point in time, possess any High School Certificate. On the day I assumed office as a teacher at ICC, Fr. Donnelly summoned me to his office and said:

> I know that you would prefer to teach science subjects like mathematics, physics and chemistry. But I will allow you to teach any of these subjects only if you agree to also teach English language.

I was astonished but promptly agreed. The results of the HSC examinations were announced in March 1968 and I obtained the best result in my set. So, I taught English to Form 3 students and Mathematics to Form 4 students. On the academic staff with me were five other ICC alumni. Three of these were my classmates: the future Ambassador Thaddeus Daniel Hart, the future University of Benin Fisheries and Aquaculture Professor Jude Oronsaye and the future President of the Surulere (Lagos) Rotary Club Anthony Osagie Egbe. The other two schoolmates were the future physician Dr. John Ebima Valentine Ogbeide and the future Pittsburgh-based counsellor, Dr. Andrew Igbineweka, who functioned as the institution's Librarian.

Teachers at ICC in 1968: GOS is standing in the middle of the back row.

The dearth of qualified teachers for the HSC programme continued even after 1967. Around March 1968, Fr. Donnelly summoned me to his office and told me that ICC had some difficulty in recruiting a chemistry teacher for the HSC class. He said that he had decided that I should teach Chemistry from that day on to the Lower Six HSC class. I took up the assignment for some time, under the mentoring oversight of Thaddeus Ogboghodo, a graduate of the University of Ibadan, before a substitute was appointed. I left the employment in August 1968, to take up my admission in September 1968 as a direct entry freshman of the University of Ibadan.

1968 ICC table tennis team: staff coach GOS seated, third from left.

PART III

TERTIARY LEVEL EDUCATION

14

AT THE PREMIER
UNIVERSITY

I began to think seriously about university education after the HSC results were released around March 1968, although the probability that I would be able to mobilize the resources to fund a three-year programme in any Nigerian university was infinitesimally small. My brother, John, identified with my ambition to obtain a university degree. His idea was that he would borrow the money for the first year at the university from money lenders, with the understanding that I would pay back the principal and interest when I completed my studies. This was akin to a student loan. Although the proposal was a good stratagem, it left out how the funds for the remaining two years would be sourced. Moreover, it was clear that if all the money for my university education would have to come from money lenders, the financial burden of repaying the cumulative principal and interest would weigh me down for many years after graduation. A fundamental consequence would then be that I would have to perish any thought of postgraduate training or marriage within a reasonable time span after my first degree programme. Nevertheless, I accepted my brother's proposal, with much trepidation.

My elder sister, Rose

My immediate senior sister, Mary

1968: GOS and his senior brother, John

Selecting a University to Attend

In 1968, there were only the following five universities in Nigeria.

1.   University of Ibadan, Ibadan

The institution, which prides itself as the nation's premier University, began its existence in 1948 as the University College Ibadan, affiliated to the University of London, UK. Administratively, its pioneer Principal was the British ecologist and entomologist Professor Kenneth Mellanby (March 26, 1908 – December 23, 1993) who trained at the University of Cambridge and University of London and was in office from 1947 to 1953. The first male hostel in the University is called Mellanby Hall, in honour of the scholar and administrator.

2.   University of Nigeria, Nsukka

Established in 1960, its pioneer Vice-Chancellor was Professor George Marion Johnson (May 22, 1900 – August 11, 1987)), an African-American lawyer and academic trained at the University of California, Berkeley, USA. His tenure was from 1960 to 1964.

3.   University of Ife, Ile-Ife

Established in 1962 as the University of Ife, Ile-Ife, its pioneer Vice-Chancellor was Omooba Professor Oladele Adebayo Ajose (1907–1978), a medical doctor and academic, who trained at the University of Glasgow, United Kingdom. His tenure was from 1962 to 1966.

4.   Ahmadu Bello University, Zaria

The institution was established in 1962. Its pioneer Vice-Chancellor was the New Zealander Dr. Norman Stanley Alexander (October 7, 1907 – March 26, 1997), a physicist who trained at the University of Cambridge. His tenure was from 1961 to 1966.

5.   University of Lagos, Lagos

Established in 1962, its pioneer Vice-Chancellor was Professor Eni Njoku (November 6, 1917 – December 22, 1974), a botanist who trained at the University of Manchester and University of London in the UK. His tenure was from 1962 to 1965.

To study in Nigeria, it was from these five universities that I was to make my choice. In reality, I had fewer than five universities to choose from. This was because, firstly, University of Nigeria, Nsukka, was at that time in a war zone and was therefore not accessible for learning; secondly, as a result of the subsisting tense political situation in the country in 1968, it appeared to me inadvisable to think of Ahmadu Bello University, Zaria, as a possible choice. I was therefore left with the three universities in the western part of Nigeria: University of Ibadan, University of Lagos and University of Ife, which was renamed Obafemi Awolowo University on May 12, 1987. But from the outset, I had fixed some selection criteria to guide my choice, the most stringent of which was that I would attend the University of Ibadan, come hell or high water. I had assumed that every university offerred every course imaginable, no matter by what name called. In my planning, I therefore settled for Engineering Physics or, at worse, any other specialisation in Engineering, as the degree programme that I would pursue at the University of Ibadan.

How did I arrive at the choice of Engineering Physics? From around August 1966 to August 1967, I was taught Physics at the HSC level by a USA Peace Corps member. Called Franklin Chance, he obtained a BS degree in Engineering Physics in 1961 at the University of Tennessee, Knoxville. Before arriving at ICC, he had participated in the Cooperative (Co-op) Education Programme at the National Aeronautics and Space Administration (NASA), with headquarters in Washington DC. He urged me to study Engineering Physics because, according to him, of its versatility in the industry and national development. As a result of the invasion of the Mid-Western Nigeria by the Biafran soldiers in August 1967, Mr. Chance returned to the US in that month. Unfortunately, he died two years later in 1969 in a motor accident in his country. When I received the prospectus of the University of Ibadan, not only did it not contain Engineering Physics but, worse still, it emerged that the institution did not offer any Engineering specialisations whatsoever. The nearest degree programme to my wish was Physics: consequently, I applied to study Physics, in respect of which I was duly offered admission. For my residence on the University campus, I was assigned to the Independence Hall. I would subsequently be allocated a shared Room B56 in the Hall. I maintained the room space B56 throughout my three-year undergraduate programme at the University of Ibadan.

1968: The B wing of the Independence Hall, University of Ibadan

My First Year at the Premier University

The second visit of my life to Ibadan occurred toward the end of September 1968 when I travelled to the city to begin my university education. Before leaving Benin City for Ibadan on one of the vehicles of the Armels Transport Company, my brother had furnished me with the money that he was loaned by some lenders for my first year at the University.

1968: The main gate of the University of Ibadan

2021: The main gate of the University of Ibadan

I joined the University of Ibadan when the psychiatrist Professor Thomas Adeoye Lambo (March 29, 1923 – March 13, 2004), trained at the University of Birmingham and University of London, UK, was Vice-Chancellor. His tenure, which straddled my undergraduate days at the institution, was from 1968 to 1971. The Registrar was Chief Nathaniel Kolawole Adamolekun (October 14, 1919 – May 1, 2000), whose tenure was from 1960 to 1972, and the (Acting) University Librarian was Mr. K. Mahmud, who was in office from 1968 to 1971. The Dean of the Faculty of Science in 1968 was the Jamaican Chemist Professor Dennis Horace Irvine (January 15, 1926 – November 26, 2005), who trained at the University of Leeds and University of Cambridge, UK, and was later the third Vice-Chancellor, from 1969 to 1982, of the University of Guyana, Georgetown, Guyana, an institution that was established on October 1, 1963. His tenure as Dean was from 1966 to 1969. He was then succeeded by Professor Olumbe Bassir (May 20, 1919 – May 23, 2001), a Sierra Leonean Biochemist, trained at the University of Liverpool, UK. As Dean of the Faculty of Science, Professor Bassir's tenure was from 1969 to 1971. The Head of the Department of Physics was Arthur James Lyon (January 12, 1918 - October 7, 1981), who obtained his PhD in 1956 at the University of Edinburgh in Scotland. Professor Lyon's tenure was from 1963 to 1969. His successor was Professor Olumuyiwa Akintola Olorunninyo Awe (November 13, 1932 – May 3, 2015), trained at the University of Ibadan and University of Cambridge, UK. Professor Awe's tenure was from March 7, 1969 to July 31, 1975. Other notable freshers with me at the University of Ibadan in 1968 were Federick Akpata, Anthony Egbe and Bernard Irusota, who were my classmates at ICC in 1965, Gregory Odigie who was my schoolmate at ICC and my childhood friend, Emmanuel Enosakhare Iyamu (November 2, 1945 – January 8, 2021). We were all happy to have been fortunate to secure, and actually take up, our places at Nigeria's premier university. Already pursuing their undergraduate programmes on campus were some of my seniors at ICC, who were in their final year in the 1968/1969 academic session, namely: Chief Dr. Roland Ehigiamusoe, former Pro-Chancellor & Chairman of the Governing Council of the University of Calabar, His Royal Highness Ogiefo Festus Iduozee, the Enogie of Evboesi, Orhionmwon Local Government Area, Edo State, and Professor Samuel Okoro, using their current titles. I had the rare honour of sharing room B56, Independence Hall, with Professor Okoro.

Before and after securing admission to the University of Ibadan, Chief Dr. Ehigiamusoe was a veritable and reliable mentor to me. During my first academic year at the University, I felt completely at home because my roommate, Professor Okoro, was always there for me. To these seniors of mine, I owe a lifelong debt of gratitude.

Matriculation at UI in 1968 as first year undergraduate.
From L-R, Emmanuel Iyamu, Frederick Akpata,
Gregory Odigie and GOS

Faculty Registration

The days before October 2, 1968, were dedicated to orientation and immersion activities for us, the freshers, and for paying all fees. I promptly settled all my official bills. On October 2, 1968, the formal registration of freshers was done. It took place in the new Chemistry lecture auditorium. A student would appear before a registration officer, who was a member of the academic staff. I appeared before Dr. Mrs. Joyce B. Redhead, a lecturer of the Department of Chemistry, whose husband, Dr. John F. Redhead, was also a lecturer in the Department of Forestry. After I handed her my letter of admission, she verified my WASC and HSC results. She then said:

> Fine! You were admitted to Physics. From your results, you can be in Mathematics, Physics or Chemistry. Would you like to change to Mathematics?

In response, I asked her why she suggested Mathematics.

> Oh! Mathematics will be easier for you than Physics or Chemistry, because either of these involves lengthy practical work daily.

I reasoned that if Engineering courses were available in the University at that time, I would certainly have been involved in practical work. Consequently, I responded that if that was the main motivation for her suggestion, I would not make any change. She then registered me for Physics, as my major subject, with Mathematics and Chemistry as my minors. With the registration completed by almost all freshers, academic activities quickly kicked-in. Not long after, all freshers were formally enrolled as University of Ibadan students in a grand matriculation ceremony. The latter was held in the Trenchard Hall, a monumental edifice named after the British military officer Hugh Montague Trenchard (February 3, 1873 – February 10, 1956), a Marshal of the Royal Air Force. For establishing the Royal Air Force, Trenchard is revered in British circles as the *Father of the Royal Air Force*.

Some of My Lecturers in My First Year

It was exciting to be studying at the University of Ibadan. The teaching and learning environments, as well as opportunities for co-curricular activities, were excellent and quite different from what I had experienced hitherto. Using their ultimate academic titles, my Physics, Mathematics and Chemistry teachers in my first year in 1968 were as follows.

Physics

> Professor Akpanoluo Ikpong Ikpong Ette (September 23, 1929 – 27 March 2015), Professor Fatai Babatunde Akanni Giwa (May 3, 1938 – 2005) and Professor Ebun

Adefunmilayo Oni [nee Adegbohungbe](May 21, 1935 – December 2, 2021);

Mathematics

Professor Sunday Osarumwense Iyahen (October 3, 1937 – January 28, 2018), Professor Monsur Akangbe Kenku (December 14, 1942- June 24, 2021), Professor Aderemi Oluyomi Kuku (March 20, 1941 – February 13, 2022), Professor Gabriel Oluremi Olaofe (December 6, 1937-February 6, 1994) and Mr. J. E. Pretty.

Chemistry

Professor Titus Olubode Bamkole, Professor Donald E. U. Ekong (December 31, 1933 - 2005), Professor Dennis Horace Irvine (January 15, 1926 - November 26, 2005) and Fr. Anthony Joseph Foley (July 25, 1916 – April 7, 1997), about whom I will say a few words later.

The quality of teaching was high. The lecturers were dedicated and demonstrated a good command of the key elements of the courses assigned to them. Examinations were held in May/June of each academic session. This meant that students accumulated lots of lecture notes in their courses throughout the entire session, all of which they were obliged to carefully review in a short period of time before the examinations. Many of these were held in the Trenchard Hall, which was also used for several other events, including Convocation activities for the award of degrees. As if to remind students that Trenchard Hall was named after a military officer, the Hall was some kind of existential academic battle ground for many a student during the University's May/June examinations, because failure to obtain an overall score above a certain threshold automatically triggered outright withdrawal from the University. Students who scored above the threshold but below the pass mark in some courses were obliged to appear for re-sit examinations in the courses. It was also the case that persistent below-average performance after the first year was a signal that a student was coasting toward a Third Class or Pass degree. Awareness by students of the life-changing significance of the examinations held in the Trenchard Hall was therefore one, but not the only, motivation for them to be hardworking and engage in continuous learning throughout their degree programmes. In my case, I had no other choice but to be diligent with my studies. The examinations were held at the end of the 1968/1969 academic year. Subsequently, I received a letter from the University stating that I was eligible to proceed to the second year of the degree programme. There was, however, no indication of the marks that I scored in the various courses which I took in Physics, Mathematics and Chemistry.

A Near Traumatic Return to the Campus

My second year at the University of Ibadan was the 1969/1970 academic session. I returned to the campus from the long vacation with absolutely no inkling as to how I would finance my studies. I needed money to buy books and to pay for the session's prescribed institutional tuition, feeding and hostel fees. But I had none. There was an ominously high probability that I might drop out of the University. I was allowed to check into my accommodation: B56, Independence Hall. I could not register officially for my courses because I needed to provide evidence of payment of the prescribed tuition fees. But I could attend classes and I did. In those days, one could even seat for the session's examinations, except that the results would not be released if one had not paid the tuition fees. My existence on the campus was marked by an overwhelming feeling of uncertainty and despondence.

In the midst of the trauma and about two weeks into the session, the Federal Government of Nigeria announced that it was launching a crash programme to produce secondary school teachers for the nation's education system. The Government would

166 PROMISE AND PROVIDENCE

offer scholarships to undergraduates who agreed to specialise in Teacher Education. Seizing the fortuitous opportunity, I picked a form to apply for one of the scholarships, even though that was tantamount to an unplanned change of programme from Physics to Teacher Education. But that was the only option available to me at that point in time to avoid dropping out of the University. To submit my application, I was obliged to furnish copies of my certificates, a copy of my first year undergraduate result, names of three referees, completed bond documents, signed consent documents from my guarantors, etc. I was finding it quite challenging to assemble the requisite documents before the deadline for submitting applications.

A Providential Solution

While still struggling with the challenge of completing and submitting the application form, with all its attachments, for a Federal Government scholarship for prospective teachers, providence intervened with two auspicious and almost simultaneous solutions. I saw an announcement on a notice board of the Department of Physics inviting applications for bursaries of the Cocoa Marketing Board of Nigeria, established in 1947. The condition for applying was that applicants must be undergraduates from cocoa-producing areas who had already completed their first year of study. This providential opportunity seemed to have been tailor-made for me, and I promptly applied. To me, all was grist that came to my mill. I was highly elated when I was invited for an interview. Barely a few days after the interview, I received a letter conveying the award of a Cocoa Marketing Board bursary to me. The bursary covered my tuition, board and accommodation fees throughout the remaining two academic sessions of my programme of study. Moving overnight from the status of an indigent student in deep financial doldrums to that of a Cocoa Marketing Board scholar was a truly miraculous transformation.

It meant that I would complete my degree programme in Physics without any financial worry, if I worked hard enough. While still basking in my providential good fortune, I received another letter that conveyed the award of a University scholarship to me, in recognition of what was adjudged by the institution as an outstanding performance in my first-year University examinations. Through these auspicious events, I became the first Benin scholar and the first alumnus of the Immaculate Conception College, Benin City, to win either the Cocoa Marketing Board bursary or the University Scholarship or both. The University scholarship covered not only my tuition, board and accommodation fees but also incorporated a book allowance. I could not have asked for anything more. But how would I operate two scholarship awards in the same institution and in respect of the same programme of study? The letter directed me to see the future High Chief Dr. Ita Ekanem-Ita (died: September 3, 2009), who was the officer in charge of scholarships in the University's Registry; he later served as the institution's Registrar from 1982 to 1994. In my discussion with Chief Ekanem-Ita, he clarified that as a University Scholar who also won, and was already utilising, the Cocoa Marketing Board bursary, I was saving the University a lot of money which it would have had to pay for my tuition, board and accommodation. Chief Ekanem-Ita then told me that the Cocoa Marketing Board Bursary would be applied to defray my tuition, board and accommodation fees, while the University would pay me a book allowance every academic year. With that arrangement, which was faithfully implemented throughout my second and third years of study, I was able to utilize the crucial elements of the two awards, to the mutual satisfaction of the University and myself.

My Second Year at UI

I took courses only in Physics and Mathematics, dropping Chemistry, in my second year. Some of my Physics teachers were Professor Olumuyiwa Awe (November 13, 1932 – May 3, 2015), who was also the Head of Department, and the future Professor Awele Maduemezia (August 7, 1934 – February 20, 2018), Professor Akinremi Ojo, Professor Ebun Adefunmilayo Oni (née Adegbohungbe), Professor Robert Michael Hudson, Professor John Otunola Oyinloye (May 29, 1939 – April 5, 2010) and Dr. Adeyinka Oladipe Sanni (1939 – 2011). In the same academic year, Dr. Anthony Guillen-Preckler (February 24, 1934 – February 20, 2011), the future Dr. Gabriel Michael M. Obi and Professor Haroon Oladipo Tejumola (July 8, 1937 - December 25, 2011), were my teachers in Mathematics. The year ran smoothly and I implemented my academic activities with determination, unwavering focus and youthful verdure.

Journey through the 1970/1971

The first term of my final year 1970/71 quickly fleeted by. We entered the last week of January 1971. I took courses only in my major subject, Physics. My teachers included the same ones who taught me Physics in my second year. I was positively influenced by all of them: they were always painstaking, thorough and firm. I looked at the horizon before me: in less than a year, I would be a graduate of the nation's premier university, exchanging the gown for the town. For me, that would be a providential achievement. Teaching and learning progressed smoothly. In addition to intensive theoretical physics work, our teachers also ensured that we had state-of-the-art hands-on practical physics training in diverse areas of the subject. As was the custom, the questions for final examinations were drafted at the University of Ibadan and moderated by external examiners, who were usually in the United Kingdom. The standard of the examinations was essentially at par with that of the University of London, under which the University of Ibadan began its existence on Sunday, January 18, 1948 as the University College Ibadan. The University's 1970/71 final year students were focused on their imminent May/June examinations.

From Student to Martyr

In the last week of January 1971, there were strident rumblings by the students of the Nnamdi Azikiwe Hall concerning the state of catering services in the Hall. The students made allegations of corruption and poor delivery of catering services against the caterer, Mrs. Grace Apampa, whose husband was also employed in the Maintenance Department of the institution, and petitioned the sitting Vice-Chancellor, Professor Thomas Adeoye Lambo calling for her immediate removal. After a few days, with no official announcement by the University of the dismissal of Mrs. Apampa, the students saw the institution's apparent inaction as evidence of its arrant insensitivity to their welfare and furiously escalated their agitation to a campus-wide demonstration on February 1, 1971. The Vice-Chancellor's response was to invite the police to restore order. Not long after the police arrived on the campus and began to take on the demonstrators, a student lay dead in front of the Queen Elizabeth II Hall. The student, who had not been involved in the demonstration, was hit in the head by a bullet as he tried to provide some assistance to an injured demonstrator. His name was Adekunle Ademuyiwa Adepeju, a 23-year old, second year student of Agricultural Economics and a member of the Mellanby Hall. I learnt about the tragedy around midday because I was in a practical Physics laboratory when the demonstrations were ongoing. To stem a further escalation of the volatile situation, the Vice-Chancellor quickly announced the closure of the University indefinitely and ordered all students, except the foreign students, to vacate the campus. I moved out of the campus and travelled back to Benin City. I did not know how the new development would affect the completion date of my undergraduate programme. That was a source of constant worry for me. Adepeju's death greatly traumatised all students throughout the country, because any of them could have been Adepeju, who became the first martyr of police brutality on a Nigerian university campus. He was buried on February 5, 1971, at the St. Anne's Anglican Church, Molete, Ibadan. About ten years after the tragic immolation of Adepeju on the altar of student activism and opaque institutional decision-making processes, in his contribution to the 1981 publication, edited by Professor Tekena N. Tamuno and entitled: *Ibadan Voices: Ibadan University in Transition,* Ibadan University Press, Ibadan, a former Registrar of the University of Ibadan from 1972 to 1981, Samuel Jemieta Okudu, provided the following graphic narration of how the University tried to manage the crisis.

> January 1971: There has been some trouble in Azikiwe Hall about food and drinks served at a Hall party. There are allegations that the Catering Manageress has fiddled with some of these. The Vice-Chancellor calls me and some other officers to discuss the crisis. A decision is taken to send the catering officer away on an indefinite leave pending thorough investigation into the allegations. The striking students are not satisfied when this decision is announced to them. The Vice-Chancellor tells them at a gathering in Trenchard Hall that he is not only sending the lady away on leave but is also assuring them that she will never be returned to Azikiwe Hall. The students are not satisfied because, as they say, they do not trust the Vice-Chancellor. The famous phrase, *credibility-gap,* is bandied about.
>
> Today is 1 February 1971. The series of meetings of the past few days have not resulted in the resolution of the crisis. Students are milling around the Administration building in a continuation of the demonstrations of the past few days. The morning wears on and the tension rises. The Police are alerted of a possible escalation of events. Unfortunately, they rush in with the appearance to do battle with such equipment as batons and wicker shields. They only succeeded in provoking students who throw missiles at them. The students, led by a hard core of militants, seize the opportunity to attack the Administration

building. The Police also call in re-enforcement and the campus, within a short time, is full of tear gas smoke. There is utter confusion but the students seem to have the upper hand against the ineffectual police effort to quel the riot.

It's one o'clock. Nearly all the windows in the Administration block have been smashed. The Vice-Chancellor and I have nowhere else to seek refuge and so we run into his closet. We are joined by my deputy, the Vice-Chancellor's secretary, and a messenger. Soon, we begin to hear shots sounding different from those of tear gas. Suddenly, everywhere becomes quiet. We summon up courage to leave our place of hiding. Only a few workers can be seen around. The Vice-Chancellor's official car has been overturned and damaged. A student has been killed with live ammunition. What a price to pay for the misunderstanding over food and drinks! What a price to pay for the so-called *credibility-gap!*

As its response, the Federal Military Government, headed by Major General Yakubu Gowon, promptly constituted the University of Ibadan Commission of Inquiry, with Boonyamin Oladiran Kazeem (August 29, 1922 – 1998), who was a Judge of the High Court of Lagos from 1967 to 1976 and subsequently a Justice of the Supreme Court of Nigeria from 1984 to 1987, as sole commissioner with full powers and authority. The terms of reference were framed as follows:

The Commission shall, with all convenient speed –
- (i) establish the immediate and remote causes of the disturbances;
- (ii) submit a detailed account of the incidents;
- (iii) ascertain the nature and assess the propriety of the measures taken to quell the disturbances with particular reference to the circumstances in which one student was killed and others were injured;
- (iv) make recommendations as to the respective degrees of responsibility of all concerned; and make any other appropriate findings.

And I hereby require the Commission to submit its report to me in Lagos within fourteen days after the date of its first sitting.

The enabling instrument of the Commission was inserted in the *Supplement to Official Gazette Extraordinary No.6, Vol. 58, 4th February, 1971* – Part B as L.N. No. 8 of 1971. At the end of the inquiry, Justice Kazeem's 187-page report and the Federal Military Government's 7-page comments (white paper) on the report were published in 1971 by the Federal Ministry of Information, Lagos. Disagreeing with several elements of the Kazeem Report and the Government White Paper on it, the National Union of Nigerian Students published a 34-page document Entitled: *Students Black Paper on the Kazeem Report* [Ibadan, Ororo Publications] in 1972. Without going into the details of these publicly available documents, it is pertinent to observe that many more students have been periodically killed on several Nigerian university campuses by armed State agents after 1971. With hardly any sanctions for the recurrent fatal extrajudicial acts, an air of impunity pervaded several units of the armed forces, as tragically exemplified by the unconscionable brutality of the Special Anti-Robbery Squad (SARS), which was a notorious component of the Nigeria Police until its ignominious disbandment by the Government in 2020.

Graduation from the Premier University

As it turned out, the student upheaval described in the foregoing did not inordinately disrupt the academic calendar because after only a few weeks of closure, the University recalled all students to the campus. It was evident that the 1970/71 academic year would end normally in June 1971. The questions for our final examinations were drafted at the University of Ibadan and moderated by external examiners, who were usually in the United Kingdom. The standard of every final year examination at the UI was essentially at par with that of the University of London, under which UI began its existence on Sunday, January 18, 1948 as the University College Ibadan (UCI). I took my final year examinations in May/June 1971. I earned the BSc Second Class

Honours (Upper Division), graduating as the best student in the 1971 cohort of 19 students. The names of my classmates are shown in the following table.

1971 BSC PHYSICS SET AT THE UNIVERSITY OF IBADAN

S/N	FORENAMES	SURNAME
1	Adeyemi Johnson	ADEBISI
2	Moses Adegbola	ADIGUN
3	Kolawole Abraham Adeyanju	AISIDA
4	Erhi Emmanuel	AKPOKODJE
5	Felix Akinloye	BABALOLA
6	Ayodele Joseph	COKER
7	Nicholas Adebayo	DADA
8	Rufus Ayodele	DAODU
9	Emmanuel Ike	EBUBE
10	Godwin Osakpemwoya Samuel	EKHAGUERE
11	Jacob Adegboyega	FARINMADE
12	Gbolahan Aderibigbe Foluso	IGE
13	Lawrence Kayode	KOMOLAFE
14	Clement Sunday Chukwudum	MGBATOGU
15	Samuel Omotayo	OJUAWO
16	Samuel Okafor	OKOLIE
17	Ayodele	OMOWUMI
18	Gabriel Babasola	ONOLAJA
19	Timothy Ayorinde Olabode	ORE

I returned to Benin City and I was employed as a Physics teacher at the Anglican Girls Grammar School, Benin City, from July to December 1971. With the savings from the employment, I subsequently paid off the loan which my elder brother took in 1968 in respect of the tuition, board and hostel fees during my first year at the University of Ibadan. Thereafter, I set my sights steadfastly on postgraduate study in the United Kingdom.

Student Spiritual Needs: The Catholic Chaplaincy at UI

The religious space on campus was essentially two dimensional, occupied by the Christian and Muslim faiths which had been imposed on various parts of Nigeria by colonialists and conquerors, to the rigid exclusion of all indigenous faiths. The Christians had their worship centres at the Chapel of the Resurrection, associated with the Anglican denomination, and the Our Lady Seat of Wisdom Chapel, owned by the Catholic Church. The University of Ibadan Central Mosque was used by the Muslims for their religious activities. As a Catholic, during most of the 49 years from 1968 to 2017, I worshiped mainly at the Our Lady Seat of Wisdom Chapel whenever I was in Ibadan. Throughout my undergraduate years at UI, the chaplain of the Our Lady Seat of Wisdom Chapel was Fr. Anthony Joseph Foley, an SMA priest born in Callan, County Kilkenny, Ireland. He obtained a BA degree in philosophy and education from UCG in 1937, was ordained a priest on December 22, 1940, in the same cohort of nineteen priests to which Fr. Joseph Patrick Donnelly belonged. Like his classmate Fr. Donnelly, he subsequently obtained a BSc degree in physics and chemistry from the UCC in 1944. Assigned by the Catholic Vicariate of Lagos to St. Gregory's College, Lagos, established in 1928, he taught English and chemistry in the school from 1946 to September 1948. Fr. Foley was appointed the Catholic Chaplain of the Our Lady Seat of Wisdom Chapel and also a lecturer in Inorganic Chemistry in the Department of Chemistry, University of Ibadan, in 1948. As a priest, his masses were business-like. Moreover, his approach to certain ecclesial matters and functions were seen by some as radical, even when it was evident that he adhered loyally at all times to his sacerdotal oath. In my first year at UI, he was in charge of our Practical Chemistry classes, as Chemistry was one of my subsidiary subjects.

Those were the days when science laboratories at the University were world-class. Easily recognised by his trademark tobacco pipe and good humour, he equipped us with high quality practical skills. Fr. Foley retired from the University in 1981, when I was already a member of staff of the institution, and was aptly honoured by the University through the naming after him of the laboratory for Practical Chemistry, where he worked for many years, as the Father Foley Laboratory. He was succeeded as chaplain by Fr. Professor Louis Joachim Munoz (October 9, 1933 – March 19, 2013), a Spaniard, ordained as a priest of the Opus Dei in Madrid, Spain, on August 9, 1959. Established on October 2, 1928 by St. Josemaría Escrivá De Balaguery Albás (January 9, 1902 – June 2, 1975), a Spanish Roman Catholic priest, the Opus Dei, a Catholic personal prelature that teaches that one's profession is a veritable path to sanctity, was introduced to Nigeria in 1965. The following year, Fr. Munoz was sent to Nigeria by St. Josemaría Escrivá to assist in strengthening the new entity. He arrived in Nigeria on August 22, 1966. As chaplain of the Our Lady Seat of Wisdom Chapel, he often visited members of the laity in their homes and I remember being his host on several occasions. His visits contributed toward strengthening the laity's spiritual and moral standing. He conducted the baptismal ceremony of my daughter, Osamweetin, at the Our Lady Seat of Wisdom Chapel, University of Ibadan, in 1986. An out-and-out scholar who was a professor of European Studies in the Faculty of Arts at the University, Fr. Munoz naturalised as a Nigerian on November 17, 2006. To support student learning and spiritual development, he laboured with other members and friends of the Opus Dei to build a male hall of residence, called the Irawo University Centre, in the Agbowo area of Ibadan.

In 2002, Fr. Munoz was succeeded by Monsignor Professor Felix Adedoyin Adeigbo (November 18, 1943 – May 13, 2014), ordained on December 21, 1969, who had been the Assistant Parish Priest. Msgr. Adeigbo initiated a number of construction projects within the premises of the Our Lady Seat of Wisdom Chapel, with the building of the Pope John Paul II Hall as the most ambitious. The erection of the Hall had not been completed when, in 2006, Msgr. Adeigbo was appointed the Rector of the Catholic Institute of West Africa (CIWA), Port Harcourt, established in 1981. He then handed over the reins of the office of Parish Priest to Fr. Ezekiel Adegboyega Owoeye (August 30, 1967 – October 1, 2021), ordained on August 7, 1993, close to his 26th birthday. After assuming office, Fr. Owoeye, who also held the post of Director of Justice, Development and Peace Commission of the Catholic Archdiocese of Ibadan, diligently implemented a number of building projects, including the completion of the Pope John Paul II Hall, a project initiated by Fr. Adeigbo. On Saturday, December 21, 2013, Fr. Owoeye led the priests who jointly officiated at the solemnisation ceremony of my daughter's (Osamweetin's) marriage to her husband, Dr. Etiowo Ekanem, at the Our Lady Seat of Wisdom Chapel, University of Ibadan. Before the marriage, Osamweetin had earned an MSc degree in Business Management at the University of Hull, UK, in 2009. Fr. Owoeye's unexpected death on October 1, 2021 was a huge blow to all parishioners, including my own family.

15

AT THE UNIVERSITY OF LONDON

With my primary, secondary and first degree university education undertaken in Nigeria, my resolve was that, all things being equal, my postgraduate training would be outside the country, probably in the UK or the USA. During my student days at the University of Ibadan, the institution operated a trimester system. The first term was from October to December, while the second and third terms were from January to March and April to June, respectively. Concerning studying in the UK, I had my sights on the University of London, which was structurally a federation of some 20 Colleges.

As soon as the University of Ibadan resumed for the first term of the 1970/71 academic year, I requested for application forms from two Colleges of the University of London toward postgraduate admission. The first institution was the Imperial College of Science & Technology, established in 1907. In July 2007, after one hundred years of its foundation, the institution became an autonomous university, independent of the University of London, with the name Imperial College of Science, Technology & Medicine. The other institution was the University College London, established in

1826, but which today goes by the name UCL. There were sections in the application forms to be completed by a candidate's Head of Department and then transmitted by the Head directly to the institutions. So, I submitted my application forms to the office of the Head, Professor Olumuyiwa Awe. I was surprised to be summoned a day later by Professor Awe. I promptly appeared before him, with much trepidation. He then said to me:

> You are applying to Imperial College London and University College London for postgraduate work. Do you not want to do your postgraduate research in this Department? From your results so far, you will certainly qualify for a University scholarship for postgraduate research here.

In reply, I explained that I wanted to do my postgraduate training abroad. Then, he said:

> Fine! I just wanted to be sure that you are aware that you could obtain a University scholarship for postgraduate research in this Department. I will complete and post your application forms.

I was grateful to Professor Awe. Not long after, I received letters of admission from the two Colleges in December 1970. With the two offers of admission coming so swiftly and so early, I did not bother any more trying to secure admission in the USA. Moreover, I was in regular correspondence with the future Professor Anthony Uyiekpen Osagie (1947–2013), who was already carrying out his PhD research activities at the University of Manchester. He advised me to choose the UK. From the binary options before me, I chose the Imperial College, London, on the following grounds. During my final year in 1970/71, one of my courses was Quantum Mechanics, which was taught by Professor Awele Maduemezia (August 7, 1934 – February 20, 2018). I took much interest in the subject principally because of its underlying mathematical foundation. As a consequence and toward identifying a possible area of research, I tried to find out more about quantum theory and its possible ramifications. In the process, I came across the branch of Mathematical Physics called Axiomatic Quantum Field Theory, which was applying cutting-edge mathematical ideas for its formulation. Exemplifying the approach was a book that was published in New York in 1964, a few years before my graduation, entitled *PCT, Spin and Statistics and All That*, jointly authored by Raymond Federick Streater of the Imperial College, London, UK, and Arthur Strong Wightman (March 30, 1922 – January 13, 2013) of Princeton University, Princeton, New Jersey, USA, with Benjamin as publishers. In the words of Professor Streater, The book broke new ground in physics, with a more thorough going involvement of advanced mathematics.

My choice of the Imperial College, London, was to enable me to work in a highly mathematical branch of Mathematical Physics with Professor Streater, whose affiliation, as stated in the book, was the Imperial College, London. Professor Wightman is credited with the formulation of the so – called Wightman Axioms of Axiomatic Quantum Field Theory.

Mid-West Government Scholar

Equipped with a BSc degree in Physics and a teaching job to match, as well as a firm offer of admission to the foreign university where I would pursue my postgraduate training, the outstanding challenge was funding. In the early 1970s, scholarships were easier to secure in respect of postgraduate training than for undergraduate education. My chances of obtaining a scholarship were further boosted by the establishment in 1970 in Benin City, just before my graduation, of the Mid-West Institute of Technology (MIT), a higher education institution, during the illustrious administration of Brigadier-General Dr. Samuel Osaigbovo Ogbemudia (September 17, 1932 –March 9, 2017), who was the Military Governor of the Mid-West State from 1967 to 1975. There was then a drive by the Government to train academic staff with PhD degrees for the MIT. I was determined to be one of those to be trained.

Accordingly, as soon as a call was made by the Ministry of Education toward the end of July 1971 for applications in respect of the Mid-West Government Postgraduate Scholarships, I promptly responded. Since the Ministry was certainly aware of the academic calendar of most universities at home and abroad, my thinking was that the process of selecting the applicants to be awarded scholarships would be such that awardees would be able to begin their postgraduate training on time during the 1971/1972 academic year. But, unexpectedly, there was an inordinate delay by the Ministry in conducting the interviewing of applicants and subsequently notifying the successful ones. The chairman of the interviewing panel was the distinguished chemist Professor Emmanuel Emovon (February 24, 1929 – February 20, 2020), who later served as the Vice-Chancellor of the University of Jos and was also a Federal Minister of Science & Technology. I received a notification of award, subject to some bond conditions, toward the end of October 1971. I was able to find some guarantors to complete the bond forms and I eventually received a contractual and firm letter of award.

Toward Travelling Abroad

As I had never travelled out of Nigeria before 1971, I needed an international passport. For that, I travelled to Lagos to apply for one. Within three days of arriving in Lagos, an international passport was issued to me and I returned to Benin City. Then I needed to secure a UK study visa, after which I could approach the Ministry for an air ticket to London. In 1971, the British High Commission in Nigeria maintained a Consulate in Benin City. So, I was issued a UK study visa in the City. But before doing so, the Visa Officer observed that the academic year had started in the UK since September. He then asked me the following two questions: "Are you sure that Imperial College is still expecting you? Would you be able to make up for the lost time of about two months?"

My answers were: "I had not been sent any letter by Imperial College indicating that I should defer my admission. I would work very hard to cover lost grounds." I was glad that the Visa Officer did not contest these answers, which I gave with much trepidation, but was kind enough to take them for their face value. He issued me the visa and wished me well.

Off to London

November 1971: GOS, in white suit, boarding a Nigeria Airways flight to
Lagos en route London, with a farewell handshake from his senior brother, John. In those
days, a person could move to the airside of the Benin airport and see off his relation even up
to the aircraft's entry door.

I flew in a Nigeria Airways aircraft from Benin City to Lagos
on Tuesday, November 16, 1971, as Convocation activities for
the conferment of first degrees were ongoing at the University
of Ibadan. I had looked eagerly forward to formally receiving
my degree in person in the iconic Trenchard Hall but the degree
was conferred on me in absentia. Around 10:00am on the next
day, Wednesday, November 17, 1971, while the Foundation Day
activities were taking place at the University of Ibadan, I was on
another Nigeria Airways flight from Lagos to London. As will
soon be evident later, I was fortunate to have been seated in the
airplane by a Nigerian lady who was returning to London after
a trip to Lagos. During our conversation, she realised that I had
never been to London. She asked me where I would be headed
after leaving the Airport and by what means. I showed her the
address of my destination and indicated that I planned to hire a
taxi. She recognised the address, which was in the vicinity of the
Queen's Park underground station along Salusbury Road, London
NW6 6NL, on the Bakerloo Line. She then observed that the
address was on her route and that there was an arrangement for
her to be picked up.

I Set My Feet on London Soil

Our aircraft landed at Heathrow Airport, London, around 5 pm. I was happy that I had fulfilled one of my life ambitions. Outside the Airport, the environment was, for me who had never travelled outside Nigeria, overly cold: the climate had changed from the tropical to the temperate. A car, with two men, was indeed already waiting to pick up the lady. She asked me to join them, after explaining to the men that I was new in London. The men welcomed me and allowed me to ride with them. I was overwhelmed by the kind gesture of the lady and the men. The car first stopped at the lady's residence, where I was given a sumptuous Nigerian meal. Thereafter, I was driven to the address of my classmate at ICC, Festus Eke, of blessed memory, to whom I had been linked by Anthony Osagie and who had graciously accepted to host me for a few days.

Next day, November 18, 1971, with Festus guiding me, I submitted a letter from the Mid-West Government about my scholarship to the Crown Agents for Oversea Governments and Administrations, established in 1833, a British public statutory corporation under the supervision of the UK Ministry of Overseas Development. By the letter, the Crown Agents, which eventually transmuted into a private non-governmental company in 1997, were authorised to pay my tuition fees directly to the Imperial College, London, and also disburse monthly allowances to me for my board, lodging and local transportation. Using the money paid to me, I bought the most urgent necessities, including winter clothing, on November 18 and 19, 1971. I was then anxious to appear at the Imperial College.

Taking up My Admission at the Imperial College

On Monday, November 22, 1971, I showed up at the Registry of the Imperial College. As I waited for an officer to attend to me, the questions which the Visa Officer asked me in Benin City suddenly began to haunt me, as they coursed repeatedly through my mind. What would I do if I was told that I had come too late to join a programme that started in mid-September? When an officer was ready to attend to me, I introduced myself and showed her my documents. She wondered why it took me so long to take up my admission, since I was almost two months late, and asked me to give her some time to contact the Head of the Department of Theoretical Physics. After a while, she came back and said:

"Your Department is ready to receive you."

I was overwhelmed with joy. I completed the registration formalities and was allocated accommodation in one of the Imperial College student residential buildings at Evelyn Gardens in the Kensington and Chelsea local authority area of London. I quickly checked into the accommodation, which was a fairly large room with somewhat poor heating, and then rushed to the Department of Theoretical Physics, where I was already being awaited. The Head of Department, Professor Paul Taunton Mathews (November 19, 1919 – February 26, 1987) who later was appointed the Vice-Chancellor of the University of Bath, welcomed me. I was shown the lecture room for my courses. I met some of the course teachers and they graciously agreed to provide me with photocopies of their lecture notes during the almost two months when I was absent. From the voluminous nature of the notes that I eventually accumulated, it was evident that I had my work cut out for me. There were about 15 of us, all male, in the programme leading to the award of the Diploma of the Imperial College (DIC). Only three members of the class, namely, an Indian, a Lebanese and me, were non–Europeans.

A few days after joining the Department, I asked Professor Mathews about Dr. Raymond Frederick Streater, who was the main reason for my choosing to study at the Imperial College. He replied that Streater had been appointed in 1969 to the Chair of Applied Mathematics at Bedford College, established in 1849, another College of the University of London located at the

Regent's Park, London. The information was quite unsettling. But the immediate challenge was securing my DIC. I put my hands firmly to the plough, working daily round the clock. Some of the other lecturers in the Department of Theoretical Physics in 1971/72 were Professor Mohammad Abdus Salam (January 29, 1926 – 21 November 21, 1996), the Pakistan-born 1979 Nobel Prize laureate in Physics, Professor Thomas Walter Bannerman Kibble (December 23, 1932 – June 2, 2016), the future Emeritus Professor Robert Delbourgo, an Australian, and the future Professor Christopher John Isham. The examinations were conducted in May/June 1972 and I passed them, in partial fulfillment of the requirements for the DIC award. To be awarded the DIC, the submission of a supervised dissertation was required. My DIC dissertation was in the area of the algebraic approach to axiomatic quantum field theory as formulated in the so-called Haag-Kastler axioms by the versatile mathematical physicists Rudolf Haag (August 17, 1922 – January 5, 2016) and Daniel Kastler (March 4, 1926 – July 8, 2015) in their joint paper of 1964 published in the *Journal of Mathematical Physics*. Daniel Kastler was the son of the 1966 Physics Nobel Prize laureate Alfred Kastler (May 3, 1902 – 7 January 7, 1984). My dissertation concerned the inequivalent, irreducible representations of certain quasi-local algebras generated by the local C*-algebras associated with a class of quantum fields. It was supervised by Professor Delbourgo. The next stage was then the PhD research work.

Choosing a PhD Supervisor

As soon as the results of the DIC examinations were released, students of my set were assigned to supervisors for their PhD research activities. I was assigned to Professor Abdus Salam, who was also the Director of the International Centre for Theoretical Physics (ICTP), Trieste, Italy, established in 1964. One year after his death in 1996, the Centre was renamed the Abdus Salam

International Centre for Theoretical Physics. Professor Salam visited the Department at Imperial College about fortnightly. On one such visit, I met him in his office about my supervision.

He immediately reeled out his research plan for me: I was to work in the area of Elementary Particle Physics and would be required to concentrate on a computational problem as, according to him, a hands-on-approach to computation was what was best for scientists from developing countries. He was of the view that if developing countries built adequate capacity in computation, they would progressively address many of their developmental problems. He then asked me what I thought. I immediately had an eerie feeling of *déjà vu:* during my HSC programme, my Principal, Fr. Donnelly, wanted me to study Zoology (to become a medical doctor) but I wanted Mathematics; seven years later, Professor Salam wanted me to conduct my PhD research in Elementary Particle Physics but I wanted Axiomatic Quantum Field Theory, which was my main motivation for choosing Imperial College. After thanking him for his research plan for me, I told him that I was actually interested in Axiomatic Quantum Field Theory and would be glad if he could assign me a research topic in that area. He replied that he could not supervise me in Axiomatic Quantum Field Theory, as none of his students was working in that area at that time. According to him, he always wanted his students to be able to interact effectively among themselves and other scientists at the ICTP. Concluding, he said that if I wanted Axiomatic Quantum Field Theory, I could go to Professor Streater at Bedford College but that if I changed my mind, I should meet him the following week at the ICTP to start my research. He assured me that I would receive some supplementary funding. Even if I had no bias for Axiomatic Quantum Field Theory, the idea of moving to Trieste, Italy, for my research was problematic: I would need to inform the Nigerian High Commission and the Crown Agents in London as well as the Ministry of Education in Benin City about my relocation; and I would need a study visa for Italy. These could not be achieved within a week or two because, for example, I would need official approval from the Ministry of Education in Benin City which would then operate as an authorization for the Crown Agents to remit my monthly scholarship allowances to me in Italy. Consequently, I contacted Professor Streater who accepted to be my supervisor. He received his PhD degree at Imperial College in 1960 under the joint supervision of Professor Salam and Professor John Claytin Taylor, a Mathematical Physicist. The latter, who received his PhD degree at the University of Cambridge, UK, in 1955, also had Professor Salam as one of his two supervisors. In passing, I recall that Professor Salam also obtained his PhD degree at the University of Cambridge, UK, in 1952, with Professor Paul Taunton Matthews, who I had mentioned above, as one of his two supervisors.

At Bedford College

I joined Bedford College in 1972 for my PhD research work under the supervision of Professor Streater. The Head of Department was Professor Paul Moritz Cohn (January 8, 1924-April 20, 2006), a renowned German-Jewish Mathematician, who published numerous articles and several books in the area of Algebra. I carried out my PhD research work from 1972 to 1975, and was awarded the degree in April 1976. During the period of my research, there was the nagging open problem in Constructive Quantum Field Theory of how to construct quantum fields that satisfied the so-called Wightman Axioms, which I alluded to above. There were several approaches to confronting the problem and some partial results were obtained by a number of authors. In 1973, using a probabilistic approach, Professor Edward Nelson (May 4, 1932 – September 10, 2014), who was of the Department of Mathematics at Princeton University, USA, established that quantum fields could be constructed from certain generalised stochastic fields endowed with the so-called Markov property.

The latter had been discovered by the Russian Mathematician and atheist, Andrei Andreyevich Markov (June 14, 1856 – July 20, 1922), who was a faculty at the state-owned St. Petersburg University in Russia. Nelson's work thereby placed Markovian fields at the core of Constructive Quantum Field Theory, while simultaneously throwing up the challenge of determining which stochastic fields had the Markov property. My thesis was motivated by the felt need to meet this challenge: it established, among other results, necessary and sufficient conditions for a certain class of generalised stochastic fields to possess a certain notion of Markov property. By applying my results, it is possible to screen an interesting class of generalised stochastic fields for the Markov property. Then, adopting Nelson's probabilistic approach for constructing quantum fields, the members of the class that test positive for the property are identified as the appropriate candidates. Specifically, my thesis, which was a conflation of elements of several branches of Mathematics such as Stochastic Analysis, Functional Analysis, Group Theory, Schwartz Distributions (also called Generalised Functions) and Partial Differential Equations, was entitled: *A Markov Property for Multicomponent Euclidean Covariant Gaussian Generalised Stochastic Fields.* Professor Christopher J. Isham, of the Imperial College, London, an expert in Quantum Gravity and the Foundations of Quantum Theory, who I already mentioned above and whose PhD thesis was supervised by Professor Paul Taunton Matthews, also at the Imperial College London, was the external examiner during my defence of the thesis on Thursday, April 22, 1976. Since I obtained my PhD degree under the supervision of Professor Streater, I am, of course, not a direct PhD student of the Nobel Laureate Professor Abdus Salam. But using the terminology of the Mathematics Genealogy Project,[8] which maintains an online, global database on the academic genealogy of mathematicians, I am classified as a descendant of Professor Salam because Professor Streater was supervised by him. I published elements of the thesis

---

8   https://genealogy.math.ndsu.nodak.edu

in several journals and carried out additional work in the areas of classical and noncommutative stochastic analysis, C*-algebras, partial *-algebras and Functional Analysis.

At some of the conferences that I attended during my PhD research programme, I met several of the mathematicians and mathematical physicists who were at the forefront of a number of the new scientific developments in the 1970s. These included icons like Israïl Moyseyovich Gel'fand (September 2, 1913 – October 5, 2009), Arthur Strong Wightman (March 30, 1922 – January 13, 2013), Richard Vincent Kadison (July 25, 1925 – August 22, 2018), Edward Nelson (May 4, 1932 – September 10, 2014), Rudolf Haag (August 17, 1922 – January 5, 2016), Hans-Jürgen Borchers (January 24, 1926 – September 10, 2011), Huzihiro Araki, Arthur Jaffe, James Gilbert Glimm, Barry Martin Simon, Oscar Eramus Lanford III (January 6, 1940 – November 16, 2013), David Pierre Ruelle, John Rider Klauder, Kalyanapuram Rangachari Parthasarathy, Klaus Schmidt, Jakob Yngvason, Geoffrey Sewell, Sergio Doplicher, John Elias Roberts (1939–2015), Sergio Albeverio, Jan Raphael Hoegh-Krohn(February 10, 1938 – January 24, 1988), Ludwig Paulary Evert Streit and Ivan F. Wilde.

A Flying Visit to Ireland

As soon as I embarked on my PhD research activities in 1972, I contacted Fr. Donnelly in Ireland to intimate him about my presence in London. I did not receive any reply from him. But one morning in November of that year, my door bell rang. To my utter surprise the visitor was Fr. Joseph Patrick Donnelly, my former Principal at ICC. He arrived in a taxi. The cab's engine was kept running, as he asked about my welfare and made some jokes. I told him that Anthony Uyiekpen Osagie (June 7, 1947 – May 22, 2013), of blessed memory, was doing his postgraduate work at the University of Manchester and that Raymond Osemwegie Elaho was engaged in his postgraduate studies at the University of London, like me. There and then, Fr. Donnelly issued an invitation, through me, to the three of us to pay him a visit during the following summer in Ireland. He informed me that he was in charge of supervising SMA activities in West Africa and that the post took him frequently to the subregion. It was all so nice. Then Fr. Donnelly got into the waiting taxi, said good bye and was off. The following summer in 1973, I wrote on behalf of Tony Osagie, Ray Elaho and myself to inform Fr. Donnelly that we were set to visit him in Ireland. He agreed to the proposed visit and even promised to take us on a tour of Ireland. But before the trip could take place, he informed me that he had to travel again to West Africa and would not be back to Ireland during the period that we had all agreed for the visit. He assured us that there was no problem as Fr. Peter Thompson was at that time in Ireland and had been requested by him to be our host. We flew to Dublin airport and were picked up by Fr. Thompson. He was a perfect host who took us on an epic tour of Ireland. From Dublin, he drove us through County Roscommon, where his parents lived, to County Galway, County Tipperary and then to County Cork. We slept at the SMA house in Cork. Before leaving Cork, we visited the Blarney Castle, built by Cormac Laidir Maccarthy (1411–1494), less than 10 kilometres away. After touring the Castle, I joined other visitors to kiss the Blarney Stone, renowned as the *Stone of Eloquence*. On our way back to Dublin to catch our return flight, Fr. Thompson drove us from Cork through County Tipperary, County Laois, County Kildare and then to Dublin. The memory of that trip lingers in my mind. We acquired a good knowledge of the geography of Ireland, a country whose land mass is less than that of the sum of the land masses of Yobe and Zamfara States and whose population in 1973 was about 3 million, which is less than the current population of Adamawa State. In 2021, the population of Ireland was about 5 million, while that of Nigeria was estimated as 213 million. Over the years, in spite of its relatively tiny population, the impact of the selfless contributions of priests of the SMA (Ireland Province) to Nigeria's national development, through their steadfast implementation of the religious mission of the SMA, quality education, affordable healthcare and diverse life-changing social services, have been truly gargantuan.

(L-R) Future Emeritus Prof Ray Elaho, GOS and Prof Tony Osagie on a visit to Ireland during their PhD research in the UK

1973: A tourist guide positioning GOS to kiss the Blarney stone at the Blarney castle, near Cork, Republic of Ireland

Arising from his appointment as the pioneer diocesan Secretary of the Diocese of Issele-Uku, Fr. Thompson left ICC in 1973 to take up the new administrative and ecclesial position. He occupied the office of diocesan Secretay for five years and left Nigeria for Ireland in 1978. He considers his service under Bishop Gbuji and his assisting to set up the structures of the Diocese of Issele-Uku as together representing the greatest joy of his missionary life. Till date, five suffragan dioceses have been established in the Archdiocese of Benin, namely: Diocese of Warri (established on March 10, 1964), Diocese of Issele-Uku (established on July 5, 1973), Diocese of Auchi (established on December 4, 2002), Diocese of Uromi (established on December 14, 2005) and Diocese of Bomadi (established on September 21, 2017).

PART IV

ENTERING MARITAL LIFE

16

SEALING A LIFELONG UNION

I met Deborah Abieyuwa, my future wife, in 1970. Born on June 21, 1952, she is the first daughter of Mr. Alexander Airhihenbuwa Ogunmu (1921-1989), a veteran primary school teacher, and Madam Comfort Aimiemwekhomwan Ogunmu (nèe Aghedo) (1926-2014), an astute trader and housewife. I was in the last academic session of my undergraduate studies at the University of Ibadan. Deborah was a classmate of my cousin Magdalene Nugbasoro at the Itohan Girls Grammar School, Benin City. Magdalene later married Prince Anslem Aisologun Akenzua, who was subsequently installed as the Enogie of Orogho in the Orhionmwon Local Government Area of Edo State. Born by an Igbanke father and a Benin mother, Deborah possessed many of the quintessential traits that I wanted to see any woman who would be my wife.

1971: Deborah as my fiancée

Before travelling from Benin City to London in November 1971, my family had met Deborah's family to indicate my interest in marrying her. In line with the Benin tradition, each family then carried out discreet enquiries about the other, regarding matters like fertility issues, treatment of spouses, longevity of marital union, existence of adverse genetic traits, character of the suitor, character of the spinster and the overall societal perception of the other family. Deborah's family graciously gave its provisional assent to my family's proposal on November 15, 1971: a traditional marriage engagement between Deborah and I was thereby approved. But the traditional solemnization of the marriage, which would make Deborah my *de jure* wife, was deferred to a mutually agreeable date, when all the obligatory traditional rites would be meticulously performed. Nevertheless, after the traditional marriage engagement, Deborah became my *de facto* wife by traditional precept.

The Reunion

1971: Deborah and GOS during courtship

Deborah joined me in London in July 1973. By tradition, Deborah was my wife, even though I had not yet paid her dowry. I planned to clear that traditional hurdle as soon as I returned to Nigeria. Also, our relationship was yet to acquire the status of a sacrament in the Catholic tradition. As Catholics, both of us were determined to work toward the solemnisation of our marriage as early as feasible.

A few days after Deborah's arrival in London, I was off to Erice, Sicily, Italy, to participate in a conference on Axiomatic Quantum Field Theory. One of the trending challenges in those days was how to construct quantum fields in four space-time dimensions that satisfied all the Wightman axioms. At the forefront of the constructive approach were Professor Arthur Michael Jaffe, whose PhD thesis was supervised by Professor Arthur Strong Wightman, and Professor James Gilbert Glimm, whose PhD thesis was supervised by Professor Richard Vincent Kadison (July 25, 1925 – August 22, 2018). Glimm and Jaffe had achieved some progress by constructing such fields in two space-time dimensions. The challenge was how to scale up the Glimm-Jaffe construction to four space-time dimensions. While the mathematical physics community tried to tackle this conundrum, Professor Edward Nelson (May 4, 1932 – September 10, 2014) introduced a probabilistic approach in 1973. He showed, as I had previously mentioned, that quantum fields could be constructed from Markov fields in any space-time dimension. The Erice conference revolved largely around how to utilise Nelson's ideas in the general study of quantum fields. On the other hand, there was the underlying question of how to characterise Markov fields. As narrated earlier, my PhD thesis was principally devoted to addressing this fundamental question.

Sacred Union in London

Deborah quickly settled down to life in London. She enrolled for a course in computing, which was a rapidly evolving specialty. On my part, my PhD research activities were gathering momentum. What engrossed my mind was the task of acquiring the key tools for accomplishing my research goals: *-algebras, stochastic analysis, measure theory, theory of distributions (generalised functions), pseudo-differential equations, complex analysis and functional analysis, especially the Hille-Yosida theory of semigroups, named after the American mathematician Carl Einar Hille (June 28, 1894 –February 12, 1980) and the Japanese mathematician Kōsaku Yosida (February 7, 1909 – June 20, 1990). Deborah was also deeply preoccupied with her studies.

Toward the end of 1975, we were in a position to embark on planning the solemnisation of our marriage: Deborah had completed her studies and I had submitted my PhD thesis in September 1975 toward its oral defence by me. We then chose March 1976 for the solemnisation activities. In planning the later, Deborah and I were of one mind: we jointly delineated some boundaries. We were aware that many in Nigeria had escalated the pomp, pageantry and financial expenses of church marriages to the stratosphere. We rejected such ostentation. We had attended some marriage ceremonies and also watched others involving some Britons in London. Guests at the ceremonies and the associated social events were often less than forty or fifty, and generally about twenty or twenty five. We resolved that our wedding ceremony would be modest. Moreover, as there is no prescription in the Bible that a bride and bridegroom must wear a gown and a suit, respectively, we decided to do away with these. Instead, we settled for Nigerian dresses as our wedding attire. Concerning guests, we invited not more than twenty. We were extremely happy that we could take these fundamental decisions between us, without outside pressure of any kind. Planning for the same wedding ceremony in Benin City or Ibadan, we would have been obliged to invite between 200 and 500 guests, provide entertainment and buy presents for the guests, rent a sizeable hall for the social activities and ensure that the hall was befittingly decorated. All these would then gulp a large amount of money, much of which could have been deplored to address other pressing needs.

The solemnisation of our marriage took place on March 20, 1976, at the Church of the Most Precious Blood and St. Edmund, King Martyr in the London Borough of Enfield. The parish priest, Fr. Norman Francis Kersey (August 3, 1918 – July 24, 1999), officiated. Born in Finchley, North London, UK, Fr. Kersey was ordained on June 19, 1943 by Coadjutor Archbishop Edward Myers (September 8, 1875 – September 13, 1956) at the Westminster Cathedral. Like many a Catholic faithful, the kind and hardworking Fr. Kersey found some of the unprecedented changes approved at the Second Ecumenical Council of the Vatican, commonly known as the Vatican II, held from October 11, 1962 to December 8, 1965, quite unexpected and unsettling. Nevertheless, in his parish, he obediently and diligently implemented the changes to the best of his ability. Vatican II is the successor to the First Ecumenical Council of the Vatican (also known as Vatican I), held from December 8, 1869 to October 20,

1870, which is credited with the existing doctrinal definition of papal infallibility and its dogmatisation.

During our pre-marriage interaction with Fr. Kersey, Deborah and I informed him that we were essentially married by Benin tradition. In the marriage certificate, he reflected this information by writing: *previously went through a form of marriage at Benin City, Nigeria, on 15th November, 1971.* A relation, Mr. Samuel Igbe, gave Deborah away. My classmate at ICC, Mr. Andrew Babatunde Eke, the future Deputy Director of the National Business and Technical Examinations Board (NABTEB), established in 1992, was my bestman while Mrs. Regina Woghiren was my wife's chief bridesmaid. As planned, we had about twenty guests. At the end of the church wedding ceremony, the guests retired to my flat at 27, All Saints Close, Off Victoria Road, Edmonton, London N9 9AT, for a modest reception.

With the ecclesial solemnisation of our marriage out of the way, what remained was the payment by me of my wife's dowry: an act that would serve as the ultimate imprimatur on the marriage, in line with the ageless mores and tradition of the Benin people. In a ceremony involving Deborah's family and mine, the traditional rite of dowry payment was performed in March 1977 at Igbanke, Edo State. A lifelong union was thereby sealed and delivered.

PART V

IN THE ACADEMIA

17

BACK TO THE PREMIER UNIVERSITY

When the euphoria associated with my successful defence in April 1976 of my PhD thesis had dissipated, it was time for me to enter the next phase of my life: pursuing my lifelong goal to join the ranks of university teachers and researchers. Academic sessions started annually in September in most parts of the world, including Nigeria, and offers of academic employments normally took effect from the beginning of an academic year. Before completing my PhD degree programme, I received several overtures from some universities asking me to consider their institutions for employment. For example, from Nigeria, I was invited to apply to the Department of Physics, University of Benin, Benin City, by the future Professor Paul Olekanma Ogbuehi (September 5, 1936 – November 27, 2016), highly revered by his professional peers as the "founding father of Optometric Education in Nigeria", who was at that time the Acting Head of Department. To evaluate the different propositions, I applied a number of metrics: annual salary, conditions of service, workplace environment, my responsibility as a Mid-West Government Scholar and the fact that my mother, who was already quite old, needed my attention and support. In the 1970's, the salaries in Nigerian universities and in many British universities were comparable: this fact acted as a veritable magnet that continually pulled many foreign scholars, comprising students and academic staff, to the Nigerian academic space in those years. As a result, there was a high level of internationalisation of many Nigerian universities, evidenced by the presence of a large number of scholars from around the globe in the Nigerian University System. Hence, from the salary perspective, not much financial advantage was likely to accrue to me if I accepted a job in the UK. Also very attractive in those days were the conditions of service and the workplace environment in Nigerian universities. On my return to Nigeria, I was expected to join the University of Benin, which was an institution established by the Mid-West Government at the time I left Nigeria for the UK in 1971, because I was a Mid-West Government scholar. But before I completed my PhD degree programme in April 1976, the University of Benin, which started as the Mid-West Institute of Technology in 1970 but later changed to its present name in April 1972, had become a Federal university on April 1, 1975. As a result, there was no State university any more in Benin City, or the entire Mid-West State, in 1976. Finally, it was evident that if I returned to Nigeria, I would be able to support my aged mother, who gave up everything so that I could have something. Consequently, I decided to return to Nigeria. To actualise this decision, I wrote to Professor Ogbuehi, informing him that I had successfully completed my PhD degree programme and was open to his invitation.

My Route to the Department of Mathematics

The whole of May and June 1976 passed by without any response from Professor Ogbuehi. It was clear that I needed to act quickly if I was to be employed in the 1976/1977 academic year which was starting in September 1976. Consequently, in July 1976, I wrote to Professor Olumuyiwa Awe, who was the Head of the

Department of Physics during my final year at the University of Ibadan, informing him that I had obtained a PhD in Mathematical Physics at the University of London and would like to join his Department at Ibadan. My thinking was that he was still the Head of the Department of Physics at the University of Ibadan, unaware that his tenure as Head had ended.

Professor Awe's reply was quite swift. Moreover, his response showed that he had done considerably far more than the request in my exploratory letter to him. After congratulating me for earning the PhD degree, he indicated that he was no longer the Head of Department but Professor Akpanoluo Ikpong Ikpong Ette (September 23, 1929 – March 27 2015), one of my past teachers; that he had discussed my interest in an appointment with Professor Ette. He disclosed that Professor Ette informed him that there was no vacancy in the Department at that point in time but that he would endeavour to contact me directly. Professor Awe also revealed that he had shown the title of my thesis to Professor Awele Maduemezia, a renowned theoretical physicist in the Department, and that Professor Maduemezia's opinion was that the subject of my thesis was in the area of mathematics, and not physics (as a matter of fact, I had done my PhD degree programme in a Department of Mathematics at the University of London). Based on Professor Maduemezia's opinion, Professor Awe, quite proactively and altruistically, contacted the Head of the Department of Mathematics, Professor Haroon Oladipo Tejumola, about the feasibility of an appointment for me. Professor Tejumola indicated that his Department was in a position to offer me a temporary appointment, which could subsequently be regularised after an interview. Professor Tejumola then promised to contact me directly on the matter. I was greatly overwhelmed by Professor Awe's unquantifiable kindness and also greatly humbled by his resolute problem-solving and results-oriented approach to dealing with the issue that I referred to him. His actions were beyond my wildest expectations. As a result of Professor Awe's generous game-changing initiatives, I soon received two letters: one from Professor Ette and the other from Professor Tejumola.

Professor Ette's letter referred to his interaction with Professor Awe regarding my quest for employment. He then expressed his congratulations to me for successfully completing my PhD degree programme but regretted that there was no vacancy in the Department at that time. He hoped that I would be employed by the Department of Mathematics and added that if I still did not secure a position by the end of September 1976, I should let him know. He then ended by saying that if the latter event occurred, he was ready to make a special case to the Vice-Chancellor to offer me a temporary employment in his Department. At that time, the Vice-Chancellor of the University of Ibadan was the eminent historian, Professor Tekena Nitonye Tamuno (January 28, 1932 - April 11, 2015).

The second letter was from Professor Tejumola. He mentioned his discussion with Professor Awe. He then said that his Department of Mathematics was ready to have me as a member of its academic staff and that he was sending a recommendation to the Vice-Chancellor to offer me a temporary employment.

The two letters by Professor Ette and Professor Tejumola were not only extremely encouraging but also immensely morale-boosting: I looked anxiously forward to receiving a letter of appointment from the Vice-Chancellor of the University of Ibadan. But I received no such letter throughout July 1976 and even throughout the first two weeks of August 1976. Was the letter being processed but possibly encountering some delays as a result of the slowly turning wheels of the university's bureaucracy? Unable to fathom why I had still not received the letter by the middle of August 1976, I decided to visit the University of Ibadan Liaison Office in London, to see what help the office could render in facilitating the delivery of the letter that I was expecting. I met the head of the Liaison Office, a British lady, explained the reason for my visit, showed her the original copy of Professor Tejumola's letter and requested her to kindly contact the Vice-Chancellor at Ibadan. After reading the letter, she told me that there was no need for her to contact the Vice-Chancellor: she revealed that the Vice-Chancellor was holding a meeting with the University Registrar in an adjoining room in the building and that I should wait to meet him. Not long, the Vice-Chancellor, Professor Tamuno, entered the waiting room where I was seated and he introduced himself. He said that it was clear that Professor Tejumola was unaware that he was not in the country when the letter was written. We had a brief discussion. Then, Professor Tamuno summoned the University Registrar, Samuel Jemieta Okudu (June 24, 1934 – 2006), and asked him to issue me a letter of temporary appointment as Lecturer Grade 2. Within about thirty minutes, I had a letter of appointment in my hand. There were provisions in the letter for air tickets for me and my family to Lagos and for transporting my personal effects to Ibadan. Thus, by happenstance, I received promptly in London that which I anxiously expected from far away Ibadan. I arrived in Lagos on Saturday, September 25, 1976. After spending a few days in Benin City with my family, I travelled to Ibadan on Thursday, September 30, 1976. I was warmly received by Professor Tejumola. He personally drove me and my wife in his car to the Premier Hotel, Ibadan, and ensured that we were checked-in. The hotel was my temporary accommodation for a while. Since my appointment took effect from October 1, 1976, a national holiday, I assumed duty on October 2, 1976. For completeness, I should mention that around the middle of September 1976, I received a letter from Professor Ogbuehi reiterating his Department's interest to employ me. But that kind gesture had been overtaken by events because, by Providence, I was already headed inexorably toward the University of Ibadan.

18

THE PREMIER UNIVERSITY AS WORKPLACE

My assumption of duty as Lecturer Grade 2 at the University of Ibadan on October 2, 1976, some twenty-eight years after the founding of the institution, was for me a defining and fulfilling moment, as it marked my continuing and, ultimately, lifelong journey through the world of academia. It was at a time when the University of Ibadan, and indeed all Nigerian universities, needed and were recruiting well trained and top-rate academics. From the 1960s, many Nigerian universities pursued staff development with steadfast determination through, for example, awarding postgraduate scholarships to their students who graduated with First Class Honours or Second Class Honours (Upper Division) while simultaneously providing cutting-edge teaching and research facilities. As I disclosed in a previous Chapter, I had resolved from the outset to carry out my postgraduate research activities outside Nigeria because my research interest was in the area of Axiomatic Quantum Field Theory: there was, in those days, no expert in Nigeria who was in a position to supervise my work in that branch of Mathematical Physics.

Signing the Institutional Register

After I was formally received on October 2, 1976 into the Department by Professor Tejumola, who was the Acting Head of the Department of Mathematics, he advised me that, as a new member of staff, I was required to sign a register at the Vice-Chancellor's Office. I complied with his advice. At the Vice-Chancellor's Office, I was ushered into the presence of the Vice-Chancellor, Professor Tamuno, who I had met in London and who approved my temporary appointment. A simple, unassuming, soft-spoken and genial person, Professor Tamuno was happy to see me again, following our brief meeting in London. He hoped that I would enjoy the academic and social life at the University. I then signed the institutional register in his presence, an act that signalled my formal entry into the University of Ibadan academia.

The University of Ibadan that I Knew

During the period from 1948 to 1970, the University of Ibadan vigorously pursued institutional, academic and student-centred capacity building activities, through highly competitive staff and student recruitment and the provision of state-of-the-art teaching, learning and research resources. The Nuffield Foundation (established in 1943), Rockefeller Foundation (established on May 14, 1913), Ford Foundation (established on January 15, 1936), British Council (established in 1934) and a number of other international non-governmental organisations (INGOs) were veritable partners of the University of Ibadan. They supplied much of the resource oxygen that fuelled the implementation of a plethora of the university's core activities. The INGOs facilitated the internationalisation of the University, through their support for inter-university cooperation, collaboration and linkages, staff and student mobility as well as funding for participation in local and foreign conferences, provision of research grants and aiding staff and student visits to internationally renowned foreign institutions for research or sabbatical leave. During the Nigerian civil war from July 6, 1967 to January 15, 1970, some of the INGOs moved out of Nigeria. After the war, even those INGOs which had offices on the campus closed shop. Additionally, with the establishment of several universities in the country after Nigeria's independence, there were other competitors for the INGOs' support and partnership. As a consequence, the quantum of resources which the University attracted from government and its partners dipped substantially.

Department of Mathematics and the University Library

With the foregoing in mind, before I left London for Ibadan to take up my appointment, I was somewhat apprehensive about whether I would have the full range of resources that I needed for my teaching and research functions in a timely and continuous manner. At the University of London (UL), I had unfettered access to the libraries of its multiple colleges and institutes. Moreover, the Bedford College Library would leverage on a UK-wide inter-library loan system to fetch for me from other institutions anywhere in Britain any books, journals or documents which were unavailable in its collection. Might there be an analogous nationwide inter-library loan system in Nigeria? Preparing for a scenario of possible scarce academic resources, I tried to equip myself as much as I could. I visited three of the foremost bookshops in London on multiple occasions to buy many of the textbooks that I considered indispensable to my teaching and research activities. The bookshops were the Dillons Booksellers, located on Gower Street, London, and founded in 1932 by Agnes Joseph Madeline Dillon (8 January 1903 – 4 April 1993), more commonly known as Una Dillon; the W&G Foyle Ltd. (simply called Foyles), located on Charing Cross Road, London, established in 1903 by two brothers called William Alfred Westropp Foyle (1885-1963) and Gilbert Foyle (1886-1971); and the H.K. Lewis & Co. Ltd. (publisher, bookseller & lending library), established in 1844, by

Henry King Lewis (1823-1898), also located on Gower Street London. Additionally, I took out subscriptions to some journals which I considered crucial to my research work. Because of the sheer weight of the numerous books and journals that I eventually accumulated, I arranged for their shipment by sea to Nigeria. At Ibadan, the two bookshops that stocked educational materials were Odusote Bookshop, located on Obafemi Awolowo Way, Oke-Ado, and the University of Ibadan Bookshop, established in the 1950s, originally as a section of the then University College Library. I was quite familiar with these bookshops, as I had patronised them during my undergraduate days at the University of Ibadan. In those days, they stocked almost all the textbooks which were prescribed by lecturers in the diverse Departments throughout the University. Moreover, whenever the need arose, each of these shops took and delivered orders in respect of books which were not available in its inventory.

State of Academic Resources

To prepare for my teaching and research activities, I visited the Departmental Library and the University Library to assess the level of available academic resources held by them. I was pleasantly surprised to find that the libraries were as richly stocked as the ones that I had used in London: several copies of each of the books that I had spent a lot of money to acquire were either in the Departmental Library or in the University Library, and sometimes in both. Moreover, the most recent copies of some of the journals in respect of which I had made costly subscriptions before leaving London were available in the University Library. It was also customary in those days for the University Librarian to issue calls throughout an academic session requesting academic staff to recommend state-of-the-art books and journals which the University Library should acquire. The strategy ensured the relevance, diversity and continuous growth of the acquisitions.

Inside the Department

As I settled down in the Department, I found myself in the midst of colleagues, some of whom had taught me during my undergraduate days. Using their titles as at 1976, my teacher-colleagues were: the Acting Head of Department, Dr. Haroon Oladipo Tejumola (July 8, 1937–December 25, 2011), Dr. Monsur Akangbe Kenku (December 14, 1942–June 24, 2021), Dr. Aderemi Oluyomi Kuku (March 20, 1941-February 13, 2022), Dr. Gabriel Oluremi Olaofe (December 6, 1937–February 6, 1994), and Dr. Anthony Guillen-Preckler (February 24, 1934–February 20, 2011). Dr. Guillen-Preckler, a Spaniard who died in 2011, arrived in Nigeria in October 1966 as a member of a team that started the apostolic work of the *Opus Dei*. The members of staff who I had never met before joining the Department were Professor Adegoke Olubummo (April 19, 1923–October 26, 1992), Dr. Charles Olusegun Adedayo Sowunmi (September 14, 1934–December 3, 2007), Dr. Uwadiegwu Boniface Chukwugozie Okafor Ejike (September 25, 1941–May 18, 2008), Dr. Samuel Akindiji Ilori, Dr. Victor Adekola Babalola (December 24, 1941–April 19, 2021), Dr. Olusola Akinyele (May 11, 1944–August 18, 2021), Dr. Timothy Olufemi Adewoye (August 15, 1948–August 17, 2018) and Dr. Olabisi Oreofe Ugbebor, using their titles as at 1976, as well as a host of expatriates from India, Switzerland, United Kingdom and the United States of America. I had not met these colleagues before my assumption of duty because as my degree major was Physics, I took only a number of prescribed ancillary mathematics courses up to my second year in the University of Ibadan. All my Nigerian colleagues listed above became full professors over the years. Academically, as I wrote elsewhere, I met a Department in which,

> there was already a deeply entrenched, thriving and balanced mathematics ecosystem, comprising several specialisations or mathematical worlds: algebra, analysis, topology, geometry, number theory, applied mathematics, differential equations, mechanics, biomathematics and numerical analysis; I was bringing

mathematical physics and noncommutative stochastic analysis on topological *-algebras to the table.[9]

Similarly, the future Professor Olabisi Oreofe Ugbebor (née Grace Olabisi Falode), an alumna of the University of Ibadan and the University of London, who joined the Department a few months before me, added measure theory and probability theory to the basket of available specialisations. Professor Ugbebor earned her PhD at the University of London in 1976. The need arose again in the early 1980s to further expand the diversity of the set of available specialisations in the Department of Mathematics by adding a branch of mathematics pertaining to decision-making and mathematical optimisation. Accordingly, operations research, which is concerned with finding optimal conditions for multi-criteria decision-making, subject to some prescribed constraints, became an additional field of specialization. Teaching and research in operations research, which has myriads of applications in diverse branches of knowledge, were introduced and pioneered in the Department by Dr. William Friday Amar Aigbe, who obtained his PhD in Hungary. The future Daudu of Ibhiolulu, Uwessan, Irrua; Esere of Irrua, Esan Central; Justice of Peace; Honorary Consul of Hungary in Lagos and recipient of the Knight's Cross of Hungarian Order of Merit, Dr. Aigbe joined the Department in 1980 as a National Youth Service Corps member and was appointed to the post of a Lecturer Grade II after his Service year. Through his exemplary teaching and research activities, operations research quickly became a very popular specialisation that annually attracted many new postgraduate students to the Department. Dr. Aigbe successfully produced two doctoral graduates in operations research before leaving the Department for the private sector. They are the future University of Ibadan Associate Professor Chukwuma Raphael Nwozo (July 24, 1951 – December 4, 2017) and the future Ebonyi State University Professor Ugochukwu Anulaobi Osisiogu.

---

9   G.O.S. Ekhaguere: A Life of Mathematics and Service, in: *Samuel Akindiji Ilori: Tributes and Reflections at Seventy,* edited by G.O.S. Ekhaguere, Deborah O.A. Ajayi and H.P. Adeyemo, pages 19-25, published by the Department of Mathematics, University of Ibadan, Ibadan, 2015.

While immersing myself in the Department of Mathematics in 1976, what was also pleasing to me was the fact that[10],

> the Department was as sophisticated in every respect as the one I had just left at the University of London, UK.

Moreover, several of my colleagues[11]

> were young and highly talented, operating at the commanding heights of their specialisations.

The mathematics research space in Nigeria was indubitably dominated and governed by the Department of Mathematics, University of Ibadan. Like me, most of my colleagues earned their PhD degrees in foreign universities. Only a few had the University of Ibadan PhD degree: these were supervised by Professor Adegoke Olubummo, Professor James Okoye Chukuka Ezeilo (January 17, 1930 – January 4, 2013) and Professor Hyman Bass, who was a member of staff of the Columbia University, New York, USA. With the exception of Functional Analysis, the specialisations in the Department were so disparate that research activities were carried out in a largely insular fashion: not many knew in reasonable detail, even after participating in the Department's weekly seminars, what their colleagues were studying and why. I did not perceive a clear and deliberate Departmental policy designed to consciously build or proactively foster a culture of research cooperation among staff: the research articles published by almost every one of us were invariably single-authored. In spite of this research management glitch, the Department's status in the world of mathematics has, over the years, been relatively enviable, even in the face of immense resource challenges. In this regard, the resources available to the Department for teaching and research began to dwindle in the mid-1980s as a result of continuous poor Federal funding of its universities, with conspicuous and inevitable adverse effects on research capacity and staff development.

---

10   *ibid.*
11   *ibid.*

The Golden Age of Mathematics at UI

What should one consider as the Department's defining era? I answered this question in the reference above[12] as follows.

> Without any reservation, I am inclined to characterise the two-decade period from 1970 to 1989 as certainly the golden years of mathematics at UI. The following persons, all male, were professors in the Department at one time or the other during the period: A. Olubummo, H.O. Tejumola, C.O.A. Sowunmi, G.O. Olaofe, A.O. Kuku, S.A. Ilori, O. Akinyele and GOS Ekhaguere. This constellation of experts, together with their non-professorial colleagues and the impressive mathematical diversity represented by their collective specialisations, ensured that the highly talented and impressionable students, who were drawn to the Department, not only from Nigeria but also from the entire continent of Africa, received world-class mathematics training. Above all, the standing of the Department in the global mathematical community and its status as the nation's foremost centre for undergraduate and postgraduate mathematics training and research were consolidated and considerably enhanced during the period. In those days, mathematics seminars flourished and formed an integral part of the continuous professional development of staff and students. Indeed, we lived from day to day, waiting longingly for the week's seminar because it was always an exciting academic experience to listen to most speakers.

Over the years, a number of scholars who were taught by me became my colleagues in the Department. Some of them are Professor Ezekiel Olusola Ayoola, Professor Victor Folarin Payne, (May 6, 1949-January 20, 2018), Professor Deborah Olayide Ajayi, Reader (Associate Professor) Chukwuma Raphael Nwozo, Reader (Associate Professor) Dr. Unanaowo Nyong Bassey, Senior Lecturer Michael Enioluwafe, Senior Lecturer Dr. Peter Olutola Arawomo, Senior Lecturer Dr. Olawale Sunday Obabiyi and Lecturer Dr. Ini Adinya. I should say a few words about the late Dr. Chukwuma Raphael Nwozo. He joined the Department of Mathematics during my tenure, from 1993 to

12   ibid.

1996, as Head. I recommended him for a temporary appointment, which was subsequently regularised, to enable me to fill a void that had unexpectedly emerged in the teaching of operations research, following Dr. Aigbe's withdrawal of service. Dr. Nwozo singlehandedly bore the enormous burden of training the rapidly increasing number of undergraduate and postgraduate students who were continuously attracted to operations research. In my view, he carried out his duties and responsibilities with outstanding commitment, innovation, dedication and unblemished integrity. Dr. Nwozo became the indisputable face of operations research, especially mathematical optimisation, not only at the University of Ibadan but also throughout the nation's higher education system.

My Progression through the Ranks

Joining the Department from the University of London, I was quite aware of the significance of research as a crucial determinant of the career path and reputation of an academic. At the University of Ibadan, a lot of premium was rightly placed on research, especially in respect of appointments and promotions. Antithetically, in those days, no official significance was attributed to teaching when evaluating a lecturer for appointment or promotion. So it was possible to secure appointment or promotion even if one was a poor teacher as long as one was good in research. In recent years, efforts have been made to carry out student evaluations of teaching and integrate their outcomes into the promotion criteria, as a way of formulating a fairly balanced appointments and promotions system.

In the midst of periodic administrative assignments, I pursued my teaching and research functions with determination and panache. In the 1970s, there was nothing like the internet, whose protocol suite the Transmission Control Protocol/Internet Protocol (TCP/IP) was standardised in 1982. Desktop or laptop computers and printers, which are ubiquitous today, were not in existence in those days.

To produce a research paper for publication, one first typed it on stencils with a typewriter, such as an IBM typewriter which had some balls with mathematical symbols. Then the stencils were printed onto paper on a stencil printer such as a *Gestetner* machine. Thereafter one posted the paper off to an international journal. The journals that I used were mainly in the UK and the USA and were of world-class. It took about two weeks for the paper to be received by the journal, which would immediately send an acknowledgement. Then the refereeing process, which could take up to one year to complete, would begin. One then received a provisional letter of acceptance, subject to the successful implementation of a number of corrections or clarifications. All told, getting a paper published in those days sometimes took up to, or sometimes exceeded, one year. The peer review process was therefore a significant factor that determined the speed of accumulating the requisite number of publications for moving from one rank to another. With the internet, it is today the new normal to submit a manuscript online and instantly receive an acknowledgement. The peer review process is often concluded within a much shorter period of time. The internet and the ease of submitting manuscripts through it for publication have led to a proliferation of journals, a large number of which are predatory and of abysmally inferior quality. This means that it is possible for a researcher to flaunt a large number of papers published in a very short time in predatory journals and then be swiftly promoted by some universities, which do not have rigorous rules for the assessment of the quality of research outputs, to the grade of professor or to employ the low quality publications to secure choice jobs. The deleterious impact of this toxic trend on national development, especially in developing countries, has been aptly characterised by the Cornell University (USA) theoretical physicist, Professor Paul Ginsparg (born: January 1, 1955), the creator of the electronic academic repository called *arXiv* for e-preprints, as follows:

Journals without quality control are destructive, especially for developing world countries where governments and universities are filling up with people with bogus scientific credentials.

For some researchers today, it is no longer 'publish or perish', which was a slogan intended to foster ethical research conduct, hard work, creativity and national development but rather what I characterise as 'publish and perish'. This phrase is intended to capture the rapidly emerging context in which many unscrupulous academic authors are perishing professionally or rapidly sliding scholastically into academic recession, in spite of publishing or flaunting long lists of publications, following the formulation by several universities of stringent criteria for combating unethical research conduct, fostering creativity and recognising authentic research works.

Moving from Grade to Grade

For promotion from one grade to the next, a candidate would inform his Head of Department of his wish to be considered. A Departmental committee would evaluate the wish and make an affirmative recommendation to the Head, if found meritorious. The Head would then send a formal recommendation for promotion to the Faculty of Science, through the Dean. At the Faculty, three assessors, within the University, would be appointed to evaluate the candidate's publications. If at least two of the assessors returned favourable verdicts, the Faculty would approve the transmission of the candidate's request, together with the assessors' reports, to the University's Appointments and Promotions Committee (UAPC). For promotions up to the grade of Senior Lecturer, the UAPC would simply ratify the positive recommendations of the assessors, in case there are no objections. In the case of promotion to the professorial cadre, namely: Reader or Professor, the UAPC would appoint three other assessors from the global academic community, outside the University, to submit evaluations of the candidate's publications, while adhering to the University's promotions criteria. The candidate's promotion would be approved by the UAPC if at least, two of the three assessors found the candidate promotable. From the foregoing, to be promoted from the grade of Senior Lecturer directly to the professorial cadre, a candidate would be assessed by three experts from within the University and three experts from outside the University. In my case, only one expert could be found within the University for the evaluation of my publications at the Faculty level; consequently two other assessors were appointed from outside the University. Hence, for the two-stage evaluation of my publications, one assessor within the University and five assessors outside the University were utilised: an exceptionally rigorous appraisal.

My progression through the ranks to the professorial cadre was as follows. With effect from October 1, 1978, I assumed the rank of Lecturer Grade 1, two years after my appointment. Then, I was promoted to the grade of Senior Lecturer with effect from October 1, 1982. From the grade of Senior Lecturer, I leapfrogged to the grade of full Professor with effect from October 1, 1988, thereby skipping the grade of Reader, also called the grade of Associate Professor in some Nigerian universities. When I retired from the University of Ibadan on May 23, 2017, I had held the position of full professor for close to twenty-eight and half years.

My Research

As I alluded above, promotions or appointments to all academic cadres in the University were, during my upward academic advancement, based exclusively on outstanding performance in research, assessed by the quality and quantity of research publications, presentations at conferences and the opinion of peers around the world. Teaching, participation in University administration and service to the outside world were neither evaluated nor incorporated in the promotions or appointments criteria, even though these were time-guzzling activities with direct impact on the time available to a person for research. That institutional mindset was largely unfair and hurtful to the career advancement of several academics who always accepted administrative assignments or positions for the overall good of the institution and the nation. Toward formulating equitable promotions or appointments criteria, the University has, in recent years, tried to construct some kind of balance between the triad: 'publication, teaching and service' (to the nation and the international community).

I joined Department of Mathematics, where everyone conducted his research almost as a recluse, with virtually no collaboration. As a mathematical physicist, with profound interest in axiomatic quantum field theory and who carried out his PhD research programme in Department of Mathematics, it was possible for me to relate with a number of the prevailing specialisations: functional analysis, especially the structure and representation theory of topological *-algebras, group theory, especially representation theory, and noncommutative stochastic analysis, including classical stochastic analysis. I employed these and other specialisations in my research. My publications were always a conflation of elements of multiple specialisations. The first indication that my research work was gradually being recognised, at least institutionally, was when I was promoted to the rank of Lecturer Grade 1 in 1978, two years after my appointment. That was a case of accelerated promotion, since it normally took a minimum of three years for such a promotion. I progressed steadily with my academic work, quickly attaining the apex of my career. Journeying through life, one soon finds, quite surprisingly, that some persons become jealous and antagonistist when they see others advancing at a pace they are unable to replicate or match. I did not allow this realisation to interfere with my diverse activities because I was always inspired by the following advice of the American entrepreneur and motivational speaker, Emanuel James Rohn (September 17, 1930 – December 5, 2009), also called Jim Rohn:

> Let others lead small lives, but not you.
> Let others argue over small things, but not you.
> Let others cry over small hurts, but not you.
> Let others leave their future in someone else's hands, but not you.

In my life journey, I am also leveraging the following observation by the iconic Irish poet and playwright, Oscar Fingal O'Flahertie Wills Wilde (October 16, 1854 – November 30, 1900):

> There is only one thing in life worse than being talked about and that is not being talked about.

With time, I discovered that, almost globally, many who make deafening noises often do not make much mathematics while many who truly make much mathematics often do not make any noise at all. As an academic, I always invited, welcomed and appreciated constructive and value-adding criticisms because they strengthened me by allowing me to take multiple perspectives on board. But there is always more than one side to every coin. When it came to how I should deal with non-academic, non-scientific or generally unconstructive criticisms, I always surmised that some of the latter probably depicted a situation where I should simply apply Hanlon's philosophical razor (by Robert Joseph Hanlon (December 28, 1932 – May 30, 1998) of Scranton, Pennsylvania):

> Never attribute to malice that which is adequately explained by stupidity [or incompetence].

Over the years, I have observed that certain criticisms were made by some critics simply out of ignorance or incompetence, or both, rather than pure malice.

At the NAMP Conference in Lausanne

With my first promotion as a huge motivation, I set my sights on movement to the grade of Senior Lecturer. Attainment of the goal was evidently contingent on steadfast and intensified research performance on my part. In 1979, I applied to attend an International Conference on Mathematical Physics, scheduled to take place from August 20-26, 1979, at the École Polytechnique Fédérale de Lausanne, Lausanne, Switzerland. Organised by the International Association of Mathematical Physics, established in 1976, a prospective participant was required to pay a registration fee. I requested for a waiver of the registration fee and the chairman of the local organising committee, Professor Phillippe Choquard, whose PhD degree was supervised by the Austrian theoretical physicist Professor Wolfgang Ernst Pauli (April 25, 1900-December 15, 1958), graciously obliged. The next set of challenges then comprised finding the airfare to Lausanne as well as the financial resources for my hotel expenses and local travel in Lausanne. I brought this conundrum to the attention of my friend, the future Emeritus Professor Benjamin Ohiomahme Elugbe, who advised me to intimate my Head of Department, Professor Tejumola, with the situation. As was his genial nature, Professor Tejumola promised to also intimate the then incumbent Vice-Chancellor, Professor Samson Olajuwon Kokumo Olayide (1928-1984), with the challenges. The pleasant outcome was that Professor Olayide graciously approved money, under the staff development fund, for my airfare to Lausanne as well as for my hotel expenses and local travel in Lausanne. Consequently, I was able to participate actively in the conference and also interact with several eminent mathematicians and mathematical physicists. One of these was an Indian who told me that he was attending the conference from Germany, where he was a Fellow of the Alexander von Humboldt Foundation (AvH Foundation), established in its present form on December 10, 1953, by the government of the Federal Republic of Germany and named after the polymath Friedrich Wilhelm Heinrich Alexander von Humboldt (September 14 176 – May 6, 1859). As I was not previously aware of the existence of the Foundation, the Indian scholar gave me some information about the entity and how to apply for a Fellowship. The number of Fellowships awarded by the AvH Foundation in the 1980s was not large. But these days, the Foundation awards annually over 700 globally competitive research Fellowships in the humanities and natural sciences, including mathematics, to scholars from all over the world who are interested in carrying out research projects of their own choice in Germany in collaboration with German hosts. Concerning its selection process, the Foundation writes as follows on its website[13]

> If you would like to become a member of the Humboldt Family, only one thing counts: your own excellent performance. There are no quotas, neither for individual countries, nor for particular academic disciplines. Our selection committees comprise academics from all fields of specialisation and they make independent decisions, based solely on the applicant's academic record.

Aware of the Foundation's rigorous selection criteria and process, it was clear that I had my work cut out, if I wanted to be a recipient of its Fellowship.

My Research Stay in Göttingen, Bielefeld, Heidelberg

Research at Gottingen

In 1982, three years after I participated in the conference in Lausanne, I was one of the recipients of the globally competitive Fellowship of the Alexander von Humboldt Foundation. Moreover, I earned the unique distinction of being the first scholar in Nigeria to be awarded the Fellowship in mathematics/mathematical physics. I chose the University of Göttingen, Göttingen (officially called Georg-August-Universität Göttingen, Göttingen),

---

13   https://www.humboldt-foundation.de/web/about-us.html

established in 1734, in the Niedersachsen State of Germany, as my host institution and Professor Hans-Jürgen Borchers (January 24, 1926-September 10, 2011) as my host, Professor Borchers was one of the foremost mathematical physicists of all time, globally recognised for his seminal contributions to the theory of operator algebras and axiomatic quantum field theory. His PhD thesis was supervised at the University of Hamburg by Professor Wilhelm Lenz (February 8, 1888-April 30, 1957), a German physicist renowned for formulating the *Ising model*. I took up the Fellowship in August 1983. On arrival in Germany, I started my German language course at the Goethe-Institut, Mannheim, in the country's Baden-Württemberg State. Some four months later, I was fairly proficient in writing, reading and speaking the language, scoring "sehr gut", in the final examination at the Institute. In December 1983, I arrived at the Institut für Theoretische Physik der Georg-August-Universität Göttingen, Göttingen, with my host Professor Borchers on hand to welcome me. At the Institute were Gerhard Christian Hegerfeldt, Jakob Yngvason, Erwin Bruening and the Peruvian, Julio Cesar Alcantara-Bode, who, like me, was beginning his Alexander von Humboldt Fellowship year under Professor Borchers.Alcantara-Bode was a professor at the Pontificia Universidad Catolica Del Peru (Pontifical Catholic University of Peru) and Instituto de Matematica y Ciencias Afines (Institute of Mathematics and Related Sciences) in Lima, Peru. At the Institute, I was assigned an office which, I was told, had once been occupied by Professor Max Born (December 11, 1882 – January 5, 1970), one of the two 1954 Nobel laureates in Physics; he helped to develop several key aspects of quantum mechanics. Born was a German-Jew. Following the genocidal persecution of German Jews, orchestrated by the Nazi Party of Germany (Nationalsozialistische Deutsche Arbeiterpartei), an ultra-right political party, which existed for about a quarter of a century from 1920 to 1945, he became a naturalised British citizen on August 31, 1939, the eve of the Second World War. My stay at the Georg-August-Universität Göttingen greatly built my research capacity. There were weekly research seminars where current trends in diverse areas of mathematics and mathematical physics were showcased and open problems highlighted. Many eminent scientists participated in the seminars or visited the Institute. One of them was Professor Yang Chen-Ning who, jointly with Professor Tsung-Dao Lee, won the Nobel Prize in Physics in 1957. These were the first Chinese to be Nobel laureates. By acquiring American citizenship in 1962, Professor Lee became the youngest American to win a Nobel Prize. About half a century after his naturalisation, Professor Lee relinquished his American citizenship on September 30, 2015, and had his Chinese citizenship reinstated. On the whole, my one-year stay at the Georg-August-Universität Göttingen was academically uplifting, as I came in contact with some iconic scholars in my areas of specialisation. The experience opened up new vistas for me in research, research methodology, problem-solving and research reporting. I was also able to actively participate in several academic networks and, consequently, to vastly expand my professional networking space. Socially, during our stay in Göttingen, my wife and I met and made friends with Dr. Godfrey and Heidi Adodo. Godfrey (December 27, 1943– July 14, 2011), who studied at the University of Heidelberg, was a diligent medical doctor, with a state-of-the-art, highly patronised and flourishing surgery. He was a relation of Admiral Augustus Akhabue Aikhomu (October 20, 1939–August 17, 2011), the erstwhile Military Vice President of Nigeria from 1986 to 1993 in the administration of General Ibrahim Badamasi Babangida, the self-styled Military President of Nigeria from August 27, 1985 to August 26 1993. In my multiple visits to Germany, no matter in which town I was staying, Godfrey always picked me up with his car to spend some time with him and his wife in his house at Theisbergstegen, located in the German State of Rheinland-Pfalz. His death in 2011 was extremely painful to me and my family.

Since his transition, my family and I have remained in very close contact with his affable and genial wife, Heidi.

Research at Bielefeld

In December 1984, following a seven-month extension of my Fellowship by the Alexander von Humboldt Foundation till June 1985, I moved on to the research centre called the Forschungszentrum Bielefeld-Bochum-Stochastik (BiBoS Research Centre), located at the Universität Bielefeld (University of Bielefeld), established in 1969, in the city of Bielefeld in the State of Nordrhein-Westfalen. My host at BiBoS was Professor Ludwig Paul Ary Evert Streit. BiBoS was coordinated by Professor Streit and Professor Sergio Albeverio, a Swiss mathematician, who was based at the Ruhr-Universität Bochum (University of Bochum), established in 1962, located in Bochum, a town also in the State of Nordrhein-Westfalen. The Centre offered me a three-month visiting professorship, sponsored by the Hannover-based Volkswagenstiftung (Volkswagen Foundation), established in 1961, which enabled me to work at BiBoS up till the end of September 1985. During my stay at BiBoS, I was privileged to meet such eminent visiting scientists like my supervisor, Professor Streater, the American mathematician Professor Richard Kadison (July 25, 1925-August 22, 2018), who made multiple fundamental contributions to the theory of operator algebras, the Polish theoretical physicist Professor Witold Karwowski, who I had earlier encountered during my research work for the PhD degree at the University of London and who, in 1985, invited me to, and hosted me in, his institution, the University of Wrocław (Uniwersytet Wrocławski), Wrocław, Poland, founded in 1945, the Belgian theoretical physicist Professor Jean-Pierre Antoine who, together with Professor Karwowski, initiated the systematic study of partial *-algebras, the Norwegian mathematician Jan Raphael Hoegh-Krohn (February 10, 1938 – January 24, 1988), who was a research collaborator of Professor Albeverio, and the French mathematician Professor Paul-André Meyer (August 21, 1934 – January 30, 2003) who contributed immensely to the development of several aspects of stochastic analysis, especially the theory of semimartingales. My research activities straddled several areas of the fields of specialisation of these scholars who were some of the authors whose trailblazing publications substantially impacted a number of my own publications in subsequent years.

In spite of the rigorous academic work that steadfastly engrossed my attention at BiBoS, it was relieving that Bielefeld, founded in 1214, was a nice city to live in and work, not minding *die Bielefeld-Verschwörung* (the Bielefeld conspiracy) which originated in 1994, almost eight centuries later, through a Usenet post by the future Professor Achim Held of the University of Kiel, satirically implying that "Bielefeld does not exist" ("Bielefeld gar nicht existiert"). Apart from the year of its foundation as evidence, a further verifiable proof of its existence ("Bielefeld gibt es doch!"), is that Bielefeld is the *Stadt* where my daughter, Osamweetin, was born.

My Research at Heidelberg

From August to December 1994, the Alexander von Humboldt Foundation afforded me the opportunity for another research visit to Germany under its *Wiedereinladung* programme. My host research institution was the oldest university in Germany: the Ruprecht-Karls-Universität Heidelberg (briefly called the University of Heidelberg), Heidelberg, established in 1386, located in the State of Baden-Württemberg. I carried out my research activities at the Institüt für Angewandte Mathematik of the University, where Professor Wilhelm Freiherr von Waldenfels (February 22 1932–March 14, 2021), an expert in stochastic analysis, was my scientific host. I worked in the area of quantum stochastic differential inclusions, a new branch of mathematical

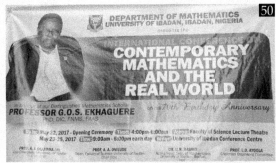

50. Poster of the international conference in my honour, May 22-25, 2017
51. Some of the dignitaries at the opening ceremony of the retirement activities for GOS, May 22, 2017
52. GOS and wife with friends at the opening ceremony of the retirement activities, May 22, 2017

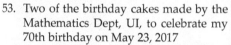

53. Two of the birthday cakes made by the Mathematics Dept, UI, to celebrate my 70th birthday on May 23, 2017

54. GOS and wife cutting the 70th birthday cake at the conference dinner, May 23, 2017

55. GOS and wife at the conference dinner, 2017

56. GOS and wife with Prof Wayne Patterson, an invited speaker at the international conference

57. GOS and wife with daughter, her husband, Dr. Etiowo Ekanem, and their children at the conference dinner, May 23, 2017

58. GOS and wife at the thanksgiving mass at St. Peter Catholic Church, Benin City, June 2017
59. GOS and wife at thanksgiving mass at St. Peter Catholic Church, Benin City, during offering, June 2017
60. Some guests at the Conference dinner, 2017
61. Prof. S.A. Ilori making some remarks at the conference dinner, May 23, 2017
62. GOS and wife in a group photo with the wives of some ICC Old Boys at the thanksgiving mass in Benin City, June 2017
63. GOS with family at conference opening ceremony, 2017

64. The high table at conference dinner, 2017
65. GOS in a group photo with some ICC Old Boys at thanksgiving mass at St Peter Catholic Church, Benin City, 2017
66. (L-R) Prof VF Payne, Prof Florentin Smarandache, GOS, Prof Wayne Patterson and Prof EO Ayoola, at the conference, 2017

physics which I pioneered in 1992. The overall academic and research space was stimulating and enabling. As in all other foreign institutions where I had previously been involved in diverse forms of research undertaking, I had unfettered access to a gamut of library and computer facilities, not mentioning the assignment to me of a comfortable office space. In the relatively conducive research bubble in which I operated, I accomplished many of my short-term research objectives. Moreover, during my stay, I was also able to interact with a number of other mathematicians in the University and beyond.

My Associateship Awards at the ICTP

From October 8 to October 16, 1984, I participated in a *Symposium on the State of Mathematics and Physics in Africa* at the International Centre for Theoretical Physics (ICTP), Trieste, Italy. Prior to the Symposium, thirty-four African scientists, concerned about the apparent poor state of Mathematics and Physics in Africa, the tepid research cooperation among African scientists and the widening scientific and technological divide between the developed countries and African nations, had met on Friday, August 26, 1983, at the ICTP and resolved to form the Society of African Physicists and Mathematicians (SAPAM). The new body was formally inaugurated during the Symposium. The Ghanaian Professor Francis Kofi Ampenyin Allotey (August 9, 1932-November 2, 2017) and the Nigerian Professor Charles Nwachukwu were elected as the inaugural President and Secretary, respectively, of SAPAM. During the period of the Symposium, I paid a courtesy call on the Director of the ICTP, Professor Abdus Salam, who had been designated as my PhD supervisor at the Imperial College, London, in 1972. He was glad to see me again and asked whether I was an Associate of the ICTP. I replied in the negative, because I was not aware that such an opportunity existed. He asked me to apply for the Associateship, remarking that there was a rigorous selection process because scholars from all Third World countries were eligible to apply. A few years later, I implemented Professor Salam's advice. I was awarded the Regular Associateship of the ICTP for the period from 1989 to 1995, an award that was funded by the Swedish Agency for Research Cooperation with Developing Countries (SAREC). The Associateship enabled me to visit the ICTP for up to three months in a year during the period of the award to carry out my research activities. After my Regular Associateship, one could then apply for the highly competitive Senior Associateship of the ICTP, also funded by SAREC. I was awarded the Senior Associateship for the period from 2001 to 2006. An amount of money was attached to my Senior Associateship such that I could visit the ICTP, for a maximum of 60 days per visit, as many times as feasible from 2001 to 2006 until the grant was exhausted. I utilised the Senior Associateship as prescribed in the award letter, visiting the ICTP multiple times between 2001 and 2006 for my research activities.

The National Mathematical Centre

The ICTP was the prototype after which the National Mathematical Centre (NMC) was modelled. Established in 1988 by the Federal Government of Nigeria, the NMC's existence was subsequently legitimised by means of Decree No. 40 of 1989, later renamed the National Mathematical Centre Act 2004 (CAP. No. 58). The expectation was that the Centre would carry out activities that were akin to those of the ICTP. Accordingly, the Act lists fifteen functions which the NMC was mandated to implement. In the early years of its existence, there were justifiable hopes that the NMC would truly become a replica of the ICTP. Unfortunately, it is widely believed among many Nigerian mathematical scientists that, in recent years, the NMC has not lived up to its billing. For example, over thirty years after its establishment, the NMC has not been able to

> establish and execute a visiting programme for mathematical
> scientists, under which mathematical scientists can visit the Centre
> for short periods, to work on their individual research problems
> using the Library, Computing and other facilities of the Centre,

as contained in and envisaged by the Act. Moreover, the NMC
ought to be a veritable hub in Nigeria for the continuous professional
development of mathematical scientists who are expected to
foster Stem (Science, Technology, Engineering and Mathematics)
education. This is feasible only if mathematics which, in the words
of the English philosopher and Franciscan friar Roger Bacon
(c. 1219- c. 1292), "is the door and key to the sciences", forms the
core of such education.

A New Generation of Researchers

My research activities in multiple branches of Mathematics and
Mathematical Physics attracted a substantial number of students
who worked under my supervision. At the BSc and MSc levels, I
supervised the projects of hundreds of students. Beyond these
levels, as I write now, eleven students have so far successfully
earned their MPhil and PhD degrees under my supervision in
the areas of quantum (noncommutative) stochastic analysis,
partial *-algebras, financial mathematics and fractal analysis. They
are: Ezekiel Olusola Ayoola (PhD, University of Ibadan: 1999),
Sadik Olaniyi Maliki (PhD, University of Ibadan: 1999), Michael
Babatunde Olorunsaiye (PhD, University of Ibadan: 2003),
Maurice Nnamdi Annorzie (MPhil, University of Ibadan: 2004;
PhD, University of Ibadan: 2015), Peace Chisara Ogbogbo [female]
(MPhil, University of Ibadan: 2009; PhD, University of Ibadan:
2016), Charles Iwebuke Nkeki (PhD, University of Ibadan: 2012),
Enahoro Alfred Owoloko (PhD, Covenant University: 2014), Ini
Adinya [female](PhD, University of Ibadan: 2019) and Adaobi
Mmachukwu Udoye [female] (PhD, University of Ibadan: 2019).
Accordingly, through my training and research capacity building

activities over the years, I helped to develop new generations of scholars who were ably qualified to replace me at retirement. As a result, I contributed in some way to the incremental realisation of UI's institutional succession plans and goals. Several of my past MPhil/PhD students have since attained the professorial cadre in the academic profession, are at the forefront of global research activities in mathematics and its applications to national development; they have themselves been successfully supervising PhD students in the institutions where they are employed.

Memorialising Past Heads of Mathematics

One of the tasks that I set myself was the memorialising and honouring of all the Heads of the Department of Mathematics who served before me by displaying their photographs in the Department. When I became the Head in 1993, the relevant persons were ten in number. The pioneer Head of Department was Professor Frederick Valentine Atkinson (January 25, 1916 – November 13, 2002), a British mathematician, whose PhD research work was supervised by Professor Edward Charles Titchmarsh (June 1, 1899 – January 18, 1963) at Oxford University, UK. His tenure was from 1948 to 1955. He was also the Dean of the Faculty of Arts from 1954 to 1955. He established the Department on a sound footing. I had hoped to find a photograph of Professor Atkinson in the Department's archive. But that was not to be: it quickly dawned on me that I had taken on a herculean task. Yet, it was not my wish to abandon the entire project. How was I to proceed? I did not know whether Professor Atkinson was alive or his whereabouts, if alive. I could not lay my hands on his photograph before I left office as Head in 1996. His successor as Head of Department was Professor Kathleen Collard (October 21, 1915 - June 2, 2009), another British mathematician, whose maiden name was Kathleen Sarginson.

In 1957, she married Patrick John Collard (April 22, 1920-June 17, 1989), who was appointed the pioneer Professor of Bacteriology at the University College Ibadan in 1954. Patrick was the second husband of Kathleen, whose first husband, Dr. Basil Geoghegan died in January 1954 shortly after their marriage; conversely, she was the second wife of Patrick whose first marriage was to Jessie Flora Robertson in 1948.

Professor Kathleen Collard's tenure as the Head of the Department of Mathematics was from 1955 to 1965. After returning to the United Kingdom, she spent many years at the University of Nottingham until her retirement in 1978. I wrote to Professor Collard for her photograph and she graciously sent it to me. When she died in 2009, her corpse was not buried because she had approved that it could be used for medical research. After Professor Kathleen Collard, every Head of the Department of Mathematics has been a Nigerian. So, it was relatively easy for me to obtain the photographs of all the Nigerian Heads before me. Professor Adegoke Olubummo (April 19, 1923 – October 26, 1992) succeeded Professor Collard in 1965. Professor Olubummo was the first Professor of Mathematics and the pioneer expert in Functional Analysis in Nigeria. His tenure was from 1965 to 1971. His successor was Professor John Oyedokun Oyelese (April 19, 1917-January 16, 1987), an accomplished statistician, who obtained his PhD degree in 1970 under the supervision of the Polish statistician Professor Jerzy Neyman (April 16, 1894-August 5, 1981) at the University of California, Berkeley, USA. Professor Oyelese's tenure was from 1971 to 1975. He handed the reins of office to Professor Haroon Oladipo Tejumola, an expert in ordinary differential equations, who taught me complex analysis in 1969. Professor Tejumola had two tenures: from 1975 to 1979 and from 1980 to 1983. His successor was Professor Charles Olusegun Adedayo Sowunmi (September 14, 1934–December 3, 2007), who introduced the rigorous study of, and research in, mathematical biology into the Department. His tenure was from 1979 to 1980, after which he was succeeded by Professor Tejumola during the latter's second-term tenure. Professor Aderemi Oluyomi Kuku, who taught me group theory in 1968, was the Head of Department after Professor Tejumola. His tenure was from 1983 to 1986. A world-class algebraist, Professor Kuku introduced the study of and research in algebraic K-theory into the Department and is regarded globally as one of the mathematicians at the forefront of the development of that branch of mathematics. He was succeeded by the two-term Head of Department, Professor Samuel Akindiji Ilori, whose two tenures were from 1986 to 1989 and 2002 to 2005. Also an algebraist, Professor Ilori is globally renowned for his work on algebraic topology. He introduced the study of, and research in, algebraic topology into the Department. Professor

Ilori's successor was Professor Victor Adekola Babalola, an expert in Functional Analysis, who was a PhD student of Professor Olubummo. Professor Babalola was a two-term Head of Department, who served from 1989 to 1991 and from 2005 to 2007. He was succeeded by Professor Gabriel Oluremi Olaofe (December 6, 1937-February 6, 1994), one of whose areas of research activities was numerical analysis. He was in office from 1991 to 1993. I succeeded Professor Olaofe and my tenure was from 1993 to 1996. A tenure normally started on August 1 and ended after two years (in the case of an Acting Head) or three years (in the case of a substantive Head) on July 31. When I left office in 1996, I had secured the photographs of all past Heads of Department of Mathematics, except that of Professor Atkinson. There was no indication that I would ever acquire his photograph. But a silver lining eventually appeared. In 2004, I organised an international conference on *Contemporary Applications of the Mathematical and Computer Sciences to Development Problems* in Lagos from February 8-11, 2004. The proceedings of the conference were edited by me and published by the International Centre for Mathematical & Computer Sciences. At the conference were participants from the USA and Europe, one of whom was Professor Wayne Patterson of Howard University, Washington DC, USA. During discussion with Professor Patterson, I mentioned rather casually that I was actively searching for a photograph of one Professor F.V. Atkinson, who was a past Head of Department of Mathematics at Ibadan. To my amazement and relief, he disclosed that Professor Atkinson was one of his former professors at the University of Toronto, Canada, before he joined Howard University. Professor Patterson then promised to send me a photograph of Professor Atkinson, an undertaking which he graciously fulfilled. Unknown to me, after leaving Ibadan in 1955, Professor Atkinson had spent most of his academic career at the University of Toronto, Canada, before his death in 2002. Through Professor Patterson, I was finally able to connect all dots. Today, the photographs of all past Heads of Department of Mathematics, from 1948 till date, are conspicuously displayed in the Department.

PART VI

SERVICE AT MULTIPLE LEVELS

19

DEFENDING THE NIGERIAN UNIVERSITY SYSTEM

I was elected in 1981 into the University of Ibadan Branch Executive Committee (UIBEC) of the Academic Staff Union of Universities (ASUU), which had its national headquarters at Mellanby Hall at that time. The future Federal Minister of Education and former Ambassador to Germany, Professor Babatunde Adeniran and the future Vice-Chancellor of the University of Nigeria, Nsukka, Professor Ginigeme Francis Mbanefo (March 21, 1942-February 8, 2017), were Chairman and Secretary, respectively, of the UIBEC. My portfolio was that of Treasurer. At that time, I was merely a Lecturer Grade 1. I saw my participation in the Committee as an opportunity to learn about, and contribute to the management of ASUU at an institutional branch level. Moreover, I also wanted to acquire some insight into the kind and variety of issues in higher education that ASUU was continually grappling with at the national level. Established in 1978 as a trade union, with all Federal and State universities in the country as its members, ASUU replaced the National Association of University Teachers (NAUT) which was formed in 1965. The future Professors Biodun Jeyifo and Timothy Uzodinma Nwala were the pioneer President and Secretary, respectively, of ASUU at the national level.

As a union, ASUU's aims and objectives are multifarious. They include:

> to defend the principles of academic freedom and university autonomy in the Nigerian University System; foster and ensure the existence of a conducive environment for quality university education; and encourage its members to be active in university and national affairs.

Others are:

> to work toward the prevalence of good labour relations between academic staff and their employers; ensure good conditions of service for its members; act as a bulwark against unfair employer practices against its members; and contribute to, and promote, national development.

Realising these ostensibly lofty aims and objectives has been at the epicentre of the Union's activities over the years, beginning with the first strike action in 1973 by the NAUT over conditions of service.

I joined the UIBEC at a time when there was again much discontent over conditions of service in public universities. The 1973 strike action by NAUT had been forcibly terminated by the military administration of Major General Yakubu Gowon, who was the Head of State: the striking university teachers were ordered back to work, under pain of losing their employment and university accommodation if they did not comply with the order. Additionally, to be accepted back, each teacher was obliged to sign a register and submit a letter to the institutional head, pledging to be of good behaviour thenceforth. With their tails literally between their legs, the teachers abandoned their strike action and scampered unconditionally back to work, thereby suffering unspeakable humiliation, resulting in a considerable loss of prestige and precedence within the Nigeria society. More traumatically, the university teachers' advantage in salary relative to what was earned by workers in such sectors as the civil service and the military was abruptly erased.

By 1981, the conditions of service, including salaries, of university teachers had abysmally deteriorated and become intolerable. The highly untenable situation had been statutorily fostered through the immersion of the university salary structure in the Unified Grading and Salary Structure (UGSS) in 1975, as recommended by a commission, which reviewed the nation's public service, headed by the future Igwe Ozuluoha I of Igboland, Chief Jerome Oputa Udoji (1912 - April 10, 2010). On September 21, 1981, ASUU declared a trade dispute with the Federal Government. The University of Ibadan Branch of ASUU was a loyal and an active participant in the dispute. At issue were the basic conditions of service of university teachers, underfunding of public universities, progressive erosion of institutional autonomy, continuous degeneration of academic freedom and rejection of the 1975 harmonisation of the salaries and conditions of service of university staff with those of the civil service. In response to the dispute, the Federal Government of President Shehu Usman Shagari (February 25, 1925-December 28, 2018) appointed a Presidential Commission on Salaries and Conditions of Service of University Staff, headed by Dr. Samuel Joseph Cookey (January 25, 1918 – July 22, 2003). The initiative was an admission by the Nigerian Government that the mission, structure, modus operandi and the unique strategic role of the university system are radically different from those of the civil service and the public corporations. It therefore recommended that, in line with its special character, the university system was entitled to conditions of service distinct from those of the civil service. That led to the creation and introduction of the University Salary Structure (USS) in 1981. I was happy to have been a member of the UIBEC of the ASUU when this landmark achievement was recorded. President Shagari's second term in office, which began on October 1, 1983, was abruptly terminated three months later by a military coup that installed Major-General

Muhammadu Buhari as the new Head of State on December 31, 1983.

After the apparent triumphant outcome, in ASUU's reckoning, of the 1981 strike action, even though not all of its demands were adequately resolved, several whirlwinds of strike actions have periodically buffeted the Nigerian University System. For example, in the decade from 1988 to 1998, ASUU engaged in strike actions on three occasions over a cumulative period of more than 9 months. My involvement in the struggle for justice in respect of one such strike action by ASUU, concerning what the Union determined was a breach of agreement by the Federal Military Government of Nigeria, is sketched in what follows.

In Court for ASUU

In 1996, I was a member of the University Management, since I was the Head of the Department of Mathematics, and a member of the University Governing Council. Nevertheless, I was active in the affairs of ASUU. My roles, of a member of Management, Council and a consummate ASUU loyalist, were seen by some as incompatible but hailed by the Union. Before the end of my tenure on July 31, 1996, ASUU embarked on a strike action on April 9, 1996, to get the Federal Military Government, led at that time by General Sani Abacha (September 20, 1943 – June 8, 1998), to review an agreement, signed with the Union on September 3, 1992, during the Military Administration of General Ibrahim Badamasi Babangida. Irked by yet another industrial action by ASUU, the Government ordered the striking academic staff back to work not later than Wednesday, June 19, 1996. At the University of Ibadan, the order was disseminated through a *Special Release* published on Wednesday, June 5, 1996. Two weeks later, the institution's Registrar & Secretary to the Council, Chief C.O. Arowolo, who would retire soon after from the University on September 30, 1996, signed the University of Ibadan *Special Release* No. 1271, of Monday June 17, 1996, which warned that the Federal Government proposed to implement the following punitive measures if staff did not return to work:

(i)   In any University where the majority of staff refuses to return to normal lectures and other normal functions on campus and also shun the path of dialogue, despite Federal Government conciliatory gesture, such a University might face the dangers of formal closure.

(ii)   Furthermore, all members of staff who are adamant on not calling off the strike will be faced with the likelihood of termination of appointment and its attendant severance of all perquisites of office, i.e. remuneration, housing accommodation, refund of research grant and the handing over of all public properties entrusted to them.

These potential consequences of sustaining the strike action until the Federal Government acceded to the Union's demands infuriated some of us. We, therefore, decided to test the legality of the threats (i) and (ii) in court by suing the Federal Government's agent, the Governing Council. Accordingly, six of us, namely: my good self, Professor Ezekiel Kayode Adesogan (October 1, 1939 - January 6, 2021), Professor Johnson Adebayo Odebiyi, Professor Jimi Olalekan Adesina, Professor Adeniyi Olumuyiwa Togun and Mr. Christopher Ogechi Uroh, as plaintiff, for themselves and other academic staff of the University of Ibadan, sued the Governing Council of the University of Ibadan, as the defendant, in Suit No. I/334/96. The case was before HON Justice T.O. Adeniran, Judge of the High Court of Oyo State (High Court No. 3). To institute the action, we had obtained a General Writ of Summons, dated June 20, 1996, against the defendant after obtaining leave of court to institute the action in a representative capacity. Our claims were twofold:

1.   A DECLARATION that the Decision of the Defendant to carry into effect the directives of the Federal Government of Nigeria as contained in the University of Ibadan Official Bulletin Special Release No. 1271 of Monday, 17 June, 1996, signed by the Registrar & Secretary to Council of University of Ibadan, is wrongful, illegal and contrary to Section 9(3) of the University of Ibadan Act, 1962, as amended and the Recovery of Premises Law Cap 111 Laws of

> Oyo State of Nigeria, 1978 as respect Academic Staff tenants of
> the University of Ibadan.

2.   AN ORDER OF INJUNCTION restraining the Defendant, their
       agents, privies from carrying into effect the directive of the Federal
       Government of Nigeria as contained in the University of Ibadan
       Bulletin Special Release No. 1271 of Monday, 17 June, 1996.

Our Counsel was the future Professor John Oluwole A.
Akintayo while Chief Ladosu Ladapo, a Senior Advocate of
Nigeria, was the Counsel for the defendant. After arguments by
our Counsel and that of the defendant, represented by Barrister
Mrs. C.M. Ososanya, the Judge restrained the defendant, in his
ruling of June 26, 1996, from

> taking any steps whatsoever which directly or seemingly render nugatory
> whatever the ultimate judgment in the case is.

The order was a great relief, as it bought us some time, while
simultaneously creating much anxiety and uncertainty in the
defendant's camp. Subsequently, the counsel for the defendant
filed a 'Preliminary Objection', through a motion on notice dated
July 16, 1996, in which two issues were articulated, namely: that

(a)   the court had no jurisdiction to entertain the suit,
       and

(b)   there was no juristic person as a defendant before
       the court.

These issues were argued on August 12, 1996, after which the
trial Judge delivered a verdict on September 12, 1996, upholding
the 'Preliminary Objection' and striking out our action. But we
had fought a good fight on behalf of the Union. We had the legal
option to appeal the judgement. We did not pursue that option for
two reasons. Firstly, it soon became apparent that the Government
did not have the will to implement the threats (i) and (ii) above,
considering the potentially immense adverse consequences on the
entire education system, beyond the Nigerian University System,
which we were defending. Secondly, the Government eventually

reached a new agreement with ASUU, leading to the suspension of the strike action on September 30, 1996, barely two and a half weeks after the court judgement of September 12, 1996.

Some Deleterious Consequences of ASUU Strike Actions

The Union was on strike on sixteen other occasions, over a cumulative period of 40 months, during the two decades from 1999 to 2019. In 2020, ASUU was involved in another strike action from March 23, 2020 to December 24, 2020. Over the years, the innumerable strike actions effectively became "weapons of mass destruction", with potentially deleterious consequences for the stability of academic calendars, teaching effectiveness, student character and learning, student mentoring, student drop-out rate, research capacity building, graduate employability, national and international image of Nigerian universities, internationalisation of Nigerian universities, integrity and global recognition of certificates awarded by Nigerian universities as well as the global competitiveness and ranking of Nigerian universities, to mention but a few of the likely fallouts for the Nigerian University System. As far as the Union was concerned, the Government was to be held liable for any adverse consequences of its strike actions.

Over the years, the probability of a strike action by ASUU increased with time, rendering students of Nigerian public universities the most strike-vulnerable and adversely strike-impacted on the continent. As a result of the often prolonged disruptions to academic activities in the nation's public universities, caused by the frequent strike actions, it was hardly possible for a student to predict when a four- or five-year degree programme would be completed. ASUU's frequent characterisation of its strike actions 'as total, comprehensive and indefinite' has unfortunately metastasised throughout the entire labour union space in Nigeria: today, every worker or student union proclaims its strike action 'as total, comprehensive and indefinite', "untill our demands are met".

As what appears to be the fundamental philosophy that undergirds ASUU's numerous strike actions, which invariably denied students vital learning opportunities and timely graduation, Professor Abiodun Ogunyemi, whose three-year tenure as ASUU President ended in May 2021, recently furnished the following rationalisation[14]:

> ASUU is strongly convinced that if academics fail to fight the cause of university education, the fate that befell public primary and secondary schools would soon become the lot of the public university system in Nigeria. ASUU's advocacy on the need to stem the continued slide into rot and decay in public universities since the 1980s has fallen on deaf ears.

Some flagship achievements of ASUU's strike actions over the years have been the creation, and periodic revision, by the Federal Government of a separate salary scale for university teachers; the establishment, by Act 16 of 2011, of the Tertiary Education Trust Fund (TETFund), formerly called the Education Trust Fund (ETF); the introduction in 2013 of the Needs Assessment Intervention Fund and the enactment of the Universities (Miscellaneous Provisions) (Amendment) Act 2003 that explicitly affirms the autonomy of Nigerian Federal universities in the following words:

> The powers of the Council shall be exercised, as in the Law and Statutes of each University and to this extent establishment circulars that are inconsistent with the Laws and Statutes of the University shall not apply to the Universities; . . .

> The Governing Council of a University shall be free in the discharge of its functions and exercise of its responsibilities for the good management, growth and development of the university.

In spite of these hard-won and laudable successes by ASUU in its defence of the Nigerian University System, the Union seemed to have taken its eyes off the ball, in respect of also working toward protecting and upholding the defining character

---

14   *Premium Times*, Abuja, February 7, 2019.

of universities, namely their 'universality'. Through what amounts to institution-capture by cabals, cliques and ethnic goons, there has been a progressive slide by some public Nigerian universities into ethnicity, parochialism, uncompromising loyalty to locality and arrant narrow-mindedness in institutional affairs, particularly the appointment of Principal Officers. It is, however, pleasing that the National Universities Commission [NUC] is acutely aware of the worrying development, as amply depicted in the following excerpt[15]:

> Professor [Abubakar Adamu] Rasheed [Executive Secretary, NUC], however, expressed dismay that many Nigerian universities were losing universal character due to ethnic and religious sentiments which had bedevilled the system. He said that it was disheartening that a federal university would be so localised to the extent that even the best hands from other regions of the country would not be given the opportunity of leadership or other positions based on sentiments that did not conform to universality system.

A nagging challenge in public universities is how to courageously restore the 'principle of universality' to the institutions in a way that is simultaneously consistent with merit, the 1995 Federal Character Commission Establishment Act and the 2003 Universities (Miscellaneous Provisions) (Amendment) Act.

ASUU's Use of Strikes for Dispute Resolution

For Nigerian public universities to realise their enormous potential, there is an urgent need to address such matters as the following. Are strike actions the only pathways to securing employer-employee agreements and their implementation? Do the Federal Government and Unions ever evaluate the adverse impact of strike actions on national development and progress? In particular, with Nigerian universities as the upstream providers of education, new knowledge and human capacity, what are the salutary or adverse

---

15   NUC *Monday Bulletin*, February 4, 2019, Vol. 14 No. 05, ISSN 0795-3089.

effects of ASUU strike actions on the downstream education providers (polytechnics, colleges of education, secondary schools and primary schools) and the nation's entire education value chain? What is the global perception of Nigerian universities? How internationalised are Nigerian universities? How long-lasting and sustainable have been the key gains from ASUU's numerous strike actions? In a rapidly changing, dynamic and unpredictable world, can every 21st century problem be solved with 20th century methods or tactics? Could ASUU devise and implement a positively disruptive approach to higher education matters, whether existing or emerging, with the strategic goal of vastly expanding the teaching and learning space for millions of prospective candidates, while simultaneously ensuring adequate and sustainable funding of public universities? While ASUU continually calls for the reform of diverse sectors of national life, especially the higher education sector, does the Union have a procedure for self-evaluation and peer-review of its activities? Is there a process or mechanism for continuously reforming ASUU? Apart from these and kindred issues which continually agitate the minds of all stakeholders of tertiary education in Nigeria, it is also necessary to constantly examine the whole issue of the impact of ASUU strike actions on graduate quality and employability.

20

ACTS OF AN INSTITUTIONAL CITIZEN

As is customary in many tertiary education institutions in Nigeria and around the world, the governance paradigm of the University of Ibadan is rooted in the 'committee system.' The most prominent committees, which may be 'ad hoc' committees or 'standing' committees, are those of the University's Senate or the University's Governing Council. Additionally there are also joint committees of Senate and Council. Under the committee system, some members of Senate, Council or Congregation are empowered to focus, in a problem-solving fashion, on the continuous implementation of a set of objectives that form a committee's terms of reference. Membership of a committee is invariably by election from a group of willing members or through selection by office (ex officio) or relevant expertise.

My Life as a Multiple Integral

Besides my work as an academic, which principally comprised teaching, research and dissemination of research outcomes through scholarly authorship as well as various forms of community service, I was also involved in a significant number of institutional, national and international initiatives, missions, tasks and assignments. As a consequence, I operated in a multidimensional space of sundry activities and events, exemplified not only by teaching and research but also by research capacity building, development of multiple generations of experts in specialised branches of mathematics and mathematical physics, continuous mentoring of students at all levels of training, scholarly publishing, institutional administration and a diversity of problem-solving services to the nation, the global academic community and the entire higher education world. The gamut of activities collectively honed several of my innate capabilities and continuously equipped me with a range of skills and experiences that I found immensely invaluable in my earthly journey. All told, my life has been, metaphorically, a 'multiple integral' of certain life-changing functions of several variables, some of which were deterministic while the others were stochastic. In the sequel, I sketch some of the multiple roles that I had the good fortune to assume.

Working with Nine Vice-Chancellors

During my statutory tenure, from October 1, 1976, to May 23, 2017, as a member of the academic staff of the University of Ibadan, I worked under nine substantive Vice-Chancellors (VCs) and four Acting Vice-Chancellors. With their tenures in parentheses, the substantive VCs were Emeritus Professor Tekena Nitonye Tamuno (December 1975 to November 1979), Professor Samson Olajuwon Kokumo Olayide (December 1979 to November 1983), Emeritus Professor Ladipo Ayodeji Banjo (December 1984 to November 1991), Professor Allen Bankole Oladunmoye Olukayode Oyediran (December 1991 to November 1995), Professor Omoniyi Adewoye (March 1996 to September 2000), Emeritus Professor Ayodele Olajide Falase (September 2000 to March 2004), Professor Adebisi Olufemi Bamiro (December 2005 to November 2010), Professor Isaac Folorunso

Adewole (December 2010 to November 2015) and Professor Abel Idowu Olayinka (December 2015 to November 2020); the Acting VCs were Emeritus Professor Ladipo Ayodeji Banjo (November 1983 to November 1984), Professor Oladosu Akanbi Ojengbede (December 1995 to March 1996), Professor Olufunso Olabode Olorunsogo (March 2000 to September 2000) and Professor Adebisi Olufemi Bamiro (March 2004 to November 2005). A VC is the chief executive officer of a university, with responsibilities that include providing academic and administrative leadership, ensuring rapid institutional development and mobilising multiple resources for the progressive realisation of the institution's vision and mission. At the sub-institutional levels (College, School, Faculty, Institute, Department, Centre, Registry, Bursary, Library, Health Service, Maintenance & Works), the heads of units are also saddled with analogous responsibilities. Through its committee system, much of the day-to-day running of a university is done collectively by its leadership at all its diverse levels as well as its teaching and non-teaching staff. Heads of academic units would normally also be 'ex officio' members of several 'ad hoc' or 'standing' committees. It is therefore often not feasible for them to seamlessly combine the additional institutional obligations with their statutory duties and responsibilities as Heads; consequently, they would invariably delegate or devolve some of their responsibilities to some of their colleagues in the units. Similarly, the running of a unit is collectively done under the leadership of its Head who would inevitably be obliged to assign roles to other members of the unit.

Computer Committee

My first institutional assignment outside the Department of Mathematics occurred during the 1977/1978 academic year. Professor Tejumola, who was the Head of Department, asked me to represent him on the Computer Committee where he was an ex officio member. The Committee was a standing committee of Senate whose terms of reference were to advise the University on computer policy and especially on the best use of [the] facilities available.

It had Professor Frank Mene Adedemisinwaye Ukoli (November 5, 1936–December 21, 2004), who was the Dean of the Faculty of Science during the 1977/1978 academic year, as Chairman. I learnt a lot about policy formulation and optimal deployment and utilisation of facilities at the University's Computing Centre. The main equipment at the Centre was a 32-bit IBM System/370 mainframe computer, manufactured by the International Business Machines Corporation (IBM), with its headquarters in Armonk, New York. The IBM is the 1924 successor of the Computing-Tabulating-Recording Company (CTR), which was established in 1911 in Endicott, New York, by Charles Ranlett Flint (January 24, 1850 – February 26, 1934) and Thomas John Watson Sr. (February 17, 1874 – June 19, 1956). The IBM System/370 employed punch cards for data processing. From 1968 to 1978, the Centre's Director was Professor Oluwumi Longe (March 20, 1932 – December 14, 2020). From 1977 till her retirement in June 2017, my wife was a member of staff of the University's Administrative Data Processing Unit (ADPU), located in the Computing Centre.

Congregation Representative

At the time I assumed duty at the University of Ibadan on October 1, 1976, there were housing and telephone shortages on campus, with sometimes adverse impact on staff effectiveness and productivity. Indeed, I was initially accommodated by the University at the Premier Hotel, Ibadan, and later at the Hotel Influential, Ibadan, which was only a stone's throw from the Premier Hotel. As a consequence of the shortages, the University had committees, which among other tasks, ensured an orderly distribution of the institution's scarce resources to eligible staff. These included the

Staff Housing Allocating Committee (SHAC) and the Telephone Committee, both of which were standing committees of Council. The SHAC had several terms of reference, principal among which was:

> to advise the University administration on the allocation of housing accommodation to newly appointed members of staff and also on applications for changing accommodation submitted by existing members of staff.

I was elected to represent Congregation on the SHAC, from August 1, 1979 to July 31, 1981. By statute, all academic members of staff, as well as all other employees who are graduates of recognised universities, are automatically members of Congregation, a body that is entitled to have representatives in Senate and some committees of Council. The chairman of the SHAC was Professor Ayodele Babajide Olukoya Desalu, a professor of anatomy. The terms of reference of the Telephone Committee were simply:

> to see to matters relating to the development of the University telephone system and the allocation of telephone [lines].

After serving on the SHAC, I was also elected to represent Congregation on the Telephone Committee from August 1, 1981, to July 31, 1983. In those days, allocating the available units of accommodation and telephone lines to a rapidly growing population of teaching and non-teaching staff, especially those who needed such facilities on account of their duties or responsibilities, represented a daunting task. The SHAC and the Telephone Committee implemented their terms of reference with steadfast attention to equity and transparency. In 1979, I was allocated the telephone number 1729 by the Telephone Committee, well before I joined the Committee. I was immensely intrigued by the number because, as first pointed out by the Indian mathematician Srinivasa Ramanujan (December 22, 1887 – April 26, 1920), who had collaborated briefly with the English mathematicians Professor Godfrey Harold Hardy (February 7, 1877 – December 1, 1947) and Professor John Edensor Littlewood (June 9, 1885-September 6, 1977), the number 1729, sometimes called a 'taxicab number' or a 'Ramanujan-Hardy number', is the smallest positive whole number that can be written in two different ways as the sum of two positive cubes: 13+123=1729=93+103. For several reasons, at the forefront of which is the currently raging nationwide insecurity, which has been forcing a growing number of staff members to apply for campus accommodation, the issue of shortage of such accommodation for staff has persisted up till this day. On the other hand, as a result of the introduction in Nigeria, on August 6, 2001 during the administration of Chief Olusegun Matthew Okikiola Aremu Obasanjo, of mobile telephony, using the Global System for Mobile Communications (GSM), with the consequent democratisation of access to telephone communication, the era of acute competition among staff or students at the University for telephone lines from the Telephone Committee eventually came to a salutary end. Accordingly, institutional and social telephone communication became seamless, although the charges by the Government-licensed mobile network operators were initially somewhat exploitatively high. In recent times, especially since 2020, the year of the berthing of the COVID-19 pandemic in Nigeria, the GSM has been quite useful in facilitating teaching and learning in the nation's secondary and tertiary education institutions.

Faculty Affairs

While merely a Lecturer Grade 1 in 1979, I was active in the affairs of the University Senate and my Faculty. I was elected to represent Congregation on Senate. That was the only route by non-professorial academic staff to Senate. I was in Senate from August 1, 1979 to July 31, 1982. After my promotion to the grade of Professor in 1988, I had a permanent seat in Senate. At the Faculty of Science, I was elected as the Sub-Dean (Physical Sciences) for the 1981/1982 academic year, during the Deanship of Professor Joseph Ibomein

Okogun, whose tenure was from August 1, 1980 to July 31, 1982. I was the Chairman of the Faculty of Science Examinations Time-Table Committee and the Chairman of the Faculty of Science Teaching Time-Table Committee. In these roles, which I assumed before the era and widespread use of desktop or laptop computers, I provided leadership toward modifying, restructuring and fine-tuning the Faculty's Examinations Time-Table and Teaching Time-Table, which are schedules with multiple constraints, to ensure that these vital academic instruments were conflict-free and optimally reliable. I was also a representative of the Dean of the Faculty of Science on a Panel of the Joint Admissions and Matriculation Board (JAMB), headquartered in Lagos in those days, where I presented, and provided justification for, the list of candidates which the Faculty had recommended for admission. I also represented the Dean on the Senate Careers Board, whose terms of reference included offering

career guidance services to undergraduates from their very first session;

explaining

the nature and content of courses offered in this University to prospective employers indicating areas of employment where they can be useful;

advising

the College/Faculties on new areas of study where there may be openings for employment;

and offering

placement service to students in their final year.

These and kindred objectives were unwaveringly pursued by the Board, where I meticulously presented the perspectives of the Faculty of Science, the oldest in any Nigerian university.

I spent the period from August 1983 to September 1985 outside Nigeria in Germany where, as narrated earlier, I was a Fellow of the Alexander von Humboldt Foundation. When I returned to the country, I needed some time to re-immerse myself in the mainstream of University business and also steadfastly implement my individual strategic plan for my upward academic mobility. Additionally, many of the elective positions at the Faculty level or in Senate or Congregation were occupied by eminently qualified colleagues, whose tenures were anything from one to four years. These and other circumstances caused a relative lull in my participation in non-academic or administrative institutional affairs when I returned to the University in 1985. My involvement in such affairs escalated in later years after my promotion to the grade of Professor.

Discipline and Career Matters

I earned my academic chair, with effect from October 1, 1988, in the Department of Mathematics during the illustrious Vice-Chancellorship of Emeritus Professor Ladipo Ayodeji Banjo, an amiable, genial, outstanding and humble scholar, administrator and mentor. With the attainment of the professorial cadre, I was elected again by Congregation to serve on the Senior Staff Disciplinary Committee (SSDC) from August 1, 1992 to July 31, 1993 and on the Appointments and Promotions Committee for Academic Staff (A&PC) from August 1, 1992 to July 31, 1994. These were standing committees of Council. The terms of reference of the SSDC included:

> to investigate, consider and determine all disciplinary cases involving members of staff of the University on USS 06 [and above [with some stated exceptions], provided always that any member of staff aggrieved by the decision of the SSDC may appeal to Council for reconsideration within twenty-one days of the decision of the SSDC.

We handled a diversity of complicated disciplinary cases, with the Vice-Chancellor Professor Allen Bankole Oladunmoye Olukayode Oyediran as chairman. The SSDC resolved the cases with unwavering attention to dispensing justice, ensuring reformation, instilling discipline and, where appropriate, meting out sanctions that were fair and commensurate. Because of the thoroughness with which the SSDC implemented its terms of reference, I cannot today recall any case decided by the Committee that was appealled to Council for a review. The Committee's work helped to safeguard institutional norms, values and principles, sustain a high standard of professional ethics within the different staff cadres and ensure that the University's image was not at any time dragged into disrepute. In the case of the A&PC, its terms of reference included:

> to consider all matters relating to appointments to, and promotions within the academic staff [with some specified exceptions] ...

and

> to make recommendations to Council on any matter that will be in the interest of the proper appointment and promotion of members of academic staff of the University.

The A&PC was therefore responsible for continually enhancing the quality of staff recruitment into the academic cadre through appointments, while simultaneously also ensuring the global competitiveness and excellence of the academic staff and their research activities, through promotions that conformed to world-class standards. The Committee carried out its functions with painstaking adherence to its terms of reference and the approved guidelines for appointments and promotions. In my view, the A&PC could not have done otherwise because no other committee had a higher potential for impugning the integrity and hard-earned reputation of the University if it did not scrupulously implement its mandate. I saw it as a great honour and an enormous responsibility to be a member of the A&PC, whose activities were capable of significantly and decisively affecting the career trajectory, velocity and development (through, for example, the provision of opportunities for sabbatical leave, study leave, leave of absence and other kinds of capacity-building initiatives) of every member of the academic staff.

Headship

I assumed office as the Head of the Department (HOD) of Mathematics on August 1, 1993. My three-year tenure ended on July 31, 1996. In the 1990s, the procedure for appointing a Head of Department (HOD) was simple: the Dean of the relevant Faculty recommended a willing Professor to the Vice-Chancellor who normally would then issue a letter of appointment to the candidate. I was appointed HOD through that procedure. In later years, the procedure changed to the following (as contained in the 2017 edition of the University's *Staff Information Handbook: Rules and Regulations Governing Conditions of Service of Staff*):

i.   When, in the Department, there is one Professor who has indicated interest in the position, that Professor shall be appointed as Head of Department provided that the Professor secures a majority of 'Yes' votes over 'No' votes from among members of the academic staff of the Department.

ii.   Where there are two or more Professors who have indicated interest in the position, there shall be an election among them and the candidate with majority of the votes shall be appointable.

viii The selection process shall involve all academic members of staff of the Department.
     The Dean of the Faculty shall be the chairman, who shall only have casting vote in the event of a tie between candidates.

ix   The Faculty Officer shall be a returning officer.

The recent innovation was intended to democratise the appointment procedure by ensuring that an HOD has the support of a majority of the academic staff of the Department. But by making voting a fundamental aspect of the procedure, there has been an inadvertent boosting of the potential for a politicisation of the appointment of HODs.

The Department of Mathematics was established in 1948 as one of the foundation academic units of the University College

Ibadan, which started its activities on January 18, 1948 as a College of the University of London. Its groundbreaking ceremony for its permanent site was performed later in the year on November 17, 1948. The post of HOD is key to the running of a university since any inappropriate actions, inexcusable acts of inaction or outright administrative failures at the departmental level would often eventually propagate upstream and potentially undermine the steady realisation of the institutional vision and mission. As HOD, my role was multifaceted and I had braced myself for it. I knew very well that I was expected to provide a strong academic leadership, administer the Department in an efficient and effective way and, generally, ensure that the Department's activities were always of high quality.

My initial action was to carefully evaluate the state of the Department. Then, based on the evaluation, I set up a structure aimed at fostering unity and single-mindedness of the entire Department in the unwavering implementation of its ternary mandates of academic, administrative and community service functions, in line with the largely unwritten, at that time, Faculty and institutional vision and mission. To secure the buy-in of my colleagues, students and other stakeholders, I constituted a number of committees and appointed an academic member of staff, with relevant expertise, as the chair of each committee: Once the committees were up and running, I was able to direct my energies toward the steady implementation of my other statutory functions with as much thoroughness as I could muster. To ensure quality decision-making, I always engaged in seamless consultations and real-time communications with staff and students. As a consequence, and also through a judicious use of scarce resources, it was possible for the Department to ramp up the quality of its teaching, research, administrative and community activities, while ensuring research integrity and ethics. As HOD, I participated actively in Faculty and institutional organs for decision-making and decision-implementation, such as the Faculty Board, Faculty Board of Studies, Senate and Congregation. I worked collaboratively with other Departments in the Faculty and the entire University to jointly formulate management frameworks, policies and solutions in respect of cross-cutting matters, especially the ones that concerned students and their affairs. I ensured, with the cooperation of all staff, that students had a rich and lasting learning experience.

I took action to enhance and then restructure the Department's existing research management activities: an intensification of postgraduate training kicked off smoothly. The University maintained its status as the institution of choice in West Africa for research work in mathematics. With a continuous influx of students from diverse Nigerian universities into the Department's MSc, MPhil and PhD programmes, I requested for and was granted permission to recruit eight additional academic staff members. As a result, there were thriving postgraduate programmes in Functional Analysis, Probability Theory, Stochastic Analysis, Algebraic Topology, K-Theory, Differential Equations (Ordinary and Partial), Mathematical Biology, Mathematical Physics and Numerical Analysis. To support research activities, the Department's Computer Committee installed several types of software for mathematics, including the flagship mathematics typesetting and publishing software called LATEX, on the Department's computers, whose number I had greatly increased. As a way of ensuring that the facilities were optimally used, I also organised computer training sessions for staff in the use of the various software types.

Securing the Department

In the 1990s, having computers and other expensive equipment in any Department in the University was often an invitation to burglary. To avoid such a situation, I installed burglarproof metal barricades throughout the Department in 1993. It was then possible for staff, who so wished, to work round the clock in their offices without any fear of burglary or attacks. Accordingly, since 1993, no burglary ever occurred in the Department. Over the years, with a substantially conducive environment for teaching and research, some of those who were recruited during my tenure, as well as others who enrolled in the Department's postgraduate training programmes and subsequently joined the Department's academic cadre, have since risen to the grades of Senior Lecturer, Reader (Associate Professor) and Professor. The Department's academic strength was thereby greatly enhanced.

Department's Global Visibility

It is in the nature of every academic Department to be always concerned about its visibility on the global scene; this is inseparably linked to its international profile, the quality of its teaching and the significance of its peer-reviewed research activities. In 1994, during my Headship, the Department was recognised as a Centre of Excellence in Mathematics in the South by *The World Academy of Sciences* (TWAS), formerly called the *Third World Academy of Sciences,* which is based in Trieste, Italy. With its status as a Centre of Excellence, the Department became a destination for top-rate mathematicians from universities of the South and thereby fostered academic mobility, research collaboration, research capacity building and academic networking between our Department and each of the visiting mathematicians' home Departments. Concerning academic staff mobility, some members of the academic staff of the Department, including myself, were actively involved in the Associateship scheme of the International Centre for Theoretical Physics, Trieste (ICTP), Italy. The Department also participated in the Federation Arrangement scheme of the ICTP. According to the ICTP, the Associateship scheme was established to provide "support for distinguished scientists in developing countries in an effort to lessen the brain-drain" and to expose "them to the most modern aspects of their scientific fields". On the other hand, the Federation Arrangement scheme enabled our Department to send academic staff (not older than 40 years) to the ICTP for visits from 60 to 150 days during a period not exceeding three years. Utilising the schemes, some of our members of staff were able to collaborate and network with mathematicians from various parts of the world. Some years later, I was also appointed a Senior Associate of the ICTP. In the words of the ICTP, the Senior Associate scheme was designed "for scientists from a developing country who have acquired international scientific status".

Normal Workplace Leadership Challenges

It is almost inevitable that an office holder would, from time to time, encounter workplace challenges, experience pressures and be involved in conflict resolution and peace building. During my tenure as HOD, my main challenge was linked to the inadequate funding of Nigerian public universities, a matter that has perennially been at the epicentre of several ASUU strike actions since the early 1980s. As a consequence, HODs, including my good self, sometimes funded Departmental activities from their own resources. The sources of pressure were mainly guardians and students. Guardians wanted their wards recommended for undergraduate admission into the Department even when they did not meet the admission criteria, especially benchmarks such as cut-off marks. It was my duty to politely explain to the guardians why it was not possible for me to bend the rules. Similarly, students who were asked to withdraw from the Department or the University often thought that such a decision could be reversed by piling a substantial amount of pressure on the HOD. I also often needed to resolve student-student, student-staff and staff-staff conflicts. I saw these as inevitable in a multicultural and multigenerational environment which the Department represented and was keen to nurture and foster.

I completed my tenure on July 31, 1996. By that time, I had already achieved a substantial ramping-up of the Department's fitness for its fundamental purpose: the steadfast implementation of its core mandate and functions.

Contributing to Postgraduate Education in Nigeria

I joined the University of Ibadan in 1976 at a time when postgraduate training in the Department of Mathematics was blooming. Indeed, some of my senior colleagues earned their PhD degrees in the Department. In those years, the mode of postgraduate training closely mimicked that of the University of London: the MSc, MPhil and PhD degrees could be earned solely through the presentation and successful defence of theses, without any course work. From about the middle of the 1980s, the requirements for the award of the MSc and MPhil degrees were revised and thereafter comprised both course work and the successful defence of an MSc project or an MPhil dissertation. The transition was feasible because the set of academic specialisations in the Department had become much enlarged and highly diversified, making it easy to introduce and operate a postgraduate curriculum in line with the American style of postgraduate education. In the case of the PhD degree programme, the main requirement for graduation remained the successful defence of a thesis, without any mandatory course work. Using the revised curriculum, a large number of candidates have earned their MSc, MPhil and PhD degrees from the Department since the 1980s. As the nation's foremost engine of postgraduate training, the University of Ibadan has been steadily and incrementally realising its principal academic aspiration of becoming a predominantly postgraduate institution. I contributed significantly to the continuous implementation of the University's postgraduate activities, especially by academically siring new generations of research-agile Nigerian mathematicians through the successful supervision of MSc, MPhil and PhD candidates in the multiple branches of mathematics in which I am a specialist. Accordingly, my MSc, MPhil and PhD students produced and defended research projects, dissertations or theses mainly in Functional Analysis, Topological Partial *-Algebras, Classical and Noncommutative Stochastic Analysis, Financial Mathematics and

Mathematical Physics. Even in statutory retirement, I continue to supervise postgraduate candidates for the MSc, MPhil and PhD degrees in my capacity as an Emeritus Professor. At the time of writing, my PhD scions are:

> Professor Ezekiel Olusola Ayoola, Associate Professor Sadik Olaniyi Maliki, Dr. Michael Babatunde Olorunsaiye, Associate Professor Maurice Nnamdi Annorzie, Associate Charles Iwebuke Nkeki, Professor Enahoro Alfred Owoloko, Dr. Chisara Peace Ogbogbo (female), Dr. Ini Adinya (female), Dr. Adaobi Mmachukwu Udoye (female).

As their own contributions toward keeping the flag of global mathematical research always flying, some of these scholars are themselves also producing PhD graduates, my academic grandscions. To foster the continuous mainstreaming of mathematical research outcomes into national development, I established, in 1999, the *International Centre for Mathematical & Computer Sciences* (ICMCS), a legal entity, registered as a non-governmental organisation at the Corporate Affairs Commission of Nigeria. Over the years, the activities of the ICMCS have contributed significantly to the ramping-up of national research capacity building in the Mathematical and Computer Sciences.

The ICMCS formulated its vision and mission statements as follows:

Vision

To be a global player and, in particular the institution of choice in Africa, for cutting edge, gender-sensitive, and applications-oriented training, research, service and partnerships in the mathematical and computer sciences.

Mission

To provide the most conducive environment in Africa for cutting edge, gender-sensitive, and applications-oriented training, research, service and partnerships in the mathematical and computer sciences.

To facilitate the orderly and agile implementation of its diverse activities, the ICMCS was structured into three Divisions, namely: Division of Mathematical Sciences, Division of Computer Sciences and Division of Extra-Mural Studies and Lifelong Learning. From the very beginning of its existence, the need to always disseminate the outcomes of its activities globally was accorded a high premium by the Centre. For example, the ICMCS has always published the peer-reviewed versions of the proceedings of its conferences. To complement the activities of the ICMCS and mainstream them throughout the entire Nigerian education system, in 2015, I established an online newspaper called *The Chronicle of Education* (TCE). Thematically focused on education at all levels (pre-tertiary and tertiary) in Nigeria, its goal was that of putting education squarely in the forefront of national development. Accordingly, the broad objective of *The Chronicle of Education* was

> to be a platform for generating and disseminating cutting-edge ideas for remodelling, repositioning, enhancing and advancing the entire Nigerian education system, in order to enable education to continually play its rightful role as the foremost agent for accelerated national and regional development.

More generally, TCE's vision and mission statements are the following:

Vision

> To be the foremost publication on education matters in Nigeria, acclaimed for always putting education squarely in the forefront of national and regional development.

Mission

> To continually map the changing Nigerian and African education landscape, with the objective of accurately depicting its full potential and dynamics, through publishing national, regional and global education news, reports, analyses, assessments, documentaries, opinions, discussions and blogs that are distinguished by their quality, relevance, creativity, objectivity and exemplary capacity to foster national and regional progress.

Through the activities of its deligent and smart staff, *The Chronicle of Education* is today recognised for assisting in fostering research, teaching and learning at all levels of education and their manifold applications to national development.

Senate and Council

In addition to the obligation of every member of Senate to participate actively in its decision-making processes and procedures, I was elected in 1994 as a member of the Senate Development Committee and Senate Curriculum Committee. These were key standing Committees of Senate. In the same year, I was also appointed by the Vice-Chancellor Professor Allen B.O.O. Oyediran as the Chairman of the Business Committee of Senate, in succession to the nematologist Professor Bamidele Fawole, who, like me, was born in Benin City. The terms of reference of the Development Committee included:

> to formulate and review policies, and establish criteria, with a view to recommending to Senate the order of priorities in the University's academic development (including periodical plans), and to keep the policies under constant review.

It was also the Committee's mandate:

> to scrutinise the annual estimates of expenditure submitted by Departments, and others, and to modify them where necessary, for presentation to Senate and through Senate to Council, provided that opportunity is afforded to each Head of Department, or a person deputed by him for the occasion, to state his case before the Committee in person.

In the case of the Senate Curriculum Committee, its terms of reference included:

> to make recommendations to Senate on the course proposals from College/Faculty Boards and Institutes, especially those which may have implications for other Colleges, Faculties or Institutes or the system in the University as a whole

and

> to advise Senate from time to time on broad matters of policy
> and principle regarding the curriculum.

As the chairman of the Business Committee, I worked with other members to collectively prepare "items of business for the consideration of Senate". This was an enormous charge because the Committee was consequently responsible for the correctness of any set of minutes presented to Senate and for formulating and structuring the agenda of a Senate meeting. The Committee also dealt with other matters that were specifically referred to it by Senate or the Chairman of Senate.

Joining the Governing Council

Before completing my tenure as HOD, I was elected by Senate as one of its four representatives on the University of Ibadan Governing Council. My tenure was with effect from August 1, 1995. Professor Allen B.O.O. Oyediran was the Vice-Chancellor, while Professor Iya Abubakar, former Federal Minister, Senator, and a 1958 alumnus of the Department of Mathematics, University of Ibadan, was Pro-Chancellor and Chairman of Council. Professor Abubakar's tenure was from October 8, 1992 to May 28, 1999. At the first meeting that I attended, members were assigned to some standing committees. Consequently, I served on the following standing committees: Board of Trustees of the International School, Projects Committee, Appointments and Promotions Committee for Senior Staff (Non-Teaching), University Housing Allocation Committee, Joint Council/Senate Committee on Naming of Buildings and Streets, Finance and General Purposes Committee and Audit Sub-Committee of the Finance and General Purposes Committee. As a member of these standing committees, I contributed toward the implementation of their terms of reference, which collectively had profound impact in diverse areas of University life.

I was also appointed by Council, on the recommendation of the Vice-Chancellor, Professor Allen B.O.O. Oyediran, as the Chairman of the Council Committee on Security (CCS). The terms of reference of the latter included that it "shall be responsible for the security of the University community". The Committee also had responsibility for defining and directing the functions of the Security Unit, as it was called in those days, dealing with the appointment and promotion of security personnel, ensuring discipline in the Security Unit, making recommendations on adequate financing of the Security Unit and enforcing any "bye-laws aimed at regulating the conduct of the University community or its visitors". My appointment as Chairman was made at a time when the campus was virtually under siege by thieves and burglars who incessantly stole high-worth teaching, learning, research and laboratory equipment from the University. At that time, the Security Unit appeared to be incapable of mounting a decisive response to the onslaught. Analysing how the thefts were perpetrated, it was clear to me that some of them had insider collusion and collaboration. I was therefore determined to deal with the menace which had made it difficult for almost every academic unit in the University to smoothly accomplish their teaching, learning and research missions. In line with the Committee's terms of reference, there were also the issues of staff discipline and the need to restructure and steer the Security Unit toward improved gender equity and enhanced operational effectiveness.

Campus Surveillance Corps and Other Innovations

To stem the widespread theft of University assets, I sought and secured the permission of the Vice-Chancellor, Professor Omoniyi Adewoye, who had succeeded Professor Allen B.O.O. Oyediran, to establish a corps of security-conscious members of staff, whose activities would complement those of the Security Unit. By August 1996, I had developed an 'operations manual' for the new body, which I christened the *Campus Surveillance Corps* (CSC). The CSC was intended to be

> a body of carefully selected volunteers from the University community, with the responsibility of assisting the Security Unit in ensuring that life and property on the campus were safe and secure.

As the CSC comprised members of staff from different units of the University, operating in mufti, they functioned as a proactive intelligence outfit. Structurally, the CSC comprised Campus Head of Operations (CHO), Deputy Campus Head of Operations (DCHO), Campus Information Officer (CIO), Deputy Campus Information Officer (DCIO), General Secretary (GS), Deputy General Secretary (DGS) and Legal Adviser (LA). Operationally, the campus was divided into Zones, with each Zone comprising not less than 50 members of the CSC, administered by a Zonal Head of Operations (ZHO), Deputy ZHO, a Zonal Information Officer (ZIO), and a Zonal Secretary (ZS). In 1997, the CHO was the linguist Professor Kola Owolabi while the Agricultural Economist Professor Somayina Gabriel Nwoko (1930-2016), was the DCHO. The CSC carried out security roles that were complementary to those of the Security Unit. Accordingly, the CSC was involved in crime-bursting activities through continuous intelligence-gathering, meticulous analysis and the implementation of strategies for preventing, checking or minimising crimes, day and night, on the campus. Additionally, the Corps had powers to apprehend criminals and then hand them over to the Security Unit.

Not long after its establishment, the CSC made a spectacular arrest. The circumstances were as follows. It was normal that laboratory equipment vendors visited laboratories in the University to solicit for patronage. A male operative of the CSC, who I will identify as CSC_OP, was in charge of an advanced research laboratory with several high-worth instruments and equipment. A certain vendor visited CSC_OP in his laboratory, ostensibly to get

CSC_OP to recommend some of the vendor's laboratory hardware for possible purchase. But, as narrated by CSC_OP, the vendor soon veered into telling CSC_OP that a certain equipment in the laboratory was worth millions of Naira and that both of them could make a lot of money by clandestinely taking the equipment out and selling it. When CSC_OP warned the vendor that there was no way the equipment could be taken out of the campus because of the additional layer of security that I had introduced, the vendor replied that taking any equipment illegally out of the campus was not, and had never been, a problem for him. The CSC_OP informed me about the imminent security breach. I then briefed the Campus Head of Operations (CHO), Professor Owolabi, and the Deputy Campus Head of Operations (DCHO), Professor Nwoko. We agreed that the CSC_OP should play along, while we finalised an arrest plan. The CSC_OP and vendor agreed on the date and time when the multi-million Naira equipment was to be stolen and I was informed. On that day, the CHO, DCHO and I positioned our cars strategically close to the laboratory. Not long, the vendor emerged around 11:00a.m. carrying a bag containing the equipment and moved swiftly to a car which then drove off at high speed. We all quickly gave chase. Eventually, the driver of the car and the vendor were arrested. The equipment was retrieved. Upon interrogation, it turned out that the driver was the official driver of one of the University's Deputy Vice- Chancellors. He was summarily dismissed from service and the vendor was prosecuted. This incident showed that many of the previous thefts of instruments and equipment in the University almost certainly had insider collusion and complicity: if CSC_OP had connived with the vendor, the latter's scheme would have succeeded, and that would have been one more campus crime that the Security Unit would have found very difficult to unravel.

I also worked to enhance the diversity of the operational security personnel. Before I became the Chairman of the Council Committee on Security, there were no women in the non-administrative section of the Security Unit: the University had a wholly male security workforce. I sought and obtained permission from the Vice-Chancellor, Professor Adewoye, to positively disrupt the prevailing status quo at that time. Accordingly, from 1997, the Security Unit began the recruitment of women into its professional workforce. With the innovation, the Security Unit was able to achieve much more because there were often occasions when only women were needed to carry out certain operations, especially intelligence gathering, thorough body-search of female suspects and the training of female recruits.

I also observed with some concern that many of the low level security personnel hardly spoke or wrote in the English Language. I needed to change the situation. This was because the first persons who visitors to the University naturally approached for information at any of its entry gates were security personnel. I sought and obtained permission from the Vice-Chancellor, Professor Adewoye, for an upward review of the minimum academic qualification for recruitment into the lowest cadre of the Security Unit from the primary school certificate to the S75, a certificate issued to a candidate who dropped out of secondary school education just before the final year or failed the West African Senior School Certificate Examination (WASSCE). Moreover, cognizant of the new recruitment academic qualification, I coordinated the introduction of a correspondingly enhanced new salary scale of the security staff.

As I indicated above, the foregoing and other changes in the University's security architecture were carried out during the tenure of the Vice-Chancellor, Professor Adewoye, who always welcomed innovations, no matter from whom they emanated. I learnt a lot from his quiet, humble, open-minded and hardworking approach to university governance. Even after his tenure, Professor Adewoye continued to be helpful to me at all times, including writing references on my behalf whenever I approached him for such.

My Role in Strategic Planning

At the dawn of this century, it was clear that the third industrial revolution (3IR), also called the digital revolution, which intensified during the last quarter of the last century, would radically change the world of learning, work and production. Indeed, a new political and economic world order has since emerged, marked by globalisation, a new world of work, a new social organisation paradigm, rapid internationalisation, global competitiveness, transnational partnerships and problem-solving regional collaborations. These developments are having multiple transformative implications for every university which must continually re-position itself for relevance, effectiveness and global competitiveness. While many countries are yet to fully absorb and apply the salient outcomes of the 3IR, the fourth industrial revolution (4IR) is already beckoning. The 4IR is characterised by the progressive merging of the continually evolving new technologies that are fuelling rapid changes in the biological, physical and digital worlds. To cope with the highly dynamic state of a rapidly changing world, every university requires a strategic plan of action that addresses key aspects of its mandate and functions. Some of the areas where clear institutional initiatives and frameworks were urgently needed included 'internationalisation and quality assurance' as well as research, 'research capacity building and research management'. I will furnish a rapid sketch of how I helped to develop institutional strategic plans and frameworks in respect of these avant-garde higher education matters.

In 2006, Professor Matthew Temitayo Shokunbi, neurosurgeon and University of Ibadan professor of anatomy, kindly invited me to present a concept paper on *internationalisation* at a seminar on *Linkages* at the University of Ibadan. At that time, Professor Shokunbi was the MacArthur Grant Liaison Officer of the University. Not long after my presentation, the future Emeritus Professor Abiola Odejide, who was the Deputy Vice-Chancellor

(Academic) from November 8, 2004 to November 7, 2006, constituted an Internationalisation Strategic Plan Committee, and appointed me as its Chair. The Committee was inaugurated in December 2006 by Professor Adigun Ajao Bolarinwa Agbaje, who succeeded Emeritus Professor Odejide as the Deputy Vice-Chancellor (Academic), and was in office from November 8, 2006 to November 30, 2010. Using their current titles at the time of writing this book, the other members of the Committee were Professor Alade Abimbade (Department of Teacher Education), Professor Olusegun George Ademowo (Institute for Advanced Medical Research and Training), Professor Victor Olusegun Adetimirin (Department of Agronomy), Mr. Ibrahim Olaniyi Aponmade (Bursary), Mrs. Margaret Aziba (Office of the Vice-Chancellor), Professor Chinedum Peace Babalola (Director, General Studies Programmes), Professor Oluyemisi A. Bamgbose (Department of Private & Business Law), Professor Francis Oisaghaede Egbokhare (Director, Distance Learning Centre), Dr. Olayinka Catherine Fatoki (Kenneth Dike Library), Mr. Olatunji M. Oladejo (Public Relations Unit), Professor Babasola Oluseyi Olugasa (Department of Veterinary Public Health & Preventive Medicine), Professor Ayodeji Emmanuel Oluleye (Chairman, ICT Committee) and Titiloye Ademola Oyejide (Department of Economics), with Mr. Suleman Olawale Oyewumi, of Office of the Deputy Vice-Chancellor (Academic)), as Secretary. The Committee formulated and adopted the following as the University's notion of *internationalisation:*

> the dual process of continually integrating international and intercultural perspectives into its [UI's] principal functions of teaching, research, management and service, so as to ensure that its staff and students are always able to operate effectively in a rapidly changing national and global scene, and simultaneously mainstreaming UI's own achievements, services and perspectives into the global academic agenda.

A *Strategic Plan for Internationalisation* (2009-2014), with the title: *Engaging a Rapidly Changing World* was produced; it represented the first-ever officially adopted strategic plan document since the University's establishment in 1948. The key objectives of the plan were to:

> foster the realisation of UI's vision and mission; re-position UI to be able to continually cope with the diverse challenges of a rapidly changing world; re-position UI to be able to continually take advantage of emerging global opportunities; strengthen the UI identity and brand in the global academic scene; produce students who are global citizens; expand opportunities for staff and students to be active players in the international academic arena; mainstream UI's own achievements, services and perspectives into the global academic agenda; continually enlarge UI's footprint in the global academic arena; and promote global peace, partnership and solidarity.

The *Internationalisation Strategic Plan* aimed at realising these objectives of the internationalisation process, underpinned by UI's core values of discipline, integrity, openness, excellence, innovation, collegiality, good quality of life, and good community relations. The document was submitted officially to Professor Agbaje, who presented it to the University administration, headed by the Vice-Chancellor, Professor Olufemi Adebisi Bamiro. *The Strategic Plan* contained several new strategic initiatives and recommendations. The diligent implementation of some of the initiatives by Professor Agbaje led to the establishment of two new structures called the Research Management Office (RMO), one of whose mandates is to "mobilise external research funds by, among other means, developing and submitting proposals which satisfy the requirements of funding agencies", and the Office of International Programmes (OIP), which handles matters related to internationalisation and partnerships. The establishment of the RMO and OIP was in line with global best practices. Professor of Community Medicine, EME Theodora Owoaje, and Professor of Psychology, Idayat Bolarinwa Udegbe, were the pioneer directors of the RMO and OIP, respectively. Professor Agbaje also appointed me as the Chairman of an 'ad hoc' Committee that formulated the University's first-ever 'Research Policy', which then triggered the production of a comprehensive institutional manual on 'Ethics Policy' in research, containing strict ethical codes and procedures, consistent with global best practices, for the manifold disciplines that underpin the University's vast training and research ecosystem: health sciences, social sciences and humanities, animal care and use, plant use and conservation, science and technology as well as teaching and learning. The 'ad hoc' Committee which formulated the 'Ethics Policy' was chaired by the Haematologist Professor Adeyinka Gladys Falusi. These developments greatly enhanced the University's profile in the highly competitive world of research and internationalisation. To make the campus secure and safe for life and property, the Strategic Plan had recommended that the University's Security Unit should be renamed the Campus Security Service (CSS) and restructured into three units called the Fire Service Unit, Intelligence Unit and Operations Unit. The recommended renaming and restructuring were smoothly implemented, during the tenure of Professor Isaac Folorunso Adewole as Vice-Chancellor, by Dr. Ganiyu Adetunji Adeniran in his capacity as the Chairman of the Council Committee on Security from November 1, 2007 to July 31, 2015.

As a follow-up to the *Strategic Plan for Internationalisation,* the University's Governing Council set up a committee, under the chairmanship of Professor Elijah Afolabi Bamgboye, to produce an institutional strategic plan that went beyond the single objective of internationalisation. I was invited to be a member of the committee. In compiling the strategic plan entitled: *Promoting Excellence in Teaching, Research & Community Service: A Five-Year Strategic Plan (2009-2014)*, I contributed the goals and objectives of the two sections on *Quality Assurance and Internationalisation.*

Quality Assurance

From the first day in office, Professor Isaac Folorunso Adewole, who was the Vice-Chancellor of the University of Ibadan from December 1, 2010 to November 30, 2015, indicated his resolve to put quality assurance on the front burner of instutional activities and promote its mainstreaming throughout all aspects of the University's teaching, learning and research functions, institutional practices as well as administrative processes and procedures. That was one of the fundamental goals that he set himself: to employ quality assurance as a mechanism for continually enlarging the University's academic footprint and improving its global visibility, ranking and networking. But quality assurance activities were by no means novel to the University of Ibadan. The institution had always fostered quality in its core functions through a diversity of quality assurance initiatives and measures. These included[16]:

> periodic programme/institutional accreditation by the National Universities Commission to ensure that the human and material resources which the University needs to implement approved programmes existed and were of an acceptable standard; approval by Senate of a research policy and a research management structure to promote high quality research; establishment of an office of Servicom on campus to foster service delivery of a high quality; the use of external examiners to enhance the quality of its examinations and validate their outcomes; compliance with the requirements of diverse professional accrediting bodies to ensure that the training received by students in professional courses was of very high standard; the development of an ethics policy to foster the highest ethical standard in the conduct of research; and the implementation of a 5-year *Internationalisation Strategic Plan*, which placed a considerable premium on quality.

But there was neither an entrenched culture of periodic self-evaluation by the institution and its units nor a dedicated outfit with responsibility for quality assurance throughout the University. Every institution aspiring to be world-class certainly needed such a framework.

16   *Quality Assurance Policy and Strategy*, University of Ibadan, Ibadan, Nigeria, 2012.

In tandem with global best practices, the Vice-Chancellor, Professor Adewole, was determined to create such a quality assurance outfit, imbued with a robust strategic vision and measurable goals for its work on quality, which was to continually ensure that all staff, students and stakeholders were always able to participate effectively in the realisation of the goals. Accordingly, he quickly established the first-ever Directorate of Quality Assurance (DQA) at the University of Ibadan. He appointed the pharmacist, Professor Oludele Adelanwa Itiola, who later became the Rector of the Moshood Abiola Polytechnic, Abeokuta (MAPOLY), as the pioneer Director. As its quality assurance motto, the DQA employed the motivating slogan: *Doing the Right Thing Right, Every Time.*

Professor Adewole also appointed me as the Chairman of a committee to produce a quality assurance strategic plan and policy that would drive the activities of the novel Directorate. Other members of the committee were: Professor Oyedunni Arulogun, Professor Talhatu Kolapo Hamzat, Professor Oludele Adelanwa Itiola, Professor Oka Obono, Dr. Peter Chukwuma Obutte, Professor Abiola Odejide, Professor Idayat Bolarinwa Udegbe, Professor Eme Theodora Owoaje, Professor Obododimma Oha and Mr. Adedokun Olufemi Ojelabi. By April 2011, the Committee had produced and submitted a document, entitled: *Quality Assurance Policy and Strategy* (QAPS), to the Vice-Chancellor. In the document, quality was defined as a binary: 'fitness for purpose and fitness of purpose'. The QAPS was designed to realise UI's aspiration of ensuring that its provisions, processes, products and services always met the purposes for which they were intended and also helped to foster national goals and objectives. The key elements of the QAPS were a meticulous definition of the functions of the DQA and a formulation of a framework for institutional quality assurance, with the DQA as the apex quality management outfit, a provision for quality assurance committees (QACs) at the unit levels and an explicit description of the functions of the QACs, as well as a set of policies, objectives and strategies which were to be implemented by the DQA and QACs. In 2013, Professor Itiola was succeeded by the civil engineer, Professor Oluwole Akinyele Agbede, as the Director of the DQA. Among its quality assurance initiatives, the DQA introduced the novel practice of semestral student evaluation of teacher performance and effectiveness, which helped to greatly improve teacher punctuality, teaching and other teacher services to students. The instrument for the evaluation was jointly designed by the DQA and the University's Centre for Excellence in Teaching and Learning (CETL), whose motto is: *promoting quality teaching and effective learning.* The pioneer Director of CETL was Professor Sikiru Adekola Babarinde, a Professor of Philosophy & Sociology in the Department of Early Childhood & Educational Foundations, who was recently the President of the Philosophers of Education Association of Nigeria. Professor Babarinde was succeeded by Professor Stephen Akinola Odebunmi of the Department of English.

Staff Recruitment, Development and Retention

In order to continually justify the University's perennial claim of being the "first and best" in Nigeria and also strengthen and enhance its national and global competitiveness, it was necessary to adopt a strategic and sustainable approach for managing diverse matters concerning the institution's human resources. To that end, toward the middle of 2011, I was invited by Professor Abel Idowu Olayinka, who was the Deputy Vice-Chancellor (Academic) in Professor Adewole's administration, to chair a committee to produce a relevant strategic plan. The other members of the committee were: Mr. Kola Ogunfolu (Secretary), Professor Simbo Daisy Amanor-Boadu (June 7, 1952 -July 31, 2019), Professor Oludele Adelanwa Itiola, Professor Adenike Osofisan, Professor Abel Olajide Olorunnisola, A.O. Abimbola, Alex Adekunle Oladeji (former Deputy Registrar at UI, later Registrar of First Technical University, Ibadan), Adedokun Olufemi Ojelabi,

Professor Segun Olugbenga Adediji, Dr. Georgina Ekpenyong, Professor Bola Udegbe, Professor Eme Theodora, Professor Abdulganiyu Olayinka Raji and Dr. Peter Chukwuma Obutte. The committee produced and submitted a document entitled: *Meeting the Human Capital Challenge in a Highly Competitive World: A Strategic Plan for Staff Recruitment, Development & Retention at the University of Ibadan (2012-2017)*. The latter outlined strategic initiatives for ensuring high quality staff recruitment, staff capacity building, continuous professional development and staff retention as well as mentoring and succession planning. Through the implementation of the plan, the University has continued to foster excellence in all aspects of its teaching, research, administration, management and community service functions, in furtherance of its goal to be a world class institution.

Managing Institutional Grants

In 1999, Nigeria was basking in the euphoria of a successful return to democratic rule, following the relinquishing of military dictatorial power by the military ruler, General Abdulsalami Abubakar and the installation on May 29, 1999 of General Olusegun Matthew Okikiola Aremu Obasanjo, who had himself been a military Head of State from February 13, 1976 to September 30, 1979, as a democratically elected President of Nigeria. With civil rule in place, Nigerians longed for a new beginning after decades of military rule that had left many sectors of the Nigerian economy in a dire state. Owing to decades of insignificant attention and poor funding, the education sector was not spared. Indeed, in his inaugural speech on May 29, 1999, the new President characterised the Nigerian nation as follows[17]:

> Our infrastructures – NEPA, NITEL, Roads, Railways, Education, Housing and other Social Services – were allowed to decay and collapse. Our country has thus been through one of its darkest periods. All these have brought the nation to a situation of chaos and near despair. This is the challenge before us.

17   Nigerian President [Olusegun] Obasanjo's inaugural speech [on Saturday, May 29, 1999], http://news.bbc.co.uk/2/hi/world/monitoring/356065.stm, accessed July 31, 2021.]

A renaissance was urgently needed in the education sector but it was not at all clear how the sector would be revitalised. The nation's premier university needed help from Government and its multiple partners.

In the year 2000, a coalition of four US Foundations with interest in and concern for higher education in Africa was formed. Calling itself the 'Partnership for Higher Education in Africa' (PHEA), it comprised the Carnegie Corporation of New York, Rockefeller Foundation and Ford Foundation, which are located in New York, as well as the Chicago-based John D. and Catherine T. MacArthur Foundation, which I will sometimes simply abbreviate as the MacArthur Foundation. The latter established an office in Nigeria in 1994 with the historian, Professor Bolanle Awe, as its pioneer Country Director. Headquartered at the Carnegie Corporation of New York, 437 Madison Avenue, New York, the PHEA was later expanded to include the following three foundations: the California-based William and Flora Hewlett Foundation, the Andrew W. Mellon Foundation with headquarters in New York, and the Kresge Foundation which is based in Troy, Michigan. According to the Partnership, its objectives were to[18]

> generate and share information about African university and higher education issues; discuss strategies for supporting universities; support universities seeking to transform themselves; encourage networking among innovative African university leaders and higher education experts; distill and share lessons learned from grant-making; and advocate for wider recognition of the importance of universities to African development.

In furtherance of these objectives, the PHEA[19]
committed a minimum of $100 million in support of African universities over the first five years, commencing in the year 2000, and pledged an additional $200 million for the second five years, through 2010.

---

18   http://www.foundation-partnership.org/index.php?id=12, accessed on November 5, 2020
19   http://www.foundation-partnership.org/index.php?id=12, accessed on November 5, 2020.

There was, however, no collective pooling of funds for project implementation: the partners individually funded projects of interest to them, although they occasionally also jointly implemented some activities, where necessary.

In Nigeria, the MacArthur Foundation, through its Global Security and Sustainability Programme (GSSP), awarded several grants to four Nigerian universities: the University of Ibadan, University of Port Harcourt, Ahmadu Bello University and Bayero University. The first grant to the University of Ibadan was made in 2001 during the tenure, from September 2000 to March 2004, of Professor Ayodele Olajide Falase as Vice-Chancellor. It was a multiyear grant of US$3,000,000 for the period from 2002 to 2004. The grant was for "staff development and University strengthening." As expected, it triggered the gradual revitalisation of some decrepit institutional structures, facilitated staff capacity building and fostered institutional renewal and strengthening. Professor Olufemi Adebisi Bamiro, who was Professor Falase's Deputy Vice-Chancellor (Administration) from November 9, 2004 to November 30, 2005, has characterised the Foundation's entry into a partnership with the University in 2001 as[20]

> a journey of hope and trust in the Vice-Chancellorship of Professor Ayodele Falase, who took over the mantle of leadership of an institution already blacklisted by critical agencies for poor management of grants.

To ensure a meticulous coordination and implementation of the planned project activities, Professor Falase established a Grant Liaison Office. The latter's duties included liaising with the MacArthur Foundation, the University community and all principal investigators as well as assisting all project teams with the implementation of their activities. He created the post of MacArthur Grant Liaison Officer (MGLO) and also established and constituted the MacArthur Foundation Grant Implementation Committee (MFGIC), with the

---

20   In *GOS Ekhaguere: A Multi-Perspective Glimpse into the Life of a Mathematician at 70*, International Centre for Mathematical & Computer Sciences, Nigeria, pages 211-212, 2017.

Vice- Chancellor as chair. Implementation reports were presented by principal investigators at the MFGIC for extensive analysis and evaluation. The MFGIC also acted as a forum for identifying any implementation challenges, proffering solutions and ensuring that implementation milestones were scrupulously met. Professor Falase appointed Professor Matthew Temitayo Shokunbi as the pioneer MGLO. Professor Shokunbi was in office from 2002 to September 30, 2005. The duties of the MGLO included general oversight of all ongoing projects, demanding, collating and processing implementation reports from principal investigators, writing and timely transmission of mandatory reports to the MacArthur Foundation as well as making presentations at meetings of the MFGIC. Professor Shokunbi was succeeded by the chemist, Professor Akinbo Akinwumi Adesomoju, as MGLO. Professor Adesomoju's tenure as MGLO was from October 1, 2005 to July 31, 2008. I assumed office as MGLO on August 1, 2008, succeeding Professor Adesomoju who had been appointed at that time as the pioneer Vice-Chancellor of the Okitipupa-based Ondo State University of Science and Technology (OSUSTECH). He subsequently became the Pro-Chancellor and Chairman of the Governing Council of OSUSTECH.

I took office at the time when Dr. Kole Shettima was the Country Director, Dr. Raoul Davion was Programme Officer (Human Rights) & Co-chair of the Africa Higher Education Initiative while Phillis Hollice was Programme Administrator (International Programmes) at the MacArthur Foundation. Moreover, Professor Jonathan Foster Fanton, appointed on September 1, 1999, was the Foundation's President. When he was informed about my appointment as MGLO, Professor Fanton sent me a letter, dated August 19, 2008, worded as follows:

> Dear Professor Ekhaguere:
>
> I wanted to congratulate you on your recent appointment as liaison officer for the collaboration between the MacArthur Foundation and University of Ibadan. I have been pleased by

the robust and candid partnership that has emerged between our institutions and look forward to continuing this tradition with the help of your coordination.

MacArthur staff Raoul Davion and Kole Shettima look forward to working with you in your new capacity, and I hope to meet with you when I am next in Nigeria.

All the best.
Sincerely,
signed

Jonathan F. Fanton
President

In my reply, I assured President Fanton that my office would endeavour to contribute "substantially, through its activities, toward enhancing the strong partnership between our two institutions". This was my firm commitment to both the MacArthur Foundation and my University at that time. President Fanton's tenure ended on June 30, 2009. He was succeeded by Professor Robert Gallucci on July 1, 2009. President Gallucci ended his five-year tenure on June 30, 2014.

My appointment as MGLO was unexpected by me. It happened as follows. After his appointment as Vice-Chancellor on December 1, 2005, Professor Bamiro needed to fill the office of Deputy Vice-Chancellor (Administration) which became vacant in May 2008. According to the University's procedure, the Vice-Chancellor would nominate two professors and present them to the University Senate which would then pick one of them through an election. I got a telephone call from Professor Bamiro informing me that I had been selected by him as one of the two professors and that he would be glad if I could accept the nomination. The second nominee was the medical statistician, Professor Elijah Afolabi Bamgboye, who was of the Department of Preventive Medicine and Primary Care (Community Medicine), College of Medicine. As my response, I told Professor Bamiro that I would reflect on his kind gesture and convey my decision. I consulted a broad spectrum of my friends and colleagues about the development. Some were of the opinion that although the playing field would definitely not be level, I should accept the nomination as an appreciation of Professor Bamiro's kind consideration. A few opined that since there were several political cliques on campus, the fact that I belonged to none of the political tendencies was a major disadvantage. Others strongly advised me not to accept the nomination, advancing a plethora of reasons, the most prominent of which was what they perceived as the absence of an unbiased electoral space on campus, whereby some contestants for electoral offices were viewed, mostly by a new generation of young lecturers who ought to be champions of equitable and unbiased elections, through lenses that were often tinted and tainted with diverse hues of ethnicity, parochialism, cliquishness, clannishness and godfatherism. Although I considered the advice as some kind of red herring, because I had won several electoral contests on campus in the past, including election into the University's Governing Council, it was evident that I was in a very difficult situation. After much reflection, I communicated a positive decision to Professor Bamiro. The date of the election was fixed for Monday, May 12, 2008, to coincide with a meeting of Senate which had been scheduled for the same day. Because many of the current social media tools were nonexistent in 2008, to reach the electorate, I relied on sending e-mails and text messages through bulk SMS (Short Message Service) as well as distributing hardcopy flyers to the voters' letterboxes. At the election, I polled 101 votes compared with 135 votes by my opponent, who was therefore declared elected. With the election behind me, I was ready to resume my international academic engagements. But about a fortnight later, I received a telephone call indicating that the Vice-Chancellor, Professor Bamiro, wanted to see me. At the Vice-Chancellor's Office, I met the then incumbent MGLO, Professor Adesomoju, the Deputy Vice-Chancellor (Academic), Professor

Agbaje, and the Vice-Chancellor himself. He informed me that he wanted to appoint me as the MGLO and wished to find out whether the idea was agreeable to me. I thanked him for the kind gesture and replied that I would like to be given some time to consider the proposal. I had not known at that time that Professor Adesomoju had been appointed as the pioneer Vice-Chancellor of the Ondo State University of Science and Technology, Okitipupa. Ultimately, I accepted the offer and assumed office on August 1, 2008.

The Liaison Office and the MGFIC were operating seamlessly at the time I took office. I only needed to sustain the trend and also ensure precision and thoroughness on my part. Moreover, it was my responsibility to enforce strict compliance by the principal investigators with the terms of the grant agreements between the University and the MacArthur Foundation. The persons who worked with me at various times during my tenure were Unity Henry Ejoh (Programme Officer), Michael Akpan (Administrative Officer), Atinuke Kawthar Ghazal (Accountant: seconded from the Bursary), Oyewale Daniel Abioye (Associate Programme Officer), Ejeh Elias Ejeh (Associate Programme Officer), Oluwaseyi Omotayo Okanlawon (Office Assistant), Abiodun Gbenga Arishe (Office Assistant), Sunday Samuel Amoo (Accounts Assistant) and Anthony Fasola (chauffeur: seconded from the Establshments Office).

MacArthur Foundation Grants

After the grant of US$3,000,000 in 2002 by the MacArthur which I mentioned earlier, the Foundation made two additional institutional grants and several project-specific grants to the University. The grants were audited almost annually by the KPMG International Cooperative, which was appointed by the MacArthur Foundation. The additional institutional grants were US$3,400,000, for the period from 2005 to 2007, and US$4,000,000, for the period from

2008 to 2010. I was directly involved in the implementation of the programmes, namely: staff development, University strengthening and community outreach programmes, associated with the later grant. Each programme was structured into multiple projects, whose implementation outcomes had significant impact on the University and the entire nation.

A New Vice-Chancellor

In the midst of the implementation of the US$4,000,000 grant, the tenure of Professor Bamiro as Vice-Chancellor expired on November 30, 2010. He was succeeded on December 1, 2010 by Professor Isaac Folorunso Adewole, a former Provost of the College of Medicine. I was fully aware that with a change in administration, there would invariably also be a change in management style, vision, priorities and tempo. In particular, a new head of an institution would usually want to install his own cabinet, by filling key positions with his loyalists, ostensibly for the smooth implementation of his vision statement. I visited Professor Adewole in the Vice-Chancellor's office about two weeks after he took office. As the head of an office with international responsibilities, I saw it as a duty to apprise him of the MacArthur Foundation grants and the state of the Liaison Office. After congratulating Professor Adewole, I let him know that I took office in 2008 but that I was ready to vacate the post in December 2010, even though my appointment was for three years, in case he had someone in mind to head the Liaison Office. I also requested that he should approve a date before the end of December 2010 for a meeting of the MFGIC, which the Vice-Chancellor normally chaired. Professor Adewole was somewhat unsettled by my offer to vacate the post of MGLO: he asked me why I thought that he would like to appoint a new MGLO. He then said: "you are remaining there". I apologised for my inadvertently unsettling proposal. He fixed a date for a meeting of the MFGIC and I went off to make the necessary arrangements for the meeting. On the day of the meeting, as part of his opening remarks, he announced that I was continuing as the MGLO and that he had brought with him a letter conveying my re-appointment for another period of three years with effect from January 1, 2011. He then pulled the letter from his pocket and delivered it to me in the presence of other members of the MFGIC. I was overwhelmed by this event which, in my view, demonstrated open-mindedness, commitment to continuous institutional improvement and progress as well as a conspicuous determination to foster quality in institutional management. Professor Adewole would later function as Nigeria's Minister of Health from November 11, 2015 to May 28, 2019.

Concerning support for other projects, the Foundation awarded two additional sets of grants to the University of Ibadan. One set of grants was for the implementation of the following six projects: Human Rights and Rule of Law (US$250,000), Monitoring and Evaluation (US$200,000), Fanton Challenge (US$250,000), Equipment for the Multidisciplinary Research Laboratory (US$400,000): the latter grant was awarded directly to the Stockholm-based International Foundation for Science (IFS)), Museum Development (US$60,000) and Strengthening of the Africa Regional Centre for Information Science (ARCIS) (US$232,000). These grants amounted to US$1,392,000, including the US$400,000 which was made directly to the IFS. The second set of grants amounted to US$5,620,000. The latter was to be utilised during the period from 2009 to 2014 for creating and funding the following five specialised centres designed to implement a number of postgraduate training and research activities: Centre For Sustainable Development (CESDEV) which was responsible for running the Masters in Development Practice (US$900,000), Centre for Petroleum, Energy Economics & Law (US$980,000), Centre for Child and Adolescent Mental Health (US$950,000), Centre for Drug Discovery, Development and Production (US$950,000) and Centre for the Control and Prevention of Zoonoses (US$890,000) as well as for supporting 'Training and Research Capacity Building in Population and Public Health', implemented in partnership with the Consortium for Advanced Research Training in Africa (CARTA) (US$950,000).

Quantum of MacArthur Grants

From 2002 to 2012, the total amount of grants awarded by the MacArthur Foundation to the University for a diversity of projects was US$17,012,000: the latter does not include the grant of US$400,000 which was paid directly by the Foundation to the IFS. At the prevailing Central Bank of Nigeria exchange rate of US$1=₦416.02, the grant amount of US$17,012,000 is equivalent to ₦7,077,332,240.00 (seven billion, seventy seven million, three hundred and thirty two thousand, two hundred and forty Naira). The grants produced several institution-transforming outcomes. I will sketch only a few of them.

New Institutional Documents and Policies

The grants strengthened the University's policy development capacity. In this regard, the following new policy and operational documents were generated in the course of project implementation:

- Internationalisation Strategic Plan (2009-2014),
- A new integrated, system-based, person-centred, community-oriented, competency-driven curriculum for the MBBS programme,
- Research Policy,
- Research Management Office Document,
- HIV/AIDS Policy,
- Sexual Harassment Policy, and
- Gender Policy.

While some of these documents outlined the University's policies on the vital issues of research, research management, HIV/

AIDS, sexual harassment and gender equity, others concerned its internationalisation strategy and the construction of a novel curriculum for the training and production of high quality medical personnel. Additionally, as knock-on effects, the diverse activities implemented by means of the MacArthur Foundation grants also inspired, to varying degrees, the formulation of the following policy and operational documents, published by the University:

- University Strategic Plan,
- ICT policy,
- Intellectual Property Policy,
- Strategic Plan for Staff Recruitment, Development and Retention,
- Authorship Policy,
- Quality Assurance Policy and Strategy.

With the foregoing array of policy and operational documents, the University was re-positioned to realize its lofty vision and mission.

New Institutional Structures

In addition to the policy documents listed in the foregoing, the following thirteen new institutional structures also emanated from the implementation of the MacArthur Foundation sponsored projects in the University:

- Research Management Office,
- Gender Mainstreaming Office,
- Office of International Programmes,
- University Advancement Centre,
- Multidisciplinary Central Research Laboratory (MCRL),
- Centre for Entrepreneurship and Innovation (CEI),
- Centre for Excellence in Teaching and Learning (CETL),
- Centre for Human Resource Development (CHRD),
- Centre for Sustainable Development (CESDEV),
- Centre for Petroleum, Energy Economics and Law (CPEEL),

- Centre for Child and Adolescent Mental Health (CCAMH),
- Centre for the Control and Prevention of Zoonoses (CCPZ),
- Centre for Drug Discovery, Development & Production (CDDDP)

These administrative and academic structures greatly strengthened the University's institutional capacity for research management, grant-hunting, internationalisation, management of gender issues, fundraising and national as well as international research collaboration.

Passing on the Baton

By the middle of 2013, I had decided that I would vacate the post of MGLO by the end of December 2013. To implement this resolve, I sent the e-mail message below on September 16, 2013, over three months before the end of my tenure, to the Vice-Chancellor, Professor Isaac Folorunso Adewole, requesting him to initiate a discreet search for my successor.

Date: Mon, Sep. 16, 2013 at 2:09 PM

Subject: Post of MGLO
The Vice-Chancellor,
University of Ibadan

My VC,

POST OF THE MacARTHUR GRANT LIAISON OFFICER

I would like, first and foremost, to thank you most sincerely for your kindness in appointing me, over two years ago, as the MacArthur Grant Liaison Officer with effect from January 1, 2011. Over the years, the appointment has afforded me an opportunity to try to contribute to some aspects of the University administration, especially grant management.

By December 31, 2013, my tenure will come to an end. In my opinion, now is probably an appropriate time for the Vice-Chancellor to initiate a quiet search for a successor, so that (s) he could be properly introduced by me to the diverse activities at the MacArthur Grant Liaison Office throughout the month of December.

In view of the sensitivity of this subject, I am sending this correspondence by e-mail, rather than as an open memorandum, to enable the Vice-Chancellor to conduct the search as discreetly as might be necessary.

I am, of course, available at your convenience for any further discussion.

Best wishes and God bless.

Ekhaguere

From a Vice-Chancellor who ostensibly did not expect the kind of decision that I had arrived at, I received the following e-mail.

Date: Wed, Sep. 18, 2013 at 1:26 AM
Subject: Re: Post of MGLO

Dear GOS,
Thank you for your mail and for bringing this up.

You never cease to amaze me.

I will get back to you.

Kind regards,

Professor Isaac F. Adewole
Vice-Chancellor, University of Ibadan, Ibadan, Nigeria
and President, African Organisation for Research and Training in Cancer

I relinquished the post of MGLO voluntarily on December 31, 2013. Before doing so, I informed my colleagues in the following words.

Dear Colleagues,

My tenure as the MacArthur Grant Liaison Officer (MGLO) at the University of Ibadan will expire at midnight of December 31, 2013. Already, my successor has been named and duly introduced to the University community in a University Bulletin. He is Professor R. A. Oderinde, a professor of chemistry and a former dean of the Faculty of Science.

As from midnight of December 31, 2013, kindly direct all correspondence relating to MacArthur Foundation grants to Professor Oderinde, who will be using the following e-mail address: mglo.unibadan@gmail.com.

My tenure as MGLO has been from August 1, 2008, to December 31, 2013. During that period, I had the good fortune of working (often remotely) with a number of staff of the MacArthur Foundation at its headquarters in Chicago and its Africa Regional Office in Abuja, as well as with fellow MGLOs at Ahmadu Bello University, Zaria, Bayero University, Kano and the University of Port Harcourt, Port Harcourt: persons, all of whom, exhibited utmost professionalism and team spirit in the conduct of Foundation affairs. In turn, I tried to ensure that my actions were correspondingly always professional, with keen attention to detail. I also coordinated the activities of all principal investigators and grantees of the MacArthur Foundation grants to the University. From almost everyone, whether at Chicago, Abuja or Ibadan, I received unstinting cooperation, consideration, support and solidarity. As I step aside, I solicit that my successor be accorded an even higher level of cooperation than I have been able to enjoy.

I held office during the indicated period as a result of two separate but consecutive appointments as MGLO by two Vice-Chancellors with consecutive tenures: Vice-Chancellor Professor Olufemi A. Bamiro (2005-2010) and Vice-Chancellor Professor Isaac F. Adewole (2010 till date). I am extremely grateful to these Vice-Chancellors for the opportunity to render some service to the University of Ibadan in the area of grant management.

While wishing everyone a New Year of joy, peace and prosperity, please accept the assurances of my highest esteem.

Ekhaguere

In response to my communication above about my departure, several persons had some things to say about my tenure. Excerpts of a dozen such statements are as follows.

1. Professor Olufemi Adebisi Bamiro, *former Vice-Chancellor, former Chairman, MacArthur Foundation Grant Implementation Committee, and former Principal Investigator Enterprise Resource Modelling Programme, University of Ibadan.*

    Congratulations on the completion of your tenure as the MGLO. Lest we forget, MacArthur Grant, from inception, was a journey of hope and trust in the Vice-Chancellorship of Professor Ayodele Falase, who took over the mantle of leadership of an institution already blacklisted by critical agencies for poor management of grants. I must therefore really commend you for building on the foundation laid by the former MGLOs – Professors Shokunbi and Adesomoju. The University has really been lucky to have you people at the helm of affairs from 2002 to the present, during which we witnessed quality projects packaging and execution leading to an unprecedented support by MacArthur. I wish you success in your future endeavours.

2. Professor E.A. Bamgboye, *former Deputy Vice-Chancellor (Administration), University of Ibadan*

    Let me join others to congratulate you on the successful completion of a two-term tenure as MGLO. You have indeed demonstrated enviable leadership and I can only wish you higher positions in this country.

3. Professor A.A.B. Agbaje, *former Deputy Vice-Chancellor (Academic) UI*

    Congrats on a wonderful tenure. I wish you all the best even as I also wish Professor Oderinde, another Oga and brother, an equally wonderful tenure.

4. Raoul Davion, *Associate Director, Girls Secondary Education, MacArthur Foundation, Chicago, USA*

    It has been a pleasure working with you, and I (belatedly) echo sentiments expressed by Kole. Thank you for all of your support.

5. Phillis Hollice, *Programme Administrator (International Programmes), MacArthur Foundation,Chicago, USA*

   GOS, it was really great working with you over the years. Having you as my "go to" person at the University really made my work so much easier in Chicago. I wish you all the best in the future!!

6. Dr. Kole Shettima, *Director, Africa Region, MacArthur Foundation*

   Congratulations on the successful completion of your tenure as Liaison Officer of UI. We appreciate all your efforts in the process of implementing projects at the University. We know it is not an easy task given the fact that you are not the Principal Investigator of the projects. We thank you for the years of service to the Foundation and wish you the best. We look forward to other opportunities we can work together.

7. Nasir Bello, *MacArthur Grant Liaison Officer, Ahmadu Bello University*

   I received your mail during the Xmas and New Year break. I had composed several responses which were equally severally discarded until this one. Permit me to on behalf of the two other GLOs at BUK and UniPort to say that we shall miss you and your frank contributions to our MacArthur GLOs meetings. We wish you all the best in your future endeavours as we hope to meet from time to time on some other University assignments.

8. Professor Labo Popoola, *Vice-Chancellor, Osun State University, Osogbo, and former Director, Centre for Sustainable Development, University of Ibadan*

   First, congratulations for the smooth sail. For me, it was a most rewarding experience working with you. As you move on, I pray for your good health and the zeal to continue serving our university and indeed humanity in other capacities.

9. Professor Olayinka Omigbodun, *Principal Investigator of the Mental Health Outreach Programme and Director, Centre for Child and Adolescent Mental Health (CCAMH)*

Congratulations Sir! I have had the opportunity to work with you through the MacArthur grant (2008-2010) in which we provided mental health care in the Ibadan Juvenile Justice system and this current grant through which a Master of Science programme in Child and Adolescent Mental Health (MSc. CAMH) was established in the University of Ibadan. Working with you has been an excellent learning experience. I am grateful for your strict scrutiny of every single request and your insistence that things should be done properly each and every time. I also treasure your wise counsel, especially on tricky issues and your patient listening to the numerous challenges and frustrations I have had to deal with. I am sure that we will continue to need this for some time to come and trust that you will understand the need for a more gradual transition.

10. Professor Wuraola Shokunbi, *Principal Investigator of the HIV/AIDS Peer Education programme*

Let me also start by congratulating you on the wedding of your daughter. Talking mathematics, you have in fact gained a son. On behalf of the team on Peer Education for HIV & AIDS Prevention we congratulate you on the remarkable leadership you provided as MGLO. Being a Mathematician, (without any bias, a genius like other mathematicians), you showed us eloquent but quiet efficiency, precision, hard work and endurance. I pray that the Almighty God will give you uncommon favour in the years to come.

11. Elias E. Ejeh, *former Associate Programme Officer, incumbent Programme Officer, MacArthur Grant Liaison Office, University of Ibadan*

Hearty cheers to you on the successful completion of your two consecutive terms as MGLO of the University of Ibadan. It was a rare privilege to have worked directly with you for two years counting, as you have impacted our lives with your many strengths that stand you out. I also congratulate the wisdom of the University administration for always making available outstanding, erudite scholars and capable hands at the helms of affairs of the MacArthur Grant Liaison Office. As an Associate Programme officer, I am aware that the MacArthur Foundation Grants to the University of Ibadan, especially under your headship has given birth to several Projects, Programmes, Institutions, Centres of Excellence and Policy documents for the University of Ibadan. All of which would not have been attainable without your due diligence, firmness, due process, accountability, foresight and strict compliance to budget line Items in administering the grants. I must quickly add that we shall miss your succinct and very objective writing skills even as a Professor of Mathematics.

12. Dr. (later Professor & Head of Department) Godson R.E.E. Ana, *Department of Environmental Health Sciences, University of Ibadan*

Thanks for your mail and congratulations on a successful tenure and monumental support for the University system and the society in general. I pray that God should grant you more wisdom, good health, renewed vigour and splendid successes in your future endeavours

As already indicated above, my successor as MGLO was the industrial chemist, Professor Rotimi Ayodele Oderinde.

21

ON NATIONAL AND TRANSNATIONAL DUTIES

ith the expiration of my tenure as Head on July 31, 1996, I returned to the mainstream of teaching, research and community service in the Department, taking on more teaching and research functions than I had been able to cope with while in office. In addition, my other responsibilities as a member of the Governing Council, Senate, Congregation and Faculty Board as well as Chairman of the Council Committee on Security were ongoing. I was therefore continuously occupied and busy, both academically and administratively. But a new vista was about to open, as my sights were gradually being directed westward toward the Association of African Universities (AAU), headquartered in Accra, Ghana.

Founded in Rabat, Morocco, on November 12, 1967, and with a membership of 385 as I write, the AAU is the apex non-governmental African organisation engaged in all aspects of higher education management on the African continent. The Association describes itself as[21]

> a prestigious network that provides a continental platform for its member universities to meet, network, share knowledge, share experiences, broker partnerships and collaborate with each other in

---

21   www.aau.org: accessed on November 18, 2020

a diversity of areas related to their areas of specialization, research interests, teaching and learning.

The organisation was not new to me. Indeed, in 1996, I had been a recipient of the Association's Staff Exchange Fellowship, by means of which I was a Visiting Professor, from April to May 1996, at the Department of Mathematics, University of the Western Cape (UWC), Bellville, South Africa. At that time, the Burundian Professor Juma Shabani was the Deputy Secretary General of the AAU and Professor Loyiso Nongxa, the Head of the Department of Mathematics at the UWC, was my host. Professor Nongxa, who would subsequently serve as the Vice-Chancellor of the University of the Witwatersrand, Johannesburg, during a ten-year period from May 19, 2003 to June 1, 2013, was extremely nice, ensuring that my visit was mutually academically beneficial; moreover, throughout my visit, he provided me with accommodation in his own house at no cost and drove me to and from the Department in his car. Prominent among other members of staff with whom I also interacted during my stay was the debonair and urbane Professor Jan Persens (1946 – 2018).

My Journey into the AAU

In February 1997, an announcement appeared in an edition of the University of Ibadan Bulletin about a call by the Association of African Universities (AAU), Accra, Ghana, for applications to fill the vacant post of Senior Programme Officer, who would be responsible for the Association's Programmes & Cooperation. I applied for the post. As my three referees, I chose Professor Akinbo Akinwumi Adesomoju, a professor of Chemistry, who was at that time the Dean of the Faculty of Science, my friend, Professor Ben Ohiomamhe Elugbe, of the Department of Linguistics & African Languages, and the mathematician Professor Samuel Akindiji Ilori, who was my senior colleague in the Department of Mathematics. A few months later, I received an invitation to attend an interview in Accra in respect of the position. Along with the invitation, the AAU also sent me some publications concerning its history and activities, as a way of ensuring that a candidate had a good knowledge of the Association. I read the publications and prepared, as best I could, for the interview. Travelling on the eve of the interview to Accra through the Murtala Muhammed International Airport, Lagos, I met two of my colleagues from the University of Ibadan and a professor from another Nigerian university who revealed that they were also candidates for the post.

On arrival in Accra, the Association accommodated us in a hotel in East Legon. On the next day, we were picked up from the hotel to the venue of the interview, where it emerged that there were altogether eight of us vying for the post: seven men and one woman. All the candidates had lofty qualifications and, additionally, were also former Deans of Faculties, Deans of Postgraduate Schools or Directors of Institutes, except myself: I was merely a former Head of Department. Since it seemed to me that the AAU wanted a former Dean to fill the post, I could not surmise why the organisation bothered to invite me. The candidates were from Egypt in North Africa and Cote D'Ivoire, Ghana and Nigeria in West Africa. Four of the eight candidates were Nigerians. The sole lady was an Egyptian. The interviewing took a whole day, as each candidate interacted with the selection panel for around an hour. I was asked questions about various aspects of higher education in Africa, including what I considered as the reasons for the apparently worsening state of higher education in a large part of the continent, what I might propose as feasible sustainable strategies for reversing the trend and how to continuously assure the quality of institutional provisions, processes and outcomes. I furnished answers to the questions as best I could. Relieved that the interview was behind us, it was much fun as those of us from Nigeria narrated our individual experiences with the panel. From the discussions, I got an insight into some of the responses by my co-interviewees. For example, someone narrated that when asked by the panel what he thought was the fundamental problem of higher education in Africa, he confidently answered that it was strikes. Pressed further by the panel to say why he considered strike actions as the fundamental problem faced by most African higher education institutions, according to him, his response was as follows: "when the teaching staff go on strike and successfully secure some concessions, the non-teaching staff would almost obligatorily also go on strike to press for parity, which in turn automatically would then force the teaching staff to start a new strike action", resulting in a progress-limiting vicious circle. To the same question, my response at the interview was that inadequate funding was the fundamental problem, with wide-ranging adverse impact on all aspects of institutional life, including teaching, learning and research activities, as well as other key statutory functions and processes. Before taking leave of the panel, I asked if I could hand over my vision statement, including my proposed strategic initiatives, toward strengthening and enhancing the post's contribution to the revitalisation of higher education on the continent. A vision statement was not requested in the call for applications, but I considered that I should let the AAU know about my vision for the Association. With the panel's response in the affirmative, I distributed copies of my four-page vision statement to the members of the panel. At the end of the interview, we were dropped off in our hotel by the Association, ready to leave Accra on the next day for Lagos by air.

A Late Night Phone Call

At about 1.30 am in the night, I received a phone call from one of the hotel's receptionists, indicating that an AAU officer wanted to speak with me. The officer was the Liberian Dr. Dominic Nmah Tarpeh (October 14, 1944 – December 5, 2018) who was the Head of Administration & Finance. He apologized for the late night visit and indicated that he had been asked to fetch me to the AAU secretariat, whose address at that time was: African Universities House, Aviation Road Extension, Airport Residential Area, Accra. Today, the Secretariat is situated on Trinity Avenue, East Legon, Accra. I dressed up and met Dr. Tarpeh at the hotel's frontdesk. He had been a member of the interview panel. Courtesies out of the way, Dr. Tarpeh handed me a letter. I was ecstatic to read that I had been selected by the panel to occupy the post. Dr. Tarpeh congratulated me. He then drove me to the AAU Secretariat in the company of another AAU officer, the Ghanaian Ms. Agnes Adjo Mawuli Apedoe, who had the title of Programme Assistant. At the Secretariat, I was again congratulated by the Association's Secretary-General, Professor Narciso Matos, a Mozmbican. He apologized for pulling me out of bed at that hour of the night. He said that the panel authorized him to do so because the alternative would have been my waiting several weeks before learning about my selection, even though the information was already available before my returning to Lagos. We then had a discussion for about 45 minutes concerning the AAU, its challenges, income streams and the core expectations of the office that I had just then been selected to occupy. Professor Matos informed me that a formal contract document would be sent to me and that I could assume duty not later than August 1997. So, providence had once more benevolently intervened at the selection interview to hand me an amazing victory. I returned to the hotel around 2.30 am. At 4.30 am, we were driven to the Kotoka International Airport, Accra, in a bus supplied by the AAU, for our 7 am flight to Lagos.

Stay at the AAU

My appointment as the Senior Programme Officer, with responsibility for Programmes & Cooperation at the AAU, had several predictable implications for my assignments and responsibilities that were ongoing at that time at the University of Ibadan. Some of them could be managed remotely while others required my physical presence at the University. While I could supervise my PhD students remotely, through e-mail correspondences and occasional face-to-face meetings, I had to resign my membership of the Governing Council and some of its standing committees as well as my office as the Chairman of the Council Committee on Security. I also needed to relinquish my teaching responsibilities, since these involved face-to-face engagements. Accordingly, I resigned from Council and, by implication, also from its sub-committees, handed over teaching duties to the Head of Department for re-assignment and then travelled to Accra in August 1997 to assume office. By virtue of my appointment, I automatically had diplomatic status with diplomatic immunity. My diplomatic car identification number, assigned to me by the Ghanaian Ministry of Foreign Affairs, was: CD 6403 P, where CD stands for Corps Diplomatique. The status conferred a lot of privileges on me throughout my stay in Ghana.

When I joined the AAU on August 1, 1997, I met a compact, but highly effective, set of employees, who were categorized as either professional or non-professional (support) staff. During my employment at the Association, the professional staff comprised the following persons: Professor Narciso Matos: (Secretary General from 1996 to 1999), Professor François Rajaoson (Secretary General from 2000 to 2003), Dr. Dominic Nmah Tarpeh (Head, Administration & Finance), Professor GOS Ekhaguere (Senior Programme Officer (Programmes & Cooperation)), Professor George Akilagpa Sawyerr (Director of Research), Mr. Zoumana Bamba (Head, Information and Communication from November 1993 to June 1999), Mr. Yawo Assigbley (Head, Information and Communication from 1999 to 2004). In terms of nationality, Professor George Akilagpa Sawyerr was a Ghanaian, Zoumana Bamba was a Burkinabe and Yawo Assigbley was a Togolese. I have already indicated above that Professor Narciso Matos and Dr. Dominic Nmah Tarpeh were nationals of Mozambique and Liberia, respectively. The Nigerian Professor Chris Ifeanyi Nwamuo was employed as a Senior Programme Officer on a special project which produced the publication: *A Study on Private Universities in Africa* (ISBN: 9988-589-15-8, Association of African Universities, 2000). Some of the key members of the non-professional staff at that time were: Ms. Alida Baeta (Executive Assistant to the Secretary General), Ms. Agnes Adjo Mawuli Apedoe (Programme Assistant), Ms. Gabrielle Hansen (Programme Assistant), Ms. Victoria Duah (Assistant Publications & Public Relations Officer), Ms. Annick Agbotame (WGHE Programme Operations Assistant), Mr. Kofi Arthiabah (Operations Assistant (IT)), who was succeeded by Mr. Benjamin Eshun (Operations Assistant (IT)), and Mr. Cozy Clottey (Principal Accounting Assistant). The abbreviation WGHE stands for Working Group on Higher Education, which was a working group of the Association for the Development of Education in Africa (ADEA). Established in 1988 by the World Bank and originally called Donors to African Education (DAE), the ADEA was primarily a forum for policy dialogue on education in Africa. Throughout my appointment at the AAU, Ms. Apedoe was my Programme Assistant and we worked harmoniously together.

Acts of Senior Programme Officer

My duties at the AAU involved coordinating several already established programmes, developing new programmes and managing any emerging opportunities for cooperation with organisations in Africa and globally. I continually appraised emerging reports, findings and developments in the global higher education world and noted their implications for the higher education sector in Africa. Moreover, in carrying out my roles, I wrote and submitted proposals to several funding agencies and worked in synergy with my colleagues to ensure that the AAU maintained continuous interaction, collaboration and cooperation with its multiple international partners. Some of these were the African Union, World Bank Group, European Union, African

Capacity Building Foundation (ACBF), Economic Community for West African States (ECOWAS), Carnegie Corporation of New York, Ford Foundation, British Council, Association for the Development of Education in Africa (ADEA), Working Group on Higher Education (WGHE), Swedish International Development Cooperation Agency (SIDA), Danish International Development Agency (DANIDA), Institute of International Education (IIE) and the Dutch Organisation for Internationalisation in Education (NUFFIC). Let me give a cursory description of some of the programmes, projects and activities that I coordinated at the AAU.

Programmes, Projects and Goals

Several programmes, projects and activities of the AAU were intended to foster teaching, learning and research as well as networking and regional cooperation among scholars and universities in Africa. I managed several of the programmes and projects at the Association. Funding came from the Association's partners and the meagre subscription fees of its members. Let me highlight some of them.

THE SMALL GRANTS FOR DISSERTATIONS AND THESE PROGRAMME

This was targeted at research students who were pursuing MSc or PhD programmes in AAU member universities. As impact, the grants helped to enhance the quality of postgraduate research on the continent, enabled students who had attained the last stages of their research activities to speedily complete their MSc or PhD programmes and also contributed to reducing the frequency of abandonment of MSc or PhD research work by students who did not have the financial resources to carry out some obligatory field work and investigations or to produce the final copies of their dissertations or theses.

The Academic Exchange Programme

I coordinated the AAU's Academic Staff Exchange programme for academic mobility, aimed at fostering networking and inter-institutional cooperation for teaching and research on the African continent. The programme enabled AAU member universities to invite scholars from other AAU member universities to carry out teaching or collaborative research activities, act as external examiners or perform other academic functions in the inviting institutions. As I mentioned earlier, I was myself a recipient in 1996 of an AAU Staff Exchange fellowship which I utilised at the University of the Western Cape, Bellville, South Africa. The Small Grants and Staff Exchange programmes contributed significantly to the continuous improvement of the quality of the academic provisions, especially the postgraduate activities, of many AAU member universities.

Quality Assurance

Concerning the overaching significance of quality assurance in African universities, I also coordinated the AAU's Quality Assurance Programme aimed at entrenching a culture of quality assurance in African higher education institutions. To that end, I authored a bilingual monograph, published by the Association in 2001, with the English title: *Quality Evaluation Guide* and the French title: *Guide d'Evaluation de la Qualite.* The Guide was intended to enable AAU member institutions to proactively carry out periodic self-evaluation and quality audit activities toward the continuous enhancement of the quality of their functions, processes and procedures. For example, I led an AAU's quality audit team that undertook a visitation to Assuit University, Assuit, Egypt, to validate the institution's self-evaluation report. Also on the invitation of Dr. Johan Brink, who coordinated Quality Assurance at the South African Universities Vice-Chancellors Association (SAUVCA), I was a member of the quality audit team that visited the Medical University of Southern Africa (MEDUNSA), Pretoria, South Africa, to validate the institution's self-evaluation process. The Quality Assurance Programme helped to entrench a culture of quality management in many AAU member universities and enhanced the global recognition and competitiveness of their provisions, degrees and graduates.

REGIONAL COOPERATION IN GRADUATE TRAINING AND RESEARCH

Consistent with the determined drive in the 1990s by African countries to foster regional and sub-regional integration on the continent, the AAU established a programme in 1998 called Regional Cooperation in Graduate Training and Research (RCGTR), under my coordination. The RCGTR was aimed at financially and programmatically supporting African universities to form active multinational networks for graduate training and research. That was because, in addition to the move toward regional and sub-regional integration in Africa, the Association had also observed that many universities on the continent had not developed a vibrant culture of cooperation and networking with their African peers in matters of graduate training and research. The RCGTR programme was designed to change the game.

First Ever African Centres of Excellence

The United States Agency for International Development (USAID) helped to realize the objectives of the RCGTR by providing sorely needed funding: it made a contribution of one million dollars (US$1,000,000) to the Working Group on Higher Education (WGHE), through the Association for the Development of Education in Africa (ADEA), in support of the RCGTR programme. The WGHE was coordinated by Dr. William Saint, who was a Higher Education Specialist at the World Bank at that time. Using a competitive and transparent process, the AAU applied part of the grant to create some regional multinational networks for graduate training and research. Toward fostering the Association's response to the social reality in much of Africa in the 1990s, especially in West Africa which was sadly marked by multiple ongoing wars in those days, a portion of the grant was dedicated *ab initio* to funding one competitively selected project that focused on humanitarian and refugee problems. This was aimed at producing experts who would be equipped with the requisite capacity to handle humanitarian and refugee issues and challenges on the continent instead of always relying on organizations outside Africa.

To the requests for proposals which I sent to all African universities in 1998, I received forty one (41) submissions for the creation of regional multinational networks for graduate training. With the aim of fostering agile responses by African nations and universities to the continent's social problems, I sent out another request for proposals in 1999 for the establishment of graduate programmes in humanitarian and refugee studies. In response, I received seven (7) proposals. Apart from focusing on solving some of Africa's development challenges, the submitted (41+7) proposals also addressed the key issue of research capacity building. Two separate panels of international experts were set up in 1998 and 1999 to select the fundable ones among the 48 proposals, using a number of criteria, including the following: leadership; verifiable institutional support for the proposal; autonomy of the decision-making process within project-hosting institutions; autonomy of decision-making process among proposed network partners; academic and scientific excellence; adequate operational arrangements; cost-effectiveness; gender equity and long-term financial sustainability. In the end, the following six proposals, comprising five (5) from the first set of forty one (41) proposals and one (1) from the second set of seven (7) proposals, were selected and funded:

1. Name of Centre: University Science, Humanities
                               and Engineering Partnerships in
                               Africa (USHEPiA).
    Lead Institution: University of Cape Town, South
                               Africa.
    Centre Leader: Professor Martin West..
    Focus of Centre: Award of Fellowships, Masters
                               and PhD degrees in Science,
                               Humanities and Engineering to
                               staff of partner institutions.
    Partner Institutions: University of Cape Town, South
                               Africa, University of Botswana,
                               Botswana, University of Dar Es
                               Salam, Tanzania, University of
                               Zimbabwe, Zimbabwe, Jomo
                               Kenyatta University, Kenya,
                               Makerere University, Uganda,
                               University of Nairobi, Kenya,
                               University of Zambia, Zambia.

2. Name of Centre: Centre d'étude Régional pour
                               l'Amélioration de l'Adaptation à la
                               Sècheresse(CERAAS), Thies, Sénégal.
    Lead Institution: Centre d'étude Régional pour
                               l'Amélioration de l'Adaptation à
                               la Sècheresse (CERAAS), Thies,
                               Sénégal.
    Centre Leader: Dr. Harold Roy-Macauley
    Focus of Centre: Graduate Programmes and
                               Collaborative Research on Semi-
                               Arid Agriculture.
    Partner Institutions: CERAAS, Senegal, Ecole
                               Nationale Supérieure d'Agriculture
                               (ENSA) de Thiès, Senegal, Abia
                               State University, Nigeria, Fourah
                               Bay College, Sierra Leone,
                               Universite Anta Diop, Senegal,
                               Université de Ougadougou,
                               Burkina Faso.

3. Name of Centre: Centre for Human Rights.
   Lead Institution: University of Pretoria, Pretoria,
                            South Africa.
   Centre Leader: Professor Christof Heyns.
   Focus of Centre: LLM and Masters degrees in
                            Humanitarian and Human Rights
                            Law in Africa.

   Partner Institutions: University of Pretoria, University
                            of Botswana, Botswana, University
                            of Dar Es Salam, Tanzania,
                            University Mauritius, Mauritius,
                            University of Namibia, Namibia,
                            University of Zambia, Zambia,
                            University of Zimbabwe,
                            Zimbabwe.

4. Name of Centre: Centre de Recherche en Sciences
                            Biologiques, Alimentaires et
                            Nutitionnnelles.
   Lead Institution: Université de Ouagadougou,
                            Ouagadougou, Burkina Faso.
   Centre Leader: Professor Alfred Traore.
   Focus of Centre: Graduate Programmes and
                            Research on Biotechnology and
                            Microbiology
   Partner Institutions: Université de Ouagadougou,
                               Burkina Faso,Université du Benin,
                            Benin, Université du Mali, Mali,
                            Université Abdou Moumouni de
                            Niamey, Niger, Université de
                            Conakry, Guinea, Université de
                            Cocody, Cote d'Ivoire.

5. Name of Centre: Department of Applied
                            Accountancy.
   Lead Institution: University of South Africa
                            (UNISA), Pretoria, South Africa.
   Centre Leader: Professor Hein F. Redelinghuys.
   Focus of Centre: Quality Assurance in Accountancy
                            in Southern Africa

Partner Institutions: UNISA, South Africa,
                                     University of Botswana, Botswana,
                                     University of Lesotho, Lesotho,
                                     University of Malawi, Malawi,
                                     University of Namibia, Namibia,
                                     University of Swaziland,
                                     Swaziland, University of
                                     Zimbabwe, Zimbabwe

6.   Name of Centre: Centre for Peace and Conflict
                                     Studies.
     Lead Institution: University of Ibadan, Ibadan,
                                     Nigeria.
     Centre Leader: Professor John Bayo Adekanye.
     Focus of Centre: Masters programme in
                                     Humanitarian and Refugee
                                     Studies.
     Partner Institutions: University of Ibadan, Nigeria,
                                     University of Burundi, Burundi,
                                     University of Conakry, Guinea,
                                     Eduardo Mondlane University,
                                     Mozambique, University of
                                     Ghana, Ghana, University of
                                     Khartoum, Sudan, University of
                                     Liberia, Liberia, University of
                                     Sierra Leone, Freetown, Sierra
                                     Leone.

These were the first ever African centres of excellence for graduate training and research. Established by the AAU, with funding from USAID, channelled through the ADEA/WGHE, they involved partnership and cooperation among 34 different African institutions. The process of creating the centres was coordinated by me. They were located in four countries, namely: Burkina Faso, Nigeria, Senegal and South Africa. As highlighted above, their areas of specialization were Engineering, Agriculture, Humanitarian and Refugee Studies, Humanitarian and Human Rights Law, Biotechnology and Accountancy. In spite of the relatively small take-off grants received by the centres, each of them was able to make a substantial impact in its area of specialization. From the outset, the AAU's expectation was that if the centres turned out to be successful pilots of innovation, change and regional cooperation, there would be a continuous scaling up of the number of new centres of excellence for graduate training and research that would be created annually. But owing to the overly high dependence of the AAU on donors for the funding of its diverse programmes at that time and also the well known short attention span of funding organizations, marked by their periodically shifting programmatic interests and focus, the expectation did not materialize in the subsequent years: no additional centres of excellence for graduate training and research were created before I left the AAU, beyond the original six listed above.

Reinventing the Wheel in 2014

The same idea that I had helped to implement at the AAU through the RCGTR programme, just before the beginning of this millennium, was reinvented some fifteen years later in 2014, when the African Centres of Excellence (ACEs) Project was launched by some African governments in partnership with the Washington-based World Bank. The West African governments of Benin, Burkina Faso, Cameroon, The Gambia, Ghana, Nigeria, Senegal and Togo launched ACE 1, comprising 22 centres, in 2014. Similarly, the East and Southern African governments of Ethiopia, Kenya, Malawi, Mozambique, Rwanda, Tanzania, Uganda and Zambia launched ACE 2, comprising 24 centres, in 2016. To fund the centres, the participating countries jointly secured loans of US$165 million and US$148 million for ACE 1 and ACE 2, respectively, from the World Bank. In 2019, the ACE Impact for Development Project was launched and funded by the following African countries: Benin, Burkina Faso, Cote d'Ivoire,

Djibouti, The Gambia, Ghana, Guinea, Niger, Nigeria, Senegal, and Togo, with a loan of US$143 million jointly funded by the Agence Française de Développement (AFD), i.e. the French Development Agency, and the World Bank. For the project implementation process, which was managed by the World Bank using a number of disbursement linked indicators (DLIs), there were a Project Steering Committee (PSC) (which comprised the AAU, the World Bank, representatives of the governments of the participating countries, project focal points and a representative of the Economic Community of West African States (ECOWAS)) and the National Steering Committees (NSCs) for oversight in the participating countries. Additionally, the Association of African Universities was designated as the Regional Facilitation Unit (RFU), with the responsibility to collect, compile and analyse data from the ACEs and forward same to the World Bank to inform grant management and disbursement decisions. To ensure smooth and effective project implementation, several of the participating countries had Project Implementation Units (PIUs); in Nigeria, the National Universities Commission was the PIU. With the substantial financial involvement of African governments as indicated above, through their subscription to World Bank loans, a selected ACE received funding ranging from US$5,000,000 to US$8,000,000, completely dwarfing the amount of US$1,000,000 (one million dollars) that was available to the AAU in 1998 and 1999 for the creation of the first ever set of multinational African centres of excellence for graduate training and research which I highlighted above. But in spite of the fact that it took close to a decade and half for the continent to return to the implementation of the fundamental goals of the RCGTR programme, it was satisfying to me that, through the ACEs Project, several African countries, together with the World Bank, have played proactive roles in the creation and project management of a number of strategically significant graduate training and research centres that are potentially indispensable for any nation's sustainable development and progress. Providentially, I also participated in the implementation of the ACE 1 project in Nigeria, in respect of those centres whose projects were in the areas of Science, Technology, Engineering and Mathematics (STEM). I shall provide additional details before long.

International Fellowships Programme

In Nigeria and many other developing countries, there is the painful reality that several demographic groups are excluded from participating in higher education for no fault of theirs but often simply on account of such factors as gender, poverty, injustice, physical disability, ethnicity, religion, race and war. As a consequence, a large number of persons from the disadvantaged groups are continually left behind in their quest for postgraduate education. I have already narrated earlier how in my own struggle to join the mainstream of the educated in Nigeria, I would not have had a primary school education without Chief Obafemi Awolowo's Free Universal Primary Education Programme (FUPEP) of 1955; I would not have had a secondary school education from 1961 to 1965 but for a Western/Midwestern Region scholarship that I providentially won; I would never have had a High School Education from 1966 to 1967 were it not for a College Scholarship awarded to me by the Immaculate Conception College, Benin City, when Fr. Joseph Patrick Donnelly was the school's Principal; and I would certainly not have obtained a postgraduate education abroad from 1971 to 1975 if I did not secure a Midwestern/ Bendel State scholarship. Concerned by the situation in developing countries with regard to access to and affordability of postgraduate education by many disadvantaged groups, the New York-based Ford Foundation launched its flagship programme, called the International Fellowships Programme (IFP), in 2001 during the tenure, from 1996 to 2007, of Ms. Susan Berresford as its President. Dr. Joan Rosalie Dassin was appointed as the

Executive Director of the Foundation's International Fellowships Fund (IFF). She was in office from August 2000 to September 2013. With an investment of some US$417 million in the IFP by the IFF within a period of 15 years, the IFP represented the largest single project ever supported by the Foundation. Its goal was to enable exceptional individuals from Africa, Middle East, Asia, Latin America and Russia, who would otherwise never have the opportunity for further studies, to pursue postgraduate degree programmes in reputable higher education institutions around the world. The implementation of the IFP in West Africa was coordinated by the AAU. Inside the AAU, I was responsible for the relevant coordination. The IFP naturally resonated spontaneously with me because of my personal experience of uncertainty and trepidation in the course of my climbing, one slippery rung at a time, up the education ladder. It was a Programme that had the potential to be life-changing for a large number of disadvantaged persons who were in dire straits educationally for no fault of theirs. I produced a set of selection criteria and some bespoke score sheets for use during the selection of potential Fellows. The documents were adopted by several other IFP sites. Before I voluntarily left the AAU in December 2001, with the Burundian Professor Athanase Bakunda as my successor, I worked seamlessly with Dr. Dassin on the IFP. My project assistant on the IFP was Ms. Araba Botchway. After leaving the AAU in December 2001, I was appointed as a Consultant to the Ford Foundation, New York. My brief was to appraise the state of the IFP, propose standards to be applied by all IFP sites and formulate comparability criteria for assessing the IFP sites. In 2003, I produced a report, commissioned by the Ford Foundation, with the title: Selection Processes at the IFP Sites: Standards, Coherent Frameworks and Comparability, that described the state of the IFP in its early days and tackled the other topics in my brief.

Some Outcomes of the IFP Project

When the activities of the IFP ended in 2013, over 300 Fellows, including 175 Nigerians, had been selected from the West African subregion and placed in appropriate academic institutions by the IFP's Placement Partners: the British Council, the Institute of International Education (IIE) and the Netherlands Universities Foundation for International Cooperation (NUFFIC). The 300 Fellows carried out their postgraduate studies in Britain, Canada, France, Switzerland, South Africa and the United States of America, obtaining Masters or PhD degrees. From 2001 to 2013, the IFP supported more than 4,305 Fellows in 22 participating countries, namely: Brazil, Chile, China, Egypt, Ghana, Guatemala, India, Indonesia, Kenya, Mexico, Mozambique, Nigeria, Palestine, Peru, Philippines, Russia, Senegal, South Africa, Tanzania, Thailand, Uganda and Vietnam. In 2014, Dr. Dassin assumed the post of Professor of International Education and Development at the Heller School of Social Policy and Management, Brandeis University, Waltham, USA. The IFP greatly fostered the inclusion of several disadvantaged demographic groups in the postgraduate higher education ecosphere, eventually producing grassroots leaders, socially committed innovators and proactive change agents, equipped with the humanitarian and technical skills to contribute to national and global development processes. I was happy that the IFP successfully achieved these outcomes for thousands of Fellows in the 22 developing countries and that I participated in its implementation.

Consultancy at the Ford Foundation Lagos

Not long after my return to Nigeria from Ghana in December 2001, I was appointed as the Higher Education Consultant to the Ford Foundation, Office for West Africa, Lagos, in July 2002, when Dr. Adhiambo Odaga was the Representative and Head of Office while Dr. Babatunde Ahonsi was the Senior Programme

Officer of the Foundation. The latter has been funding a variety of projects in Nigeria since 1958. My responsibilities were wide-ranging and revolved around the Nigerian Higher Education System (NHES). They encompassed, for example, the implementation of Foundation-approved higher education projects; formulating and proposing strategies for addressing a diversity of existing and emerging challenges in the higher education sector; dealing with matters connected with the curriculum, teaching, learning, research and assessment in relation to graduate employability, the world of work and national development; and proposing initiatives for ensuring the continuous improvement of the NHES. At that time, it was generally agreed by most stakeholders that the NHES was far from being fit for purpose and, consequently, in great need of proactive and transformational interventions that would revitalize, strengthen and re-position it for the effective and sustainable discharge of its mandate. In what follows, I adumbrate the key elements of three of the multiple projects which I implemented in Nigeria with funding from the Ford Foundation.

Pipeline Issues in the Nigerian Education System

Over the years, among some of the glaring and enduring indicators of the state of the Nigerian Education System (NES) have been the number of out-of-school children of primary school age and the number of learners who dropped out of school at some level of education every year. Over time, far from declining, these numbers have escalated into millions. Aware of these and other worrying statistics, the Foundation decided to fund a project to investigate and document some of the fundamental challenges in the NES. Accordingly, my first project as a Ford Foundation Higher Education Consultant was a study to determine the ease of entry into and progression through Nigeria's education pipeline from one end to the other. As a major outcome of the project, I produced a documentation of the nature and types of obstructions, obstacles and constraints encountered by a learner in the education pipeline from the primary to the higher education level and also a set of problem-solving initiatives and recommendations for removing the impediments. These were contained in a monograph, authored by me and published by the Ford Foundation in 2003, with the title: *The Education Pipeline in Nigeria: A Research Report and Synthesis of Consultations* (ISBN 9966-813-02-0). In reviewing the publication, Dr. Alison Bernstein (June 8, 1947 - June 30, 2016), who was the Foundation's Vice President responsible for its programme on Knowledge, Creativity and Freedom, wrote:

> the author does an exceptional job to provide the background, sort through the difficulties and propose potential solutions relevant to the educational system in Nigeria, Africa's most populous nation.

The publication was widely distributed by the Ford Foundation to its partners and Nigerian stakeholders.

Mapping Higher Education Resources in Nigeria

The second project which I implemented with the Foundation's funding was a mapping of the accessible resources in higher education in Nigerian universities. The outcomes of the project were documented in a monograph, authored by me and published by the Ford Foundation (Office for East Africa), with the title: *Mapping and Inventory of Resources in Higher Education in Africa: West African Regional Report (Nigeria)*, The Ford Foundation (Office for East Africa), 2004, ISBN 9966-813-04-7. As I wrote in its Section on Introduction and Methodology, the monograph furnished

> some insight into the state of higher education resources in Nigeria as well as the existing capacity of the available experts and institutions to actively contribute to the global pool of knowledge in the field of higher education studies.

In the words of Dr. Anne-Marea Griffin, who was the Principal Editor and Programme Consultant of the Ford Foundation's

African Higher Education Initiative, under which the project was funded,

> we have managed to produce directories that serve as appropriate launching pads for the increased amounts of data that are yet to come.

The resource audit beamed a searchlight on the fundamental resource gaps and shortfalls in the Nigerian Higher Education System. The publication was also widely disseminated by The Ford Foundation to its partners and Nigerian stakeholders.

Teaching Innovation Awards

The third major project I carried out with a grant from the Ford Foundation was called the Ford Foundation Teaching Innovation Awards Programme (FF-TIAP). The FF-TIAP was a novel initiative to identify, acclaim and reward Nigerian university teachers who were transferring knowledge innovatively to students and inspiring, mentoring and grooming them to be dedicated to the pursuit of learning and knowledge acquisition. As a pilot, the FF-TIAP focused on fostering teaching and curriculum innovation in science, engineering and technology. To this end, the project involved an awards-competition among twenty Nigerian universities, differentiated by ownership (Federal, State or Private) and geopolitical zone. The search was for

> teachers in Nigerian universities whose activities, in spite of the numerous challenges they continually faced, were substantially enriching and deepening student learning experience through their performance in classroom teaching, innovation and creativity in curriculum design and delivery, as well as a steadfast commitment to student advising and mentoring.

For the competition, a transparent bottom-up approach was adopted, with the selection process at each participating university overseen by an Institutional Selection Committee (ISC) chaired by a Deputy Vice-Chancellor. The selection criteria, which were approved by the participating universities, revolved around the core topics: innovation and creativity in curriculum design; classroom teaching and curriculum delivery; and commitment to the advising and mentoring of students and colleagues. At the national level, applying the selection criteria, the selection process was managed by a National Selection Committee (NSC) of distinguished Nigerians. The NSC was constituted as follows. Emeritus Professor Ayo Banjo, a former Vice-Chancellor of the University of Ibadan, was the Chairman. The other members were: Professor GOS Ekhaguere, Mrs. Eugenia Abu, Professor Ado Dan-Isa, Dr. Babatunde Ahonsi, Dr. Anthony Marinho, Professor Anthony Uyi Osagie and Professor Bobboi Umar. Professor Ekhaguere also functioned as the Secretary of the NSC.

The Ford Foundation Teaching Innovation Awards ceremony was held at the Ladi Kwali Hall, Abuja Sheraton and Towers, Abuja, FCT, on Thursday, October 29, 2009. Five academics from four Nigerian universities emerged as award-winners. In the order of merit, beginning from the first to the fifth position, the awardees were: Professor Abdulkarim Salawu Ahmed (Ahmed Bello University, Zaria), Dr. Mohammed Dauda (University of Maiduguri, Maiduguri), Professor Peter Benson Uche Chukwugaeme Achi (Federal University of Technology, Owerri), Dr. Charles Korede Ayo (Covenant University, Ota) and Dr. Aderemi Aaron-Anthony Atayero (Covenant University, Ota). Among the large number of participants who were present at the award ceremony were the Minister of State for Education, Hajiya Aishatu Dukku, Attorney General of the Federation and Minister of Justice, Mr. Michael Aondoakaa, Minister of Information and Communication, Professor Dora Nkem Akunyili (July 14, 1954-June 7, 2014), Minister of Labour and Productivity, Prince Adetokunbo Kayode, Minister of State for Health, Dr. Aliyu Idi Hong, former Minister of Education, Mrs. Chinwe Nora Obaji and former Minister of Education, Professor Chibuike Maduike, as well as the Chairman of the NUC, Professor Shehu Galadanci,

Executive Secretary of the NUC, Professor Julius Amioba Okojie, former Executive Secretary of the NUC from 1979 to 1981, Dr. Abel Ibude Guobadia (June 28, 1932-February 5, 2011), former Executive Secretary of the NUC from 1981 to 1986, Alhaji Yahya Aliyu, former Executive Secretary of the NUC from 1986 to 1996, Professor Idris Abdulkadir, and former Executive Secretary of the NUC from 2001 to 2006, Professor Peter Okebukola. From the Ford Foundation (Office for West Africa) were Dr. Joseph Gitari, who stood in for the Foundation's Representative, Dr. Adhiambo Odaga, and Dr. Babatunde Ahonsi, Senior Programme Officer at the Foundation.

The outcomes of the FF-TIAP are contained in a monograph, authored by me and published in 2010 by the International Centre for Mathematical & Computer Sciences with the title: *Teaching Innovation in Nigerian Universities: Report of a Project Funded by the Ford Foundation*. A follow-up national conference was organized by me and held at the Redeemer's University at its temporary site at Mowe, Ogun State, from April 17-20, 2012, during the tenure of Professor Zacchaeus Debo Adeyewa as the Vice-Chancellor of the institution. With me as the editor, the proceedings of the conference were published in the same year 2012 by the International Centre for Mathematical & Computer Sciences (www.icmcs.org), with the title: *Teaching and Research Innovation in Nigerian Universities* (ISBN: 978 37246 3 0). On the whole, the project, conference and several knock-on activities collectively induced improvements in the quality of teaching, research, mentoring and student learning experience, thereby fostering national development and progress.

Postgraduate Research in the Nigerian University System

The state of the Nigerian University System (NUS), together with relevant strategies for continuously improving it, has been of immense concern to me over the years. Among the nagging issues that needed continuous attention were teaching innovation, learning resources, research capacity building, research integrity, application of research to national development, curriculum design and implementation, quality assurance and strategic planning. Accordingly, within the NUS, I participated in several projects and activities, beyond my statutory role as a teacher and researcher, at the National Universities Commission (NUC), whose enabling law is the NUC Act Cap 81 of 2004, and at the Tertiary Education Trust Fund (TETFund), established by an Act in 2011. Let me sketch rapidly a number of them.

Participation in some NUC Activities

A notable flagship programme of the NUC was the Nigerian Universities Doctoral Theses Award Scheme (NUDTAS), into which an earlier scheme called the Nigerian Universities Postgraduate Theses Award Scheme (NUPTAS) had transformed. The objective of NUDTAS was to identify and reward postgraduate students who produced outstanding PhD theses in Nigerian universities. NUDTAS was therefore an instrument for stimulating scholarship through research work of high quality, ensuring academic excellence, fostering competition among doctoral students in Nigerian universities and entrenching a sustainable culture of continuous commitment to the strategic development and application of research by scholars throughout the NUS. To select deserving candidates for awards, it was necessary to institute a process that ensured diligent scrutiny and assessment. This was accomplished by means of multiple panels of subject specialists, comprising Professors from Nigerian universities, which were set up by the NUC from time to time. Through invitations from the NUC on three distinct occasions, I played an active role in three selection processes. These were in September 2009, December 2011 and October 2013, when I participated in the assessments of the doctoral theses in the mathematical sciences. The theses had been approved by some Nigerian universities for the award of PhD degrees in the seven years 2006 and 2007; 2008 and 2009; and 2010, 2011 and 2012. I was involved in the assessments during the tenure of Professor Julius Amioba Okojie as the Executive Secretary of the NUC, with Professor Onyemaechi Valentine Ekechukwu as the Director of Research & Innovation and also the coordinator of NUDTAS. The latter was successful in many ways. Indeed, over the years, it propelled a continually increasing level of thoroughness in the supervision of doctoral theses in the NUS, the steadfast upgrading of the available institutional resources for research activities in Nigerian universities, the adoption and implementation of international best practices in the delivery of research training in the NUS and the continuous improvement of the global competitiveness of the PhD graduates produced by Nigerian universities as a result of the progressive escalation of the quality of their theses. I was glad to have contributed, through my participation in NUDTAS, to the delivery of these laudable outcomes.

Consultant on the ACEs Project

As already mentioned above, the NUC appointed me, in August 2017, as the Country-based Science, Technology, Engineering and Mathematics (STEM) Consultant and a Member of the Scientific Advisory Team for the STEM-related Africa Centres of Excellence (ACEs) in Nigeria. My appointment was during the tenure of Professor Abubakar Adamu Rasheed, who assumed office on August 3, 2016, as the Executive Secretary of the NUC. Dr. Joshua Atah was the National Coordinator of both the ACE Project and the Sustainable Procurement Environmental and Social Standards Enhancement (SPESSE) Project at the NUC. Broadly, my responsibilities included: participating in Supervision Missions by the World Bank to the STEM ACEs; assisting with the technical and scientific aspects of the implementation plans, including quality assurance and accreditation issues at the STEM

ACEs; and assisting in the strengthening of the operational and scientific relationships among the STEM ACEs, on the one hand, and their home institutions; relevant academic, scientific and research development partners with focus on STEM, on the other hand. Under the ACE 1 Project, there were three STEM ACEs in Nigeria, namely: the Pan African Materials Institute (PAMI) located at the African University of Science and Technology, Abuja, which had Professor Peter Azikiwe Onwualu and Dr. Olusola Odusanya as Centre Leader and Co-Leader, respectively; the OAU ICT Driven Knowledge Park (OAK PARK), Obafemi Awolowo University, Ile-Ife, whose Deputy Vice-Chancellor (Academic) and Professor Ganiyu Adesola Aderounmu were the Centre Leader and Co-Leader, respectively; and the Africa Centre of Excellence in Oilfield Chemicals Research (ACE-CEFOR), University of Port Harcourt, Port Harcourt with Professor Ogbonna Friday Joel as the Centre Leader. I carried out my responsibilities as a Consultant in two of the three STEM ACEs in Nigeria, namely: PAMI and OAK PARK. Briefly, PAMI's training and research activities revolved around the development of biomaterials for health care; energy issues, especially the development of organic solar cells and organic light emitting devices (OLEDs) as well as energy storage materials; water filtration, mineral processing, corrosion in oil and gas facilities and the development of sustainable building materials. In the case of OAK PARK, its training and research activities were focused on software matters and their applications for national and regional development. Toward the realization of its multiple objectives, this ACE established a number of laboratories such as those for data communication and cloud computing, intelligent system and information system engineering, software engineering, computer engineering and cybersecurity. Through their diverse training and research activities, which attracted a sizable number of students from West Africa and Central Africa annually, PAMI and OAK PARK contributed significantly to the enhancement of regional cooperation in graduate training and research.

Funding and Fostering National Research

Nigeria, unlike, for example, the so-called Asian Tigers, is yet to fully exploit the natural dynamic between research and national development: research drives national development which, in turn, funds research and its uptake. Consequently, the pace of the nation's development and progress has been slow, largely because of the nation's apparent tepid commitment to problem-solving and mission-oriented research activities and also an inadequate attention to steadfastly ensuring a high degree of uptake of research outcomes. Given its huge natural endowment with both human and material resources and in spite of owning a diversity of infrastructure for fundamental and applied research, it has been utterly confounding that the most populous black country in the entire world remains largely underdeveloped. The vast investment on research infrastructure over time has not yielded substantial developmental benefits to the nation because research activities in almost all of the nation's public research facilities have not been adequately and sustainably funded. As a consequence, the quantum of resources for research has invariably not been such as could ever propel Nigeria into the elite rank of continental or global leaders in research, or significantly contribute to the nation's rapid development.

Notwithstanding the huge scarcity of adequate research funding, several public research institutes and tertiary educational institutions have, nevertheless, been innovative, as evidenced by several research outcomes with potential positive impact on national development. But the nation is not gleaning the expected full benefits of its institutions' research findings principally because there are no viable and sustainable routes from laboratory to market: this is marked by an inadequate uptake of many game-changing research outcomes by Nigerian industries, entrepreneurs or venture capitalists. With a large proportion of the research findings ending up pathetically on library shelves with no uptake, a slow pace of national development is engendered, leading to Nigeria's unending reliance on other nations for sorely-needed solutions to its developmental challenges.

Let me also mention another factor that has become accentuated in recent times: in order to secure a respectable position in the so-called global university ranking, many Nigerian universities seem to be constrained to conduct only that kind of research whose outcomes are publishable in foreign journals with high impact factors. As a result, their research findings and innovations are often not directly aimed at solving the nation's pressing challenges but rather the problems that are considered interesting by the foreign journals. Therefore, while such research findings are fit for publication but would often not address national development issues, they become globally available to flagship industries, with limitless capacity for research uptake, in developed countries. This situation, which is becoming deeply entrenched in the nation's research ecosphere, was glaring during the COVID-19 pandemic in the year 2020 when Nigeria could not develop any life-saving vaccine to address the lethal virus but placed all its hopes precariously on the benevolence of, or agreements with, its global partners. For the research outcomes of the nation's research establishments to continually have the desired handshake with national development, some of the fundamental prerequisites are adequate funding of viable research activities, provision of state-of-the-art research infrastructure, continuous research capacity-building, research management and a sustainable pursuit of mission-oriented research goals, within the context of a quintuple helix: the academia, government, industry, civil society and the environment. A Nigerian government organisation that has recently stepped forward to ensure that the national research enterprise continually advances national development is the Tertiary Education Trust Fund (TETFund), established by the TETFund Act of 2011. A principal goal of the TETFund is to strengthen and expand research activities in Nigerian public tertiary education institutions and also foster research and development initiatives in Nigeria. Accordingly, the TETFund periodically calls for research proposals from scholars in Nigerian tertiary education institutions and thereafter select some of the proposals, through a transparent and competitive process, for funding. A request for proposals would often elicit thousands of submissions. To manage the inherent selection process, the TETFund established the TETFund National Research Fund Screening and Monitoring Committee (NRFS&MC). I was appointed as a member of the NRFS&MC on June 21, 2019, during the tenure of Professor Suleiman Elias Bogoro as the Executive Secretary of TETFund. As conveyed in the letter of appointment, the chairman of the NRFS&MC was Professor Olufemi Adebisi Bamiro, former Vice-Chancellor of the University of Ibadan. The functions of the NRFS&MC were to:

> pre-qualify applications for research grants from academics in beneficiary institutions to ensure that they are in compliance with approved templates for accessing TETFund NRF Grant; categorise pre-qualified research proposals into streams and disciplines to ease appointing Assessors/Reviewers; recommend pre-qualified and categorised proposals; serve as members of the NRF Proposal Defense Panel; and carry out any other responsibilities as may be assigned by the Fund.

For the effective implementation of these responsibilities, the NRFS&MC was structured into three Subcommittees, namely: Humanities and Social Sciences (HSS), Science, Engineering, Technology and Innovation (SETI) and Cross-Cutting (CC). I served on the SETI Subcommittee which initially had Professor Israel Folorunso Adu (July 4, 1944 – June 9, 2020) as its chair and was responsible for processing the proposals from eleven research thematic areas. Following his unexpected demise on June 9, 2020, Professor Adu was succeeded by Professor Abdullahi Abdu Zuru who had been a Vice-Chancellor of two institutions: Usman Danfodio University, Sokoto, and Kebbi State University of Science and Technology (KSUST), Aliero. The proposals were

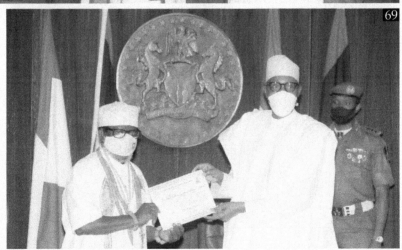

67. GOS (3rd from left) as a member of the Governing Council of the National Mathematical Centre, Abuja, 2018
68. President Muhammadu Buhari decorating GOS with the NNOM medal, February 8, 2022
69. President Muhammadu Buhari handing GOS the NNOM certificate, February 8, 2022

70. My 18-karat-gold NNOM medal, Feb 8, 2022

THE NIGERIAN NATIONAL MERIT AWARD (NNMA)

Established by Act 53 of 1979 as amended by
Act 96 of 1992 (CAP 122 LFN. 2004)

To *Prof. Godwin Osakpemwoya Samuel Ekhaguere* (NNOM)

Instrument of Conferment of the Nigerian National Order of Merit (NNOM)

In exercise of the powers vested in me as President, Commander-in-Chief of the Armed Forces of the Federal Republic of Nigeria under Section (8) of the NNMA Act and having been adjudged by the Governing Board of the NNMA to be deserving of this highest National Prize for Academic and Intellectual attainment, I HEREBY confer on you to have and enjoy, the title, **Dignity** and all privileges of the Nigerian National Order of Merit (NNOM), Given at Abuja under the Public Seal and joint hands of the President, Federal Republic of Nigeria and the Chairman, Governing Board of the NNMA.

this ___8th___ day of ___February,___ 20 ___22___

Chairman, Governing Board of the NNMA

President, Federal Republic of Nigeria

71. My NNOM certificate dated February 8, 2022

72. GOS (3rd from left) in a group photo with President Muhammadu Buhari (4th from left), February 8, 2022
73. GOS and wife in a group photo with some members of the NNMA Board and Engr. Isaac Uhunmwagho, Prof. Oye Gureje and Prof. Union Edebiri, February 8, 2022

74. GOS and wife with friends after thanksgiving at the Our Lady Seat of Wisdom Chapel, UI, Feb 20, 2022
75. GOS and wife with Parish Priest and friends after thanksgiving at the Our Lady Seat of Wisdom Chapel, UI, February 20, 2022

76. Award-winning professors of mathematics (front, L-R) Prof. A.O. Kuku (NNOM) and Prof. GOS Ekhaguere (NNOM), (back) Prof. O.D. Makinde (MFR)
77. Brave and audacious - GOS with a lion and its cub in Bangkok, Thailand 2001

78. The high table at the grand reception, with the chairman, "Lord" Matthias Ogunsuyi speaking

79. Some members of the ICCOBA Executive Council in a group photo with GOS and his wife. Fifth from right is ICCOBA President, Engr. Ighodalo Johnson Edetanlen

80.   The Speaker of the Edo State House of Assembly, Hon. Marcus Onobun, who represented His Excellency Godwin N. Obaseki, Executive Governor of Edo State, presenting a plaque to GOS on behalf of ICCOBA

81.   Some guests at the grand reception held at the Protea Hotel, Benin City

82. Standing first from the left is the media icon, Soni Irabor, who was the master ceremony at the reception

83. Some ICCOBA65 members at the reception. Standing, from left to right, with neck bands, are Roderick G.B. Smart, Engr. Isaac I. Uhunmwagho, Sir Lawrence Ohiowele, Noble Sir Alexander Vlachos, Andrew Iloh and Ambassador Thaddeus Daniel Hart

84

85

84. "Lord" Matthias Ogunsuyi, Chairman at the reception, standing to the left of GOS, in a group photo with some members of the ICCOBA Executive Council

85. Barrister Bernard Irusota and GOS at the grand reception

86. GOS and wife with Mr. and Mrs. Enobakhare of the University of Benin, Benin City, at the grand reception

86

Congratulations

Prof. G.O.S.EKHAGUERE

We congratulate you on the conferment of the Nigerian
National Order of Merit Award by His Excellency,
President Mohammadu Buhari.

We are proud of your stellar accomplishment.

His Excellency Godwin Obaseki
Governor, Edo State

87. Governor Godwin Obaseki's congratulations published in *The Vanguard*,
February 10, 2022

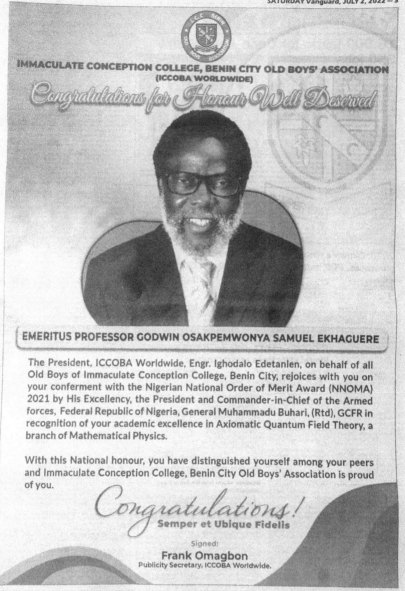

IMMACULATE CONCEPTION COLLEGE, BENIN CITY OLD BOYS' ASSOCIATION
(ICCOBA WORLDWIDE)

Congratulations for Honour Well Deserved

EMERITUS PROFESSOR GODWIN OSAKPEMWONYA SAMUEL EKHAGUERE

The President, ICCOBA Worldwide, Engr. Ighodalo Edetanlen, on behalf of all Old Boys of Immaculate Conception College, Benin City, rejoices with you on your conferment with the Nigerian National Order of Merit Award (NNOMA) 2021 by His Excellency, the President and Commander-in-Chief of the Armed forces, Federal Republic of Nigeria, General Muhammadu Buhari, (Rtd), GCFR in recognition of your academic excellence in Axiomatic Quantum Field Theory, a branch of Mathematical Physics.

With this National honour, you have distinguished yourself among your peers and Immaculate Conception College, Benin City Old Boys' Association is proud of you.

Congratulations!
Semper et Ubique Fidelis

Signed:
Frank Omagbon
Publicity Secretary, ICCOBA Worldwide.

88. The ICCOBA congratulatory message to GOS published in *The Vanguard* Newspaper on July 2, 2022

expected to address interesting research problems with potential impact on national development through the likely scalability of their expected products or outcomes. The upper limit of a grant for the implementation of a successful proposal was set at ₦50,000,000 (fifty million Naira). However, based on their individual budgets and how convincing the associated budget items were, the grants made by TETFund to several proposals were sometimes less than the indicated maximum. Beyond recommending successful proposals for the award of grants, the NRFS&MC also undertook the monitoring and evaluation of the projects to ensure timely implementation of the planned activities as well as the full and high quality realization of their expected outcomes. I was involved in carrying out these post-award functions as a member of the SETI Subcommittee.

Founding of NAMP

My PhD degree was in mathematical physics. I obtained the degree in 1976. It was in that same year that the International Association of Mathematical Physics (IAMP) was founded with the goal of promoting research in mathematical physics. Membership of IAMP was open to mathematicians and physicists. I was very much aware of the activities of IAMP: I longed very much for an academic association like IAMP in Nigeria. I discussed this desire on several occasions with Professor Awele Maduemezia, a theoretical physicist, who was one of my teachers and later my colleague at the University of Ibadan. But at that time, only a few persons in the country could broadly be described as mathematical physicists. Notable among them were Professor Awele Maduemezia, Professor Alexander Obiefoka Enukora Animalu, Dr. Gabriel Oluremi Olaofe (December 6, 1937-February 6, 1994), Dr. Robert Akin Ojo, Dr. GOS Ekhaguere and Dr. Oluwole Aderogba Adetunji Odundun (died: July 15, 2014), all of whom became full professors in later years.

It was evident that forming a learned society, akin to the IAMP, in Nigeria in those days was bound to be difficult, if a strict definition of a "mathematical physicist" was applied. As one of my career goals was to steadfastly expand and strengthen my academic networks through active participation in scientific conferences, I attended an International Conference, organized by the IAMP, at the École Polytechnique Fédérale de Lausanne, Lausanne, Switzerland from August 20 – 26, 1979. Before then, to try to realize my craving for an academic body of mathematical physicists in Nigeria, I wrote a letter to Professor Maduemezia in May 1979 to propose the holding of a colloquium on mathematical physics before the end of the year. That was because I was keenly aware that most academic associations were formed during conferences. I was elated that Professor Maduemezia wasted no time in endorsing my idea. Accordingly, the first National Colloquium on Mathematical Physics was held at the Department of Physics, University of Ibadan from December 12-15, 1979, with thirty one participants from the College of Technology, Ilorin, and eight of the thirteen universities that existed in the country at that time. The eight universities were Ahmadu Bello University, Zaria, Bayero University, Kano, University of Ibadan, University of Ife, Ile-Ife (later: Obafemi Awolowo University, Ile-Ife), University of Ilorin, University of Lagos, University of Maiduguri and the University of Nigeria, Nsukka. The idea of forming an academic body of mathematical physicists in Nigeria was tabled, discussed and approved during the colloquium at a meeting held on December 13, 1979, at which 22 of the 31 participants were present. It was also agreed to define "mathematical physicist" broadly as:

> any scientist who applies fairly rigorous mathematics to physics, chemistry, engineering, or other sciences and also any mathematician whose results have direct applicability in physics, chemistry, engineering and so forth.

A motion for the establishment of a body of mathematical physicists was moved by Dr. Odundun of the Department of Physics, University of Ife, Ile-Ife, and seconded by Dr. Jacob Adetunji of the Department of Physics, Ahmadu Bello University, Zaria. The motion was unanimously carried. Its wording was as follows:

> That those here present constitute themselves into a body to be known as and called the Nigerian Association of Mathematical Physics (NAMP).

The new body elected the following persons (using their 1979 academic titles) to form its inaugural Executive Council:

President:	Professor Awele Maduemezia
Secretary:	Dr. GOS Ekhaguere
Treasurer:	Dr. Gabriel Oluremi Olaofe
Ex-Officio members:	Professor John Chukwuemeka Amazigo, Professor Muneer Ahmad Rashid, Dr. Clement Olaloye Folayan (April 1, 1914 - December 22, 2018).

The Council promptly immersed itself in its functions. It organized a NAMP colloquium annually and established an academic periodical called: *The Journal of the Nigerian Association of Mathematical Physics* (JNAMP). Within a short time, NAMP had grown its membership significantly and it had become an internationally respected academic association. I held the post of Secretary of NAMP for some 19 years from 1979 to 1998. I was succeeded as Secretary in 1998 by Professor Vincent Ele Asor. Simultaneously, Professor John Ovuezirie Akeraino Idiodi, of the University of Benin, Benin City, took over from Professor Balogun Chike-Obi, of the Department of Physics, University of Ilorin, Ilorin, as Editor-in-Chief of JNAMP. Professor Idiodi rebranded JNAMP, ensured its uninterrupted timely publication and introduced a second periodical called: *Transactions of the*

Nigerian Association of Mathematical Physics (TNAMP). It continues to gladden my heart that the small academic tree that I helped to plant in 1979 has not stopped growing but has endured and is in full bloom. One of the activities organized by the Department of Mathematics, University of Ibadan, to mark my retirement in 2017 from the University, upon my attainment at the age of 70 years, was an International Conference on Contemporary Mathematics and the Real World, where some specially invited Nigerian and foreign mathematicians, as well as many other experts from several branches of the mathematical sciences, made landmark presentations on diverse branches of contemporary mathematics and its applications to the real world. Volume 6 of the *Transactions of the Nigerian Association of Mathematical Physics* is a 392-page festschrift, containing all the peer-reviewed papers presented at the Conference; the volume was published by NAMP in January 2018 in my honour.

Founding of the NMS

Some three years after the founding of NAMP in 1979, the Nigerian Mathematical Society (NMS) was established in 1982 when I was a Senior Lecturer at the University of Ibadan. Unlike the case of NAMP, where a broad notion of a "mathematical physicist" had to be adopted because the number of persons who could strictly be called mathematical physicists was very small, there was a significant number of mathematicians in Nigeria in 1982. This was because research in mathematics had started 34 years earlier in 1948 when the Department of Mathematics was established as one of the foundation Departments of the University of Ibadan. The founding of the NMS was principally through the efforts of the mathematics icon, Professor Adegoke Olubummo (April 19, 1923 – October 26, 1992). He was elected as the pioneer President of the NMS, during a conference at the University of Ibadan where the body was formed in 1982. He was in office from 1982 to 1984. Like NAMP, the NMS also simultaneously created an academic periodical called the *Journal of the Nigerian Mathematical Society* (JNMS). The pioneer Editor-in-Chief of the JNMS was Professor Haroon Oladipo Tejumola (July 8, 1937 - December 25, 2011), who was in office from 1982 to 1990 and also from 1997 to 2000. I held the post of Vice President of the NMS from 1995 to 1997 during the tenure, abridged by his death in 1997, of Professor Rufus Fidelis Adetunji Abiodun (1931-1997) as the President of the NMS.

Founding of IORMS

By 2011, as with my involvement with the creation of NAMP, some of us began to discuss the establishment of an academic association for practitioners of Operations Research, a multidisciplinary branch of knowledge with pervasive applications. We chose the name of the body as the Institute of Operational Research and Management Sciences (IORMS). In June 2014, IORMS was formally registered, under the Companies and Allied Matters Act (CAMA), Part C, of 1990, by the Corporate Affairs Commission and issued a certificate of incorporation. The following seven persons were the pioneer members of the Board of Trustees (BoT) of IORMS: Professor Joseph Funso Akingbade (September 9, 1940 – May 7, 2017) (University of Lagos), Professor GOS Ekhaguere (University of Ibadan), Professor Adamu Idama (August 1, 1948-April 19, 2017) (Modibbo Adama University, Yola), Professor Rasheed Kola Ojikutu (University of Lagos), Chief Felix Amadi, Dr. Mrs. Dixon Ogbechie and Professor Mojeed Olayide Abass, with Mr. Moses Olusola Okesola as the IORMS Registrar and Secretary to the BoT. An official launching of IORMS and the induction of the pioneer members occurred at the University of Lagos, MBA Campus, Edmund Crescent, Yaba, Lagos, on November 2, 2015. Through its conferences, workshops and seminars, IORMS has, since its certification, been promoting operations research and management sciences in Nigeria, grooming the next generation of experts in a discipline that is versatile in applications, while also forging strong bonds with the private and public sectors of the economy toward national development.

Governance at the NMC

The National Mathematical Centre (NMC), Abuja, was established on January 1, 1988 by the Federal Government of Nigeria, but its enabling law (now an Act of the National Assembly which is CAP 58 of Federal Laws of Nigeria 2004) was promulgated on December 12, 1989, as Decree 40. Accorded the status of an inter-university centre, its principal officers are deemed to be of the same ranks as their counterparts in a Nigerian university. The NMC was created to be the hub and engine for the development of the mathematical sciences in Nigeria through training and research activities. I was appointed as a member of the 5th Governing Council of the National Mathematical Centre, Abuja on March 15, 2018, by President Muhammadu Buhari, through a letter written by the Honorable Minister of Education, Mallam Adamu. The other members of Council were: Professor Buba Garegy Bajoga, Pro-Chancellor & Chairman; Professor Stephen Ejugwu Onah, Professor Garba Uba Goje, Professor Romanus Ibeawuchi Keke, Professor Gregory Maksha Wajiga, Professor David O. Adewumi, Professor Micah Okwuchukwu Osilike, Dr. Matthew Otafugbe Adaji, Mr. I.M. Yaraki, Dr. (Mrs.) Amina Muhammed Bello Shamaki, Professor Hadiza Shehu Galadanci and Mr. Salifu Matthew Atayi (who was replaced by Mrs. E. O. Adedigba on August 30, 2019, following his retirement from the Federal Civil Service), with Mallam Aliyu Muhammed Biu, the NMC Registrar, as the Secretary.

At the inaugural meeting of Council on April 23, 2018, the NMC Director, Professor Onah, gave an overview of the state of the Centre. It was immediately evident that the NMC had achieved a lot since its foundation. But as a result of a raft of unresolved funding, systemic and structural issues over the years, the Centre had not significantly realized the vision underlying its establishment, which was that it should be essentially a mirror image of the Abdus Salam International Centre for Theoretical Physics (ICTP), Trieste, Italy. For example, it was shocking to learn from the Director's briefing that the NMC had never had a strategic plan to guide the implementation of its multiple activities since its establishment in 1988. Council felt that operating a flagship institution like the NMC without a strategic plan was akin to groping in the dark, with no objective metrics to measure performance and quality of outcomes or to make evidence-based prognosis of the future trajectory or direction of the Centre. It was therefore not surprising that the NMC had continually punched below its weight. To turn the situation around, Council immediately approved the setting up of an ad hoc Committee to develop a strategic plan: the first ever for the Centre. Council also approved that I should be the Chair of the ad hoc Committee. The other members of the Committee were Professor Stephen Ejugwi Onah, Professor Garba Uba Goje, Professor Gregory Maksha Wajiga and Professor David O. Adewumi, with Mallam Aliyu Mohammed Biu as member & Secretary.

The Committee adopted an inclusive and participatory bottom-up approach, involving the staff and stakeholders of the NMC, in the process of developing the Centre's Strategic Plan. This was to ensure that the staff and stakeholders fully assumed effective ownership of the implementation of all the strategic initiatives proposed by the Committee. In the end, the Committee produced a Strategic Plan (SP), in two versions, an abridged version and a full version, for the five-year period from 2020 to 2024. The full version had the title: *Expanding the Frontiers of Training and Research in the Mathematical Sciences: Goals and Framework for Implementation, Monitoring and Evaluation* (64 pages) while the abridged version was entitled: *Expanding the Frontiers of Training and Research in the Mathematical*

Sciences: Goals, Objectives, Strategic Initiatives and Key Expected Outcomes (30 pages). The SP was designed to enable the NMC to achieve some carefully selected SMARTER (Specific, Measurable, Achievable, Relevant, Time-bound, Evaluated, Reviewed) goals and objectives by implementing some strategic initiatives within a specified timeframe. Council received and approved the SP during its two-day meeting from March 9-10, 2020. The SP also contained revised versions of the NMC's vision and mission statements as well as a number of initiatives for addressing some of the longstanding systemic and structural impediments that had hindered the realization of the Centre's fundamental goals and objectives.

Power to Establish State and Private Universities

For a long time in Nigeria, the establishment of universities was the exclusive legislative preserve of the nation's Federal Government. But in 1979, there was some liberalization, allowing the States of the Federation to establish universities through laws enacted by their respective Houses of Assembly. To this end, Item K27 on the Concurrent Legislative List of the 1979 Constitution of Nigeria contained the following provision:

> . . . a House of Assembly shall have power to make Laws for the State with respect to the establishment of an institution for purposes of university, professional or technological education.

Moreover, Item K28 on the same List stated as follows:

> Nothing in the foregoing paragraphs of this item shall be construed so as to limit the powers of a House of Assembly to make laws for the State with respect to technical, vocational, post-primary, primary or other forms of education, including establishment of institutions for the pursuit of such education.

Relying on these constitutional provisions, Professor Ambrose Folorunso Alli (September 22, 1929 – September 22, 1989) established the Bendel State University, Ekpoma, in 1981 as the first State university in Nigeria. The name of the institution changed to Edo State University, Ekpoma, in 1992 when Edo State was created. It was again renamed Ambrose Alli University, Ekpoma, in 1999 in honour of Professor Ambrose Folorunso Alli. The higher education landscape was further expanded, enabling the establishment of private universities, through the Education (National Minimum Standards and Establishment of Institutions) Act of 1985, whose Section 20 had the following provision:

> 20. PERSONS WHO MAY ESTABLISH INSTITUTIONS OF HIGHER LEARNING
>
> An institution of higher learning may be sponsored or owned by the Government of the Federation or of a State or by a local government or by any of the following,that is-
>
> (a) by a company incorporated in Nigeria; or
> (b) by an individual or association of individuals who are citizens of Nigeria and who satisfy the criteria set out in the Schedule to this Act for establishment of institutions.

This provision empowered States, companies, individuals or associations to establish universities, thereby greatly expanding the tertiary education space in Nigeria.

The Dominican University

Riding the crest of this auspicious Act, the nation's first three private universities, Babcock University, Ilishan-Remo, Ogun State, Igbinedion University, Okada, Edo State, and Madonna University, Okija, Anambra State, were licensed on May 10, 1999, by the Federal Government. Since then, the number of private universities, of diverse ownership, in Nigeria has grown significantly. I was involved in the planning activities toward the founding, and subsequently also the governance, of a faith-based university in the country. The institution, called the Dominican University (DU), Ibadan, was established by the Province of Saint Joseph the Worker, Nigeria & Ghana of the Order of Preachers (OP), commonly called the Dominicans. The OP was founded in France by St. Dominic

De Guzman (August 8, 1170 – August 6, 1221) and approved on December 22, 1216 by Pope Honorius III (1150 – March 18, 1227), born Cencio Savelli. Established in 1993, the Province operated an academic outfit at Ibadan, called the Dominican Institute, for the ecclesial formation of new generations of priests and reverend sisters. The Institute offered a number of degree programmes, in affiliation with the University of Ibadan. The Dominicans are known for their centuries-old culture of intellectualism and scholarship, having produced a large number of theologians and philosophers in the Catholic Church. In 2008, some staff of the Dominican Institute and its proprietor began a project to creat a private university.

I was invited by Fr. Professor Joseph Peter Kenny, OP (January 12, 1936 – January 28, 2013), who was the Institute's Dean of Studies, and Fr. Kenneth Nkadi, OP, to join the Project Implementation Committee (PIC). I had known Fr. Kenny, whose grandparents were Irish-American, for several years as a colleague at the University of Ibadan, where he was a professor of Religious Studies until his retirement on September 30, 2001. He was a globally acclaimed expert in Islamic and Arabic Studies as well as inter-religious dialogue: this earned him many academic accolades and also the nickname Alhaji. His students, friends and colleagues often addressed him as "Fr. Professor Alhaji Joseph Kenny" or "Ave Joe". A polyglot, he was proficient in thirteen languages: Arabic, Dutch, English, French, German, Greek, Hausa, Hebrew, Italian, Latin, Portuguese, Spanish and Yoruba. Fr. Kenny often said the evening Mass on Sundays at the Our Lady Seat of Wisdom Catholic Chapel, University of Ibadan. As I preferred evening Masses to morning Masses, we often met on Sundays. He said Masses in a business-like manner. As a result, he was often called *Father Sharp Sharp*. Moreover, his short and incisive homilies were written and then published on his personal website. I have attended Masses by many a priest whose homilies were overly long, rambling, unfocused, devoid of substance or impact and delivered using mannerisms that are associated with Pentecostal denominations. In my view, the creeping infusion of elements of Pentecostalism into homilies in the Catholic Church poses a significant threat to the Church's highly revered tradition.

In the PIC, I was involved with Fr. Kenny and others in developing the Academic Brief of the proposed Dominican University. I was also responsible for defending the Academic Brief at the NUC or during inspection or evaluation visits by NUC teams to the Dominican Institute. By 2012, steady progress was being made toward the goal of establishing the Dominican University before Fr. Kenny travelled to the USA in the summer of that year. When I did not hear from him for some time, I sent him an e-mail message on August 20, 2012, with the following content.

Date: Aug 20, 2012, 2:33 PM
Subject: Greetings

How are you doing, Father? Are you back to Ibadan, or when will you be back?

Best wishes.

GOS

In less than an hour, I received the following response from him:

Date: Aug 20, 2012, 3:18 PM
Subject: Re: Greetings

What a happy surprise! Good to hear from you, GOS.

I am still in US - DC area - should have been back to Nigeria two weeks ago, but for a health scare, which tests (so far) have dissipated as negative. I had to reschedule my flight to middle of October, and am locked into that.

   Are you in US? For now, I am at my brother's – house: phone 703-***-**** [my editing].

Best wishes and prayers,

Joseph Kenny OP

I was greatly relieved that what Fr. Kenny described as a "health scare" had, according to him, "dissipated as negative". But when I visited the Dominican Institute toward the end of October 2012 and asked about him, I received the unsettling news that he was seriously unwell. So I quickly sent him the following message.

Date: Oct 30, 2012, 3:40 PM
Subject: Best wishes for a quick recovery

Dear Father,
I have received the unexpected news of your ill-health with great sadness. On behalf of myself and family, I send you our best wishes and God's favour for a quick and complete recovery.
God bless.

GOS

But his reply, which was uncharacteristically slow in coming, further alarmed me because I received the following e-mail message after over a fortnight.

Date: Nov 18, 2012, 8:35 PM
Subject: Re: Best wishes for a quick recovery

Thanks a million GOS. I am down. I had a stroke over here "banged up abroad". I am afraid I am grounded in nursing home for the foreseeable future. I have no idea when or if I can return to Nigeria.
Got news of Justina Ogwu's death - prayers.
This is first of a rare access to internet.
Love,

Joseph Kenny OP

Sadly, Fr. Kenny's premonition soon materialised: he died on January 28, 2013, the Feast of St. Thomas Aquinas, in Washington DC. In line with his lifelong selflessness and generosity, he requested that, instead of bringing flowers to his funeral, donations should be made to the Dominican University of Nigeria Development Fund (USA). He also asked that his remains be flown to Nigeria and interred in the grounds of the Dominican Community, Ibadan, where the Dominican Institute, Ibadan, was collocated.

The Dominican University was granted a Provisional Licence in November 2016 by the Federal Government of Nigeria. I wished that Fr. Kenny, who had worked very hard to establish the DU, was physically present at the NUC during the delivery of the Licence to the new institution, the first University to be founded in Africa by the Order of Preachers.

Governance at DU

On January 12, 2017, I was appointed as one of the pioneer members of the Governing Council of the Dominican University by the Prior Provincial of the Order of Preachers (OP) & Chancellor of the University, Fr. Charles Ukwe, OP. The Council was inaugurated on February 23, 2017, and had Mr. Peter Obi, former Governor of Anambra State, as Pro-Chancellor & Chairman of Council. The other members of Council were: Professor Anthony Alaba Akinwale, OP, Professor Ibi Ajayi, Professor Ngozi Osarenren, Professor Godfrey Nzamujo, OP, Mr. Peter Amangbo, Mr. Patrick Akinwuntan, with the Registrar Fr. Kenneth Nkadi, OP, as Secretary. At the end of a selection exercise by Council, Fr. Professor Anthony Alaba Akinwale, OP, was appointed the pioneer Vice-Chancellor of the Dominican University on August 21, 2017, for a renewable period of two years. The appointment was renewed retroactively on February 13, 2020 for a further period of three years until August 21, 2022. A Full Licence was granted to the Dominican University, Ibadan, in June 2020.

For a newly established University which needed to move fast and establish enduring processes, procedures, frameworks and policies in all areas of institutional governance, a Governing Council was crucial. But I was somewhat disappointed that Council met infrequently and, even so, mainly outside the location of the Dominican University, far away in Lagos. Moreover, every meeting lasted only a few hours. I noticed that several of the members were not familiar with the normal business and functions of a Governing Council. More worrying, standing committees, which are invariably a Council's workhorses, were not formed, as a result of which Council always took decisions about any matter in plenary. My assessment was that the University would have made much more progress if all the organs of Council were established and operated in line with the institution's enabling law. Nonetheless, the University is making steady progress with the implementation of its academic activities.

The institution, whose motto is *In Veritate Libertas* is, for now, structured academically into two faculties, namely: the Faculty of Sciences, comprising the Department of Physical & Mathematical Sciences, Department of Chemical Sciences and the Department of Biological Sciences, and the Faculty of Humanities, Social and Management Sciences, comprising the Department of Philosophy & Religious Studies, Department of Mass Communication, Department of Accountancy & Business Administration and the Department of Economics. The student population has been growing steadily since the foundation of the University, while crucial state-of-the-art institutional structures are continually being expanded or erected. If it sustains the rapid progress that it is making, there is every hope that DU will eventually realize its lofty mission:

> to assist Nigeria to achieve the greatness her potential warrants by bringing together peoples of ethnic, religious and cultural diversity, into an academic community conducive to research, teaching and learning, to become a driving force for solidarity and authentic development of a new humanity.

The Order of Preachers has a rich intellectual and scholastic tradition, exemplified by Thomas Aquinas (1225 – March 7, 1274), an eminent Doctor of the Catholic Church, who was an Italian Dominican friar and priest.

22

A GLIMPSE INTO
NATIONAL POLITICS

I did not become significantly aware of the practical aspects of politics in Nigeria until the nation's 1979 elections because I was relatively young when the earlier elections were held. The country operated a federal system of governance, with the Northern, Eastern, Western and Mid-Western regions as its constitutionally recognised federating units. But this mode of governance was abrogated on May 24, 1966, when General Johnson Thomas Umunnakwe Aguiyi-Ironsi (March 3, 1924-July 29, 1966) promulgated the Unification Decree No. 34 of 1966, which contained the following declaration that explicitly annulled the federal structure:

> The Federal Military Government hereby decrees as follows:
>
> 1. Subject to the provisions of this Decree, Nigeria shall on 24th May 1966 (in this decree referred to as 'the appointed day') cease to be a Federation and shall accordingly as from that day be a Republic, by the name of the Republic of Nigeria, consisting of the whole of the territory which immediately before that day was comprised in the Federation. *Supplement to Official Gazette Extraordinary No. 51, Vol. 53, 24th May, 1966 — Part A*

This decree is regarded by many as one of General Aguiyi-Ironsi's most controversial acts as a Military Head of State. He was succeeded on July 29, 1966, through another coup, by General Yakubu "Jack" Gowon who then repealed the Decree 34 and replaced it with Decree 9 of August 31, 1966. The latter contained the following provision:

> The National Military Government hereby decree as follows:
>
> 1.   (1) Subject to the provisions of this Decree, Nigeria shall as from 1st September 1966 (in this Decree referred: to as "the appointed day") again be a Federation in accordance with Sections 2 and 3 of the Constitution of the Federation; and accordingly the following Decrees are hereby repealed as from the appointed day, that is to say –
>
>   (a)   the Constitution(Suspension and Modification) (No. 2) Decree 1966;
>   (b)   the Constitution (Suspension and Modification) (No. 5) Decree 1966 (in this Decree referred to as "Decree No. 34") ; and
>   (c)   the Constitution (Suspension and Modification) (No. 6) Decree 1966.
>   *Supplement to Official Gazette Extraordinary No. 85, Vol. 53, 1st September, 1966 – Part A*

Nonetheless, in practical terms, several elements of Decree 34 have remained in force, in one form or other, till this day, with Nigeria being today neither truly unitary nor truly federal.

From 1966 to 1999, some 33 years, there were only brief periods of democratic rule, namely: the Second Republic from October 1, 1979 to December 31, 1983, and the Third Republic from January 1992 to August 27, 1993. By contrast, military dictatorship extended over long periods of time. The military administrations were installed by coups d'etat, some of which led to untold loss of lives. On July 30, 1975, General Gowon was ousted in a coup d'etat that installed Brigadier (later General) Murtala Muhammed (November 8, 1938 – February 13, 1976) as the military Head of State. General Muhammed was assassinated in a failed coup on February 13, 1976, leading to his replacement as the Head of

State by his deputy, Lt. General Olusegun Obasanjo. The nation experienced some respite from coups d'etat, until December 31, 1983, when a democratically elected civilian administration headed by Alhaji Shehu Usman Aliyu Shagari (February 25, 1925 – December 28, 2018) was overthrown on December 31, 1983, and replaced by General Mohammadu Buhari as the military Head of State. Ironically, General Buhari would subsequently be democratically elected as the President of Nigeria, with a two-term tenure from May 29, 2015 to May 28, 2023. Through a coup d'etat on August 27, 1985, General Buhari's military administration was replaced by the military administration headed by General Ibrahim Badamasi Babangida. In December 1985, there was an allegation by the General Babangida administration of a conspiracy to carry out a coup d'etat under the leadership of Major General Mamman Jiya Vatsa (December 3, 1940 – March 5, 1986) and some other officers. The officers were tried, convicted and executed by firing squad. Finally, there was a failed coup d'etat led by Major Gideon Gwaza Orkar (October 4, 1952 - July 27, 1990) on April 22, 1990. I always tell my friends that apart from the two coups d'etat in January and July 1966 which were staged when I was studying for the Higher School Certificate, no attempted coup d'etat succeeded whenever I was in the country. Thus, while the coups d'etat in 1975, 1983 and 1985 succeeded when I was in the United Kingdom, Germany and Switzerland, respectively, the attempted coups d'etat of 1985 (allegedly by Major General Vatsa) and 1990 (allegedly by Major Orkar) both failed when I was in Nigeria, with disastrous consequences for the alleged planners.

On December 12, 1959, parliamentary elections were held in Nigeria, when I was barely twelve years old. The first electoral event organised by Nigeria after its Independence from Britain in 1960 was a constitutional referendum on July 13, 1963, through which the Mid-Western Region was created on August 9, 1963, when I was sixteen years old and a student in Form 3 at ICC. The area which formed the Mid-Western Region had been a part of the

Western Region before the plebiscite. The referendum of February 11, 1961, through which Northern Cameroons was integrated into Nigeria, was organised by the United Nations. The next set of parliamentary elections in Nigeria took place in 1964 and 1965. The elections were successfully held throughout Nigeria on December 30, 1964, except in a number of constituencies in the Eastern Region, Mid-Western Region and Lagos. The constituencies had boycotted the December 1964 elections but eventually held their elections on March 18, 1965, when I was under eighteen years of age. Not long after those elections, a military coup generally associated with Major Chukwuma Kaduna Nzeogwu, whose main accomplices were Majors Adewale Ademoyega, Chris Anuforo, Humphrey Chukwuka, Emmanuel Ifeajuna, Don Okafor and Timothy Onwuatuegwu, occurred on January 15, 1966, abruptly dismantling the country's budding democratic system. As the prime movers and implementers of the coup were predominantly of the Igbo ethic nationality, the coup has over the years been seen by many as an *Igbo coup*, although the Ndigbo have laboured somewhat unsuccessfully to shake off this characterisation.

About twenty years after the pre-independence elections of 1959 and after the military had ruled the country for thirteen years, starting from January 15, 1966, the 1979 elections were held under the supervision of the Federal Electoral Commission (FEDECO), which was headed by Chief Michael Okon Nsa Ani (November 30, 1917 – December 18 1985). Chief Ani was appointed by General Olusegun Matthew Okikiola Aremu Obasanjo; he held the post from 1976 to 1979. For the Second Republic which started on October 1, 1979, the country had adopted, almost hook, line, and sinker, a variant of the American presidential style of governance, with a bicameral legislature comprising a 95-member Senate and a 449-member House of Representatives at the national level as well as 19 unicameral legislative Houses of Assembly at the sub-national level. The 1979 constitution provided for a President for the entire nation and also a Governor for each of the nineteen States, into which Nigeria was reconfigured by the military regime of General Murtala Ramat Mohammed (November 8, 1938-February 13, 1976) when he created seven new States on February 3, 1976. With the lifting of the ban on politics by the military on September 21, 1978, the march to the 1979 elections began. For me, the elections would be the first national electoral contest in which I was qualified to vote or be voted for. I was therefore eager to see the contest begin.

Political Parties

Six political parties threw their hats into the ring. Two of them, the Unity Party of Nigeria (UPN) and the Nigerian Peoples Party (NPP) announced their existence on September 22, 1978, while the National Party of Nigeria (NPN) was formed on September 20, 1978 and launched on September 24, 1978. The Peoples Redemption Party (PRP) declared its existence on September 27, 1978 and the Nigeria Advance Party (NAP) was unveiled on October 13, 1978. Finally, the Great Nigerian Peoples Party (GNPP), which split from the Nigerian Peoples Party (NPP), announced its existence in October 1978. After reviewing the parties and their manifestoes, I pitched my camp with the UPN, which was led by Chief Obafemi Jeremiah Oyeniyi Awolowo, who also emerged as the party's presidential candidate. The UPN's ideology was essentially social welfarism. Its manifesto revolved around the following set of four goals which it marketed as its *cardinal programmes:*

1. free education at all levels for all, with effect from October 1, 1979;
2. integrated rural development, aimed at feeding some 60 million Nigerians [the population of the country in 1979 was 71.36 million];
3. provision of free health facilities for all Nigerians; and
4. full employment for all Nigerians.

I could easily identify with the first goal, because as I narrated earlier, I had providentially benefitted from the Free Universal Primary Education Programme (FUPEP) which Chief Awolowo introduced in 1955, when he was the Premier of the Western Region. The other three goals were laudable but it was evident that their implementation would require the continuous mobilisation and deployment of a vast amount of human and material resources. Although there were criticisms in some quarters as to the feasibility of the UPN's manifesto, aware of his proverbial self-discipline, integrity, industry and patriotism, many citizens, including some of his political opponents, were quick to concede that Chief Awolowo certainly had the requisite leadership capacity to accomplish his party's four cardinal programmes.

Politics on Campus and National Elections

On the University of Ibadan campus, a UPN support group sprouted in no time, with Otunba Professor Olusegun Odunuga (1937-April 13, 2013) and Professor Tunde Adeniran as the leaders. Other members of the group of about forty academics (using their ultimate titles) included: Professor Moses Airen Amayo, Professor Tola Atinwo, Professor Ben Elugbe and me. As the canvassing for votes progressed, members of the group helped with campaign ideas and the popularisation of the Party within their respective networks. Three of us, Professor Tunde Adeniran, Professor Tola Atinmo and me worked directly with the UPN's gubernatorial candidate for Oyo State, Chief James Ajibola Idowu Adegoke Ige (September 13, 1930 – December 23, 2001), fondly addressed as Chief Bola Ige. We observed political rallies held by Chief Ige, noted the reactions and critical comments by some potential voters and then produced strategies for addressing their expectations. Three of us, Professor Moses Airen Amayo, Professor Ben Elugbe and me from Bendel State, also interacted with the UPN's Bendel State gubernatorial candidate, Professor

Ambrose Folorunso Alli (September 22, 1929 – September 22, 1989). In the end, Chief Ige was elected as the Governor of Oyo State in the nation's Second Republic, whose lifespan was from October 1, 1979 to December 31, 1983. His main opponent was Chief Osuolale Abimbola Richard Akinjide (November 4, 1931 – April 21, 2020) of the National Party of Nigeria, whose running mate was Prince Afolabi Oyeleke Agboola (1937-March 9, 2005). Chief Ige was in office from October 1, 1979 to September 30, 1983, with Chief Sunday Afolabi (1931 – May 10, 2004) as his Deputy. His attempt to secure a second term was unsuccessful, as he was defeated by the mathematician, Dr. Victor Omololu Sowemimo Olunloyo, of the National Party of Nigeria. Similarly, Professor Alli was elected as the Governor of Bendel State, with Chief Demas Onoliobakpovwa Akpore (August 4, 1928 – December 28, 1993) as his Deputy. He was in office from October 1, 1979 to September 30, 1983. Professor Alli's attempt to secure a second term was also unsuccessful, as he was defeated by the former Military Administrator of the Mid-West State, Dr. Samuel Osaigbovo Ogbemudia (September 17, 1932 – March 9, 2017), of the National Party of Nigeria.

The presidential election, which was held on August 11, 1979, was particularly interesting, not merely because the associated office was the ultimate prize of the 1979 elections but largely because it morphed into an epic legal contest between the candidates, Chief Obafemi Awolowo and Alhaji Shehu Usman Aliyu Shagari (February 25, 1925 – December 28, 2018), of the two main political parties UPN and NPN, respectively. In the end Alhaji Shagari, who had been declared as the President-elect by the FEDECO Chief Returning Officer, Bishop Chief Frederick Louis Oke Menkiti (February 5, 1929 – May 29, 2014) on August 16, 1979, based on the determination that Alhaji Shagari, who secured 5,688,857 (or 33.77% of) votes as against Chief Awolowo's 4,916,651 (or 29.18% of) votes, had also secured the constitutionally mandatory geographical spread of "...not less than one-quarter of the votes cast at the election in each of at least two-thirds of all the states within the federation". As the number of States in Nigeria in 1979 was 19, the core issue became, unexpectedly, the meaning of two-thirds of 19 States, as it was evident that Alhaji Shagari, who successfully garnered one-quarter of the votes cast in the 12 States of Bauchi, Bendel, Benue, Borno, Cross River, Gongola, Kaduna, Kwara, Niger, Plateau, Rivers and Sokoto, had not secured one-quarter, but rather less than one-fifth, of the total votes cast in Kano, which represented the thirteenth State in descending order of magnitude of the votes cast by the States for him. In a nutshell, Chief Awolowo's contention that two-thirds of 19 States is 13 States, and not $12^2/_3$ States, was not accepted by both a three-person Presidential Election Petitions Tribunal (PEPT), led by Justice Boonyamin Oladiran Kazeem (August 29, 1922 – 1998), and a full composition of the Supreme Court of Nigeria, that comprised seven Justices, with Justice Chief Atanda Fatai-Williams (October 22, 1918–April 10, 2002) presiding. Accordingly, Alhaji Shagari was judicially declared the winner of the 1979 Presidential Election. The PEPT's judgment was delivered on September 10, 1979, while that of the Supreme Court was rendered about a fortnight later on September 26, 1979, a few days shy of the inauguration of the Second Republic. The verdict was a huge disappointment to all supporters of the UPN, not excluding our support group. During his campaign visit to Ibadan in 1979, some members of the UPN support group on the University of Ibadan campus, led by Professor Olusegun Odunuga including Professor Tunde Adeniran, Professor Ben Elugbe and me, visited Chief Awolowo at his residence in the Oke-Bola area of the city. Meeting the statesman face-to-face, and not simply in textbooks, journals or newspapers, was a defining event for me. The encounter was the first and, unfortunately, the only one that I was privileged to have with the sage and icon. We looked forward to the next round of elections which would be due in 1983. The 1983 presidential elections were held in Nigeria on August 6, 1983, and the contestants were: Alhaji Shehu Shagari (National Party of Nigeria), Chief Obafemi Awolowo (Unity Party of Nigeria), Dr. Nnamdi Azikwe (November 16, 1904 – May 11, 1996), (Nigeria Peoples Party), Alhaji Khalifa Hassan Yusuf (1937–2019) (Peoples Redemption Party), Alhaji Waziri Kolo Ibrahim (February 26, 1926 – 1992) (Great Nigeria Peoples Party) and Dr. Tunji Braithwaite (September 13, 1933 – March 28, 2016) (Nigerian Advance Party). But substantially, the two frontline contestants were Alhaji Shehu Shagari, who secured 12,081,471 votes, or equivalently 47.5% of the total votes cast, and Chief Obafemi Awolowo, who garnered 7,907,209 votes, which represented 31.2% of the total votes cast. Once again, Alhaji Shehu Shagari won the 1983 presidential elections and was inaugurated as President on October 1, 1983. By October 1983, Chief Awolowo was already over 74 years old. It was clear that the door to his active participation in future presidential contests was then barely ajar, if not gradually closing. Providentially, the distinguished lawyer, administrator, strategist and eminent politician died some four years later, with his presidential ambition unrealised. Acknowledged nationwide as a politician in a class of his own, compared with his competitors for the nation's highest office, Chief Awolowo was truly "the best President that Nigeria never had", an epitaph that is sometimes attributed to Chief Chukwuemeka Odumegwu Ojukwu. Nevertheless, with his sterling performance as the Premier of the Western Region, through his successful implementation of a raft of life-changing programmes, including the free primary education initiative, innovative agricultural schemes, novel industrial projects and poverty-reducing welfare plans in his Region, the former Premier of the Western Region had triumphantly bequeathed to the nation and posterity a legacy of several proofs of concept of the feasibility and potential benefits of the UPN's four cardinal programmes which he would certainly have implemented in multiple areas of national development.

The New Democratic Space

After the 1979 elections, the nation's democratic space expanded extensively. Nigeria was reconnected to the global democratic ecosystem. A sense of freedom and relief pervaded the country. The nation's non-governmental organisations became more active and vibrant, new democracy-fostering entities were formed and many communities embarked on the pursuit of their constitutional rights which had been suppressed for years by shear force or military decrees. However, a lingering political issue was the status of Bendel State, formerly called the Mid-West State, as a component of the Federal Republic of Nigeria.

In 1982, the Edo people of Bendel State launched a highly coordinated agitation for a State of their own, called Edo State. The demand for Edo State was spear-headed by His Royal Majesty, Omon'Oba N'edo Ukuakpolokpolo, Oba Erediuwa II (1923 – 2016), born Prince Solomon Aiseokhuoba Igbinoghodua Akenzua and crowned as the 39th Oba of the Benin Kingdom on March 23, 1979. Edo people in Ibadan and Lagos quickly identified with the clamour. Let me sketch the motivation for the agitation. The Mid-West Region was created constitutionally on August 9, 1963 through a plebiscite, thereby becoming one of Nigeria's four federating regions. But its position in the Federation began to deteriorate in 1967 when, from being 1 of 4 Regions, the Mid-West became only 1 of 12 States on May 27, 1967, during General Yakubu Gowon's administration, which simply changed the name Mid-West State to Bendel State; then only 1 of 19 States on February 3, 1976, when General Murtala Mohammed created 7 more States. To facilitate the struggle for the creation of Edo State, we formed the *Edo State Movement, Ibadan Extra-Territorial Zone*, comprising the present Oyo, Osun and part of Kwara States. I was the Chairman of the Movement, which was launched at the Liberty Stadium, Ibadan. Witnessed by a tumultuous crowd of Edo indigenes and their well-wishers, His Royal Majesty Oba

Erediuwa II was the Chairman at the launching. We had hoped
that the Edo State would be quickly created. But that did not
happen throughout 1982. In 1983, a military coup on December
31, 1983 abruptly ended the tenure of the democratic government
headed by Alhaji Shehu Shagari and brought General Muhammadu
Buhari into office. All political activities, ncluding agitations
for State creation, were banned by the new military regime. On
August 27, 1985, the military administration of General Buhari
was removed in another coup which installed General Ibrahim
Badamasi Babangida as the Head of State. The Edo people and
the whole of the Bendel State were somewhat demoralised when
General Ibrahim Badamasi Babangida created two more States on
September 23, 1987, making Nigeria a 21-State country, with the
Bendel State remaining intact. It was evident that the Bendel State
was being relegated in the nation's political affairs, because being
only 1 of 21 States instead of 1 of 4 Regions, the State and every
Bendelite had become more remote from the Federal Government
in 1987 than in 1963 when it was created constitutionally.

In 1991, a group of Bendel State academics at the University
of Ibadan decided to make an open demand for the restructuring
of their State into several States. I was one of the academics.
We met several times in my house, with Professor Joseph Ukpea
Akpokodje, professor of Veterinary Surgery & Reproduction,
always in the Chair. Eventually, we produced a statement. Through
the benevolence of Olorogun Michael Christopher Onajirevbe
Ibru (December 25, 1930 – September 6, 2016), a foremost
Urhobo Bendelite born in Agbarha Otor, who was the head of a
business conglomerate called the Ibru Organisation, the statement
was published in *The Guardian*, a Nigerian newspaper at his own
expence. In it, the academics made the following plea for redress:

> It is evident from the above that Bendel State (i.e. the former
> Mid-West Region) has not been fairly treated so far. Something
> should be done in the name of justice and fairplay to reassure
> Bendelites. At least 3 States should be created from Bendel. This,
> we believe, would ameliorate the existing situation.

Fortunately, this plea was partly answered. On August 27, 1991, General Babangida, who called himself Military President of Nigeria and was in office from August 27, 1985 to August 26, 1993, created 9 more States, including Edo and Delta States into which the Bendel State (i.e. the Mid-Western Region) had been remodelled, 28 years after the creation of the Mid-Western Region, thereby making Nigeria a country of 30 States. The academics' demand for the creation of three States, which they envisaged as Anioma State, Delta State and Edo State, from the Bendel State was not implemented, as Anioma State was not created but incorporated into the Delta State. In the twilight of his administration, condemned and vilified by most Nigerians for annulling the June 12, 1993 presidential election on July 4, 1993, General Babandiga hastily appointed Oloye Ernest Adegunle Oladeinde Shonekan (May 9, 1936 – January 11, 2022) as the President of an Interim National Government (ING) to which he transferred power. Oloye Shonekan was in office from August 26, 1993 to November 17, 1993. To conclude this brief historical insight into the reconfiguring of Nigeria into multiple States, General Sani Abacha (September 20, 1943 – June 8, 1998), who replaced Oloye Shonekan as Head of State and was in office from November 17, 1993 to June 8, 1998, created six additional States on October 1, 1996, thereby bequeathing the existing 36-State structure to the nation. With the indicated sequence of periodic changes to the political structure of the country, the distribution of States among the pre-1966 four Regions of Nigeria is today the following: the Western Region plus Lagos became 6 States, the Mid-Western Region, also called Bendel State for a long time, was partitioned into only 2 States, the Eastern Region was remodelled as 9 States while the Northern Region was resolved into 19 States. After the creation of Edo State and Delta State, those of us who contributed to the realisation of this outcome were satisfied that our struggle had been partially fruitful, since we had also expected the creation of Anioma State as the third State from Bendel State.

As far as I know, none of us asked for, or were appointed, to any political office nor lobbied for any elective position: as contained in the publication of the Bendel State academics at the University of Ibadan, our sole motivation was to ensure 'justice and fairplay' for all Bendelites within a prosperous and rapidly transforming Nigerian nation.

PART VII

STATUTORY RETIREMENT

23

FROM GOWN TO TOWN

It was quite stunning to me how fleeting and evanescent time had been. From my arrival at the University of Ibadan in 1968 at the age of 21 years for my undergraduate studies, which I completed in 1971, through my appointment in 1976, aged 29 years, at the same institution, as a Lecturer in Mathematics, to my retirement in 2017 when I was 70 years old, the cumulative timespan appeared to me as very short. But, as there was no stopping or slowing down the inexorable march of time, the point in history had ultimately arrived for me to step aside or exit the system statutorily.

Notice of Retirement

As if to rub in the fact that I had reached my retirement age and must leave the University, I was issued *a notice of retirement* by the University's Registry with the following content.

From: Deputy Registrar
       Establishments (Academic Staff)

To: Professor G.O.S. Ekhaguere
       Department of Mathematics

Date: 10/05/2017

Notice of Retirement

It has been observed in our records that you will be retiring with
effect from 23 May, 2017 from the service of the University of
Ibadan on age limit, i.e. 70 years.

  I am directed to advise you to kindly tender your letter of
notice of retirement with immediate effect.

  Thank you.

Signed
[by a subordinate of the Deputy Registrar]

Since my retirement was not voluntary but statutorily obligatory,
as the Registry knew very well, why was there a demand for a
'notice of retirement' from me? Evidently, my appointment would
automatically elapse as soon as I attained 70 years of age. What
was unclear to me was whether I would be prevented from retiring
if I did not tender a "letter of notice of retirement". What was the
meaning of and need for the military command: "with immediate
effect"? Should a person who had been in the academic trenches
for over four decades, always holding the banner of the University
of Ibadan very high, be sent a memorandum of that kind?

  As I was retiring, new generations of mathematicians, some of
whom I had helped to groom and mentor over the years, had happily
already competently stepped up to the plate, both professionally
and administratively; they were renowned academicians in their
own right. Some of them had attained the professorial cadre and
were themselves also involved in the mentoring of a large number
of undergraduate and postgraduate students, while others were
pursuing their careers with steadfast determination and substantial
success.

24

WHO OTHERS SAY I AM

My retirement date was Tuesday, May 23, 2017, the day that I attained 70 years of age. I had served at the University of Ibadan for close to 41 years. During that period, I rose from the grade of lecturer through the grade of Senior Lecturer to the grade of Professor of Mathematics. Unknown to me, the Department of Mathematics had worked out an elaborate plan to mark my 70th birthday anniversary and retirement. When the plan was revealed to me by Professor Ezekiel Olusola Ayoola, a former PhD student of mine, and Associate Professor (Reader) Chukwuma Raphael Nwozo, one of my close friends, I was overwhelmed by the evident collegiality, kind gesture, solicitude and consideration. The plan was binary and comprised the compilation of a *book of tributes* and the organisation of an *International Conference on Contemporary Mathematics and the Real World*. A programme of activities was meticulously worked out.

Collegial Solidarity

A global invitation for tributes from my schoolmates at the secondary or higher levels of education; my students at all levels of education; my professional colleagues, institutionally, nationally and internationally; persons who worked with me in any establishment or institution; persons who worked with me in various committees, institutionally, nationally and internationally, and persons mentored by me, whether directly or remotely, was issued by the Department, which also made a formal announcement of the conference, in the form of a call for papers from prospective participants. An impressive number of tributes were received. Their compilation and editing by Professor Ayoola, who had graciously accepted the onerous role of Editor, were soon under way. Over 55 tributes were received. At the end of the editing, design and structuring processes, a xxviii+287-page volume, with the title: *GOS Ekhaguere: A Multi-Perspective Glimpse into the Life of a Mathematician at 70,* edited by Ezekiel Olusola Ayoola, was published in October 2017 by the International Centre for Mathematical and Computer Sciences, Lagos, Nigeria, with ISBN: 978-37246-6-5. Rationalising the decision of the Department of Mathematics to implement a set of activities in my honour, Professor Ayoola wrote as follows in the book:

> ... GOS contributed immensely in putting our University in the global mathematical map through his teaching, research and community service over the years. In fact, he is the founding father of what is currently known as the Ibadan School of Quantum Stochastic Analysis. Concerning this book, invitations were extended to a carefully selected list of potential contributors drawn from diverse backgrounds. ...This book provides a rare glimpse into the life of Professor GOS Ekhaguere at 70 from the multiple perspectives of people who have interacted with him in diverse ways over the years. Collectively, the contributors artfully paint an extremely vivid picture of the person and character of Professor Ekhaguere... I invite you to drink freely from the fountain of deep insights of some of our top-rate academic minds into the life of one of their own, our very own GOS.

I was, of course, very happy to read the book. It contained tributes and reminiscences by my colleagues, schoolmates, friends, students and relations with whom I had interacted professionally, administratively, educationally or socially over the years. In the apt words of Professor Isaac Folorunso Adewole, former Vice-Chancellor of the University of Ibadan from December 1, 2010 to November 30, 2015, who kindly wrote one of the volume's multiple forewords, in spite of his myriads of responsibilities as the Federal Minister of Health at that time, the tributes

> highlighted his character, nature, skills and numerous qualities, including those outside his routine academic life. The authors have him keenly dissected and painstakingly analysed.

Excerpts from the Book
Some excerpts from the book are the following.

PROFESSOR ISAAC FOLORUNSO ADEWOLE
former Honourable Minister of Health,
former Vice-Chancellor of the University of Ibadan

Excerpts from Foreword 1

It is a great honour and privilege for me to write a Foreword to this great compilation in honour of Professor GOS Ekhaguere to mark his 70 years of sojourn on mother planet. I have known and interacted with him for many years during his academic exploits in the University of Ibadan. He lived out his academic life on the campus in Ibadan except for the brief period that his international assignments took him away to Ghana and other countries. . . .The book offers panoramic perspectives of the man popularly called "GOS". It highlights his character, nature, skills and numerous qualities, including those outside his routine academic life. The authors have him keenly dissected and painstakingly analysed. Over and over, I hear ringing superlatives such as thorough, gentle, down to earth, soft spoken, diligent, humane, role model, intelligent, supportive, great, colossus, humble and hardworking. I'm not at all surprised that he is described as a good teacher, mentor and an inspiration. . . .I wish I could clone GOS, then I would have found a key weapon for making our University System better and more productive. This work is an excellent way to celebrate a patriotic and detribalised Nigerian for traversing the University of Ibadan, Nigeria and Planet Earth with great guts. May his legacy of honesty, hard work, humility, thoroughness, integrity and diligence live forever.

Professor Abel Idowu Olayinka
former Vice-Chancellor, University of Ibadan
former Deputy Vice-Chancellor (Academic),
former Dean, Postgraduate (now The Postgraduate College)

Excerpts from Foreword 2

It gives me great pleasure to write a Foreword to this Book of Tributes in honour of someone whom many of us have always admired and looked up to as a senior colleague and mentor, Professor GOS Ekhaguere, in commemoration of his 70th birthday and formal retirement from the services of our *alma mater* and great institution, the University of Ibadan. In doing this, I will like to specially commend the efforts of the different contributors who have attempted to bring to the fore their different perspectives of the life and career accomplishments of this foremost and erudite mathematical physicist, renowned scholar of immense national and international repute and a very humane person.

... In the course of his career, Professor Ekhaguere has taught, supervised and mentored countless undergraduate and postgraduate students, many of whom are now eminent scholars and researchers in their own right. ...The young GOS Ekhaguere came here as an undegraduate student of Physics in the Faculty of Science nearly fifty years ago. He is stepping aside as a distinguished Professor of Mathematical Physics. You have performed exceedingly well, without any blemish to your hard-earned reputation built over many decades of honesty, hard work, diligence and attention to details. The University of Ibadan, our common heritage, our dear country and the entire academic community are eternally grateful to you.

PROFESSOR OLUFEMI BAMIRO,
former Vice-Chancellor University of Ibadan

Excerpts from Foreword 3

It is indeed a great honour to be asked to write a Foreword to this publication containing tributes by highly respected minds in the academia to celebrate the great mathematician – Godwin Osapemwoya Samuel – popularly called GOS, to mark his 70 years on this side of the great divide. Many people, including me, have taken GOS to be his first name. It is symptomatic of the warmth that he naturally exhibits while relating to people. It is, therefore, not surprising to see the array of colleagues, former students and relations who have chosen to say one thing or the other about him in this publication. ...I make haste to observe that much of what has been written, is to my mind, just expatiating on the attributes of the great man: a great teacher as attested to by his students; a mentor and role model to so many; an accomplished researcher who has traversed all the continents through collaborative research works, attendance of conferences; an unusual administrator who has applied his analytical mind to the diverse administrative responsibilities at Ibadan and beyond; an activist with commitment to justice and fair play; and very much more in the service of academia and humanity, as covered in the publication. ... To GOS, our great friend, the fire is still very much in you to help pilot this generation further through the identified headwinds. May God grant you that grace as I urge, not only our budding mathematicians, but also, the young academics in various disciplines, to digest this publication and learn from the life and works of GOS. He has shown clearly that through hard work and perseverances, one can provide meaningful service to his or her profession and humanity and, thereby, gain national and international recognition that will stand one in good stead beyond retirement.

EMERITUS PROFESSOR DANIEL SUNDAY IZEVBAYE
former President, Nigerian Academy of Letters,
former Provost of the College of Arts, Social Sciences and Law, University of Ibadan,
former Dean, Faculty of Arts, University of Ibadan,
former Dean, Faculty of Humanities, Bowen University

Excerpts from Foreword 4

I feel highly honoured at being invited to write a Foreword for this *Festschrift* in honour of Professor GOS Ekhaguere. The invitation could not be for a lack of candidates given that the response from contributors distinguished in their own professions has been overwhelming. ...The testimonies of many of the contributors to this *Festschrift* shows that GOS's application of his administrative skill and research expertise is so sophisticated and cosmopolitan that it transcends cognate fields and extends into new areas that are not directly related to his discipline. ...It is no surprise that in an era of specialisation, he always finished each stage of his education – from Higher School Certificate to PhD, on an "interdisciplinary" emphasis, with a combination of Mathematics and Physics. The effect of this profound passion for Mathematics is predictable; it takes over the whole being and determines character and personality, such that a first meeting with acquaintances leaves an impression of his personality that is as enduring as it is with old friends and colleagues. That is unusual for such a soft-spoken person. It is no surprise that the one recurrent answer that his interpreters seek is the secret of his success – how, for example, he has managed to resist the logical consequence of his profound commitment to mathematics from turning him into a rigid "mathematical" man, and managed to retain his humanity and humility as "a gifted scholar and gentleman", as Professor Ayo Banjo puts it. Professor Oka Obono offers an answer that is fascinating because it strikes so close to the mark: "It is not easy to separate who he is from what he does and how or why he does it. He is a whole and total person." As Emeritus Professor Janice Oluwoye and many other contributors testify, GOS gets totally immersed in a project when duty or professional interest calls. ...I should now present my own birthday wish. If it seems somewhat extravagant to a mathematician who is also a committed Catholic, remember it is offered with all sincerity. GOS, for the benefit of our developing science culture, may the years of your life – and of others like you – extend well beyond the seventy and eighty at which the Psalmist circumscribes the time capsule of our brief stop on earth, and be blessed with both the strength and the wisdom of the long-lived Patriarchs before you.

EMERITUS PROFESSOR AYO BANJO,
Chairman, Board of the National Universities Commission, Nigeria
former Pro-Chancellor & Chairman of Council University of Port Harcourt, Nigeria,
former Pro-Chancellor and Chairman of Council, University of Ilorin, Nigeria
former Vice-Chancellor, University of Ibadan, Nigeria

A Man with a Gentle Mien and Scholarly Bearing

It gives me enormous pleasure to be given the opportunity to pay tribute to Professor Ekhaguere on his attainment of seventy years. ...I had, naturally, been aware of GOS's presence on the campus of the University of Ibadan for many years, being struck by his gentle mien and scholarly bearing; but in due course, two episodes brought us closer together to confirm my first impressions of a truly gifted scholar and gentleman. ...GOS's standing in the

University had been enhanced by the excellent job he had done in running the University's MacArthur Foundation-sponsored programmes. Everyone knew of the commitment he exhibited in that office and of his impeccable administration there. It so happened that a committee of the Nigerian Academy of Letters invited me to deliver a lecture on university rankings, which the Academy was planning in collaboration with the Nigerian Universities Commission. There was not too much time to plan the lecture, but my mind went immediately to GOS. I thought he would be an excellent resource person, and indeed I suggested that he should be recognised as the joint author of the paper that I was going to read. ...I do believe that GOS has been a great asset to the Department of Mathematics, and to the University of Ibadan in general. As he approaches the retirement age, one wishes there could be ways of retaining his talents in the university a little longer. Happy birthday, GOS!

EMERITUS PROFESSOR ABIOLA ODEJIDE,
former Deputy Vice-Chancellor (Academic) , University of Ibadan, Ibadan,
former Director, Distance Learning Centre, University of Ibadan,
former Head, Gender Mainstreaming Programme. University of Ibadan

An Epitome of Forthrightness, Integrity and Good Work Ethic

I congratulate a worthy colleague, Professor GOS Ekhaguere, on his 70th birthday, which is a landmark event. I respect him for his forthrightness, integrity, work ethics and commitment to the upliftment of our great University. I cannot forget our first close encounter. The year was 2004. I had turned up on his office doorsteps (with an entourage) to canvass for votes to become Deputy Vice-Chancellor (Academic) of the University. He firmly, but softly, requested my "fans club" to wait outside while he asked me a few pointed questions about what I thought should be the vision and mission of higher education in Nigeria. We had a short discussion on "fitness for purpose" and "fitness of purpose." I would like to think he was persuaded that I knew what the job entailed. ...Over the next few years, I interacted with him when he was the MacArthur Foundation Grant Liaison Officer (MGLO) and continued to be impressed by his efficiency, attention to details and support for the different projects. He was very supportive of the Gender Mainstreaming Programme of which I was Principal Investigator and found time to attend our workshops. He was also instrumental to the successful formulation of the Strategic Plan for the Internationalisation of the University and other critical programmes which have helped to place our university on the global map. Professor, I salute your intellect, hard work and unassuming manner as you promote excellence in higher education.

PROFESSOR OKA MARTIN OBONO,
Director, Centre for Human Resource Development, University of Ibadan
former Director, Institute for Peace and Strategic Studies, University of Ibadan

A Quiet Introduction to Ekhaguere

In reminiscing about a colleague's accomplishments, it is often easy to overlook how far these accomplishments express his basic humanity. With Professor GOS Ekhaguere, this is not the case. The man's life is interwoven with his work. It is not easy to separate who he is from what he does and how or why he does it. His achievements are, therefore, forms in which his interior worlds are externalised. Accordingly, his life can be understood, so to speak, as a function of mathematics. He intuitively sees most problems as amenable to a calculated approach and, in this respect, it is fair to say that Ekhaguere is a modern Leibniz. ...Ekhaguere is, for me, the quintessential scholar. He is at once basic and complex, simple and profound. I admire him because his type doesn't come frequently in the annals of civilisation. How many Ekhagueres like Ekhaguere do you know? How many times have you felt in his presence that you stood in the presence of greatness? Perhaps it is part of cosmic justice that such persons are so few and so rare. They are so few and far between in order that a reflective society would perpetually query itself. It must ask questions. What did the society do with the talents it had? What did it do with greatness when it encountered it? What did this community do with Mathematics when Mathematics became flesh and dwelt among us? ..."If only we had four more people like you...." . That mournful nullity. When you had Professor GOS Ekhaguere, what did you do with him? Did you do all you could with him? Did you do all you should have done? Therein lies equity and universal justice – the other side of the equation. Therein lies our current dilemma and our not-so-quiet introduction to penance and repentance.

PROFESSOR ROTIMI AYODELE ODERINDE
MacArthur Grant Liaison Officer, &
Professor of Industrial Chemistry, University of Ibadan, Ibadan

> *Seest thou a man diligent in his business? he shall stand before kings; he shall not stand before mean men. – Prov. 22:29*

He is Diligence Personified

My immediate predecessor as MacArthur Grant Liaison Officer (MGLO), University of Ibadan, Professor G.O.S. Ekhaguere, popularly referred to as "GOS", is a fine gentleman and an erudite scholar of many parts. How does one start to write about a colossus? No matter how much one may claim to know Professor Ekhaguere, one can only know in part what makes this man of integrity the person that he is. It gives me great delight to write a tribute on this quintessential gentleman, a teacher of teachers, a great mathematician, a devout Catholic, a patriot, a simple and great leader of people. His outstanding leadership as the Liaison Officer during his tenure in office with the support of the MacArthur Foundation and the University administration gave rise to several University policy documents, namely, Internationalisation Strategic Plan (2009-2014), A New Integrated, System-Based, Person-Centred, Community-Oriented, Competency-Driven Curriculum for the MBBS Programme, Research Policy, Research Management Office Document, HIV & AIDS Policy, Sexual Harassment Policy, Gender Policy. Also under him and with the support of the MacArthur Foundation Grants and the University administration, he chaired and pioneered the establishment of the following offices and programmes, namely, Research Management Office, Gender Mainstreaming Office, Office of International Programmes, University Advancement Centre, Multi-disciplinary Central Research Laboratory (MCRL), Centre for Entrepreneurship and Innovation (CEI), Centre for Excellence in Teaching and Learning (CETL), and Centre for Human Resource Development (CHRD). There is hardly a Committee of Senate of the University of Ibadan to which Professor Ekhaguere has not made some significant contribution. He is a man with deep insight, versatility, multitasking and is widely consulted in Nigeria and abroad. Since my assumption of duty as the current MGLO, the office has had cause to seek his second opinion on a lot of technical issues, including our institutional grant-seeking activities for the MacArthur 100 and Change Grant challenge and the British Council-SPHEIR proposal. His wise counsel and guidance can never be wished away no matter how hard you try. When in need of a sincere and critical perspective on issues, Professor Ekhaguere is the right person to go to. His evaluation is likely to appear daunting, but it remains the best way to go. Professor Ekhaguere pays attention to details and is almost a perfectionist. He never stops to amaze me with the profundity of his writings. An email from GOS would always stand out conspicuously by itself. It is a popular opinion that he has distinguished himself in all the qualities of leadership which I believe, without doubt, are ingrained in his person. ... It is worthy of note that at 70 he continues to play leading roles with diligence in all endeavours that involves him. With his vigour and youthful strength I still believe that the very best is yet to come. Our country, Nigeria, is in dire need of many more of your sterling attributes. Seventy hearty cheers to you and happy birthday!

PROFESSOR DEBORAH O. AJAYI
former Acting Head, Department of Mathematics, University of Ibadan

He Taught Me Hard Work and Discipline

It is a great privilege and honour to write a tribute on my distinguished teacher and senior colleague Professor GOS Ekhaguere. I got to know Professor GOS during my postgraduate studies in 1987. He taught us MAT 720, the only required course for all Master students in the Department. Although Professor GOS taught the cause with all carefulness, his very serious look and disciplined attitude sent fear down our spines. He was an excellent teacher. The course was so well taught that many of us can still recall with ease those things he taught us. After I was employed in 1990, I was attached to him to take tutorials of an analysis course that Professor GOS taught. He made me work out all the tutorial questions before taking the classes. This got me established in the course and imbibed in me the attitude of hard work and discipline. Later on we travelled together to Benin Republic in 1993 for a conference and also we met at the International Centre for Theoretical Physics (ICTP), Italy, during one of his visits as a senior associate. These two occasions particularly showed me another side of Professor GOS as very caring and fatherly. In Italy, he had compelled one of us, Professor Ayoola, to see me off to the airport. This gender-sensitive side of Professor GOS underlies the fact that he is one of the only two males (the other being Professor S.A. Ilori, my PhD supervisor) each of whom has produced a Mathematics female PhD holder in the Department of Mathematics, University of Ibadan, which has graduated over 50 PhDs, including only two female PhDs, since 1971. He must have been very patient to accomplish this feat. Professor GOS is indeed a distinguished mathematician, an excellent teacher and a role model, who is fatherly, caring, disciplined, patient and hardworking. I convey my congratulations to Professor GOS and pray that the Lord will grant him long life in good health to continue to be a blessing to this generation.

PROFESSOR CHINEDUM PEACE BABALOLA,
*Vice-Chancellor of Chrisland University, Abeokuta,
former Dean, Faculty of Pharmacy, University of Ibadan*

GOS: A Strong, Effective and Impactful Leader

Who is GOS Ekhaguere and how much of him do I know? I know GOS, first of all, as a genius and a Professor of Mathematics in University of Ibadan. I know GOS as an extremely intelligent man and yet humble, quiet and soft-spoken I know GOS as a strong, effective and impactful leader. I know GOS as a very strict disciplinarian, yet he will not bark at you. I know GOS as a focused man and yet sees other things going around him. I know GOS as a man of very high integrity and so will not bend rules. I know GOS as a very thorough man and so will not tolerate carelessness. I know him as a very punctual person and so will not tolerate lateness. I know him as a very strong young-looking man yet he is 70 and so does not look it at all!!

AMBASSADOR PROFESSOR TUNDE ADENIRAN
Professor of Political Science
former Minister of Education
former Ambassador to the Federal Republic of Germany

A Mathematician with a Socio-Political Purpose

Before I am charged, let me establish my qualification on three premises: GOS Ekhaguere and I have been friends for almost forty years. Secondly, as philosophers, we share common ancestry through Plato and Aristotle of the Hellenic period. Thirdly, we have both been "conspirators" and "comrades" in the national theatre of political action. ... It was delightful and a great credit to the academic community to see GOS Ekhaguere during the Second Republic playing technical and constructive roles in socio-political engineering. Having joined the staff of the University of Ibadan in October 1976 he had, by 1979, "found his feet" on campus and could look out to see what was needed to add value to the unfolding democratisation process. Professor Segun Odunuga and I assembled what was apparently a formidable group of about forty scholars who believed in the populist manifesto and people-oriented programmes of the Unity Party of Nigeria (UPN). GOS was among the most resourceful in the group which included Tola Atinmo from Medicine, Femi Otubanjo from the Social Sciences, Ben Elugbe from the Arts, Soji Ofi from Technology, etc. The group was involved in strategic planning and in writing position papers to assist Uncle Bola Ige of the Old Oyo State and other South Western State leaders as well as Papa Obafemi Awolowo at the national level before and after the 1979 general elections. A most humble, unassuming and self-effacing personality, GOS dazzled many of us with his knowledge of political issues and the social consequences of policy options. With his precise and dispassionate analysis, he brought mathematics to bear on the exposition of issues. ... May the tribe of Ekhaguere multiply in our society for the sake of tomorrow.

PROFESSOR WAYNE PATTERSON
Professor of Computer Science,
Howard University, Washington, DC USA

An Exemplar of a Mathematician

I am honoured to have this opportunity to reflect on my relationship with GOS and to indicate the great value that I place on our relationship. ...I first met GOS close to 20 years ago when I was involved in organising an International Conference involving numerous leaders in graduate education in the United States and in about 25 African countries. At the time, GOS was a leading official in the Association of African Universities, in Accra. ...I have had the good fortune to maintain and expand on my relationship with GOS in the many years since that time. We realised at one point we had similar mathematics backgrounds, and I have often pointed to GOS as an exemplar of a mathematician doing exceptional research in a very challenging research environment. ...Most recently, I was asked by Professor Evans Harrell, editor of the *International Association of Mathematical Physics News Bulletin,* to contribute an article emerging from a panel at which I spoke last year at the Annual Meeting of the AAAS (American Association for the Advancement of Science). The article he requested, on "The Advancement of Mathematics, Physics and Computer Science in Developing Countries," appeared in the October 2016 issue of that newsletter. In order not to project only my own views, I solicited contributions from several distinguished colleagues in these fields from Africa, Latin America, and Asia. GOS's contribution was typically thorough, detailed and extremely thoughtful (This newsletter and the indicated article are online at http:// www.iamp.org/bulletins/Bulletin-Oct2016-screen.pdf). ...I am very honoured to have been invited to give a presentation at this Conference mentioned above in honour of GOS's 70th birthday (although by appearance I could believe it would really be his 50th birthday). I look forward to the conference in May in Ibadan and I will be very pleased to give a presentation on what I view as an emerging research area in what we now call "Behavioural Cybersecurity."

PROFESSOR NINUOLA AKINWANDE
President, Nigerian Mathematical Society (NMS),
former Head, Department of Mathematics, Federal University of Technology, Minna

He is an Inspiration and a Problem-Solver

The President, Council and Members of the Nigerian Mathematical Society (NMS) join the family and the University of Ibadan community to celebrate our dearly beloved icon, colleague, father and mentor, Professor Godwin Osakpemwoya Samuel (GOS) Ekhaguere, on the occasion marking his 70th birthday. Professor Ekhaguere has continued to play a significant role in the re-invigoration of the NMS and remains a veritable source of encouragement to many of us. He was at a time the Vice-President of the Society and was recently conferred with the Fellowship of the Nigerian Mathematical Society, FNMS, an honour well deserved. Professor Ekhaguere is a distinguished Mathematician who has opened up research areas in the field of Mathematical Physics (areas where angels fear to tread). These areas include Algebras and Partial Algebras, Classical and Non-Commutative Stochastic Analysis, Financial Mathematics and Mathematical Modelling. As a Mathematics teacher, he is highly inspiring, always taking the pains to write details of his lectures with his beautiful handwriting for the students. Great mathematical minds are problem-solvers and Professor Ekhaguere has consistently demonstrated this in every challenging position he has been privileged to occupy within and outside the academic communities. We celebrate this great mathematician and wish him long life so he can continue to make further contributions to the frontiers of mathematics and services to humanity in general. Happy birthday!!!

EMERITUS PROFESSOR WITOLD KARWOWSKI
University of Zielona Góra,
Institute of Physics, Zielona Góra, Poland

My Good Friend and an Outstanding Scientist

I first met Professor Ekhaguere in 1972. He was not a professor then, no. He was rather a student of mathematics at the London University and I was a British Council scholar. Our advisor was Professor R.F. Streater at Bedford College. Some years later, we were participating in a research project at the Centre for Interdisciplinary Research of the Bielefeld University in Bielefeld, Germany. He was so kind to visit the Institute for Theoretical Physics of the Wroclaw University in Wroclaw, Poland where I worked. The last time we met in Nigeria was at a conference. Although our getting together occurs very rarely, I consider him my good friend and an outstanding scientist. GOS, I wish you all the best on this occasion of your 70th anniversary.

ENGR. ISAAC I. UHUNMWAGHO
Chairman, EFEX Executive/Efosa Express Ltd.
Benin City, Edo State, Nigeria

He Set the Benchmark and Standard for Academic Excellence

It gives me great pleasure and a sense of nostalgia to wish my friend a Happy 70th Birthday. GOS and I were "small boys" in the early 1960s and I wish to make some comments about my fellow "small boy" during that era. So here it goes. ...GOS was a unique student in our class because he set the benchmark and standard for academic excellence for the rest of us. Right from Form 1 and at such a young age, he had a lot of unique features, part of which were the initials of his name – GOS. He was the only one who was called by his initials rather than his name Godwin. This singular factor distinguished him but how he managed to stamp that name on himself so early in life still beats my imagination. ...I also grew to appreciate the special qualities of GOS. Apart from just being a brilliant student, he was a young gentleman with an impeccable character. He had very little time for trivialities and was an excellent time-manager. He did not need to burn the midnight oil as he was naturally brainy. He was generally well-organised, soft-spoken and avoided loud and noisy environment. I can still remember his beautiful handwriting. He was witty and had a canny sense of humour. ...May the good Lord grant GOS many more fulfilling years ahead in good health and happiness. Amen.

AMBASSADOR THADDEUS DAN HART
Rtd Permanent Secretary, Ministry of Foreign Affairs,
Former Ambassador to The Netherlands, Former Ambassador to Brazil,
Senior Special Assistant to the President of Nigeria on International Relations (2007-2015),
Member, Class of '65 Immaculate Conception College, Benin City, Nigeria

He Was Very Friendly, Humble and a Good Team Player

For many of us members of the graduating class of 1965 of the Immaculate Conception College, Benin City, there was something extraordinary about the personality of GOS as we fondly called him. GOS was the cleverest boy and the "all-rounder" of the class from the inception of our academic career at the college; he always led the class in our tests and examinations. Most remarkable was his casual and seemingly effortless manner of achieving his academic feats. ...GOS was restrained in his physical exertions;

not one to engage in unnecessary quarrels and fisticuffs. He was very friendly and humble, a good team player who was always disposed to helping his mates out of their academic difficulties. He was about as removed from the student fashion consciousness and the fun-loving ethos of the 60s as it is possible to imagine. But he was not all work and no play. His favourite sport was table-tennis (ping-pong) which he played with relish. He was a regular member of the college table-tennis team and participated in several inter-collegiate competitions. So strong was his power of mental concentration and motor coordination that he was always a difficult opponent to beat in a table-tennis encounter. He was also an avid chess player. ...His overwhelming combination of intellectual power, simplicity and humour earned him great respect and popularity among the entire student population, members of staff and our school Principal, the great Rev. Father J. Donnelly. GOS was obviously a cut above the others, the ideal student par excellence in his years at college. ...GOS, thank you for bringing such great honour to our nation, the University of Ibadan and our alma mater. God bless you and your family.

THE RT. HON. CHEVALIER DR. E.J.S. UUJAMHAN,
former President, Nigerian Society of Engineers,
former Vice President (African Region), World Federation of Engineering Organisations
Chairman, Board of Trustees, Nigerian Society of Engineers,
Principal Partner/CEO, Oska-Jo & Partners Ltd

He's a Marvel and Would Have Shone as a Star in Any Field!

I really don't know if mine is a tribute or a reflection on where our paths crossed especially in the formative years of our lives, but I must thank God for you that in spite of your health challenges in the sixties, you are today enjoying that promised three scores years and ten (Psalm 90:10). My wife and I and, indeed my entire family, congratulate you and look forward to your gathering enough strength to attaining four scores and beyond. ...GOS, although I eventually went to Ahmadu Bello University, Zaria, for my Mechanical Engineering degree, you strenuously wished I attended the University of Ibadan to read Mathematics, for which I also got admission, but UI was not offering Engineering at the time. Looking back now, you should certainly have been a wonderful and creative Engineer but I thank God that you have excelled in your chosen line of studies, obtaining a first degree in Physics but ending up as one of the greatest Mathematical Physicists of our generation. With all my exploits in Engineering Mathematics, do you know that I did not even understand one line of your first book in Mathematical Physics? I keep on wondering where this "son of Joseph, the Carpenter" got all these wisdom from. Is it from No. 34 Siluko Road, or the flowery gardens of UI? We all know you as GOS, not knowing for a long time that they were indeed your initials. The "os" in small letters always followed the big "G". Those of us that have been opportune to read your essays wonder whether these were works of a Mathematician or that of a literary giant. I tried to transform your "learn one new word a day" philosophy to many but I never succeeded. You could have been a star in any field. You are a marvel. . . . My wife and I have enjoyed every moment of our long relationship with you, always displaying a quiet confident disposition imbued with knowledge and thoughtfulness. Congratulations, GOS, as we pray to join you in ten years' time for your four scores reserved for those who are strong!!

PROFESSOR DANIEL AISAGBONBUOMWAN ENOBAKHARE
Former President of the Entomological Society of Nigeria,
former Head, Department of Crop Science, Faculty of Agriculture,
University of Benin, Benin City

His Motto? Semper et Ubique Fidelis

It is with pleasure and indeed to the glory of God that I seize this opportunity to say what I know of this rare gem and genius born about 70 years ago in Benin City, Edo State, Nigeria. I knew Professor Godwin Osakpemwonya Samuel Ekhaguere in Immaculate Conception College (ICC) Benin City as a student of the College. He was in his final School Certificate year in 1965 while I was in the second year in the same College. After his West African School Certificate year, he was admitted for Higher School for two years in the same College. I was also in the Higher School class after him in ICC, a Catholic School where the Principal, Rev. Fr. Joseph Donnelly (Irish) trained us like seminarians. ...I recall that while we were both in Immaculate Conception College, Benin City, he gave me homework and taught me how to study. I remember very many instances when students would bring Mathematics puzzles for him to solve. We were astonished at his ingenuity and readiness to solve problems without referring to any textbook or deriving answers from formulas. ... He had brilliant classmates in the Lower and Higher School Certificate classes who were also my friends. As usual in our college, there was competition among students for academic positions in the class. GOS, as he was popularly called, was always in the first position both in the Lower and Higher Schools. ...I am proud of you for your steadfastness to the motto of our college – *Semper et ubique fidelis,* i.e. always and everywhere, be faithful.

PROFESSOR ADEOLA ADENIKINJU
Director, Centre for Petroleum, Energy Economics and Law,
University of Ibadan, Ibadan

Behold a Brother, Mentor and Friend!

I am pleased to write this tribute to an erudite scholar par excellence, a man of integrity, honesty, hard work, humility, with a passion for excellence. Professor GOS is an icon, an administrator, firm but fair to all, a mentor and a friend, a godly, disciplined man. My path crossed the path of Professor Ekhaguere when he was the MGLO. His incisive comments and suggestions, eyes for details, willingness to listen to the other side of the argument, and readiness to always assist have endeared him to me and many others. He is loyal to his friends and will always be there to offer support and encouragement. Sir, I am proud to call you a mentor, a brother and a friend. God will add to your years, strength and wisdom and continuous service to humanity and those the Lord has brought along your way. I am glad I met you. Happy 70th Birthday.

PROFESSOR EZEKIEL OLUSOLA AYOOLA
former member of the University of Ibadan Governing Council,
former Head, Department of Mathematics , University of Ibadan, Ibadan

He is a Mathematical Phenomenon

It is with great pleasure that I write this tribute on the occasion of the 70th birthday anniversary and the formal retirement from the University of Ibadan of Professor GOS Ekhaguere. I first came in contact with Professor Ekhaguere during my undergraduate years in the early 1980s. At that time, he made an indelible impression on most of us as a very serious academic who enjoyed learning and imparting mathematical knowledge to his students. He explained serious and complicated mathematical structures and principles in such a simplified manner that he stimulated my interest in taking up career as a professional mathematician. As providence will have it, Professor Ekhaguere was divinely appointed to supervise my doctoral research which I began in 1993. ...Professor Ekhaguere belongs to a rare breed of multi-talented mathematicians. His research interests cover a broad spectrum of mathematical topics. He is well-known in the global and local mathematical communities as an erudite researcher in mathematical physics, functional analysis, non-commutative stochastic analysis, partial *algebras and mathematical finance. These are mathematical sub-disciplines that cut across the pure and the applied areas. His research activities are always fundamental, breaking new grounds at the frontier. His seminal paper on Lipschitzian Quantum Stochastic Differential inclusions published in 1992 in the well-known *International Journal of Theoretical Physics remains* the foundation of further research on the qualitative and quantitative properties and applications of solutions of this class of equations and inclusions to concrete problems all over the world. I wish to state that my PhD thesis on the numerical procedures for solving quantum stochastic differential equations (QSDE), supervised by Professor Ekhaguere and concluded in December 1998, was firmly built on the foundation of this paper. ...Professor Ekhaguere remains my mentor, teacher and an excellent role model. He easily and effortlessly makes his wealth of experience both in academic and administrative matters available to us. He remains an example of manpower resources that our nation refuses to utilise optimally at the national level simply because he is not the type of person that engages in do-or-die efforts to obtain political recognition. He refused to join the bandwagon of the movement of academics to other lands during the brain drain era in the late 80s to early 90s, despite the fact that he has far more than what it takes to move away from the country to more rewarding academic appointments abroad. His decision to remain in this country has turned to be an unquantifiable benefit for us his former students. ...We look up to you for continued leadership in our profession.

PROFESSOR DELE LAYIWOLA
former Director, Institute of African Studies
University of Ibadan, Ibadan

Man of Figures, Man of Letters

I knew Professor GOS Ekhaguere (the quiet, unassuming mathematician, a man of figures and a man of letters), when he first served on the governing council of the university. His batch of councillors preceded ours by two sets. During his tenure, he was the Chairman of the Council Committee on Security. His innovations were path-breaking and the qualities of leadership in him were evident. I, like a few others, had hoped that he might have had a shot at the Vice-Chancellory but events dictated otherwise. He is always calm and composed and he always had his wits about him. He has shown, over time, that he could be entrusted with very sensitive and crucial responsibilities as he has always delivered on his beat. I do not know him to be a hustler. He is always civil and minds his own business. I have extrapolated that his career progression threw some light on his practicality as a person and as an academic knowing that he first studied physics and then chose to experiment with greater abstraction by careering into mathematics. This shows that he is capable of bold experimentation and can be independent and eminently practical. Professor Ekhaguere is a successful family man; a totally decent husband and a proud grandfather. My family and I send him 70 hearty cheers and pray that we would all be here to celebrate with him when he is 90 and, peradventure, present him with a walking stick at his centenary. *Iselogbe. Ughatosayo o. Ugha kakabokhion Omae.* Dear big brother, Enjoy your day.

PROFESSOR CALEB ADEBAYO FOLORUNSO
former Head, Department of Archaeology and Anthropology,
University of Ibadan, Ibadan

He is Immune to Materialism

On behalf of my wife and children, I wish to congratulate Professor GOS Ekhaguere on the occasion of his clocking the age of seventy years. Professor Ekhaguere represents one of the finest academics of Ibadan. I have found Professor Ekhaguere to be very humble, gentle and soft-spoken but he would not compromise standards on the altar of kindness. I had been on several panels, committees and bodies chaired by Professor Ekhaguere and I have never seen him openly expressing anger. He treated everyone with respect even when some individuals had consistently defaulted in meeting set targets in the submission of reports. The expression of his frustration in such cases would not go beyond reporting to the Committee at meetings about those who had defaulted in submitting reports. He is very accommodating and would bend backwards to encourage people to meet up on responsibilities entrusted to them rather than expressing disappointments in people. The contributions of Professor Ekhaguere at meetings in the Faculty of Science had also been succinct and unambiguous. He had always complained about the continuous fall in standards in both the physical and intellectual landscape of our campus and he had always proffered solutions. He is not sentimental in his judgment and that may make him to be mistaken for being too demanding or insensitive to other persons' aspirations. It should be noted that he equally recognises and rewards hard work. Professor Ekhaguere represents part of the vestiges of what we came to know as the true academics and scholars at the University of Ibadan. He had been immune to the spirit of materialism that invaded Nigerian Universities from the 1990s. He maintains a decent and simple lifestyle befitting an academic who is contented with his calling and closing his eyes to the temptation of going after questionable riches that had pervaded town and gown. He is a shining example for us to follow. I wish him well as he steps into the septuagenarian caucus.

PROFESSOR SIKIRU ADEKOLA BABARINDE
former Director, Centre for Excellence in Teaching and Learning
University of Ibadan, Ibadan,
former Head, Department of Teacher Education, University of Ibadan in Ibadan

He Exemplifies the Immensity of Our National Possibilities

It is a wonderful privilege for me to contribute to this publication to mark the retirement of an icon in academics, Professor GOS Ekhaguere. I was not an undergraduate student of the University of Ibadan, so I did not know Professor Ekhaguere as a teacher. I am also not in the sciences and had no opportunity to relate to him within the domain of his discipline. Nevertheless, I came to know him fairly well as a researcher and administrator and, later, as a worthy mentor. Professor Ekhaguere was the MacArthur Grant Liaison Officer (MGLO) when I was the Principal Investigator (PI) of a project titled "Capacity Building in Pedagogical Skills", which was the project that eventually developed into the University of Ibadan Centre for Excellence in Teaching and Learning and later midwifed the Faculty Development in Nigeria. As grants manager, Professor Ekhaguere was detailed, inspiring, and gentle but firm. Throughout the period he served in that capacity, I never heard anyone speak ill of him. Even when one of his staff became almost impossible to deal with, Professor handled the situation with a calm, reassuring and dignified manner. I recall one such occasion when his staff raised a question and insinuation bothering on personal integrity about my project. I got so provoked that I was determined to fight that official and the establishment. But my meeting with Professor Ekhaguere, the MGLO, immediately doused the fire. I entered his office, spoiling for "war", but Professor left his chair, came to sit beside me and calmly said, "Professor of Pedagogy, you should not operate at the same level with my staff, if anything needed clarifications, make such known to me and I shall review it". And with that, a further breakdown was averted and the matter was laid to rest. Such was Professor Ekhaguere as an administrator. He was firm but humane. ...He is not just a mathematician. If he was, I might not have known much about him. He has translated his scholarship in mathematics into grant raising and management and has moved into the broad area of educational policy, advocacy, management and research. Always unassuming, soft-spoken, ready to offer expert opinion on topical issues in grant writing, research and management, Professor Ekhaguere will continue to be regarded as an icon of the old block who places scholarship above politicking, who is a universal citizen above petty ethnic and religious inclinations. Ever since he knew me as a devout Muslim, he has never failed to send me special greetings to mark major Islamic festivals despite being a devout Christian himself. In an age when highly revered academics are following the unenlightened crowd into a retreat into primordial cocoon of bias and prejudice, he has stood apart from such crowd to remain a shining light and hope to this university and beyond. ... To you, sir, on this special occasion I dedicate the immortal words of B.K.S. Iyengar, "The hardness of a diamond is part of its usefulness, but its true value is in the light that shines through it", and that of Benjamin Disraeli, "The greatest good you can do for another is not just to share your riches but to reveal to him his own". Thank you for your invaluable contributions to humanity.

DR. ALFRED E. OWOLOKO (RIP)
Senior Lecturer,
Department of Mathematics, Covenant University, Ota

His Lecture Was Always an Awesome Experience

Professor Ekhaguere is a father, teacher, mentor and motivator to me. He is different things to different people. Before meeting him in person, I had heard so much about him. One striking remark I always heard about him from another respectable professor from the University of Benin, was that "Professor Ekhaguere is one Benin man that is making us proud at the University of Ibadan (UI)". A one-hour discussion with him is like reading ten books on a given topic. My very first encounter with him was at his residence at UI. We got talking, because I wanted him to be my PhD supervisor. The first thing that caught my attention in that discussion was the way he described a stochastic process. I have been taught stochastic process at the undergraduate and postgraduate levels, but nobody ever gave me a vivid picture of what a stochastic process was as he did that day. It was an experience I will never forget. I have since adopted that description whenever I am opportune to teach any course relating to stochastic processes. Every time I listen to Professor teach (I was only opportune to have him teach me at the PhD level), it was always an awesome experience. His lectures were never boring; you always had something new to learn in the course of the lectures. He demonstrated this ability of his during his inaugural lecture: for the one-hour or so that the lecture lasted, everybody in the auditorium paid rapt attention all through the lecture. He supervised my PhD work, which was a rare privilege. Though the programme was tough, at the end, Professor succeeded in bringing out the very best in me. Whenever I look at my thesis, I am always filled with joy that I encountered such an erudite scholar in life. Professor, sir, as you celebrate your 70th birthday today, may the Almighty God keep and give you more glorious years ahead in Jesus' name. My family and I love you so dearly. Be blessed of the Lord. Amen.

OSAMWEETIN IMANE EKANEM (NÉE EKHAGUERE)
Business Analyst, Work Force Software, Milton Keynes, UK

Dad is the Simplest, Kindest, Humblest and Most Humorous Man I Know

I would not have thought that writing about my dad would be very challenging; not because there is nothing to write but because there is a lot to write with very few words to express how great a man and father he is. My father is the simplest, kindest, humblest and most humorous man I know. This man has not only sacrificed for his immediate family but also for those outside his family. Those who do not know my Dad as well as I do, find him very serious, non-smiling, very quiet and strict. Whilst their impressions of him are very true (my husband will agree), he is the funniest person ever with a great sense of humour. The funny thing is that, everything he does and says in the house is extremely funny to the extent that it is almost impossible to reconcile his professional personality with his personality at home. His close friends will tell you that, GOS has a way of infusing humour into everything he says. An example of my dad's humility is highlighted in the snippet of an email sent to me in 2009 by someone who shares our surname who had been helped in faraway America, as a result of my dad's assistance to one of his former students who assumed this young man was related to my dad.

> Osa,
>
> I am not sure; your dad is however the most popular Ekhaguere I know and he is all over the internet as a mathematician. I had a teacher who helped my math improve because your dad helped him, so even though I have never met your dad, I have benefitted from his example. Cheers. David Ekpenede Ekhaguere

I must say that as I live my life daily, two of the greatest things I have learnt from my dad are that hard work doesn't kill and humility pays. These values have stayed with me and I will be passing them on to my children as well. I hope now that as my dad retires from "active academic service" that he would display more of his fun personality, relax more and not stay up all night studying and writing. Above all, I wish my dad many more years in health and happiness.

An Electronic Encounter with a Namesake

As a precursor to the statement "I had a teacher who helped my math improve because your dad helped him" by David Ekpenede Ekhaguere (born: October 29, 1966) highlighted by my daughter in the foregoing excerpt, David had sent me an e-mail message on Thursday, February 11, 1999, with the subject: *Thanks for the good name,* and the following contents:

Subject: Thanks for the good name
Date sent: Thu,11 Feb 1999 23:15:28-0800

I am an Ekhaguere and very proud of it: thanks to you. Several years ago in Sapele, while in boarding school at Eziafa Grammar School, my life was dramatically changed because I have this last name. I was an excellent Arts student, excelling in English, Literature and all the Arts. My grades in Math were horrible and I could not break the cycle of poor Math grades, barely passing. Then in my junior year of school (class four), I met a young graduate of Ibadan who was serving his National Youth Service Corps and happened to be my Math teacher. He saw the name and my grades and called me to his office to scold me. Then he told me how my relative (you) had changed his life by teaching him Math, and what a great inspiration to him you are. He is Ibo. I forget his name but always remember trying to convince him I wasn't going to ever excel in Math. He then put me on a strict 1-hour a day diet of Math with his supervision, no food, nothing until I solve one problem a day for days, maybe even weeks. I resented him and this unknown relative that had caused this suffering. Finally after several weeks of painstaking, stressful 1-hour a day sessions, I finally figured one problem, then another. In a few weeks soon it became one or more problems a week, soon it was several a week, then he let me on my own. Soon I solved several weekly algebra, then geometry, trig and then it became intoxicating several hours a day even neglecting my other classes and responsibilities. That year later I passed Math and improved from a low grade that year earlier of 47% to 88%, barely passing my other courses. Well with much training and balance I switched to sciences from arts and took calculus, physics, etc. also because my Dad is an engineer. Finally I graduated and got an A1 in Math, scoring the highest in the State. I graduated also [with] an A3 in calculus, A1 in physics and etc. I went to med school for a while in A.B.U Zaria (s.b.s). Well long story short, I am an engineer now in America and have done contracts for Texas Instruments, Abbott Labs, and Canon as an Engineer, currently doing and building planes and choppers using a lot of calculations and Mathematics. Though we might not be related, I am proud to have this name, and want to thank you for how you have affected my life, from the bottom of my heart. Thank you.

[The writer shares the same surname with me, but we are not blood relatives.]

Although over the years, I received testimonies from time to time from some of my past students about how the mention of my name had opened certain doors for them at crucial moments, I was quite happy to learn from the e-mail message that my name changed the life-trajectory of a person I had never met. David Ekpenede Ekhaguere, who was headed for a career outside the specialization of science, eventually became an engineer, attaining the position of Principal Systems & Project Engineer at Cape Canaveral, Florida, USA, and continually acquiring multiple USA patents that protect some of his engineering innovations.

Moving out of the Campus

Retirement, as a remarkable milestone of an earthly journey, always brings about several life-changes for any public servant, especially one who had lived during most of his career years on a university campus in an accommodation provided by the institution. My wife and I were in that potentially unsettling position: for much of the 40 years from 1978 till 2018, we lived on the campus, with relatively good security, healthcare and other municipal facilities. I joined the University of Ibadan on October 1, 1976, while my wife was employed by the University on October 1, 1978. I retired from the institution on May 23, 2017; my wife retired a month later on June 21, 2017. Several years before our retirement, we needed to decide whether we would be remaining in Ibadan or relocating to our hometown Benin City, where I already had a house, which I christened Providence Villa; the latter was built with the unstinting help of my trusted friend, Sir Professor Daniel Enobakhare, and his dear wife, Lady Felicia Enobakhare: the couple bore, altruistically and graciously, the full and unpleasant brunt of the meticulous supervision of every aspect and detail of the construction. Returning to Benin City was challenging because we had been away from the town for a very long time. Apart from members of our families and some ICC schoolmates who lived in Benin City, many of our friends, colleagues, and confidants, as well as my past students, were largely in Ibadan and other adjoining towns. Although we visited Benin City from time to time, the visits were few, intermittent and brisk: they were mainly at weekends, except when we had some official duties to perform in the city. Additionally, over the years, the number of our contacts in Benin City had been diminishing. Meeting our past schoolmates during such visits always evoked ecstasy and nostalgia.

We decided to remain in Ibadan after retiring. Associated with this decision were the questions relating to whether we would simply move into a rented accommodation or build a house in the city. We settled for the latter option. Toward implementing this choice, I acquired a piece of land at the Ajoda New Town, Ibadan, from the Government of Oyo State. It was always frightful to think about how my family and I would adjust to living off-campus. I started building a house on the piece of land in 2006. I did not have millions and millions of Naira to implement the project nor to contract a building firm. Deploying whatever I could appropriate from time to time from my monthly salaries and the honoraria that I received occasionally for performing various services within the national and global academic community, I forged on steadily with the project, using direct labour and personally ensuring fidelity to the approved building plan. Eleven years later in 2017, the house, in the form of a duplex, was ready. But I should quickly admit that without the unstinted and selfless assistance of my deceased colleague, Associate Professor Chukwuma Raphael Nwozo, who helped to identify the right calibre of technical workers and meticulously ensured that all the materials employed in the construction were fit-for-purpose, it might have taken much longer than eleven years to complete the project. As had become the burden of every private house owner in Nigeria, we equipped the one-story building with a borehole and a source of solar energy, in addition to a standby electricity generator, to ensure uninterrupted water and electricity supply. I also contracted a security firm to provide round-the-clock professional security services for the compound. These were hallmarks of Government failure to provide basic services to Nigerians, including me. Elsewhere in the world, I would not be the one to personally provide fundamental municipal necessities as water, electricity and security, in respect of which I spent a substantial amount of my lean resources. Together with my family, I moved into the house in June 2018, thereby terminating my continuous residence on the University of Ibadan campus for almost 40 years from 1978 to 2018. Our experience about living in the new abode has been pleasant but expensive, because of the continually escalating cost of the multiple municipal services that I am obliged to provide on my own.

PART VIII

A YEAR LIKE NO OTHER

25

A GLOBAL HEALTH
CHALLENGE

The first two years after my retirement were interesting and potentially adventurous. There were unknown challenges and unpredictable uncertainties associated with my having to live thenceforth off-campus, after some 40 years of continuous residency on the University campus. As I cautiously dipped my toes into the somewhat tepid waters of my newfound freedom outside the formal world of work, it was clear that I was immersing myself in a whole new world in my continuing earthly journey. My financial ties with the University of Ibadan had been severed with effect from May 23, 2017. Thenceforth, liability for paying my monthly pension entitlements was to be borne by the Stanbic IBTC Pension Managers Limited, a Pension Funds Administrator (PFA), incorporated on May 19, 2004, as a subsidiary of Stanbic IBTC Holdings Plc. But with recurrent scary tales of the mistreatment of diverse classes of Government pensioners, through aperiodic or outright non-payment, or at best an inordinate delay in the payment, of their pension entitlements, it was not at all certain what fate awaited me. Fortunately, my PFA discharged its obligations to me with exemplary professionalism: unlike the situation where the University sometimes paid my monthly salary between the last week of a month and the first week of the following month, the PFA remitted my monthly pension to my bank account between the 11th and 15th day of every month with clockwork precision. This made financial planning feasible. Moreover, with occasional engagements here and there, I also earned some honoraria from time to time. By 2019, I had settled into my new routine and looked forward with ample confidence and enthusiasm to the imminent year 2020.

A Global Health Challenge

But 2020 turned out to be a year like no other since my birth. It was a year when the entire world was shaken to its foundations: a pandemic of an infectious disease, caused by a novel coronavirus, had struck various parts of the globe. The virus was spread through droplets of saliva or discharges from the nose when an infected person coughed or sneezed. The exceptionally vulnerable groups were identified as persons above 60 years in age, especially those with certain underlying morbidities or are immunocompromised, while the superspreaders were young persons, who were invariably asymptomatic. Initially, the World Health Organization (WHO) characterized the outbreak on January 30, 2020, as no more than a Public Health Emergency of International Concern (PHEIC). On February 11, 2020, WHO gave the virus the official name of SARS-CoV-2, a coronavirus that is transmitted from animals to people, while the disease caused by it was christened COVID-19, an abbreviation of "coronavirus disease 2019", formed by combining the letters CO, VI and D extracted from "COrona", "VIrus" and "Disease", respectively. Confronted with the rather astonishing speed of transmission of the virus, both nationally and internationally, the increasing number of hospitalisations and the continually rising death toll across nations, especially in Italy, USA and some other countries, WHO re-characterized the viral disease on March 11, 2020, as a global pandemic. This underlined the substantial risk that the disease posed to every nation.

In Nigeria, the index case was a male Italian from Milan who tested positive for COVID-19 on February 27, 2020 in Lagos. On March 9, 2020, a Nigerian male at Ewekoro, Ogun State, who had some contact with the index case, also tested positive for COVID-19. It was then evident that the globally dreaded COVID-19 ship had since berthed in Nigeria. To disrupt the transmission of the virus, there were actions to be taken responsibly by the Government and the citizens. On its part, Government set up a Presidential Task Force on COVID-19 (PTF-COVID-19), chaired by the Secretary to the Government of the Federation, Boss Mustapha, to coordinate its response. With no cure for, or a vaccine against, SARS-CoV-2 anywhere in the entire world in 2020, nations were naturally in a palpable state of panic and uncertainty. The response designed by the PTF-COVID-19 was essentially mimetic: it involved the wholesale mimicry of the responses in China, Europe, South Africa, South Korea and the USA. The first fatality in Nigeria was a former employee of the Pipelines and Product Marketing Company; he died on March 23, 2020.

The PTF-COVID-19 embarked on a nationwide campaign to build and entrench public awareness about the mode of infection and transmission of SARS-CoV-2, while also prescribing a number of so-called non-pharmaceutical preventive measures, such as hand-washing, use of hand sanitizers and face masks as well as avoidance of crowded gatherings, which all residents in Nigeria were to adopt at all times. Government also traced, tested and, where necessary, isolated and treated persons who had been in contact with the infected.

In Nigeria, President Muhammadu Buhari made a nationwide broadcast about SARS-CoV-2 on March 29, 2020. Relying on the Quarantine Act (CAP Q2 LFN 2004), he signed the COVID-19 Regulations, 2020 on March 30, 2020, imposing "restriction/ cessation of movement in Lagos, FCT and Ogun State" for an "initial period of 14 days with effect from 11:00pm on Monday, 30th March, 2020". The Regulations also contained the following:

All citizens in these areas [Lagos, FCT and Ogun State] are to stay in their homes. Travel to or from other States should be postponed. All businesses and offices within these locations should be fully closed during this period.

This particular regulation was quickly expanded into a nationwide interstate lockdown by the Nigerian Governors Forum, effective from April 23, 2020 to May 7, 2020. To earn the description of a year like no other, some other distinguishing characteristics of 2020 were the

- fearsome velocity of transmission of COVID-19,
- unprecedented loss of lives in several countries, which had not occurred since the plague of 1919,
- unparalleled disruption of educational activities and calendars at all levels of education,
- abrupt postponement of public examinations (WAEC, NECO, JAMB, UTME) and shutting down of NYSC orientation camps across Nigeria,
- unplanned resort to remote and virtual teaching and learning systems in many countries across the globe,
- unmatched disruptions of national and global economies,
- traumatic lockdowns in countries across the globe,
- sudden moratoria on social activities and travel within countries,
- atypical curtailment of international travel by several countries, enforced with effect from various dates in February 2020,
- multiple reports of mindless violations of citizens' human rights in a number of countries, including Nigeria.

The overall adverse impact of these unprecedented developments was exacerbated by the:

- weak state of the Nigerian economy in which unemployment and inflation figures were already spiralling,

- pervasive poverty in the land, marked by a poverty index of 70% of the Nigerian population,

- relatively deplorable state of the Nigerian health sector,

- glaring unpreparedness of the Nigerian education system for a sudden and almost wholesale adoption of the virual mode for teaching, learning, conferences, workshops, seminars and administration,

- inadequate attention to research and development activities by successive Nigerian governments,

- numerous fault lines and vulnerabilities in the Nigerian development processes, including the choice, location and implementation of national projects,

- paucity of game-changing people-centred services and assets.

A number of the measures implemented by the PTF-COVID-19 inevitably inflicted unforeseen, painful and hope-depleting hardship on many, some of whom were retrenched from their jobs or placed on reduced pay. Concomitantly, the initiatives simultaneously precipitated a phenomenal rise in the prevalence of psychological morbidities in the country. Additionally, many persons on tourist visits, business trips or pleasure cruises were locked down in foreign countries or on the high seas. Only narrowly did I escape being locked down in Dubai, United Arab Republic, in February 2020. Around the world, some national economies, including the Nigerian, slipped into recession. For someone like me who only recently retired from service and was still working to establish himself in a new phase of his life, the pandemic and the multiple occurrences associated with it were utterly destabilizing.

Combating the Pandemic

With a rapidly rising death toll from the pandemic, the world needed to urgently combat the COVID-19 infection by significantly slowing down its aggressive propagation or even completely eliminating the scourge. Accordingly, there were frenetic efforts by some globally renowned pharmaceutical companies to develop appropriate vaccines. By the end of December 2020, less than two years into the pandemic, the World Health Organization granted its first approval for an Emergency Use Listing (EUL) of a vaccine. By June 2021, the body had issued EUL approvals for the following COVID-19 vaccines: Pfizer/BioNtech Comirnaty (produced by Pfizer Inc, New York, USA and BioNTech SE, Mainz, Germany, with EUL approval on December 31, 2020), SII/Covishield and AstraZeneca/AZD1222 (produced by Oxford University, UK and AstraZeneca, Cambridge, UK, with EUL approval on February 16, 2021), Janssen/Ad26.COV 2.S (produced by Janssen Vaccines, Netherlands and Janssen Pharmaceuticals, Belgium, with EUL approval on March 12, 2021), Moderna (mRNA 1273) (produced by Moderna Inc, Cambridge, USA, with EUL approval on April 30, 2021), Sinopharm (produced by Beijing Bio-Institute of Biological Products Co. Ltd, China, with EUL approval on May 7, 2021) and Sinovac-CoronaVac (produced by Sinovac Biotech Ltd, China, with EUL approval on June 1, 2021). Overwhelmed by the unprecedentedly desperate situation created by the pandemic, a scramble by nations for access to the vaccines was inevitable. Unfortunately, vaccine nationalism then set in. This is the my-country-first approach to vaccine access adopted by the rich nations of the global north, through which those nations prioritised the vaccination of their own citizens over and above that of the citizens of the poor countries of the global south, not minding the potential global consequences. This ethically repugnant conduct by the wealthy nations was rigorously implemented by buying up most of the vaccines produced by pharmaceutical companies, leaving almost nothing for the poor nations. In that way, the rich nations unabashedly abandoned the high ideals of global equity, fairness, good conscience, cooperation, collaboration, solidarity, altruism and togetherness, in a world that was routinely portrayed as a global village, exposed by the pandemic to be tragically bereft of global solidarity or solicitude. As a result, the rich nations' behaviour posed an existential threat to poor nations and simultaneously reduced the prospects of an early end to the COVID-19 pandemic, because, in any pandemic, no one is safe until and unless everyone is safe. To illustrate the inequity in the relative access to the COVID-19 vaccine, as at November 4, 2021, the percentages of the populations of some of the countries of the northern hemisphere that had been partly or fully vaccinated were as follows: United States of America (66%), Germany (69%), United Kingdom (73%), France (76%), Italy (77%), Japan (78%), Canada (79%), Spain (81%) and Portugal (89%), using data from Our World in Data[22]. By contrast, the corresponding percentages for some African countries were as follows: Tanzania (1.4%), Nigeria (2.7%), Ethiopia (3.1%), Kenya (6.8%), Egypt (18%) and South Africa (26%). Providentially, while the cumulative deaths in, for example, the United States of America and the United Kingdom were 744,398 and 141,395, respectively, as at November 5, 2021, the corresponding figure for Nigeria was mercifully 2902, relying on data from the WHO[23].

The Pandemic Lives on

On April 6, 2021, Boss Mustapha announced the renaming of the PTF-COVID-19 as the Presidential Steering Committee on COVID-19 (PSC-COVID-19) with effect from April 1, 2021. According to him,

> ...the structure of the PSC-COVID-19 shall reflect the new focus of the response with a targeted approach on vaccine oversight,

22   https://ourworldindata.org/covid-vaccinations
23   https://covid19.who.int/table

risk communication, international travel quarantine processes and sub-national engagement.

... the tenure of the presidential steering committee shall last till December 31, 2021.

Pandemics are, unfortunately, not one-off events. Accordingly, there is the nonzero probability that other pandemics might occur again and again in the future, perhaps with unimaginable virulence, a much higher transmission speed and an enormous disruptive capacity. What will it take for the world, especially Nigeria, to be able to respond speedily and effectively to future pandemics?

Travelling in the Midst of a Pandemic

The COVID-19 years, 2020 and 2021, were unusually challenging. I narrowly escaped a potentially expensive lockdown in Dubai (United Arab Emirates) in 2020. Travelling from Nigeria to Europe or returning from Europe to Nigeria became unusually expensive and fatiguing. For my wife and I to travel to the United Kingdom in April 2021, each of us was required to take a COVID-19 test at a cost of ₦55,000, book for and subsequently take two COVID-19 tests, while self-isolating for eight days, on arrival in the UK at a cost of £210 (British pound sterling), complete and submit a passenger locator form before arrival in the UK, take another COVID-19 test at a cost of £100 before departing the UK to Nigeria, complete and submit an online NCDC form and book for a COVID-19 test in Ibadan at a cost of ₦39,500. Boarding a plane, or freedom to carry out one's business on arrival at one's destination, was contingent on the COVID-19 tests being negative. All told, for COVID-19 tests alone, my wife and I paid the equivalent of ₦527,482.80, using the exchange rate of ₦545.94 to £1 published by the Central Bank of Nigeria[24]. Additionally, we also had to cope with airfares that had been substantially marked up.

---

24   https://www.cbn.gov.ng/rates/exchratebycurrency.asp?beginrec=1&currencytype=&endrec=100

26

A LIFELONG
APPOINTMENT

Providentially, the year 2021 ended spectacularly for me in several ways, including sustained good health.

Emeritus Professorship

In November 2019, I was informed separately by Professor Deborah Olayide Ade Ajayi, the Head of the Department of Mathematics, and Professor Ezekiel Olusola Ayoola, former Head of the Department of Mathematics, former member of the University of Ibadan Governing Council and later the Deputy Vice-Chancellor (Administration), that there had been a call by the University for nominations by Faculty Boards and Boards of Institutes of suitable retired Professors for possible appointment as Emeritus Professors and that the Department had decided to nominate my colleague Professor Samuel Akindiji Ilori and me for consideration. Spontaneously, I told Professor Ajayi and later Professor Ayoola that, to increase the chances of success, it would be better for the Department to nominate only one candidate, who should be Professor Ilori. My reasons were that my colleague was senior to me by age, date of professorial appointment and also date of retirement. He was the substantive Head of the Department of Mathematics when my professorial promotion was announced. I was willing to wait for nomination during the next call, which could occur in 2023 after two years even though that was not a certainty because it was contingent on the existence of vacancies for new Emeritus Professors.

Vacancies are declared biennially by the University of Ibadan if, and only if, the total number of surviving Emeritus Professors is less than 15% of the total number of serving Professors. Professor Ajayi and Professor Ayoola must have been greatly surprised by my proposal because becoming an Emeritus Professor is a major aspiration of many a retired professor at the University of Ibadan. The two Professors insisted that the Department would not change its mind because, according to them, Professor Ilori and I were qualified to be nominated as Emeritus Professors by the Department.

With the rejection of my position, I provided all the information requested for nomination. Professor Ayoola did a yeoman's job in meticulously coordinating the Departmental nomination process and also defending the nominations at the Faculty Board of Science. The latter also ensured that the nominations rigorously met all the stipulated University requirements for the appointment of Emeritus Professors. The University's *Staff Information Handbook* (SIHB), published in 2003 and reviewed in 2017, contains fundamental details of the procedure for such appointments, including the following: expectations from Emeritus Professors, guidelines for the appointment of Emeritus Professors, procedure for nomination and a structured list of criteria for the award of Emeritus Professorships. The SIHB also contained the following:

The appointment of Emeritus Professor is for life.

i)   The total number of awards should not exceed 15% of the total number of Professors in the University.

iv)   Only persons who have been Professors for at least 15 years, at least 10 of which must have been spent as a

Professor of this University, must be recommended for award.

v)   Appointment of Emeritus Professors shall be made biennially provided there are vacancies.

The processing of our nominations was disrupted for close to two years by the SARS-CoV-2 pandemic. Eventually, I was honoured with a lifelong appointment by the Governing Council of the University of Ibadan in July 2021 as an Emeritus Professor of Mathematics, together with my colleague, Professor Samuel Akindiji Ilori. Only the two of us were nominated for appointment as Emeritus Professors by the Faculty Board of Science. At the University of Ibadan with about 500 Professors, the appointment of Emeritus Professors is highly competitive because of a number of requirements such as:

> To be considered appointable, candidates must have a minimum of 70% overall score and they will be ranked for selection purposes. They must also satisfy all the criteria.

In its recommendation to the University Senate by the Special Committee on the Appointment of Emeritus Professors, composed of a representative of professorial rank from each Faculty/Institute and chaired by the Deputy Vice-Chancellor (Research, Innovation and Strategic Partnerships), I was scored 98%, well beyond the required minimum score of 70% for appointability. The recommendation was endorsed by the University Senate to the University Governing Council, which finally made the appointment. Seven other Professors, besides Professor Ilori and I, were also appointed as Emeritus Professors in 2021. Through our appointments, Professor Ilori and I achieved the unique and enviable distinction of being the first Emeritus Professors of Mathematics at the University of Ibadan since its establishment in 1948.

27

A NATIONAL ACADEMIC
LAUREL

For the year 2021, I was the sole winner of the Nigerian National Order of Merit (NNOM) award, established through the Nigerian National Merit Award Act No. 96 of 1992, whose precursor was Act No. 53 of 1979,

> to be given to deserving citizens of Nigeria for intellectual and academic attainments that contribute to national endeavours in science, technology, medicine, the humanities, arts and culture and any other field of human endeavour whatsoever.

My journey to the award was by pure happenstance. A call for nominations for the NNOM award had been issued by the Board of the Nigerian National Merit Award (NNMA), with March 31, 2021 as the deadline. But I was not aware of the announcement, which included the following key elements:

> The Award is open to all citizens of Nigeria at home and abroad.

> The Award emphasizes distinct merit and upright morality, as this is the highest Merit Award in the Country.

> Successful candidates will be notified about the outcomes of the process between October and November 2021, to be followed by an official public announcement latest two weeks from the date of Investiture.

The Investiture of NNOM Awardee(s) is personally conducted by the President of the Federal Republic of Nigeria.

Not long after the request for nominations, some eminent Professors outside the University of Ibadan altruistically drew my attention to the announcement and urged me to join the contest for the 2021 NNOM award. It was quite humbling to be identified by the iconic Professors as someone who ought to throw his hat into the ring of the monumental academic and intellectual competition. After expressing my profound gratitude to the highly esteemed Professors, I gave them my word that I would participate in the 2021 contest. Thereafter, I was formally and enthusiastically nominated for the award by two eminent scholars: Professor Ninuola Ifeoluwa Akinwade, Fellow of the Nigerian Mathematical Society, former President of the Nigerian Mathematical Society and former Head, Department of Mathematics, Federal University of Technology, Minna, and Professor Ezekiel Oluyemi Oladiran, Fellow of the New York Academy of Science and former Head, Department of Physics, University of Ibadan. To my nominators, I owe much gratitude. I submitted my application for the NNOM award well before the deadline. From April to mid-November 2021, I did not receive any communication from the NNMA Board, not even an acknowledgement of receipt of my application. Luckily, I had sent my consignment through a reputable courier service and was therefore able to track its delivery to, and receipt by, the Board.

A NNOM Laureate Emerges

On November 25, 2021, I received a telephone call from the Secretary of the NNMA Board, Mr. Ibrahim Namadi, informing me that I had won the year 2021 NNOM award, Nigeria's highest intellectual and academic laurel, conceived as the nation's analogue of the Nobel Prize. The latter was endowed by the Swede Alfred Bernhard Nobel (October 21, 1833 – December 10, 1896) and was first awarded in 1901 to six laureates, namely: the German

Mechanical Engineer and Physicist, Professor Wilhelm Conrad Röntgen (March 27, 1845 – February 10, 1923) for Physics, Professor Jacobus Henricus Van 'Thoff (August 30, 1852 – March 1, 1911) for Chemistry, Professor Emil Adolf Von Behring (March 15, 1854 – March 31, 1917) for Medicine, René François Armand (Sully) Prudhomme (March 16, 1839 – September 6, 1907) for Literature, and two Peace laureates: Jean-Henri Dunant [commonly called: Henry Dunant] (May 8, 1828 – October 30, 1910) and Frédéric Passy (May 20, 1822 – June 12, 1912).

In Nigeria, the inaugural NNOM awards were made to four eminent laureates in 1979, namely: Professor Chinua Achebe (November 16, 1930 – March 21, 2013), Professor Olawale Teslim Elias (November 11, 1914 – August 14, 1991)., Alhaji Abubakar Imam (February 1, 1911 – 1981) and Professor Adeoye Thomas Lambo (March 29, 1923 – March 13, 2004). Since there is no Nobel Prize in Mathematics, I was highly delighted to be orally informed that I won the 2021 NNOM award.

Formal Letter of Award

On January 21, 2022, I received yet another phone call from Mr. Ibrahim Namadi informing me that, consequent upon the official approval by President Muhammadu Buhari, GCFR, of the recommendations by the NNMA Governing Board, the Chairman of the Board, Professor Shekarau Yakubu Aku, held a press conference on that day to announce the winners of the NNOM awards for the two years 2020 and 2021. The announcement was published by a number of newspapers with global offline or online circulation, especially the *Independent* (on January 21, 2022), *The Punch* (on January 21, 2022), The Sun (on January 21, 2022), *The Guardian* (on January 22, 2022), *TheCable* (on January 22, 2022) and *The Nation* (on January 25, 2022). According to Professor Aku, two scholars won the NNOM award for the year 2020, namely: Dr. Oluyinka Olurotimi Olutoye in Medicine and the late

Professor Charles Ejike Chidume (August 11, 1947 – October 7, 2021) in Science. He announced me as the sole NNOM award winner in Science for the year 2011. Subsequently, I received a formal letter of award from Professor Aku, dated January 25, 2022, with the subject: Conferment of the Nigerian National Order of Merit (NNOM) Award, 2021 on Professor Godwin Osakpemwoya Samuel Ekhaguere in the Field of Science, and the opening statement:

> I am pleased to inform you that His Excellency, the President, Commander-in-Chief of the Armed Forces of the Federal Republic of Nigeria, Muhammadu Buhari, GCFR, has approved the recommendation of the Governing Board of NNMA to confer on you the Nigerian National Order of Merit (NNOM) for the year 2021. The Nigerian National Order of Merit is an order of dignity, which entitles you as a recipient to: (i) use the designation Nigerian National Order of Merit (NNOM) after your name; . . . The date for your investiture and other event(s) lined up for the occasion will be communicated to you as soon as possible.

President Muhammadu Buhari subsequently approved February 8, 2022, as the date for the formal investiture of Dr. Olutoye, Professor Chidume and me as NNOM laureates at the Council Chambers, Presidential Villa, Aso Rock, Abuja.

Investiture as NNOM Laureate

The award letter contained the information that I was entitled to have five guests at the investiture. My daughter in the United Kingdom and a number of my colleagues in Nigeria were eager to be my guests. But as a result of the very short notice for the investiture, it was impossible for them to realise their wish. I felt extremely honoured that, in spite of their multiple daily engagements, two persons readily accepted to be my guests, namely: Professor Unionmwan Edebiri, FNITI, OFR, a retired Professor of French and Barrister-at-Law, and Engr. Isaac Izogie Uhunmwagho,

President of the Public Transport Owners of Nigeria Association (PTONA) and Chairman/Chief Executive Officer of Efex Executive, a division of Efosa Express Limited. Professor Edebiri was one of the eminent professors who altruistically asked me to apply for the NNOM award. I was extremely happy that he was able to attend my investiture. Engr. Uhunwagho, who obtained a First Class Honours degree from the Teesside University (formerly Teesside Polytechnic), Middlesbrough, Tees Valley, UK, was my classmate at the Immaculate Conception College, Benin City, as I had previously indicated. Endowed with grace, a large heart, team spirit, altruism and uncommon empathy, he always showed me filial affection and friendliness from our school days. He is recognised and highly respected by my schoolmates as a unifier and the prime implementer of multiple initiatives aimed at fostering continuous and seamless interaction, collegiality, solidarity and collective empathy among various ICCOBA groups. I was eager to have this lifelong friend of mine by my side during the historic moment. Happily, Engr. Uhunmwagho graciously attended the conferment of the NNOM on me by President Muhammadu Buhari on February 8, 2022. With the President were the Secretary to the Government of the Federation, Mr. Boss Mustapha, Minister of Special Duties, Senator George Akume, Minister of Information, Culture and Tourism, Alhaji Lai Mohammed, Chairman, Governing Board of the Nigerian National Merit Award (NNMA), Professor Shekarau Yakubu Aku, members of the Governing Board of the NNMA, and the Special Adviser to the President (Media & Publicity), Femi Adesina. In the evening of the same day, there was a dinner in honour of the three 2020 and 2021 NNOM awardees, with the Vice President Professor Yemi Osinbajo, SAN, GCON, as chairman. The speeches delivered by President Muhammadu Buhari and the Chairman of the NNMA Governing Board, Professor Shekarau Yakubu Aku, at the investiture and the Vice President Professor Yemi Osinbajo's speech at the dinner are presented in the Appendix. In his own speech, the Minister of Special Duties and Intergovernmental Affairs, Senator George Akume, gave an insight into the highly competitive nature of the NNOM award. According to the *The Guardian* of February 9, 2022:

> Minister of Special Duties and Intergovernmental Affairs, George Akume, said the three emerged winners, following a selection process from over 1,200 applications received by the NNOM Governing Board.

I had the unique honour of giving a brief and impromptu acceptance speech on behalf of the three new NNOM laureates The grand investiture ceremony was reported both online and offline in the Nigerian media, including *The Guardian* (February 9, 2022), *New Telegraph* (February 8, 2022), *TheCable* (February 8, 2022), *ThisDay* (February 8, 2022), Channels Television (February 8, 2022), Radio Nigeria (February 8, 2022), *Premium Times* (February 8, 2022), *BusinessDay* (February 8, 2022), *Daily Trust* (February 8, 2022), *Daily Trust* (February 8, 2022), *The Nigerian Tribune* (February 8, 2022), The NTA (February 9, 2022), *The Punch* (February 9, 2022), *News Express* (February 9, 2022), *Vanguard* (February 14, 202266) and *Leadership* (February 18, 2022).

Following the conferment of the NNOM on me, I received countless congratulatory messages from my colleagues, nationally and globally, schoolmates at the diverse levels of education that I traversed over the years, relations and well-wishers, including the first female Provost of the College of Medicine, Professor Olayinka Olusola Omigbodun (née Banjo). The President of the Nigerian Mathematical Society (NMS), Professor Bashir Ali, also sent me a congratulatory message on behalf of all members of the NMS and its Governing Council. Above all, His Excellency, Godwin Nogheghase Obaseki, the Governor of Edo State, my State of origin, graciously congratulated me through a full page publication in the *Vanguard* newspaper of February 10, 2022. The Governor also sent me the following message:

> We congratulate you on the conferment of the Nigerian National Order of Merit (NNOM) Award for science by His

Excellency, President Muhammadu Buhari, in recognition of your groundbreaking achievements in mathematical physics.

Your emergence as a laureate of the country's most prestigious award for intellectual and academic contributions, from an original list of 1,200 applicants, is a proof of your exceptional brilliance and accomplishment, which is worthy of emulation especially by the younger generation. By creating and pioneering the theory of Quantum Stochastic Differential Inclusions (QSDIs), you have formulated new pathways which can be deployed in resolving outstanding problems in mathematics.

In Edo, we recognize the importance of youth participation in Science, Technology, Engineering and Mathematics (STEM) fields and have prioritized the revamp[ing] of the education sector to enable our youths compete with their peers internationally. Your impressive body of work, which has put our nation and our state on the global stage, will invariably open a vista of opportunities to expand knowledge, and further the advancement and promotion of scholarly causes.

Congratulations.

HIS EXCELLENCY, GODWIN OBASEKI,
Governor, Edo State

Led by its President, Engr. Ighodalo Johnson Edetanlen, the Immaculate Conception College Old Boys Association (ICCOBA) would not be outdone by other well-wishers in the midst of the huge avalanche of goodwill, amity, collegiality and fellowship that rushed my way, following my investiture as a NNOM laureate on February 8, 2022. Accordingly, on July 2, 2022, ICCOBA organised a grand reception in my honour, at the prestigious Protea Hotel, Benin City, with the Executive Governor of Edo State, His Excellency Godwin Nogheghase Obaseki, represented by the Speaker of the Edo State House of Assembly, . Marcus Onobun, as the Special Guest of Honour, the Archbishop of the Archdiocese of Benin, His Grace Augustine Obiora Akubeze, represented by the Very Rev. Father Pascal Omono, Rector of St. Paul's Seminary, Benin-City, as Guest of Honour and the Omo n'Oba n'Edo Uku Akpolokpolo, Oba

Ewuare n'Ogidigan II, represented by three eminent Chiefs, as the Royal Father of the Day. The Chairman of the occasion was "Lord" Matthias Ogunsuyi, who was my Godfather when the sacrament of Confirmation was administered to me by Bishop Patrick Joseph Kelly in 1963: he graciously accepted to be a last-minute substitute for the Deputy Inspector General of Police, Parry Osayande (rtd.), the substantive Chairman, who was inevitably absent. The keynote address was delivered by my classmate, His Excellency, Ambassador Thaddeus Daniel Hart, a former Permanent Secretary of the Federal Ministry of Foreign Affairs. An Old Boy of ICC, Soni Irabor, the nationally and globally recognised media icon, who is the owner and chief executive officer of the Soni Irabor Institute of Media and Communications located in Lagos, was the Master of Ceremony. All my classmates (ICCOBA65) participated assiduously in ensuring that the epochal reception was a resounding success. The ICCOBA presented me with a plaque to mark my NNOM award. It also graciously created prizes in my name for outstanding performances in Mathematics by Senior Secondary School and Junior Secondary School students at the Immaculate Conception College, Benin City, and actually made the first awards to two high flying Mathematics students of the school during the event. Some Old Boys of ICC also individually presented me with some gifts. One of my academic progenitors at ICC, Dr. Ralph Ebehiremhen Ebhojie, of the 1959 set, kindly gave me a copy of his highly enlightening autobiography. As the icing on the cake, Hon. Barrister Victor Osarenren, of the 1969 set and a former Chairman of Uhunmwode Local Government of Edo State, kindly gave me an expensive and historically significant gift, namely a bronze bust of Queen Idia, the mother of Oba Esigie, the 17th Oba of Benin, whose reign was from 1504 to 1550. I had always wished that I owned such an iconic artwork: fortunately for me, Hon. Osarenren's benevolence morphed amazingly into the full realisation of my fervent dream.

At the event, I proffered two suggestions: one to the Edo State Government and the other to the Federal Government of Nigeria.

My proposal to the Edo State Government concerned the sustainable development and utilisation of Science, Technology, Engineering and Mathematics (STEM) as drivers of national transformation and development, especially the rapid expansion of employment opportunities, continuous wealth-creation and impactful national progress. The proposal was formulated as follows.

> Edo State, as well as every sub-national government, should first and foremost develop and implement a long-term policy and a strategic plan relating to the advancement of the teaching, learning and application of STEM in its educational institutions at all levels. To ensure the seamless coordination of the key strategic activities, including mission-oriented research that can produce measurable outputs and outcomes with game-changing national impact and transformation, it would be advisable that sub-national governments, including Edo State, establish properly funded analogues of the Federal Ministry of Science, Technology & Innovation. The key strategic objective would be to mainstream technology into all aspects of human enterprises through technology incubation, commercialisation and uptake in Edo State and beyond. As the process of developing and utilising technology is capital-intensive, the objective will be achieved through a sustained triple-helix partnership among the Edo State Government, its tertiary education institutions and its society, especially the private sector, which continually fosters scientific expertise, innovation, technology-uptake and the infusion of capital into the technology generation and utilisation process. As a sustainable strategy for accumulating the needed capital, the Edo State Government could adopt a whole-of-society approach by setting up an analogue of the Tertiary Education Trust Fund (TETFund), probably christened: Edo State STEM Fund (ED-STEMFund). ED-STEMFund would be funded through the annual remittance by businesses and enterprises operating in and taxable by Edo State of, say, 2% of their annual profits. Properly structured and administered, this will ramp up, and also firmly entrench, technology dissemination, absorption and utilisation in Edo State. If the Edo State Government adopts this suggestion, it would be the first sub-national government in the country to implement a strategy for the sustainable mainstreaming of STEM into its developmental agenda.

My suggestion to the Federal Government of Nigeria was to entrench steadfast national development, harmony and progress.

> . . . in a country that is increasingly becoming fissile, as a result of snowballing political, religious, security and ethnic challenges, it is often difficult for citizens to pursue their life goals in an atmosphere of peace, safety and happiness. To progressively change this undesirable state of affairs will require a whole-of-society approach that steadfastly fosters conflict prevention and resolution, peace-building and national cohesion for national progress. When persons or organisations work toward achieving these nationally beneficial outcomes, they ought to be duly recognised through a competitive and distinguishing award, undergirded by some carefully formulated eligibility and selection criteria. That is why I am hereby proposing the establishment of a Nigeria National Prize for Peace which will be administered by a Governing Board that is distinct from the Governing Board of the Nigerian National Merit Award (NNMA), whose focus is, and should remain, the rewarding of academic and intellectual excellence.

In my view, Nigeria was long overdue for such a Prize. I therefore looked forward to the eventual institution by the Federal Government of the *Nigeria National Prize for Peace*, which would be the Nigerian analogue of the globally recognised *Nobel Prize for Peace*.

Through my investiture, I became the 79th NNOM laureate since the enactment of the NNMA Act No. 53 of 1979. Mathematically, the prime number 79 is both a happy number (since it eventually transforms into 1 when it is progressively replaced by the sum of the squares of each of its two digits, i.e.: $79 \rightarrow 72+92 = 130 \rightarrow 12+32+02 = 10 \rightarrow 12+02 = 1$) and an emirp (since the number 97, obtained by reversing its digits, is also a prime number). Some other happy numbers in my life are 1959 (my final year at the primary school level); 1967 (my final year at the Higher School level); and 1976 (my matrimonial year, which was also the year of my appointment as a lecturer at the University of Ibadan). On the other hand, 1965 (the year that I experienced a significant health challenge) is mathematically not a happy number. The conferment of the NNOM on me showed that my humble contributions to mathematics and mathematical physics were appreciated and recognised nationally, as had been the case internationally through multiple scholarships, sponsorships, fellowships, visiting positions and honours that I received over the years. I dedicated the award to the eminent Professors who altruistically initiated the idea that I should join the contest for the 2021 NNOM award, the professors who enthusiastically nominated me for the award, all my schoolmates, teachers, mentors and students at the various levels of education where I have been active over the years as a student or teacher; the University of Ibadan, a wonderful academic world, where I hold the lifelong appointment of Emeritus Professorship; my workplace colleagues; my international academic friends and the multiple institutions around the world where I held diverse visiting positions. Like Professor Max Born (December 11, 1882 – January 5, 1970), whose former office was allocated to me during my visit at the Institute for Theoretical Physics, University of Göttingen, Göttingen, Germany, and who was a joint winner of the 1954 Nobel Prize in Physics for his seminal contributions to the foundations of Quantum Mechanics, much of the work for which I was honoured was undergirded by the fundamental axioms of Quantum Field Theory.

A Non-Technical Sketch of My Mathematical Footprint

As a mathematician and mathematical physicist, my research activities fundamentally concern the continuous search for novel mathematical structures and related interesting theorems, as well as their diverse applications to the real world, including national development. This is because some existing mathematical results are often too restrictive in their scope, owing to the nature of their underlying hypotheses, to be applicable in a rapidly changing world. Thus, through reliance on its inherent self-evaluation and self-renewal mechanism, mathematics is always fit for purpose, as it continually drives the expansion of its own frontiers as well as those of other disciplines. An important outcome is the building of mathematical paradigms of real world systems, with game-changing impact on national development and progress. My own research interests and activities are principally in the fields of mathematical physics, with emphasis on quantum field theory, dynamical systems, and applications to natural phenomena; noncommutative stochastic analysis, with emphasis on quantum stochastic (ordinary/partial) differential and integral equations, and their applications; topological partial *-algebras, with emphasis on their structure, representations and applications; and financial mathematics, with emphasis on financial contracts, real options, risk analysis and sensitivity analysis. Toward fostering national research capacity building and strategic institutional succession planning, I have successfully supervised a substantial number of MSc, MPhil and PhD students in these branches of knowledge.

Some of the work for which the 2021 NNOM was awarded to me concerns my research activities in mathematical physics, a discipline that straddles mathematics and physics, and noncommutative stochastic analysis, which straddles functional analysis and stochastic analysis. I have innovatively created some new directions in mathematics and deployed their outcomes to solve a number of outstanding problems in the branch of mathematical physics called axiomatic quantum field theory. My groundbreaking innovations harmonized multiple elements of quantum field theory, partial *-algebras and classical stochastic differential inclusions, thereby opening up a novel pathway to rigorous research into quantum stochastic differential inclusions and the dynamics of quantum systems. Besides being of independent mathematical interest, my novel mathematical contributions have important concrete applications in quantum stochastic differential equations with discontinuous coefficients, quantum computing, quantum cryptography, quantum biology and the dynamics of open quantum systems, where many features of subatomic-scale systems are increasingly being utilized to create novel and optimally-performing, game-changing products that are beneficial to all nations, including Nigeria.

Over the years, the University of Ibadan has supplied an appreciable number of scholars to the national pool of NNOM laureates. In the Faculty of Science, three persons have so far won the NNOM award. They are the physicist and my former teacher (who taught me Mechanics in 1968), Professor Ikpong Akpanoluo Ette (NNOM: 2002), the mathematician and my former teacher (who taught me Group Theory in 1968), Professor Oluyomi Aderemi Kuku (NNOM: 2009) and me, Professor GOS Ekhaguere (NNOM: 2021). Through receiving the NNOM award, I also made history in some other ways. I am the second Edo academic to win the NNOM award, the first Edo NNOM laureate being the versatile Professor Francis Abiola Irele (May 22, 1936 – July 2, 2017), an indigene of Uokha in the Owan West Local Government Area of Edo State, who won the NNOM award in 2013. Professor Irele was the first Edo NNOM laureate in the Humanities and I am the first Edo NNOM laureate in Science. Moreover, I am the first indigene of the Benin kingdom and also the first alumnus of ICC to win the NNOM award.

Professor Charles Ejike Chidume

I would be utterly negligent if I did not pay tribute to my friend Professor Charles Ejike Chidume (August 11, 1947 – October 7, 2021), on whom the 2020 NNOM award in Science was, sadly, conferred posthumously. Professionally, we were quite close. Our mathematical paths crossed on several occasions at numerous conferences and at the International Centre for Theoretical Physics, Trieste, Italy, where I was a Senior Associate. He was an iconic mathematician, one of the shining lights in the Nigerian mathematical firmament, with his globally recognised work in Nonlinear Analysis, within the broad area of Functional Analysis. Through his multiple invitations to me to teach some courses at the African University of Science & Technology, Abuja, I was a Visiting Professor on several occasions at the institution's Mathematics Institute which he headed. Professor Chidume is sorely missed by the nation and the global mathematics community, not minding that his unique and game-changing contributions to mathematics are imperishable and eternal.

EPILOGUE

You only live once, but if you do it right, once is enough.
Mae West[25]

In my life journey, I encountered multiple situations, institutions and persons, with substantial impact on the nature, range and quality of service that I have so far been able to render to humanity. Accordingly, many persons and institutions have played significant trajectory-determining roles in my life. Consequently, a monumental challenge immediately emerges: who and which institutions should be explicitly mentioned in this autobiography? First and foremost, I acknowledge the awesome providential solutions to the many apparently insurmountable problems that I faced during the journey and I am eternally grateful to the Almighty for the modest achievements that I was eventually able to record.

Compiling the details of facts and events concerning aspects of my life was awfully challenging, especially in respect of those events which occurred well over half a century ago, because of the high standard of precision that I set for the work and also since I

---

25   American stage and film actress, playwright, screenwriter and singer; born MARY JANE WEST (August 17, 1893 – November 22, 1980).

did not consciously accumulate any notes during the period. I was amazed about how my recollection of certain important facts and events had become somewhat fuzzy or nebulous. Consequently, it was necessary that I fact-checked my narration with multiple other witnesses and sources.

During my days as a student from 1961 to 1967 at the Immaculate Conception College (ICC), Benin City, our teachers were chiefly identified by their surnames. In writing this book, I needed additional information about the teachers, many of whom were Irish. In respect of the clerical staff, all of whom were priests of the Societas Missionum ad Afros (SMA), founded by Fr. Melchior De Marion Bréssillac (December 2, 1813 – June 25, 1859), I contacted Fr. Fachtna O'Driscoll, who was the Superior General of the SMA from 2013 to 2019. In spite of his enormous responsibilities, Fr. Fachtna O'Driscoll swiftly referred me to Fr. Michael Mccabe, the former Provincial of the Irish Province from 2013 to 2019. Fr. Mccabe would, in turn, link me with Fr. Edmund Michael Hogan [Eamonn Hogain], the Archivist of the Irish Province of the SMA. Fr. Mccabe was succeeded in 2019 by Fr. Malachy Flanagan as the Provincial of the Irish Province. For almost two years, I worked closely with Fr. Hogan to collaboratively unearth several important pieces of information about all my past teachers who were SMA priests. I am therefore infinitely grateful to Fr. O'Driscoll, Fr. Mccabe, Fr. Flangan and Fr. Hogan for their unflinching support at crucial moments throughout the implementation of this project. I was also interested in some of the non-clerical Irish teachers at ICC. In my search, I found out that Mr. Owen Gerard [Gerry] Murtagh, who taught English Language until he left the school in the first quarter of 1966, had also taught the same subject at St. Laurence College, Loughlinstown, Dublin, Ireland, established in 1967 by the Marianist Order, and retired there in 2002. I thank Bro. Jim Contadino, Mr. Ronan Coffey and Ms. Carol Byrne, who were the school's Chair of the Board of Management, Principal and

Secretary, respectively, for their assistance in facilitating my reunion electronically with Mr. Murtagh in 2019 after 53 years. Thereafter, Mr. Murtagh and I engaged in regular electronic correspondence through which we reminisced with nostalgia on our days and roles at ICC.

I was able to enroll as a student of ICC in 1961 because I was a Western/Mid-Western Region Scholar. I am, of course, thankful to the Governments of the Western and Mid-Western Regions of Nigeria of the 1960s. I had narrated how illness dealt me a bad hand in 1965, the final year of my secondary school education at ICC. My illness surprised both my school and family. Besides its enormous potential to abruptly halt my graduation in that year, the unexpected ordeal was harrowing. I am thankful to all members of my family because they stood firmly by me throughout my travail. I single out my niece, Ms. Patience Erhabor (nee Okuonrobo) and my cousin, Mr. Dauda Lawani, for special praise in acknowledgement of their extraordinary roles in ensuring that I regained my health and completed my secondary school education. As I had recounted, at the school level, the Principal, Fr. Joseph Patrick Donnelly ((July 26, 1916-June 11, 1992)), worked assiduously to find a quick remedy for my illness to enable me to write my final year examinations. Providentially, he succeeded and I was able to participate in the 1965 West African School Certificate Examinations (WASCE). Moreover, from a financial standpoint, it was evident that I would not be able to pursue my education beyond the West African School Certificate level. But after the release of the WASCE results, in which I performed well, the Principal offered me a College Scholarship that enabled me to pursue my Higher School Certificate education and recalibrate my academic trajectory. Although Fr. Donnelly is no longer alive today, for his many acts of empathy and kindness to me at defining moments in my life, I remain eternally in his debt.

Occasionally, when I needed certain kinds of information, I turned to some of my classmates and other alumni of ICC.

Prominent among them were Professor Daniel Aisagbonbuomwan Enobakhare, Loius Idahosa, Andrew Iloh, Paul Guobadia, Engr. David Olotu, Engr. Isaac Uhunmwagho, Engr. Alexander Vlachos and Michael Uchidiuno. These persons supplied me with their own recollections of certain events. I am grateful to all of them for their assistance. More generally, I greatly appreciate every kind of help that I received from all my classmates, whose names appear later, and my eminent teachers when we were co-occupants of the unique academic space called ICC from 1961 to 1965.

In total, I spent over 44 years, initially as a student and later as a teacher, at the University of Ibadan, a wonderful academic world. During the period, I interacted with academic colleagues around the world, facilitated by multiple scholarships, sponsorships and other awards. Consequently, I am naturally indebted to a large number of persons and organizations throughout the global academic space. My joining the University of Ibadan in 1976 as a lecturer was not planned but an act of Province, in respect of which I tender my profound gratitude to Professor Takena Tamuno (January 28, 1932 – April 11, 2015), who was the Vice-Chancellor from December 1975 to November 1979, Mr. Samuel Jemieta Okudu, the institutional Registrar from 1972 to 1981, two former Heads of the Department of Physics, Emeritus Professor Olumuyiwa Awe and Professor Akpanoluo Ikpong Ikpong Ette, and Professor Haroon Oladipo Tejumola (July 8, 1937 – 2012), former Head of the Department of Mathematics. But for these eminent intellectuals, my academic career might have followed a different employment trajectory. Once at the University of Ibadan, I had game-changing interactions with many colleagues and members of the institutional leadership such as Professor Samson Olajuwon Kokumo Olayide), who was the Vice-Chancellor from December 1979 to November 1983 and who approved funding for my participation at a conference in Switzerland where I learnt for the first time about the Alexander von Humboldt-Stiftung; Emeritus Professor Ladipo Ayodeji Banjo, during whose tenure as Vice-Chancellor, from December 1, 1984 to November 30 1991, I was promoted to the grade of Professor in 1988 and with whom I have had the rare privilege of significant collaborations on several occasions; Professor Allen Bankole Oladunmoye Olukayode Oyediran who, as Vice-Chancellor from December 1991 to November 1995, appointed me as the Head of the Department of Mathematics in 1993 and also as the Chairman of the Business Committee of Senate in 1994; furthermore, I was appointed the Chairman of the Council Committee on Security in 1995 by the University of Ibadan Governing Council, of which I was a member, arising from his recommendation; Professor Omoniyi Adewoye with whom I worked seamlessly in my capacity as the Chairman of the Council Committee on Security during part of his tenure as Vice-Chancellor from March 25, 1996 to March 25, 2000; Emeritus Professor Ayodele Olajide Falase, Vice-Chancellor from September 2000 to March 2004, who graciously supported the approval by the Appointments and Promotions Committee of my applications for leave of absence from the University during the period from 1998 to 2001 when I was at the Association of African Universities (AAU), Accra, Ghana; Professor Adebisi Olufemi Bamiro, Vice-Chancellor from December 1, 2005 to November 30, 2010, who nominated me for the post of Deputy Vice-Chancellor (Administration), which eluded me electorally, and subsequently appointed me as the MacArthur Grant Liaison Officer in 2008; Professor Isaac Folorunso Adewole, Vice-Chancellor from December 1, 2010 to November 30, 2015, who re-appointed me as the MacArthur Grant Liaison Officer; Professor Abel Idowu Olayinka, Vice-Chancellor from December 1, 2015 to November 30, 2020, for offering me a one-year contract appointment after my retirement; and all the University of Ibadan officials with whom I had interacted in diverse roles over the years. I must also deeply acknowledge the positive influence, on my teaching and research activities, of all my undergraduate and postgraduate students who, through their incisive contributions to classroom activities and often surprisingly innovative perspectives, were some of my academic whetting stones over the years. I express my appreciation to my colleagues at the University of Ibadan, especially in the Department of Mathematics and the entire Faculty of Science, with whom I have interacted at multiple levels over the years, for their collegiality, exemplary solidarity, superb team spirit, scholarly partnership and unstinted goal-orientated strategic collaboration.

At the continental level, I worked harmoniously with many colleagues from various parts of Africa and visited multiple institutions in Africa during my tenure as a professional in charge of the coordination of several higher education programmes of the Association of African Universities. My appreciation goes to all the members of staff at the AAU during my tenure from 1997 to 2001, especially the Mozambican Professor Narciso Matos, who was the Association's Secretary-General from 1996 to 1999, Professor George Akilagpa Sawyerr who was the Director of Research, Dr. Dominic Nmah Tarpeh (October 14, 1944 – December 5, 2018) who was the Head, Administration & Finance, Professor Chris Ifeanyi Nwamuo who was a Senior Programme Officer on a special project, Mr. Benjamin Eshun who was the Operations Assistant (IT) and Mr. Cozy Clottey, who was the Principal Accounting Assistant. In their midst, my intercultural workplace skills were immensely expanded, diversified and honed. Still on the continent but outside the AAU, I express my gratitude to Professor Loyiso Nongxa, who was my host at the Department of Mathematics, University of the Western Cape (UWC), Bellville, Cape Town, South Africa, during my visit to the institution in 1996 under the AAU's academic exchange programme. Even though he had not known me very much at that time, Professor Nongxa, who later became the Vice-Chancellor of the University of the Witwatersrand, Johannesburg, fraternally provided me accommodation in his own house. During my stay, I also interacted with the amiable Professor Jan Persens (1946 – 2018), who was Professor Nongxa's colleague. In subsequent years, Professor

Persens and I participated in some higher education problem-solving initiatives, jointly organized by Professor Orlando Leroy Taylor and Professor Wayne Patterson, both of Howard University, Washington, DC, at the Rockefeller Foundation Bellagio Center, Bellagio, Italy.

At the global level, first and foremost, I acknowledge the enormous contribution by Professor Raymond Frederick Streater, my PhD supervisor at the University of London, UK, toward building my research capacity in Mathematical Physics and also for introducing me to many of the icons in the field in the 1970s. I should similarly express my appreciation to my teeming foreign friends, teachers and professional colleagues, especially Professor Wayne Patterson, my friend of many years, who travelled all the way from Howard University, Washington DC, USA, to participate in the academic and social activities that marked my 70th birthday anniversary in 2017; Professor Orlando Leroy Taylor and Professor Wayne Patterson for inviting me to several higher education activities coordinated by both of them; Professor Hans-Jürgen Borchers (January 24, 1926 – September 10, 2011), who was my host at the University of Göttingen, Göttingen, Germany, as a Fellow of the Alexander von Humboldt Foundation; Professor Wilhelm Freiherr Von Waldenfels, who was my host at the University of Heidelberg as a "Wiedereinladung" Fellow of the Alexander von Humboldt Foundation; Professor Sergio Albeverio and Professor Ludwig Paulary Evert Streit who were my hosts at the Forschungszentrum Bielefeld-Bochum-Stochastik (BiBoS), University of Bielefeld; Professor Dr. Heinz-Dietrich Doebner who was my host at the Technische Universität Clausthal-Zellerfeld, Germany; Emeritus Professor Witold Karwowski, who was my host at the University of Wrocław, Wrocław, Poland; Professor Judith Sheila Eatson, President of the Council for Higher Education Accreditation (CHEA), for my appointment as a member of the International Commission of CHEA; Emeritus Professor Steven Davis, Executive Director of the Academics for Higher Education & Development (AHED),

Montreal, Canada, for my appointment as a member of the Advisory Board of AHED; Professor John Ola-Oluwa Adeyeye who kindly paid my annual subscription fees to the American Mathematical Society on several occasions; Professor Livinus Ugochukwu Uko who provided me with accommodation in his house in Atlanta during my participation in the Southern Regional Algebra Conference at Clayton State University, Morrow, Georgia, USA; funding agencies and foundations, especially the Alexander von Humboldt Foundation, Volkswagen Foundation, The Ford Foundation, The Rockefeller Foundation, Deutsche Forshungsgemeinshaft, Swedish Agency for Research Cooperation with Developing Countries, Japanese Society for the Promotion of Science, London Mathematical Society, North Atlantic Treaty Organisation (NATO), Council for Higher Education Accreditation (CHEA) and the Global Alliance for Transnational Education (GATE), for multiple awards and sponsorships that contributed immensely to the advancement of my academic career and the enlargement of my academic footprint; institutions and research centres around the world in which I conducted research, gave seminars or taught students as a visiting scientist/professor; the professional societies of which I have been a member over the years, especially the Nigerian Mathematical Society, Nigerian Association of Mathematical Physics, London Mathematical Society and the American Mathematical Society.

I benefitted immensely from my numerous institutional colleagues, especially those of the Department of Mathematics and the Faculty of Science, who demonstrated admirable team spirit, collegiality and solidarity at all times. In many ways, I was truly fortunate to have lived a substantial part of my life in the midst such persons. I also thank the Department of Mathematics and the Faculty of Science for their kind recognition of my academic contributions to the University, the nation and the global community by unanimously recommending me to the Senate of the University of Ibadan for appointment to the lifelong position of Emeritus Professor.

I am also grateful to Professor Oluseyi Ezekiel Awe, Mr. Suleman Olawale Oyewumi and Mrs. Morenike Afolabi, who held the positions of Head of the Department of Physics, Deputy Registrar (Examinations, Records and Administrative Data Processing) and Deputy Registrar (Senate, Admission and Affiliated Institutions), respectively, at the University of Ibadan when I was writing this autobiography, for their kind and ready assistance.

To Professor Wayne Patterson, a person who has always had my back, I am immensely indebted for so kindly and readily accepting my request to provide a Foreword to this book. In 2017, he travelled all the way from the USA to participate in the diverse activities, especially as a speaker at the International Conference on Contemporary Mathematics and the Real World, that marked my statutory retirement from the University of Ibadan. I also thank Emeritus Professor Ben Elugbe and His Excellency, Ambassador Professor Tunde Adeniran, two of my best friends, with whom I have had a continually growing and beneficial friendship over the years, for expressing their opinions about this book by each contributing a Foreword.

For accepting to write a review of this book at an extremely short notice, I owe much appreciation to Oka Martin Obono, Professor of Sociology and Ethnodemography, University of Ibadan, and the Obol Kògbóónghà K'Ékpòn of Yakurr, Cross River State. He has always risen spontaneously and altruistically to the occasion whenever I sought his assistance.

Nationally, I humbly express my profound gratitude to the President of the Federal Republic of Nigeria, Muhammadu Buhari, GCFR, for conferring the Nigerian National Order of Merit (NNOM), the highest academic and intellectual award in the country, on me on February 8, 2022.

Finally, I greatly appreciate my wife, Deborah Abieyuwa, my daughter, Osamweetin Imane, her husband, Dr. Etiowo Ekanem, my grandchildren and my wonderful in-laws, Professor Asukwo Davis Ekanem and Professor (Mrs.) Professor Ima-Obong

Ekanem, for their steadfast support and cooperation throughout various segments of my life, especially when I was writing this book.

EXCURSUS

Address by His Excellency, Muhammadu Buhari, President of the Federal Republic of Nigeria, at the Investiture for the Conferment of the Year 2020 & 2021 Nigeria National Order of Merit (NNOM) Award on Awardees, Held on Tuesday, 8th February, 2022 at the State House Council Chambers, Presidential Villa, Abuja

It is my pleasure to address you this morning on this occasion of the conferment of the Nigerian National Order of Merit (NNOM) Award for year 2020 and year 2021 on deserving recipients.

2. The two-year combined award is being conferred on three distinguished Nigerians who have been adjudged worthy of the Honour by the Governing Board of the Nigerian National Merit Award. The NNOM Award is the highest and most prestigious Award bestowed by our dear nation on its citizens, at home and in the diaspora, for creative, intellectual and academic contributions that have national as well as global significance.

3. On behalf of the Nation, I am very proud to welcome the new Laureates to the prestigious league of highly honoured citizens. I also want to assure you that we will continue to celebrate and hold up your achievement as a shining example worthy of emulation by our up-coming young men and women.

4. Since the Nigerian National Merit Award (NNMA) was established 43 years ago, the addition of these three recipients will bring the total number of recipients to only 79. This is clear evidence of the high standards of the Award and an undeniable testimony of the strict adherence to quality and the merit-driven evaluation procedure for selecting laureates.

5. It also underscores the high expectations of the nation that the new recipients of the Award, like their predecessors, shall continue to hold the banners of creativity and intellectual excellence very high.

6. Please endeavour, at all times, to serve as beacons of hope and aspiration for the younger generation of Nigerians, reminding them that our survival and collective future as a nation ultimately rests on our being active participants in global developmental efforts, especially in science and technology.

7. Let me congratulate the three distinguished recipients of the Nigerian National Order of Merit (NNOM) Award for years 2020 and 2021. I must also express our appreciation for the patience of the 2020 Award winners, who had to wait close to two years to receive their Award due to the emergence of Covid-19 in 2020 and the total lockdown of the country which invariably made it difficult for the assessment process to hold then but was later held concurrently last year alongside with the 2021 applications.

8. On behalf of the Federal Government and indeed the entire nation, I congratulate the three recipients namely:

    Dr. Oluyinka Olurotimi Olutoye - Medicine (2020);
    Late Professor Charles Ejike Chidume - Science (2020) and
    Professor Godwin O. Samuel Ekhaguere - Science (2021)

9. I wish to seize this opportunity to congratulate your families, friends, associates and well-wishers, who have come to share with you the joy of today's milestone achievement.

10. I enjoin all our youths to emulate your good works by dedicating themselves to excellence and strive to contribute their quota to the arduous task of getting Nigeria on the top bracket of outstanding nations.

11. I wish to congratulate members of the Governing Board of the Nigerian National Merit Award under the Chairmanship of Professor Shekarau Yakubu Aku, as well as members of the Four Specialized Committees of Assessors and External Assessors for their integrity and transparency, and for the excellent work they have done.

12. The noble idea of constituting the Assessors Committees, whose membership is not disclosed to the public, ensures credibility that

could be emulated by other Government Agencies performing similar functions.

13. The fact that transparency and love for the nation have been the hallmark of your stewardship is well borne out by the fact that the NNOM Award is one of the enduring national legacies that are held in high regard globally and nationally and your decisions have been well acclaimed and controversy-free over the years.

14. Let me assure you that the Government and people of Nigeria appreciate your efforts and I enjoin you all to keep up the good work.

15. The Chairman, Governing Board mentioned in his speech the concern of the Nigerian National Merit Award over the dwindling budgetary allocation to the Agency and how it is constituting a constraint to the agency in carrying out its mandatory functions.

16. I wish to state that financial constraint is a general global issue and Nigeria is not excluded from it. I wish to assure you that we will do what we can to give special intervention as was done in year 2020 to the NNMA, within [the] limited resources available.

17. This administration is aware of the focal place that the NNMA occupy and the calibre of all laureates produced by the Agency, hence we will do everything possible to maintain and sustain the Agency.

18. I wish to reassure you that this Administration is fully committed to giving the NNMA the recognition that it deserves, by immortalising its recipients who have taken this country to greater heights both in Nigeria and in the diaspora.

19. We are a nation keen on fostering excellence across board and we will continue to celebrate those who have attained measurable levels of excellence in their professional life.

20. I thank you all and wish you God's abundant blessings in all your endeavours.

God bless the Federal Republic of Nigeria.

◊ ◊ ◊

Address of the Chairman, Governing Board of NNMA, Professor Shekarau Yakubu Aku, FAENG , FNSE, FSESN, at the 2020 & 2021 NNOM Investiture Held at the State House Council Chambers, Presidential Villa, Abuja on 8th February, 2022.

Protocols

I am extremely delighted to be here at this august event of the conferment of the Nigerian National Order of Merit (NNOM) Award on three outstanding Nigerians for the year 2020 and 2021 joint Award.

2.   The Nigerian National Order of Merit is the highest and most prestigious award bestowed by Nigeria on its citizens for creative, intellectual and academic contributions that are of national and global importance, and it is being conferred on any deserving distinguished nominee(s) who have been adjudged worthy of the award by the Governing Board of the Nigerian National Merit Award.

3.   The recipients of the NNOM Award are people who have made outstanding and valuable contributions to national and global attainments in all fields of human endeavour divided into four areas – Medicine, Science Engineering / Technology and the humanities, including education and culture.

4.   Since its inception forty-three (43) years ago, the Nigerian National Merit Award has identified and selected 76 awardees and with the conferment of these three winners today it will bring the total of the NNOM Awardees in the nation to seventy-nine (79). Each one of them has epitomised the finest of Nigeria's capacity for innovation and creativity.

5.   I am exceedingly proud to welcome the new Laureates namely, Professor Oluyinka Olurotimi Olutoye, Professor Godwin Osakpemwoya Samuel Ekhaguere and Late Professor Charles Ejike Chidume to this prestigious league of citizens.

6.   On behalf of the Governing Board of the NNMA, Members of the Board's four Specialised Committees of Assessors and External Assessors, I congratulate you on this great achievement. You are not just a national treasure; you are now important milestone in the history of Nigeria's upward path.

7.   I wish to humbly express my heartfelt appreciations to the President for graciously giving this day to honour these distinguished Nigerians

who have done the country proud. I wish to also acknowledged the contributions of all past Chairmen, members of the previous Governing Board of the NNMA who have always given their fullest support at all times to the activities of the NNMA.

8. I also wish to commend the current members of the Governing Board of the NNMA, and Laureates of the Nigerian National Order of Merit, the Four Specialised Committees of Assessors and the Secretariat of the NNMA, all of whom have given their best to ensure that our clarion call to serve the nation is achieved.

9. As the government is clearly aware, education is the foundational tool for national development in a knowledge-driven world and deserves to be given priority attention.

10. Hence I wish to seize this opportunity on behalf of the Governing Board of the NNMA, to acknowledge and appreciate the support being enjoyed by this agency under the present administration and also to appeal to the President for timely and adequate funding to this agency, given the perennial financial constraints faced by NNMA.

11. It is unfortunate also that the cut down of NNMA's capital budget will further create untold financial hardship on achieving the core mandate of the NNMA.

12. It is in view of this, that we therefore use this avenue to solicit the further support and consideration of the Federal government to look into the special needs of the NNMA as an agency and reconsider the important nature of responsibility the agency is saddled with, and give a special consensus for the upward review of the Agency's allocation.

13. It might interest you to note that in 2018 ₦203,000,000.00 was allocated to the NNMA, in 2019 the sum of ₦130,000,000.00 was allocated, in 2020 ₦70,000,000.00 was allocated, in 2021 ₦71,000,000.00 and then for the current year 2022 it is only the sum of ₦52,000,000.00 that has been appropriated to the NNMA. Looking at this asymmetrical fall in the budgetary allocation of the NNMA vis-à-vis the mandate of the NNMA, it is obvious that the funding is grossly inadequate and most of the times we have to go cap in hand to beg for funds from sister agencies which is not too good.

14. Your Excellency may wish to also kindly note that the recipients of the NNOM Award are expected to be given a cash reward of 10 million

each, and we have four fields of endeavours, that is, Science, Medicine, Engineering/Technology and the Humanities, so if these four fields present at least one (1) candidate each that brings it to 4 awardees and by implication 40million of the allocation is already gone and the balance of 10million will now be what the agency is left with to carry out its mandatory functions like the meetings of the Governing Board, the Four Specialised Committees of Assessors meetings, meetings of the Chairmen of the Four Specialised Committees of Assessors, Finance & General Purpose Committees meetings, Appointment & Promotion Committees meetings and other activities of the Secretariat.

15.   In view of the aforementioned, we are appealing that

    i.   A special Presidential consideration and intervention be made for increase of budgetary allocation to the NNMA in order to enhance its performance which it has upheld throughout its existence despite the financial difficulties it is experiencing.

    ii.   An immediate release of ₦ 50million to the Agency to enable us pay the awardees as well as offset other debts incurred in the course of preparing for this programme.

16.   The flag of this nation on positive achievements of its citizens need to be broadcast home and abroad and the NNOM Award being the highest in the country is in the best position to further portray Nigeria in good light to the world and this can only be sustained through the NNMA delivering on its mandate of "recognising, promoting and rewarding academic achievements in all field of human endeavours"

17.   Your Excellency, Sir, we know you as a man of honour and a man who loves hard working people and today we are pleased that you make out this time to honour these deserving Nigerians with the prestigious NNOM Award and that indeed will motivate and encourage our youths to aspire to be great people in the future.

18.   Thank you for your time. God bless you and God bless the Federal Republic of Nigeria.

PROFESSOR SHEKARAU YAKUBU AKU, FAENG, FNSE, FSESN
Chairman, Governing Board, NNMA

Speech Delivered by His Excellency, Prof. Yemi Osinbajo, SAN, GCON, Vice President, Federal Republic Of Nigeria, at the Special Dinner in Honour of Recipients of 2020/2021 Nigerian National Order of Merit Award on Tuesday, February 8, 2022 at Transcorp Hilton Hotel

Protocols

I am honoured to join you this evening at this special dinner event to celebrate three distinguished Nigerians who earlier today were conferred the prestigious National Order of Merit Award by His Excellency, President Muhammadu Buhari.

But here this evening we are honoured also by the company of some past National merit award laureates.

* Professor Augustine M.O. Esogbue, (NNOM 2006 Award Recipient in Engineering/Technology);
* Professor Oye Gureje, (2008 NNOM Recipient in Medicine), &
* Professor Samuel Chukwunonyerem Ohaegbulam (2012 NNOM Award Recipient in Medicine) and is currently also one of the Board members, of our Governing Board of the NNMA.
  I am delighted to observe that since this Award was instituted in 1979, we now have 79 distinguished Nigerians who are Laureates of the Nigerian National Order of Merit (NNOM).
  This evening we celebrate the three latest laureates –
* Prof. Olayinka O. Olutoye, who is honoured for his unique contributions to the field of fetal surgery;
* Prof. Godwin O. Samuel Ekhaguere for pioneering new approaches in the branch of Mathematical Physics known as Axiomatic Quantum Field Theory; and
* Prof. Charles Ejike Chidume for his outstanding contributions in Mathematics, Physics and Engineering. Professor Chidume's Award is posthumous as he sadly passed on before the conferment. May his memory always be blessed.

The contributions of our new laureates have had a real-world impact in their respective fields.

Professor Chidume's work has generated practical applications in understanding how System Thinking is used in Project Management, Logistics and Modelling. It also addresses a wide range of problems in economics, finance, image reconstruction, ecology, transportation, network elasticity and optimisation.

Professor Olutoye is a fetal and paediatric surgeon who led a team of surgeons in 2016, in a feat that has been hailed as the first of its kind, to perform a surgical procedure on a fetus with a tumour that developed before birth and grew from a baby's tailbone. The procedure involved bringing the fetus out of the mother's womb, removing the tumor during a 5-hour operation, and placing the fetus back in the mother's womb and the mother then carried the baby to a full term. His work on fetal anatomy including the healing wounds in fetuses is broadening understanding of how we can address wounds even in adults.

Professor Ekhaguere's work has deepened the understanding of the fundamental architecture of the universe and the fabric of reality itself. In addition to this, he has provided strong leadership for efforts to build research capacity in Mathematical Sciences in Nigeria.

These are probably just cursory simplifications of the significance of our Awardees' achievements. What is indisputable is that each of them has broadened the horizons of knowledge in their respective fields of endeavour.

But two things stand out in these particular awards especially when we refer to these high achieving Nigerians.

The first is that this is one of those occasions where we gather to celebrate people not on account of their wealth, power or status, but on account of their real achievements, their achievements that make a difference in the lives of so many not only here but in other parts of the world.

At the heart of the rationale for these awards is the idea that a nation perpetuates the sort of behaviour that it rewards. Promoting the growth of innovation, diligence, productivity and related values requires that the practitioners and exemplars of such values are adequately rewarded and celebrated. This is what the Merit Awards are all about. They are all about celebrating what we want to attract to this nation, celebrating what we want to enthrone in this nation which is excellence, innovation and hard work.

Second is that, in reflecting upon the glittering cast of Nigerians that have received this award over the years, I have been struck by at least one thing, and that is [not only] the variety of achievements but also by the diversity of origins of those who have earned these awards. The award selection process is entirely indifferent to the confessional persuasions, ethnic origins or partisan allegiances of the recipients. It is sensitive only to the quality of their accomplishments.

Often in our national discourse, we tend to juxtapose the idea of merit with that of representation as though they are mutually exclusive and it is suggested that there is an inherently natural disparity in the geographical distribution of talent. But that is not so. What these distinguished arrays of laureates from all over our country that have been assembled over the years show us is that the Nigerian genius for achievement can be found in every corner of our country.

Two imperatives immediately spring forth from such a realisation. The first is that we must ensure that we provide opportunities on a mass scale to enable all our citizens actualise their highest potential. And in this effort, we must pay more attention in particular to the education of girls, because this is the half of our population that has been neglected especially with respect to education. In so doing, we will renew our pantheon of world-beating achievers in every generation and continually rediscover the human capital for perpetual national growth.

Secondly, I am reminded of one of the past Order of Merit Laureates, Professor Chinua Achebe, who admonished us to always pick our first eleven for national tasks, our best eleven. In his words, "whenever merit is set aside by prejudice of whatever origin, individual citizens, as well as the nation itself, are victimised." If the pantheon of Order of Merit laureates reflects a representative meritocracy, is it not possible to apply the same standards in selecting those that we choose for leadership at all levels?

Democracy grants us not just the right to freely choose our leaders but the opportunity to choose the best of us irrespective of any sectional or sectarian considerations.

So, today's awardees and their predecessors represent the zenith of accomplishment; their exploits tell us what we are truly capable of as a people of the greatest heights, greatest achievements in the fields of science, the arts and every other aspect of human endeavour, and that we would soar as high as we wish so long as we do not subject ourselves to the gravitational pull of parochialism and prejudice.

If we are truly able to make these standards that we see today, the accomplishments that we see today, mainstream in our society and in the ways that we define our national traits, then we must apply the same principles that informed their selection in recruiting those who will represent this nation in every endeavour, whether it is in sports, or the public service.

Let me once again congratulate all the laureates of the NNMA and their families, the Chairman and members of Governing Board of the NNMA and indeed all associates of the NNMA. We wish you safe travels as you return to your homes.

Thank you.

◊ ◊ ◊

President Buhari: Nigeria's Collective Future Rests on Active Participation in Science and Technology, Confers NNOM Award on Three Scholars

President Muhammadu Buhari on Tuesday in Abuja conferred the Nigerian National Order of Merit (NNOM) Award for years 2020 and 2021 on three Nigerians who distinguished themselves in the field of medicine and science, expressing the belief that Nigeria's collective future rests on active participation in science and technology.

Conferring the award on the recipients, Dr. Oluyika Olurotimi Olutoye, Medicine (2020); the late Professor Charles Ejike Chidume, Science (2020) and Professor Godwin O. Samuel Ekhaguere, Science (2021), the President said he was very proud to welcome the new Laureates to the prestigious league of highly honoured citizens.

He said the nation would continue to celebrate and trumpet the scholars' achievements as a shining example worthy of emulation by the upcoming young men and women in the country.

> Please endeavour, at all times, to serve as beacons of hope and aspiration for the younger generation of Nigerians, reminding them that our survival and collective future as a nation ultimately rests on our being active participants in global developmental efforts, especially in science and technology," he told the recipients.

The President noted that since the Nigerian National Merit Award (NNMA) was established 43 years ago, the addition of the three recipients would bring the total number of recipients to only 79, confirming the high standards of the Award and undeniable testimony of the strict adherence to quality and the merit-driven evaluation procedure for selecting laureates.

He added that the integrity of the Award also underscores the high expectations of the nation that the new recipients, like their predecessors, would continue to hold the banners of creativity and intellectual excellence very high.

While congratulating the three awardees, the President expressed the government's appreciation for the patience of the 2020 Award winners, who had to wait close to two years to receive their Award due to the emergence of Covid-19 in 2020.

The president recounted that the total lockdown of the country, in 2020, made it difficult for the assessment process to hold then but was later held concurrently last year alongside with the 2021 applications.

Recognising families, friends, associates and well-wishers, who were present at the Council Chambers in State House to share the joy of the awardees, the President enjoined youths in the country to emulate the good works of the laureates by dedicating themselves to "excellence and strive to contribute their quota to the arduous task of getting Nigeria on the top bracket of outstanding nations."

The President also congratulated members of the Governing Board of the NNMA under the Chairmanship of Prof. Shekarau Yakubu Aku, as well as members of the Four Specialised Committees of Assessors and External Assessors for their integrity and transparency, and for the excellent work they have done.

"The noble idea of constituting the Assessors Committees, whose membership is not disclosed to the public, ensures credibility that could be emulated by other Government Agencies performing similar functions.

The fact that transparency and love for the Nation have been the hallmark of your stewardship is well borne out by the fact that the NNOM Award is one of the enduring national legacies that are held in high regard globally and nationally and your decisions have been well acclaimed and controversy-free over the years.

Let me assure you that the Government and People of Nigeria appreciate your efforts and I enjoin you all to keep up the good work."

On the request of the Chairman of the Governing Board over the dwindling budgetary allocation to the Agency and how it is constraining the agency in carrying out its mandatory functions, President Buhari promised that the Federal Government would provide special intervention as was done in year 2020 to the NNMA, within limited resources available.

Acknowledging the focal place that NNMA occupy and the calibre of all laureates produced by the Agency, the President assured that the Federal Government would do everything possible to maintain and sustain the Agency.

"I wish to reassure you that this Administration is fully committed to giving the NNMA the recognition that it deserves, by immortalising its recipients who have taken this country to greater heights both in Nigeria and in the diaspora.

We are a nation keen on fostering excellence across board and we will continue to celebrate those who have attained measurable levels of excellence in their professional life," he said.

The Minister of Special Duties and Intergovernmental Affairs, Sen. George Akume said the three intellectuals emerged winners for the 2020 and 2021 Award after the selection process, from the over 1,200 applications received by the NNOM Governing Board during the period under consideration.

"It is important to state that Prof. Charles Ejike Chidume died after he was selected and recommended for approval to Mr. President and he will be given the award posthumously," he said.

The Minister called on Nigerian universities to rise up to the challenge and continue to lead in innovative research targeted at providing solutions to the myriad of problems affecting the country, especially post COVID-19 era.

In his remarks, the Chairman NNMA Governing Board, Prof. Aku announced that recipients of the prestigious award bestowed by Nigeria on its citizens for creative, intellectual and academic contributions that are of national and global importance receive a cash reward of ₦10 million each.

The recipients of the award are divided into four areas- Medicine, Science, Engineering and Technology, and the Humanities, including Education and Culture, Prof. Aku said.

ABRIDGED CITATION OF RECIPIENTS

Prof. Olutoye, recipient of the 2020 NNOM Award for science, is credited to have led a team which performed ground-breaking surgical procedures on foetuses before they were born.

In 2016, in a feat that has been hailed as the first by an African, he performed a surgical procedure on a foetus with sacrococcygeal teratoma, which is a tumour that develops before birth and grows from a baby's tailbone.

Olutoye received his medical degree at the University of Ife (now Obafemi Awolowo University, Ile-Ife) in 1988 with distinctions in anatomy and pathology, interned at the Lagos State University, before proceeding to the United States for specialised training in surgery.

He is currently the Surgeon-in-Chief at the Nationwide Children's Hospital in Columbus, Ohio, United States.

Prof. Chidume, recipient of the 2020 NNOM posthumous Award for science, was the Acting President of the African University of Science and Technology, Abuja before his demise on October 7, 2021.

The works of the globally renowned Professor of Mathematics encompass several fields including Nonlinear Functional Analysis, Nonlinear Operator Theory and Differential Equations, Nonlinear Optimisation.

He bagged his bachelor's degree in Mathematics from the University of Nigeria, Nsukka in 1973, M.Sc in Mathematics in 1977 from the Queen's University Kingston, Ontario, Canada and Ph.D in Mathematics from the Ohio State University, Columbus, Ohio, United States.

Prof Ekhaguere, recipient of the 2021 NNOM Award for science, is a professor of Mathematical Physics. He created and pioneered the theory of Quantum Stochastic Differential Inclusion (QSDIs) that has greatly improved the entire Science Community's understanding of those pathological quantum systems whose governing equations involve discontinuous coefficients.

Prof. Ekhaguere holds a Bachelor's Degree in Physics from the University of Ibadan, 1971, DIC in Mathematical Physics from Imperial College of Science and Technology, London, UK in 1974 and PhD in Mathematical Physics from University of London (Bedford College), London, UK in 1976.

FEMI ADESINA
Special Adviser to the President
(Media & Publicity)
February 8, 2022

Buhari confers award on ace Nigerian surgeon, scientists

By Terhemba Daka and Sodiq Omolaoye, Abuja

09 February 2022 | 4:08 am

2020 Award Winner, the late Prof. Charles Ejike Chidume, who was represented by his son, Dr. Okechukwu Chidume (left); 2022 Award Winner, Prof. Oluyinka Olutoye, who was represented by his father, Oba Olufemi Olutoye; Award winner of 2021 Nigerian National Order of Merit, Prof. Godwin Ekhaguere; President Muhammadu Buhari, Secretary to the Government of the Federation, Boss Mustapha; Minister of Special Duties, Sen. George Akume and Chairman, Nigerian National Merit Award (NNOM), Prof. Shekarau Yakubu Aku during the presentation of the awards at the Presidential Villa in Abuja...yesterday.
PHOTO: PHILIP OJISUA

President Muhammadu Buhari, yesterday, conferred the Nigerian National Order of Merit (NNOM) Award for years 2020 and 2021 on three Nigerians who distinguished themselves in the fields of medicine and science.

This came as Federal Government reviewed the Science, Technology and Innovation (STI) Policy 2012, with a view to improving impact of the sector to the nation's economic development.

Minister of Science, Technology and Innovation, Ogbonnaya Onu, made the disclosure when the committee on review of operational guidelines on Energy Research Centres submitted their report to the ministry in Abuja, yesterday.

Onu noted that the review will determine the roadmap on development of STI and how it will affect every sector of economic and national life.

While conferring the award on the recipients: Dr. Oluyinka Olurotimi Olutoye, Medicine (2020); the late Prof. Charles Ejike Chidume, Science (2020) and Prof. Godwin O. Samuel Ekhaguere, Science (2021), the President said he was very proud to welcome the new laureates to the prestigious league of highly honoured citizens.

He said the nation would continue to celebrate and trumpet the scholars' achievements as shining example worthy of emulation by upcoming young men and women in the country.

Minister of Special Duties and Intergovernmental Affairs, George Akume, said the three emerged winners, following a selection process from over 1,200 applications received by the NNOM Governing Board.

Olutoye is credited with leading a team that performed groundbreaking surgical procedures on foetuses before they were born. In 2016, in a feat that has been hailed as the first by an African, he performed a surgical procedure on a foetus with sacrococcygeal teratoma, which is a tumour that develops before birth and grows from a baby's tailbone.

The works of Chidume, a globally renowned professor of mathematics, encompass several fields including Nonlinear Functional Analysis, Nonlinear Operator Theory and Differential Equations, Nonlinear Optimisation.

Ekhaguere is a professor of mathematical physics. He created and pioneered the theory of Quantum Stochastic Differential Inclusion (QSDIs) that has greatly improved the entire science community's understanding of pathological quantum systems whose governing equation involves discontinuous coefficient.

https://guardian.ng/news/buhari-confers-award-on-ace-nigerian-surgeon-scientists/

Times PREMIUM

Buhari confers merit awards on three Nigerian scholars

Mr. Buhari said the nation would continue to celebrate and trumpet the scholars' achievements as a shining example worthy of emulation by the upcoming young men and women in the country.

By Agency Report
February 8, 2022

President Muhammadu Buhari has conferred the Nigerian National Order of Merit (NNOM) Award for years 2020 and 2021 on three Nigerians who distinguished themselves in the field of medicine and science.

The President stated this when he conferred the award on the recipients: Oluyinka Olutoye, Medicine (2020); the late Charles Chidume, Science (2020) and Godwin Ekhaguere, Science (2021) in the Presidential Villa, Abuja, on Tuesday.

While expressing the belief that Nigeria's collective future rests on active participation in science and technology, Mr. Buhari said he was very proud to welcome the new Laureates to the prestigious league of highly honoured citizens.

He said the nation would continue to celebrate and trumpet the scholars' achievements as a shining example worthy of emulation by the upcoming young men and women in the country.

"Please endeavour, at all times, to serve as beacons of hope and aspiration for the younger generation of Nigerians, reminding them that our survival and collective future as a nation ultimately rests on our being active participants in global developmental efforts, especially in science and technology," he told the recipients.

He noted that since the Nigerian National Merit Award (NNMA) was established 43 years ago, the addition of the three recipients would bring the total number of recipients to 79.

The president confirmed the high standards of the award and undeniable testimony of the strict adherence to quality and the merit-driven evaluation procedure for selecting laureates.

According to him, "the integrity of the Award also underscores the high expectations of the nation that the new recipients, like their predecessors, would continue to hold the banners of creativity and intellectual excellence very high".

While congratulating the three awardees, the President expressed the government's appreciation for the patience of the 2020 Award winners, who had to wait close to two years to receive their awards due to the emergence of COVID-19 in 2020.

The President recounted that the total lockdown of the country in 2020 made it difficult for the assessment process to hold then but was later held concurrently last year alongside the 2021 applications.

He enjoined youths in the country to emulate the good works of the laureates by dedicating themselves to "excellence and strive to contribute their quota to the arduous task of getting Nigeria on the top bracket of outstanding nations."

He recognised families, friends, associates and well-wishers, who were present at the Council Chambers in State House to share the joy of the awardees.

The president also congratulated members of the Governing Board of the NNMA under the Chairmanship of Shekarau Aku, a professor, as well as members of the Four Specialised Committees of Assessors and External Assessors for their integrity and transparency, and for the excellent work they have done.

"The noble idea of constituting the Assessors Committees, whose membership is not disclosed to the public, ensures credibility that could be emulated by other government agencies performing similar functions," Mr. Buhari said.

"The fact that transparency and love for the nation have been the hallmark of your stewardship is well borne out by the fact that the NNOM Award is one of the enduring national legacies that are held in high regard globally and nationally and your decisions have been well acclaimed and controversy-free over the years.

"Let me assure you that the government and people of Nigeria appreciate your efforts and I enjoin you all to keep up the good work."

On the request of the Chairman of the Governing Board over the dwindling budgetary allocation to the agency and how it is constraining the agency in carrying out its mandatory functions, Mr. Buhari promised that the Federal Government would provide special intervention as was done in year 2020 to the NNMA within limited resources available.

He acknowledged the focal place that NNMA occupy and the calibre of all laureates produced by the agency.

The President assured that the Federal Government would do everything possible to maintain and sustain the agency.

"I wish to reassure you that this administration is fully committed to giving the NNMA the recognition that it deserves by immortalising its recipients who have taken this country to greater heights both in Nigeria and in the diaspora.

"We are a nation keen on fostering excellence across board and we will continue to celebrate those who have attained measurable levels of excellence in their professional life, " he said.

Selection process

Meanwhile, the Minister of Special Duties and Intergovernmental Affairs, George Akume, said the three intellectuals emerged winners for the 2020 and 2021 Award after the selection process from the over 1,200 applications received by the NNOM Governing Board during the period under consideration.

"It is important to state that Prof. Charles Ejike Chidume died after he was selected and recommended for approval to Mr. President and he will be given the award posthumously," he said.

https://www.premiumtimesng.com/news/headlines/510452-buhari-confers-merit-awards-on-three-nigerian-scholars.html

ABBREVIATIONS AND ACRONYMS

AAU	Association of African Universities, Accra, Ghana
ADEA	Association for the Development of Education in Africa
BA	Bachelor of Arts
BOT	Board of Trustees
BS	Bachelor of Science (chiefly American abbreviation)
BSc	Bachelor of Science (chiefly British abbreviation)
CAMA	Companies and Allied Matters Act 1990
CBN	Central Bank of Nigeria
CETL	Centre for Excellence in Teaching and Learning
CHEA	Council for Higher Education Accreditation, Washington DC
CRIN	Cocoa Research Institute of Nigeria
CSN	Community School, NIFOR
CSW	Community School, WAIFOR
DLI	Disbursement Linked Indicator
DU	Dominican University, Ibadan
ECOWAS	Economic Community of West African States
ETF	Education Trust Fund
FCT	Federal Capital Territory
FEDECO	Federal Electoral Commission
FF-TIAP	The Ford Foundation Teaching Innovation Awards Programme
Fr.	Reverend Father
FUPEP	Free Universal Primary Education Programme
GATE	Global Alliance for Transnational Education
GSSP	Global Security and Sustainability Programme
IAMP	International Association of Mathematical Physics
ICC	Immaculate Conception College, Benin City, Edo State

ICCOBA	Immaculate Conception College Old Boys Association
ICTP	Abdus Salam International Centre for Mathematical Physics, Trieste, Italy
IFF	International Fellowships Fund
IFP	International Fellowships Programme
IIE	Institute of International Education
ING	Interim National Government
IORMS	Institute of Operational Research and Management Sciences of Nigeria
ISBN	International Standard Book Number
ISC	Institutional Selection Committee
JD	Joseph Patrick Donnelly
JNAMP	Journal of the Nigerian Association of Mathematical Physics
JNMS	Journal of the Nigerian Mathematical Society
MEDUNSA	Medical University of Southern Africa, Pretoria, South Africa
MFGIC	MacArthur Foundation Grant Implementation Committee
MFR	Member of the Order of the Federal Republic
MGLO	MacArthur Grant Liaison Officer
MS	Master of Science (chiefly American abbreviation)
MSc	Master of Science (chiefly British abbreviation)
NAMP	Nigerian Association of Mathematical Physics
NASA	National Aeronautics and Space Administration, Washington DC, USA
NEPA	National Electricity Power Authority
NES	Nigerian Education Sector
NHES	Nigerian Higher Education System
NIFOR	Nigerian Institute for Oil Palm Research

NITEL	Nigerian Telecommunications Limited
NITR	Nigerian Institute for Trypanosomiasis Research
NMS	Nigerian Mathematical Society
NNMA	Nigerian National Merit Award
NNOM	Nigerian National Order of Merit
NRFS&MC	TETFund National Research Fund Screening and Monitoring Committee
NSC	National Steering Committee
NSC	National Selection Committee
NUDTAS	Nigerian Universities Doctoral Theses Award Scheme
NUFFIC	Netherlands Universities Foundation for International Cooperation
NUPTAS	Nigerian Universities Postgraduate Theses Award Scheme
NUS	Nigerian University System
OAK PARK	OAU ICT Driven Knowledge Park, Obafemi Awolowo University, Ile-Ife
OP	Order of Preachers
OPRS	Oil Palm Research Station
PAMI	Pan African Materials Institute, African University of Science & Technology, Abuja
PEPT	Presidential Election Petitions Tribunal
PFA	Pension Funds Administrators
PhD	Doctor of Philosophy
PHEA	Partnership for Higher Education in Africa
PHEIC	Public Health Emergency of International Concern
PIC	Project Implementation Committee (Dominican University, Ibadan)
PIU	Project Implementation Unit
PSC	Project Steering Committee

PSC-COVID-19	Presidential Steering Committee on COVID-19
PTF-COVID-19	Presidential Task Force on COVID-19
RCGTR	Regional Cooperation in Graduate Training and Research
RFU	Regional Facilitation Unit
RRIN	Rubber Research Institute of Nigeria
SETI	Science, Engineering, Technology and Innovation
SIHB	Staff Information Handbook
SMA	Societas Missionum ad Afros (Société des Missions Africaines)
SMARTER	Specific, Measurable, Achievable, Relevant, Time-bound, Evaluated, Reviewed
SP	Strategic Plan
SPESSE	Sustainable Procurement Environmental and Social Standards Enhancement
STEM	Science, Technology, Engineering and Mathematics
TETFund	Tertiary Education Trust Fund
TNAMP	Transactions of the Nigerian Association of Mathematical Physics
UI	University of Ibadan
UK	United Kingdom
USAID	United States Agency for International Development
UWC	University of the Western Cape, Bellville, South Africa
WAEC	West African Examinations Council
WAIFOR	West African Institute for Oil Palm Research
WARO	West African Research Organisation
WASC	West African School Certificate
WASCE	West African School Certificate Examination
WGHE	Working Group on Higher Education
WHO	World Health Organisation

INDEX

Lightning Source UK Ltd.
Milton Keynes UK
UKHW020926281122
412977UK00016B/1006